D0605393

WHOSE
KEEPER?

WHOSE
KEEPER?

*Social Science
and Moral Obligation*

ALAN WOLFE

UNIVERSITY OF CALIFORNIA PRESS
BERKELEY   LOS ANGELES   LONDON

University of California Press
Berkeley and Los Angeles, California

University of California Press, Ltd.
London, England

© 1989 by
The Regents of the University of California

Library of Congress Cataloging-in-Publication Data

Wolfe, Alan, 1942–
  Whose Keeper? : social science and moral obligation / Alan Wolfe.
    p. cm.
  Bibliography: p.
  Includes index.
  ISBN 0-520-06551-4 (alk. paper)
  1. Social ethics. 2. Political ethics. 3. Social sciences—Moral
and ethical aspects. 4. Social sciences and state. 5. Welfare state.
6. Capitalism. I. Title.
HM216.W65 1989
300—dc19   88-37389
                                              CIP

Printed in the United States of America
1 2 3 4 5 6 7 8 9

*This book is dedicated to
Jytte, Rebekka, and Jan*

Contents

List of Tables

List of Figures

Acknowledgments

A book about obligations will inevitably incur many. I certainly have, and I wish to take this opportunity to acknowledge debts accumulated along the way.

My first is to two research assistants, both of whom not only did what I asked of them, but also became so engaged in the project that they chose their own avenues to investigate and offered substantive criticisms as well. Daniel Poor of the Graduate Center of the City University of New York was indispensable to this book in ways too numerous to mention; he knows what they are and also how much I appreciate his help. Kasper Lippert-Rasmussen of the Institute of Political Science, University of Århus, enthusiastically helped me with a variety of tasks during my stay in Denmark.

I am also indebted to the funding agencies that made it financially possible for me to learn more about Scandinavian societies. The Research Foundation of the City University of New York provided three grants; these enabled me to spend the academic year 1984–85 in Denmark learning the language, and 1987–88 in Scandinavia consulting documents, visiting libraries, and talking to people. Further support for the first year came from the Commission for the International Exchange of Scholars, which permitted me to be a visiting professor at the University of Copenhagen. Additional support for the second year came from the Center for the Study of Philanthropy, the Association of American Colleges, the Research Foundation of the University of Århus, and the National Endowment for the Humanities. I am grateful to all these institutions.

Travel within Scandinavia was facilitated by numerous individuals and institutions. In Denmark, the Institute of Political Science at the University of Århus was my base in 1987–88. I want to thank the two directors of the Institute during that period, Søren Risbjerg Thomsen and Palle Svensson, for their help in securing me a good office, providing state-of-the-art word-processing facilities, and helping with last-minute travel funds. Lise Togeby, Erik Albæk, Jørgen Grønegaard Christiansen, Jørn Loftager, Nils Mortensen, Henrik Kaare Nielsen, and Finn Arler were especially helpful as critics of my manuscript. Steen Bengtsson of the Danish Institute for Social Research made it possible for me to meet specialists in many of the subjects about which I was writing and opened the doors of the Institute's library to me. Birte Siim helped arrange a presentation of these ideas at Ålborg University and was an especially intelligent critic of my work.

William Lafferty of the Institute for Political Science, University of Oslo, in conjunction with Knut Midgaard, enabled me to present my work to a seminar on social science theory for Norwegian social scientists. Lafferty pointed me toward important Norwegian materials and introduced me to people at the Institute for Applied Social Research in Oslo. I am also grateful to Håkon Laurentzen for his hospitality at the Institute. Ulf Himmelstrand and Göran Svensson of the Institute for Sociology, University of Uppsala, and Tom Burns of the Swedish Collegium for Advanced Study in the Social Sciences provided opportunities for presentations of the ideas in this book at their respective institutions. Walter Korpi, Robert Erikson, Joakim Palm, Gösta Rehn, and Stefan Svallfors of the Institute for Social Research, University of Stockholm, provided an office in which to work and an atmosphere for discussion of my ideas. I am also indebted to Hans Erik Ohlsson, Gunilla Dahlberg, Berit Kemvall-Ljung, and Bengt-Erik Andersson. None of these people are, of course, responsible for any of my interpretations of recent Scandinavian experience. Indeed, I expect that they would all disagree with most parts of it.

At Queens College, Dean Helen Cairns and Dean James Mittelman were instrumental in securing financial help and release time from teaching. Charles Smith was an especially good critic. I am also grateful to Sharon Zukin, Paul DiMaggio, and Allan Silver for criticisms at an early stage in the project. Thanks also are due the anonymous readers of the manuscript for the University of California Press, one of whom suggested that I contact Kathryn Pyne Addelson. This turned out to be good advice, for her comments were a stimulus to the completion of the book. Thanks to Naomi Schneider, Anne Canright, Mary Renaud, and Mary Lamprech of the University of California Press for their help in the preparation of the book. Book publishing, like so many other things I will be discussing in what follows, can be organized by either the state or the market. I am glad that this book could be produced and distributed by individuals interested in something more than the bottom line.

My wife, Jytte Klausen, supported me through criticism, for which I am more than grateful. This book represents a change in both subject matter and political perspective from my earlier work. Readers familiar with my previous books may conclude that these changes are not so much the product of intellectual maturation, but instead a result of getting married and having children. They may well be right.

Århus, Denmark
June 1988

Introduction

Introduction: Modernity and Its Discontents

Modernity's Paradox

Capitalist economics and liberal democratic politics have given many citizens of Western societies two unique gifts: freedom from economics and liberation from politics. Raised by economic growth from the consciousness of scarcity, they can forget the nitty-gritty of survival and contemplate the building of culture. Released by politics from politics, they can, unlike those who lived before them, lead their lives unaware of the struggles for power taking place around them. The middle classes of Western societies, unconstrained by a real or imagined state of nature, are in a position to make for themselves the kind of social world they desire.

Yet for all its success, modernity is an ambivalent condition. There is, not far beneath the surface, a sense that something is missing: economic growth and political freedom do not seem enough. Max Weber's image of a society without a soul has become something of a popular lament. People are not always articulate about their discontents, but numerous signs—unstable voting patterns, a return to religious orthodoxy, increases in antisocial behavior, opposition to scientific and technological advance, a withdrawal from public issues into private worlds, and the rise of irrationality—indicate, for reasons both sound and unsound, a feeling of discontent with progress.[1] Capitalist economics and liberal democratic politics have prepared the basis for the good life, but its actual attainment seems just beyond the possible.

The discontents of modernity may have to do with the difficulty facing liberal democratic citizens whenever they make their daily decisions. Severed from traditions and ties of place, they are free to make choices about how to lead their lives irrespective of the actions of others, yet, because they live in complex societies organized by large states and even larger economies, they are dependent on everyone around them to make their societies work. The essence of the liberal condition is freedom, yet a people who are completely free are a people unencumbered by obligations, whereas economic growth, democratic government, and therefore freedom itself are produced through extensive, and quite encumbered, dependence on others. Unlike Rousseau's natural man, who was born free but was everywhere in chains, modern social individuals are born into chains of interdependence but yearn, most of the time, to be free.

The citizens of capitalist liberal democracies understand the freedom they possess, appreciate its value, defend its prerogatives. But they are confused when it comes to recognizing the social obligations that make their freedom possible in the first place. They are, in a word, unclear about the moral codes by which they ought to live. A moral code is a set of rules that define people's obligations to one another. Neither the liberal market nor the democratic state is comfortable with explicit discussions of the obligations such codes ought to impose. Both view social obligation as a by-product of individual action. Both prefer present benefits to sacrifices for future generations. Both emphasize rights rather than obligations. Both value procedures over purpose. When capitalism and liberal democracy combine, people are given the potential to determine for themselves what their obligations to others ought to be, but are then given few satisfactory guidelines on how to fulfill them.

Despite their discomfort in discussing moral obligation, modern liberal democrats have a greater need to do so than any people who came before. While the distinction between traditional and modern societies can be overdone, there is little doubt that smaller-scale societies characterized by handed-down authority present the problem of moral obligation in a different light than do those that value individual mobility and economic and political rights. In the former kind of society, moral obligations tend to be both tightly inscribed and limited in scope. On the one hand, rules are expected to be strictly followed; on the other, the number of others to whom the rules are expected to apply are limited—by blood, geography, ethnicity, or political boundaries. Moral obligation is "easy" in a double sense: individuals themselves are not called on to act as moral agents, since authority structures formulate rules of social interaction for them, and the others to whom they are tied by those rules are known to them or share with them certain known characteristics.

Both the scope and the specificity of moral obligations change as societies become more modern. The sheer complexity of modern forms of social organization creates an ever-widening circle of newer obligations beyond those of family and locality. Modern liberal democrats, for one, have obligations to perfect strangers, to those passing others who populate the bureaucracies and urban living arrangements of all Western societies.[2] They have further obligations, at yet another remove from the traditional milieu, to what has been called the "generalized other,"[3] a term that might include, for example, those who will live in the future and will therefore be dependent on decisions made by the present generation. To be modern is to face the consequences of decisions made by complete strangers while making decisions that will affect the lives of people one will never know. The scope of moral obligation—especially at a time when issues of possible nuclear war, limitations on economic growth, and ecological destruction are public concerns—seems to be without limits.

Yet if modernity expands the scope of moral obligations, it also thins their specificity. Rather than following narrowly inscribed rules that are expected to be applied strictly and with little tolerance for ambiguity, modern liberal democrats find themselves facing unprecedented moral dilemmas without firm agreement, not merely about what their moral rules *are*, but even about where they can be *found*. Religion, to take the most prominent example, is certainly no longer the source of moral authority it once was. Even when one can pronounce the modern age a bit less secular owing to an upsurge in religious affiliation and belief, authoritative moral codes based on God's commands no longer guide much conduct in the modern world. Neither in Italy nor in the United States can the Catholic church assume that its positions on moral issues will be followed by the bulk of its membership; splits between Orthodox and non-Orthodox Jews have made it clear that agreement within that religion on morality is nonexistent; and Protestant theology has become either highly secular or too strict to be obeyed even by its own preachers.

Nor is philosophy an adequate source of ideas about moral behavior. Moral philosophy, especially in Great Britain and the United States, has developed into an effort to establish the rule of reason, to search for universal standards of justice. (One looks for procedure, rules that regulate not only what we do but also how we do it, ironically making morality morally neutral.) The result, William Sullivan has written, is "a mistrust of the moral meanings embodied in tradition and contingent, historical experience."[4] Relying on logic, argumentative ability, and abstract formulations of universal criteria of justice, contemporary moral philosophy, for all its brilliance, tends toward obfuscation or restatements of the obvious. Thus a recent exploration into the thickets of moral obligation (one of the better ones, actually), wishing to make a case that protection of the vulnerable demands a special moral responsibility, relies on logic and on argument against competing moral philosophers—not content to argue instead that we have a special responsibility to the vulnerable simply because it is right.[5]

Literature, furthermore, can no longer be counted on to serve as a guide to moral understandings. "For our time," Lionel Trilling once wrote, "the most effective agent of the moral imagination has been the novel of the last two hundred years."[6] Yet the novel of manners and morals, the tradition from Jane Austen to E. M. Forster that explored so deeply questions of social obligation, has become an anachronism, replaced, as John Gardner noted, by introspective, if not narcissistic, explorations of inner worlds.[7] In one of his political essays, E. M. Forster said that modern people needed to "combine the new economy and the old morality."[8] That is precisely what no one today seems to know how to do. The question of personal responsibility that Forster explored in such microscopic detail in his great moral novel *Howard's End* seems old-fashioned to contemporary readers, who, like that novel's antagonist Henry Wilcox, believe that "as civilization moves forward, the shoe is bound to pinch in places, and it's absurd to pretend that anyone is responsible personally."[9]

Finally, modern politics, like modern literature, has also lost much of its moral sensibility. The left, which once prided itself on its ethical awareness, no longer speaks a resonant language of moral obligation. Its great objective, the welfare state, gave material benefits to modern people and created an important presumption in favor of equality, but the ethical energy that inspired its early years has for some time been on the wane. Where the welfare state has achieved its greatest success—in Scandinavia— is also where the welfare state has difficulty expressing a compelling moral vision, as I will argue in Chapters 5 and 6. Social democracy there and elsewhere has become defensive, holding on to the gains of the past, unwilling to stake out a terrain for the future. It often represents quite well the interests of its major constituency, the labor movement, but it has difficulty speaking of solidarity within classes, let alone solidarity between them.

The moral exhaustion of the left should be good news to the right, but such does not appear to be the case. The libertarian right, which believes that the market will solve all problems, is, of all political ideologies in the modern world, the most amoral, unwilling even to allow the possibility that people have any obligations other than to themselves. This moral nihilism is in contrast to the position of the fundamentalist right, for if market theories are all choice and no values, groups like the Moral Majority are all values and no choice. The religious right does have a moral vision, but it is one so confining in its calls for blind obedience to a handed-down moral code that it would negate all the gains of freedom that modern people have acquired. Nor, finally, do those known as "neoconservative" possess an appropriate moral language for modern politics. They ought to, for as former socialists they understand the need for binding ties in society (unlike the libertarian right), while as conservatives they insist on tradition and the importance of morality (unlike the relativistic left). Although there are neoconservatives who have ventured into moral-issue thickets (see Chapter 4), most have preferred to turn their attention from moral questions of how society *should* work to practical ones of how it actually does.

When uncertainty about how to treat others is compounded by a greater number of others to treat, moral obligation under modern conditions becomes ever more complicated. Because they are free but at the same time unsure what it means to be obligated, modern liberal democrats need one another more but trust one another less. At a time when they have difficulty appreciating the past, they are called on to respect the needs of future generations. When they seem not to know how to preserve small families, they must strengthen large societies. As local communities disintegrate, a world community becomes more necessary than ever. Modern people need to care about the fates of strangers, yet do not even know how to treat their loved ones. Moral rules seem to evaporate the more they are needed. The paradox of modernity is that the more people depend on one another owing to an ever-widening circle of obligations, the fewer are the agreed-upon guidelines for organizing moral rules that can account for those obligations.

Three Theories of Moral Regulation

The decline of traditional notions about moral obligation (rooted in notions of Christian charity or faith in the virtue of an upper class) is often, especially by those of conservative disposition, seen as the cause of modernity's unease. The distance between the need for a moral code and the inability of modern societies to find one becomes a problem so incapable of solution that the forces of modernity which produced it ought to be distrusted, if not condemned. From such a perspective, the things that make modern liberal democracies rich and stable will always lack meaning, while things that give people meaning will have no effect on what makes their societies rich and stable. It is a short step from such a conclusion to a pre-modern nostalgia for some kind of organic moral community that is alleged to have been destroyed by the forces of modernity (or to a postmodern "deconstructive" consciousness that is distrustful of the binding power of any moral rules, indeed of any rational and intellectual understanding of modernity and its dilemmas).

Traditional morality, however, is not the only morality. Precisely because the moral codes of yesterday constrained the potential of an individual's self-development, they cannot be effective guides for the social ties that make contemporary Western societies work. Economic growth and political democracy are, presumably, here to stay, and so long as they are, moral ideas that protect the few against the many or call on large numbers to stultify their human potential are neither likely to be effective nor justifiable. The problem is not that modernity undermines morality but that modernity displaces moral discourse into new—one is tempted to say modern—forms.

In looking to religion, philosophy, literature, or politics to find the rules of moral obligation, we look in the wrong place. There is an arena in which modern liberal democrats discuss problems of moral obligation, and often with surprising vigor. I will argue in this book that liberal democracies have done away neither with moral codes nor with institutions and practices that embody them. The gap between the need for codes of moral obligation and the reality of societies that are confused about where these codes can be found is filled, however uncomfortably, by the contemporary social sciences.[10] Even those social sciences that pride themselves on rigorous value neutrality, insisting that they are only describing how people do act, not advocating how they should, contain implicit (and often explicit) statements of what people's obligations to one another should be. (The reliance on numbers, statistical techniques, and algebraic reasoning so common in modern social science journals is not, in my opinion, an alternative to moral philosophy but its continuation, an extension of an effort that began with Hobbes and Hume to systematize moral reasoning, greatly aided, these days, by a host of new technologies.) Adam Smith, the founder of modern economics, was by trade a professor of moral philosophy. His followers, though themselves often unwilling to admit it, have the same calling.

For all their tendency toward jargon and abstraction, the ideas of social scientists remain the most common guideposts for moral obligation in a secular, nonliterary age. (Witness the popularity of Milton Friedman's ideas on television or on the best-seller lists, let alone the constant attempts of mass media to find academic experts to comment on one social trend after another.) Moreover, the social sciences contain not only a moral theory of how people should act toward one another, but also a large body of empirical information about how they actually do. As the Kinsey Reports first illustrated, and as every survey since demonstrates again, when all are interested in how others behave but few are secure that they are behaving correctly, social scientists are the closest we have to savants. The contemporary social sciences, despite occasional claims to the contrary, have not done especially well as predictive sciences. One reason they nonetheless continue to flourish is because they are a particularly modern form of secular religion, involving, in their own idiosyncratic language, fundamental questions of what kind of people we who are modern are.

If the social sciences are taken as the theater of moral debate in modern society, the problem facing modern liberal democrats is not a lack of moral guidelines but a plentitude. Instead of having one source for their moral codes, they have at least three: economics, political science, and sociology. (I have not included anthropology in this list, not out of lack of respect—quite the contrary, actually—but because its focus on modern societies tends to be indirect.) Corresponding to each are three sets of institutions or practices charged with the maintenance of moral responsibility: those of the market, the state, and what was once called civil society. When the theory of each social science is linked to the practices it favors, quite distinct approaches to the problem of how to structure obligations to the self and others emerge.

Society works best, says the economic approach, when there exists a mechanism for enabling people to maximize rationally their self-interest. Yet it is an extremely rare economist who stops at the point of simply asserting the ethical benefits of self-interest; most continue on to make a point about obligations to others as well: because the pursuit of my self-interest contributes to some collective good—economic growth or some form of welfare optimality—my obligation to you is to do what is best for me. That way of thinking about obligations, responds the political approach, is naive. People are not, as James Madison once told us, angels, and given the chance to escape their obligations to others, they will. Therefore, some restraint on their desires is necessary; if obligations to the community as a whole are not regulated by government, they will not exist at all. Both your ideas are too pessimistic, answers the sociological approach. People have a remarkable capacity, given them by the societies they create, to develop their own rules of cooperation and solidarity. The trick is to find a way to trust them so that they will do it. (It ought to be clear that not all economists share the economic approach, not all political scientists the political, and so on; if the disciplinary names are used from time to time in what follows, then, it is for stylistic, not intellectual, reasons.)

In comparing these three approaches to moral obligation, one is tempted to judge them on the basis of whether individual rights or collective needs are given the highest priority. By that standard, the economic approach would be valued by those placing an ethical primacy on freedom above any other value, and structuralist sociology or conservative political theory would be valued by those who emphasize obligations to the group before individual rights. Yet this debate, which goes on endlessly in social theory, tends to obscure an important point: all three approaches, because they seek to address the condition of modern liberal democrats, are theories of regulation as well as theories of freedom. It is certainly true that modern people have obtained, and value highly, individual freedom. But they also have obtained, even if they find them more frustrating and often seem to value them less, complex societies and large-scale institutions that provide them with jobs, wealth, and goods. Modernity would be just as thoroughly destroyed by complete freedom as it would be by complete regimentation.[11] Because the fear of anarchy is at least as strong as the fear of authority in the development of the social sciences, rationalizing the art of saying no is as important to their development as justifying the desire to say yes.

To be relevant to modern conditions of social complexity, any theory of moral obligation needs to develop an adequate explanation of why people must take into account the effects of their actions on one another. The economic approach, although emphasizing self-interest, does not deny such interdependence. Individual action is generally viewed as purposive, directed toward some goal (such as the creation of wealth) that is beyond the capacity of any one individual to produce independently. Milton Friedman, for example, points out that "specialization of function and division of labor" could not advance if productive units were households and if we relied only on barter. "In a modern society," he notes, "we have gone much farther." Modern economies force us to rely on cooperation, Friedman argues. "Fundamentally, there are only two ways of co-ordinating the economic activities of millions. One is central direction involving the use of coercion—the technique of the army and of the modern totalitarian state. The other is voluntary cooperation of individuals—the technique of the market place." [12]

Economists with a somewhat more complex theoretical approach, however, recognize that the market is anything but a voluntary mechanism for organizing obligations to others. As two other defenders of the market put it, "Only the romantic anarchist thinks there is a 'natural harmony' among persons that will eliminate all conflict in the absence of rules. . . . Rules define the private spaces within which each of us can carry on our own activities." [13] One of the enormous advantages of relying on the market to structure obligations to others is that it is an extremely efficient mechanism for insuring obedience to such rules. Gary Becker has expressed it as follows: "Prices and other market instruments allocate the scarce resources within a society and thereby constrain the desires of participants and coordinate their actions. In the economic approach, these market instruments perform most, if not all, of the functions assigned to 'structure' in sociological theory." [14]

The traditional critique of structural theories in sociology—that they have an overdeveloped conception of man so constrained by society that he has little autonomy and discretion [15]—would seem, from Becker's remarks, to apply as well to economic theories stressing individual choice. It actually applies more. Economic approaches to moral regulation, indeed most sets of moral assumptions based on the premises of rational choice or methodological individualism, tell me that I am free to find the best way to satisfy my obligations to others. If I fail to do so, however, there are always back-up mechanisms—prices in economics, constitutions in public-choice theory, mass society in the theories of sociologists influenced by economics—to insure that I eventually will. There is one major difference between these back-up mechanisms and the emphasis on social structure and norms found in sociology: it becomes enormously difficult for me to negotiate between my individual needs and the constraints placed on them when the latter are hazy at best, hidden at worst. I am forced, so long as I operate by individualistic moral codes, to organize my obligations to others by having a conversation with an authority I cannot see. The invisible hand is clenched into an invisible fist.

The opposite problem exists with those theories of moral regulation that emphasize collective obligation over individual freedom. In some contemporary political science, as well as in the Durkheimian reification of society or various forms of structuralism, obligations to groups tend to weaken the moral character of individuals. When, for example, government collects my taxes and distributes the money to others, it not only assumes responsibilities that would otherwise be mine, but it also decides to whom my obligations ought to extend. I am, therefore, not obligated to real people living real lives around me; instead my obligation is to follow rules, the moral purpose of which is often lost to me. Because my obligations are abstract and impersonal, I am tempted to avoid them if I can, and the collective rule-making authority, knowing full well of my temptation, will rely on its coercive powers to prevent me from doing so. Little of this would matter if modern states were simply administrative substitutes for society. The suspicion that they are not lies at the heart of the difficulty facing the political approach to moral regulation. When I rely on the state to organize my obligations for me I can be sure that my fate will be linked to others, but I lose a good deal of control over deciding how. Because modern states, even liberal democratic ones, are not, as Benjamin Barber has emphasized, very good on talk,[16] to the degree that I rely on government to structure my obligations to others I can see an authority with which I cannot converse.

Liberal democracies face discontents because they tend to rely on either individualistic moral codes associated with the market or collective moral codes associated with the state, yet neither set of codes can successfully address all the issues that confront society. Should older people support bond projects that will build schools that benefit younger couples? Should younger couples oppose increases in social security benefits that help older people? How do mothers best satisfy their obligations to their children—by staying home and nurturing them or by enhancing their own self-esteem in a career? Do we best serve the interests of those who come after us by saving parkland or by enhancing economic growth? Ought we to give to charity if the decisions of many others to give to charity might be used as an excuse to cut back government programs that have a charitable intent? Should the land of farmers be saved, even if one result would be to preserve inefficient farms? If we do not save inefficient farms, who should pay the costs, including suicides and mental illness, of farmers whose market inefficiencies stand in the way of economic progress? Should individuals maximize the collective good by paying a fair tax share or seek to maximize self-interest by cheating? Should government take responsibility for unemployment, even if the risk might be permanent dependence on the state? Will a firm contribute more to society by closing a branch in an area of high unemployment, thereby causing considerable suffering, and then opening another branch that creates new jobs somewhere else? Ought culture—ranging from opera and ballet to sports and rock music—to be produced and preserved based on the market principle of sufficient demand, thus risking the neglect of at-first unpopular works, or should we rely instead on government funding, thus risking bureaucratization and possible censorship? Should we, to improve the quality of our air and water, stop relying on "indignant tirades about social responsibility" and instead charge firms for the right to pollute, thereby "harnessing the 'base' motive of material self-interest to promote the common good"?[17] Is the best solution to the drug crisis to legalize drugs or to try and enforce laws against their use? Some societies rely more on the market to answer these questions, while others rely on the state. Yet both kinds of answers, because they tend to remove from the process of moral decision-making a sense of the individual's personal stake in the fate of others, often have consequences that are surprisingly similar.

To illustrate, consider just one question: how should a society insure that its members feel an obligation to work for their collective defense against external enemies? During the 1960s, Americans relied on government to insure their national defense; a compulsory system of conscription, complete with stiff penalties for avoiding obligation, was used to raise the army that fought in Vietnam. Americans were never asked their opinion about whether the war in Vietnam was necessary for their survival as a nation. Political leaders, whose power lay in their command over the resources of government, simply drafted young men, often against their will, and asked them to die for goals that the leaders themselves were incapable of publicly articulating. No wonder avoidance of obligation, as a presidential commission later established, was the rule, not the exception, and the drafting of people created resentment and inefficiency within the armed services.[18] Reliance on the coercive powers inherent in government for the defense of the society, premised on a distrust of people's own sense of mutual loyalty and obligation, simply encouraged large numbers of people to forget about obligation entirely.

In the aftermath of Vietnam, public thinking about military obligations swung full circle. "The significant fact of the past decade," Charles Moskos wrote in 1984, "has been the almost complete triumph of economic man over citizen soldier in military manpower policy."[19] The military began to follow the advice of Milton Friedman, Walter Oi, and other economists who had argued that creating a system of monetary incentives would insure an efficient match between personnel and needs.[20] Yet it turned out that rewarding self-interest also created problems of obligation to society. Those who were better off, and presumably therefore more obligated to everyone else, avoided obligation entirely, leaving the armed forces to those for whom service was the only available job.[21] The market was, like the state, viewed as one of only two realistic methods of recruiting people to defend their society. Exactly like reliance on the state, however, use of the market, by creating a separate sphere of military life divorced from civilian life, also weakened the concept of obligation to one's country.[22] Americans, in short, were expected to believe in the survival of their society, but the two methods used to strengthen that belief (no modern society would ever rely on a purely volunteer army) seemed to have the exact opposite effect.

Neither individualistic nor collectivist accounts of moral obligation, as this example shows, are without substantial problems. As Amy Gutmann has put it, using only slightly different terms, "Most conservative moralists set their moral sights too low, inviting blind obedience to authority; most liberal moralists set them too high, inviting disillusionment with morality."[23] The limitations of both the market and the state as codes of moral obligation may help explain why political sentiment in modern society is characterized, as Albert Hirschman has argued, by "shifting involvements."[24] When obsessed with efficiency and cost, modern liberal democrats look for market solutions to their problems; when precisely those concerns with efficiency and cost lead to problems of inequality and injustice, they turn to the state. One course offers a solution to the problems the other creates, yet simultaneously creates problems that the other offers to solve.

Although there are obvious and important differences between the market and the state, they also share similar logics, which is why, as in the case of military recruitment, they often have similar results. Neither speaks well of obligations to other people simply as people, treating them instead as citizens or as opportunities. Neither puts its emphasis on the bonds that tie people together because they want to be tied together without regard for their immediate self-interest or for some external authority having the power to enforce those ties. Finally—and the point I will emphasize most in what follows—neither wishes to recognize one of the very things that make liberal democrats modern: that people are capable of participating in the making of their own moral rules. Modern liberal democracies face so many frustrations because their economic and political accomplishments create potentials that the operating logic of their moral codes denies.

In the face of approaches to moral regulation that no longer seem as promising as they once were, it makes sense to try to find a way of thinking about obligations to others that puts into better balance individual needs and collective restraints. Such an approach—to the degree that it calls on individuals to rely on self-restraint, ties of solidarity with others, community norms, and voluntary altruism—finds its roots in a historic concern with civil society. What was once a three-sided debate has become, as markets and states have both expanded, two-sided. Sociology itself has contributed to this narrowing of options, because it has found in markets and states seeming solutions to its own moral ambivalence. A third way to think about moral obligation cannot overcome the discontents of modernity, but it can give to people a moral code that, unlike those stressing either individualism or collective obligations, enriches a decision-making process that too often leaves modern people feeling incomplete. To revive notions of moral agency associated with civil society is to begin the development of a language appropriate to addressing the paradox of modernity and to move us away from techniques that seek to displace moral obligations by treating them purely as questions of economic efficiency or public policy.

The Withering Away of Civil Society

Learning how to behave in modern society is not only difficult, but there are also few trusted signposts to guide the way. No one can ever be sure in advance how behavior in one part of society will affect behavior in any other. So great is the potential for unanticipated consequences and perverse outcomes that any effort to regulate society directly seems cumbersome, if not utopian. The uncertainty of the moral choices we must make every day enhances the attraction of the market and the state. (Simultaneously, this uncertainty makes economics and political science seem far more realistic and in greater accord with modern people's understanding of human nature than sociology.)

The market responds to the sense that consequences are best managed when left unanticipated, while the state offers to take choice out of individual hands and give it to the experts. Thus, if housing and other costs are allowed to rise because there are no controls on the market, women must go to work to earn extra income, and the question of how they should treat their obligations to the next generation is decided, without anyone really seeming to decide it. Similarly, if fiduciary experts tell us we need to raise the social security tax to keep the fund from going bankrupt, our obligation to the previous generation is resolved for us, and we need neither praise nor blame ourselves for whatever results. To the degree that the market and the state offer relief to the complexity of social coordination, they promise the possibility of reconciling the paradox of modernity behind the scenes. Both make the whole business of moral regulation seem easier than, in fact, it is.

Because they are conspicuously less demanding, the state and the market eventually come to be viewed as the only forms of regulation that modern people have at their disposal, especially in the economic organization of their society. As one sociologist puts it, "Under modern conditions . . . , the options are sharply reduced. Specifically, the basic option is whether economic processes are to be governed by market mechanisms or by mechanisms of political allocation. In social-scientific parlance, this is the option between market economies and command economies."[25] Yet there did exist, at the very start of the modern period, an alternative to both the market and the state. That alternative was called "civil society," a term with so many different meanings and used in so many different contexts that, before it can be used again, some clarification is in order.

In the eighteenth century, thinkers who unleashed modern bourgeois consciousness, such as Adam Smith, Adam Ferguson, and David Hume, believed that civil society was the realm that protected the individual against the (monarchical or feudal) state. Society was, in their view, a precious—and precarious—creation. "It is here that a man is made to forget his weakness, his cares of safety, and his subsistence, and to act from those passions which make him discover his force," wrote Adam Ferguson.[26] Modern people, taking advantage of what Ferguson called "the gift of society to man,"[27] were no longer at the mercy of nature. All progress, not only in commercial affairs but also in the possibility of curbing the passions and creating mutual sympathy, hinged on the mutual interdependence that men could obtain by leaving a state of nature. When Durkheim wrote of society as a secular god, he was reiterating a notion that found its first expression in the Scottish Enlightenment.

Like any god, society could be demanding. In return for the benefits it offers, it imposes obligations. "The general obligation," Hume wrote, "which binds us to government, is the interest and necessities of society;

and this obligation is very strong."[28] Therefore, in addition to our "natural" obligations, such as loving children, Hume wrote of justice and morality, obligations undertaken "from a sense of obligation when we consider the necessities of human society."[29] But how, if we are to be as secular as Hume was on his deathbed,[30] do we come to appreciate these necessities? The hopes of the theorists of civil society lay in a rational understanding of what made society work—what today we would call social science. In the writings of Montesquieu, for example, who has been called "the first moralist with a sociological perspective,"[31] we witness the idea that a science of society can help us use modern intelligence to organize our obligations to others. The thinkers of the Scottish Enlightenment, who were deeply influenced by Montesquieu, were confident that "constant and universal principles of human nature," as Hume called them, would make possible a modern moral order:

> The mutual dependence of men is so great in all societies that scarce any human action is entirely complete in itself, or is performed without some reference to the actions of others, which are requisite to make it answer fully the intention of the agent. . . . In proportion as men extend their dealings and render their intercourse with others more complicated, they always comprehend in their schemes of life a greater variety of voluntary actions which they expect from the proper motives to cooperate with their own.[32]

For the thinkers of the Scottish Enlightenment, civil society was coterminous with what today we call "the private sector," a realm of personal autonomy in which people could be free to develop their own methods of moral accounting. The ethical superiority of what would come to be called capitalism was due to the moral energy unleashed by the idea that people are responsible for their own actions. Yet it was also clear to these thinkers, as I will argue in Chapter 1, that to the degree that capitalism encouraged pure selfishness, it ran the risk of destroying this very moral potential. The new economic order being created during the late eighteenth and early nineteenth centuries strengthened individual freedom, but it also made obvious the degree to which people in civil society were interdependent. Hegel, for example, like Ferguson and Hume, argued that the selfish energies unleashed by the market create "a system of complete interdependence, wherein the livelihood, happiness, and legal status of one man is interwoven with the livelihood, happiness, and rights of all."[33] Freedom, from this point of view, did not exist in opposition to society; rather, civil society, by forcing people to recognize the reality of their interdependence, made freedom possible. Freedom was a social, not a natural, phenomenon, something that existed only through the recognition, rather than the denial, of obligations to others.

Given this understanding of the relationship between civil society and moral potential, the development of capitalism through the nineteenth century—although seen by most theorists, including Marx, as a progressive force—also contained the potential to destroy the very civil society it helped create. In the eighteenth century the greatest threat to civil society was the old order symbolized by the state, against which both liberalism and the market were allies. By the mid–nineteenth century the old order was passing, and the moral autonomy of civil society began to be threatened from a new direction. Because the market, capitalism's greatest achievement, placed a monetary value on all things, it increasingly came to be viewed as undermining the ability of people to find and protect an authenticity that was uniquely their own. If an eighteenth-century theorist of civil society were to have appeared in the middle of the nineteenth century looking for a place where individuals could create their own moral rules, he would have found it neither in the private sector nor in the public.

In the nineteenth century, as a result of these developments, the meaning of civil society began to change. No longer a dualistic conception, it became tripartite, standing between the market and the state, embodying neither the self-interest of the one nor the coercive authority of the other. This idea was already implicit, if in somewhat different form, in Hegel, who viewed civil society as a place of transition from the realm of particularism to that of the universal. Other thinkers found in civil society an alternative to both markets and states. Alexis de Tocqueville, for example, anxious to guard against the centralizing power of the state, did not look to "industrial callings" (which, he felt, might reproduce the aristocracy of old) but instead paid attention to ideas of voluntarism and localism. Late-nineteenth-century liberals, wanting to reject laissez-faire but suspicious of governmental collectivism, discovered in pluralism a modified notion of civil society. Certain Marxists, especially Antonio Gramsci, were attracted to the idea of civil society as an alternative to Leninism. And the classical thinkers in the sociological tradition all used civil society as the focal point of their critique of modernity. Emile Durkheim and Max Weber were both strongly influenced by Hegel, and the notion of civil society lay also at the heart of Tönnies's notion of *Gemeinschaft,* Simmel's fear of the influence of large numbers, Cooley's concept of the primary group, the emphasis on local communities in the Chicago school sociology of Robert A. Park, and the concept of a lifeworld developed by Jürgen Habermas. If there is one underlying theme that unifies the themes in sociology that never developed the resiliency of concepts such as the market or the state—such as organic solidarity, the collective conscience, the generalized other, sociability, and the gift relationship—it would be the idea of civil society.

Although civil society seems to have all but disappeared from the modern political imagination, it has in recent years begun once again to attract attention.[34] No doubt the reason for this appeal is an increasing feeling that modernity's two greatest social instruments, the market and the state, have become more problematic. Under extreme conditions of state oppression there can be no question of the power of the ideal of civil society. In Eastern Europe especially, where, in the words of Claude Lefort, "the new society is thought to make the formation of classes or groups with antagonistic interests impossible,"[35] the pluralistic vision associated with civil society seeks to protect an autonomous social realm against political authority.[36] Georg Konrad suggests that "civil society is the antithesis of military society" and that "antipolitics"—his name for morality—"is the ethos of civil society."[37] Adam Michnik writes of Solidarity in Poland:

> The essence of the spontaneously growing Independent and Self-governing Labor Union Solidarity lay in the restoration of social ties, self-organization aimed at guaranteeing the defense of labor, civil, and national rights. For the first time in the history of communist rule in Poland "civil society" was being restored, and it was reaching a compromise with the state.[38]

One need not equate the oppression that exists in Eastern Europe with the imperfections of capitalism in the West to argue that the tripartite theory of civil society can serve as an alternative both to the market under capitalism and to the state under socialism. Contemporary capitalist societies bear little resemblance to the moral world of the Scottish Enlightenment. Composed more of bureaucratic firms than self-motivated individuals, these societies rationalize away personal responsibility rather than extend its realm. Instead of broadening the recognition of mutual interdependence, they deny it, arguing that capitalism is not the product of society but the result of a natural order determined by animalistic instincts. Rather than understanding that economic self-interest is made possible only because obligations are part of a preexisting moral order, they increasingly organize the moral order by the same principles that organize the economy. The more extensively capitalism develops, the more the social world that makes capitalism possible comes to be taken for granted rather than viewed as a gift toward which the utmost care ought to be given. Societies organized by the market need a theory of civil society as much as societies organized by the state, or else their social ecologies will become as damaged as their natural ecologies.[39]

But given the confused meanings associated with the term, how ought civil society be understood? There is certainly a temptation, when faced with the limits of the market and the state as moral codes, to reject both in favor of some preexisting moral community that may never have existed or, if it did exist, was so oppressive that its members thought only of escape. That meaning of civil society is emphatically *not* the one that will be discussed here. Not only is it unrealistic to expect that modern liberal democracies will somehow stop relying on the market and the state, but it is also unfair to ask modern liberal democrats to do without these organizing structures. The market, for all its problems, does promote individual choice, thereby enabling people to act as the creators of their own moral rules. The state, no matter how critical one may be of its authority, not only creates a certain level of security without which modern life would be impossible but, as the Scandinavian societies show, also promotes equality and generally creates a better life for most. Markets and states are here to stay, and it is not my intention to say otherwise.

Moreover, it is anything but axiomatic that the morality of civil society is more "moral" than that of the market or the state. For Hegel, the family was a crucial component of civil society, yet when husbands beat wives and parents abuse children, state intervention ought to take precedence over the sanctity of the family. Theorists of civil society have often put their faith in community, yet when communities practice racial segregation or close their borders, it would be difficult to deny that the market's emphasis on openness is preferable. Even when relations in civil society are based on reciprocity and altruism, they can satisfy obligations to immediate group members to the exclusion of obligations to strangers and hypothetical others. We became modern, in short, for a reason.

There is, however, another meaning to civil society that, instead of embodying some nostalgic hope for a passing order, is more relevant than ever to modern liberal democrats. The themes so important to Ferguson, Hume, and Smith, which later came to be embodied in some of the sociologists influenced by American pragmatism (especially George Herbert Mead), were those of autonomy and responsibility. We learn how to act toward others because civil society brings us into contact with people in such a way that we are forced to recognize our dependence on them. We ourselves have to take responsibility for our moral obligations, and we do so through this gift called society that we make for ourselves. What makes us modern, in short, is that we are capable of acting as our own moral agents. If modernity means a withering away of such institutions as the tight-knit family and the local community that once taught the moral rules of interdependence, modern people must simply work harder to find such rules for themselves. If we do not, then we sacrifice what is modern about us—often, and ironically, in the name of modernity itself.

Modernity's paradox is a paradox indeed. It cannot be resolved either by welcoming markets and states enthusiastically or by rejecting them completely. The question facing modern liberal democrats is whether they can live in societies organized by states and markets yet also recognize (more than they have) that reliance on states and markets does not absolve them of responsibility for their obligations to others—on the contrary, this responsibility becomes all the more necessary. Such a recognition can come, as it did in the days of Ferguson and Hume, only when those whose business is the understanding of society remind liberal democrats of their obligation to protect the social order that makes their freedom possible.

Moral Obligations: Inward and Outward

My aim in this book is to make three points that I hope will contribute to a revival of a sociological approach to moral regulation. The first is a theoretical one: to recall that neither the market nor the state was ever expected to operate without the moral ties found in civil society (see Chapters 1 and 4). Markets flourish in a moral order defined by noneconomic ties of trust and solidarity; markets are necessary for modernity, but they tend to destroy what makes them work. Similarly, the liberal theory of the state was neither purely liberal, for its originators relied on preexisting moral ties to temper the bleakness of the social contract, nor purely statist, because it assumed a strong society. Like the market, the liberal state survives by basing itself on other things than its theory demands.

There has never existed, until the present, a pure theory of either the market or the state. When we look more closely at recent efforts to develop both—such as the effort by the Chicago school of economics to extend the principle of rational choice to all social realms, not just to those we understand as economic; the cognitive treatments of moral obligation found in the work of John Rawls or Lawrence Kohlberg; the justification for state authority associated with conservative political theorists such as Lawrence

Mead; or modern forms of the social democratic welfare state that organize moral relations as well as economic ones—we find that markets and states organized without civil society tend to develop in ways quite contrary to their original intentions.

The second point I wish to make is that as modern societies come to rely ever more thoroughly on either the market or the state to organize their codes of moral obligation, living with the paradoxes of modernity will become increasingly difficult. What makes modern liberal democracy such a frustrating condition is that the less we live in tightly bound communities organized by strong social ties, the greater is our need to recognize our dependence on others, even perfect strangers. To be modern, in short, requires that we extend the "inward" moral rules of civil society "outward" to the realm of nonintimate and distant social relations. Yet states and markets—both of which are "outward" moral codes organizing obligations to distant others—operate in exactly the opposite fashion in their codification of the business of moral obligation, for they have begun to organize "inward" relationships once associated with civil society, such as matters involving the family, the local community, and friendship and other informal networks. (In Jürgen Habermas's language, this process represents the colonization of the lifeworld by system logics.)[40] Civil society is increasingly squeezed from two directions, raising the question of whether, as a result, people are more confused about how to balance obligations to those they love with obligations to strangers and distant others.

Being modern will always require some way of linking both intimate and distant obligations. Although in theory that balance could just as easily be found by extending outward obligations inward, the proper balance will more realistically be found by extending inward obligations outward. The contribution that a sociological approach can make to discussions of moral obligation is to emphasize that no abstract and formal rules exist specifying what we owe others and others owe us. Instead, moral obligation ought to be viewed as a socially constructed practice, as something we learn through the actual experience of trying to live together with other people. It is for this reason that we ought to worry about the weakness of civil society vis-à-vis the market and the state, for the more we rely on impersonal mechanisms of moral obligation, the more out of practice we become as moral agents capable of finding our own ways to resolve the paradoxes of modernity. We need civil society—families, communities, friendship networks, solidaristic workplace ties, voluntarism, spontaneous groups and movements—not to reject, but to complete the project of modernity.

Has civil society been weakened in the shadow of the market and the state? To answer this question in greater detail, I will look at some trends taking place in societies that rely on either the state or the market for their primary moral codes. No society, of course, relies completely on one or the other. Indeed, for all the opposition between them, markets and states reinforce each other in practice. Government, for example, made possible the rapid expansion of private capitalism in the United States, whereas private capitalism provides the surplus that makes possible the welfare states of Western Europe. A similar convergence of economic and political forces operates in the intimate sector of society: when women enter the labor market, government often steps in to provide child care. Yet although the workings of markets and states cannot be separated from each other, it is also true that some societies tend to rely more on the former, while others increasingly use the latter. The United States stands, along with Great Britain, at one end of this pole of experience, with the Scandinavian welfare states at the other.

In the United States numerous relationships, such as those of family, community, and education, that traditionally have been organized by civil society have lately begun to be organized instead by the logic of the market. This is a recent development, and its full implications are barely understood. Moreover, it is at this point still a tendency, not an accomplished phenomenon, and it is possible that in the future the tendency will reverse itself and civil society will once again be strengthened. Nonetheless, as I argue in Chapter 2, this increasing intrusion of the market into civil society raises fundamental questions about obligations to strangers and hypothetical others. Will present generations, under the increasing influence of the market, be able to consider the needs of future generations? What will happen to altruistic instincts, such as giving to charity and voluntary participation, when self-interest becomes more of a moral code in the intimate sphere of society? Does reliance on the market make it more difficult for individuals to restrain their desires in order to share cultural understandings with others? Increased reliance on the market in the intimate sphere of society, in short, reopens the whole question of what makes a distant social order possible.

The penetration of the market into civil society has its parallel in other societies that, far more than the United States, rely on government to express the rules of moral obligation. In order to examine empirically the consequences of using the state as a moral code, I turn in Chapters 5 and 6 to the Scandinavian countries. Just as the extended reach of the market in the United States is a very recent development, the past fifteen years have witnessed a change in the character of the Scandinavian welfare state. Instead of relying on transfer payments, in which the wealthy are taxed to redistribute income to the less wealthy, the state has begun to provide services and build institutions—used disproportionately by the middle class—that perform activities once considered within the realm of civil society. Here too the process is incomplete, but this new welfare state also squeezes families, communities, and social networks, albeit from a different direction than that of the market. Will families be able to function well when government assumes some of their most important functions, including the raising of small children? What will happen to individual altruistic instincts if private charity is replaced by collective benefits administered impersonally? Can obligations to future generations be met when political approaches to moral regulation, based on an interest-group understanding of rewards and benefits, give priority to those who are already organized over those not yet born? Will a sense of obligation continue to encourage the expression of solidarity to others when temptations to cheat on taxes or seek private solutions to public problems become overwhelming?

There is little doubt, at least in this observer's opinion, that the welfare state does a better job than the market of organizing obligations to strangers, yet changes in the intimate sphere in Scandinavia do raise questions about the moral character of the welfare state never anticipated by its founders (and surprisingly similar as well to the problems of market-centered societies). We have, neither in Scandinavia nor in the United States, reached a state of pure capitalism or pure statism, but we are far enough along to understand why the business of being moral and modern simultaneously is so demanding.

The third and last point I wish to make, then, is that instead of serving as a nostalgic reminder of a past that probably never was, sociology ought to recover the moral tradition that was at the heart of the Scottish Enlightenment and was inherited by its nineteenth- and early-twentieth-century practitioners (Chapter 7). The problems that arise from relying on markets and states are compounded because both forces view the moral agent as a rule-follower, not a rule-maker. In the sociological tradition—and even then only in that part which rejects an emphasis on social structure in favor of the notion that ordinary people create moral rules through everyday interaction with others—lies an understanding of moral agency that allows us to bring people back in to modernity, to begin to give them the control in the making of moral rules that the market and the state promised but never delivered (Chapter 8). We would in any case need an understanding of moral obligation based on individuals' ability to contribute to the rules that regulate their behavior; yet as the moral dilemmas faced by liberal democrats intensify in their seriousness—as symbolized by such new moral issues as abortion and AIDS—this understanding becomes more pressing than ever (Chapter 9).

Because social scientists are moral philosophers in disguise, even theoretical discussions of the implicit moral messages they deliver have repercussions in society as a whole. It could turn out to be the case that, as popular as the economic approach is now and the political approach was recently, sociology—a discipline at the moment somewhat lacking in academic prestige—may yet have something to say if the moral limits of the market and the state are increasingly found wanting. My purpose in writing this book is to recall what I take to be the major moral message of the sociological tradition: to maintain their freedom and security, modern liberal democrats need to remind themselves of what a precious gift society is. Society does not carry out our obligations to others for us, but instead creates the possibility that we can carry those obligations out ourselves. If we choose not to do so, we deny what is social about us and are left only with something resembling the state of nature. In that case, it ought not be surprising why modern liberal democrats, for all the wealth their economies have generated and stability their governments have delivered, sometimes wonder what it all means.

Market

ONE

The Dubious Triumph of Economic Man

Can Bourgeois Society Survive Bourgeois Man?

For all that has been said and done in its name, "the market" was rarely discussed by those presumed to have praised it. Adam Smith in *The Wealth of Nations,* which is generally considered a hymn to the efficiencies of the market, rarely uses the term, preferring instead the more general word *exchange.* (When Smith does use the term, he seems to mean it in a physical sense, as in his claim that the division of labor "is limited by the extent of the market," that is, by the size of the economic unit within which production or exchange is taking place.)[1] Smith was not alone in his failure to discuss how markets actually behave. Joseph Schumpeter's massive *History of Economic Analysis,* as Bernard Barber has pointed out, contains no index entry for "the market," and Karl Marx, like Smith, generally assumed that circulation and exchange took place somewhere but never actually specified where.[2]

The tendency of eighteenth-century political economists—and even of those who came later—to ignore the workings of markets may well be because the societies in which they wrote did not have very many of them. Adam Smith witnessed the rise of the factory but was a stranger to a system in which markets were expected to constitute the sole method of exchange. Custom, trust, price regulation, personal contacts, and production for use were far more common in 1776 than was the exotic notion that people should maximize their self-interest through economic interaction with total strangers.[3] As a consequence of the factory system national markets did develop, but only after a revolution in production filtered down

27

through society. A recent exploration of the capitalist transformation of the West notes that the development of markets took place gradually over a very long period, but picks 1880 as a date when "markets were taken for granted as a basic feature of modern economies"—nearly 120 years after *The Wealth of Nations.*[4]

If the classical political economists rarely talked about markets as concrete entities, they talked even less about "the market," an abstract process of calculating the economic gains and losses associated with individual decision-making. Their image of the individual was not as a solitary atom acting from rational choice, but as a person embedded in the kinds of social relations we associate with civil society. Adam Smith believed that a society could break through the restrictions imposed first by absolutism and then by mercantilism, thereby advancing human progress by liberating individuals to develop their own capacities. But this did not mean to Smith, any more than it did to his philosophical contemporaries, that all human action should from this point forward be based on the instrumental quest for self-interest. As Irving Kristol has pointed out, economic man was "never thought to be a whole man, only a man-in-the-marketplace. Smith never celebrated self-interest per se as a human motive, he merely pointed to its utility in a population that wished to improve its condition."[5]

The thinkers of the Scottish Enlightenment, Adam Smith among them, were sociologists as well as economists.[6] As a protosociologist, Smith assumed that a traditional morality and a well-defined social structure would so curb human passions as to permit a realm in which people could be free to pursue their own self-interest; and this pursuit of self-interest was possible only because individuals could be sure that there was a social fabric responsible for all. "Man has almost constant occasion for the help of his brethren," Smith wrote, before adding, in the more often quoted second half of that sentence: "it is in vain for him to expect it from their benevolence only." It was not from any unalterable "original principles in human nature" that man got his famous tendency to "truck, barter, and exchange," but rather from "the . . . faculties of reason and speech"—faculties that, requiring other people for their realization, are at least partly sociological.[7]

The "other" Adam Smith—the sociologist, not the economist—is more easily perceived in *The Theory of Moral Sentiments* than in *The Wealth of Nations,* even though Smith saw both books as part of a unified system of thought. The very opening of Smith's work in moral philosophy establishes a sociological approach: "How selfish soever man may be supposed, there are evidently some principles in his nature, which interest him in the fortune of others, and render their happiness necessary to him, though he derives nothing from it except the pleasure of seeing it." To establish a moral framework while simultaneously respecting individualism, Smith developed the concept of the impartial spectator, who must "endeavor, as much as he can, to put himself in the situation of the other, and to bring home to himself every little circumstance of distress which can possibly occur to the sufferer." (Far from radical individualism, Smith's moral philosophy resembles the philosophies of the American social psychologists Charles Horton Cooley and George Herbert Mead.) We must, says Smith, learn sympathy through empathy. This great founder of capitalist economics even went so far as to suggest that a "disposition to admire, and almost to worship, the rich and the powerful, and to despise, or, at least, to neglect persons of poor and mean condition, though necessary both to establish and to maintain the distinction of ranks and order in society, is, at the same time, the great and most universal cause of the corruption of our moral sentiments."[8] Commercial society, from this point of view, was always on the brink of moral bankruptcy.

The political economists of the eighteenth century were not justifying a capitalist society; their aim was to provide the rationale for a capitalist *economy* within a *society* held together by a nonbourgeois (or, more precisely, early-bourgeois) morality. The difference between a realm of morality organized by economic principles and one organized by the principles of civil society becomes clear in Smith's treatment of friendship. In societies characterized by feudal or absolutist social relations, friendships were formed out of what Smith called *necessitudo*—they were "imposed by the necessity of the situation." In more modern "commercial countries," however, people could join together based on "a natural sympathy" that would enrich and deepen their moral obligations to one another. As Allan Silver, on whose analysis of Smith's treatment of friendship I have relied, concludes, "Smith's model of friendship rests not on calculative and utilitarian exchanges between parties to interpersonal contracts—which, in the context of friendship, are redolent more of patron-client relations than of market exchange—but on generalized mechanisms of 'sympathy.'" Because sympathy "generates a kind of social lubrication throughout civil society," commercial societies are organized by a paradox: only by preserving a realm of morality against all forms of instrumentalism, including the instrumentalism of economic calculation itself, could a society be free to allow economic calculation to take place.[9]

Markets, then, could be reconciled with the early-bourgeois vision of the political economists, but *the* market could not. Specific markets made it possible for people to come together and "truck, barter, and exchange" until they made the best mutual deal. But the market as a metaphor for a process of exchange that would serve as a moral model for all of society's interaction would have been a foreign idea to Adam Smith. In *a* market, friends can rely on their knowledge of one another and the trust they have developed to smooth over economic transaction. But in *the* market, friends are forced to treat one another as potential impediments to self-interest. If we organize all our social relations by the same logic we use in seeking a good bargain, we cannot even have friends, for everyone else interferes with our ability to calculate conditions that will maximize our self-interest. Take away the paradox that was clear to Adam Smith and one takes away what, to Smith, was one of the greatest sources of progress in the modern world: a private space in which authenticity and individuality could flourish. It is not simply that Adam Smith never thought to extend the principle of self-interest to all social relations; on the contrary, Smith recognized that to do so would destroy the very realm of morality that made economic self-interest possible in the first place.

As Adam Smith's ideas have foreshadowed, there has never existed, properly speaking, such a thing as a capitalist society, since the rules that structured capitalist economic interactions required noncapitalist moral values in society as a whole. It can surprise only those uncomfortable with paradox that capitalism lived its first hundred years off the precapitalist morality it inherited from traditional religion and social structure, just as it lived its second hundred years off the moral capital of social democracy. From precapitalist traditions there developed an emphasis on self-restraint, charity, and the organic unity of society that held to a minimum the damage caused by the pursuit of self-interest. From the postcapitalist ideology of the welfare state there developed a concern with solidarity, protection of the weak, and the organic unity of society that filled in the moral gap at just about the same time that religious, family, and community bonds weakened. One reason capitalism was able to flourish was that it could always count on those *not* committed to its vision to provide the morality that made it work, whether they were the aristocrats of the passing order or the socialists of the coming one. Civil society has always made economic man possible.

Thus it is of more than passing importance that a number of contemporary economists have begun to argue that *all* social relations in modern society are (and should be) organized by rational decision makers seeking advantage over others. In the justifications for capitalism offered by Milton Friedman and his disciples, claims are made not for a capitalist *economy*

within a society held together by noncapitalist values but, for the first time
in Western intellectual history, for a specifically capitalist *society*, in which
market freedom will serve as the moral code defining every form of social
interaction. Some contemporary economists, in other words, see bourgeois man as unconstrained by any form of noneconomic moral obligation. This new moral vision raises a question never contemplated by Adam
Smith: can bourgeois society survive the advent of bourgeois man? An examination of what is being said by the University of Chicago school of
economics suggests that it cannot.

Morality and the Market

Chicago school economists certainly do not represent the discipline of
economics as a whole, since many leading economic theorists—Herbert
Simon, Kenneth Arrow, Amartya Sen, and others—have pointed out the
paradoxes of rationality, the possibility of market failure, the need for a
welfare economics dealing with group benefits, and the limits of economic
man.[10] Even among economists who share many of the assumptions of the
Chicago school there are major controversies and differences of opinion,
such as whether one can assume that rational choosers have perfect information or whether individuals who make decisions do so within hierarchies and institutions.[11] One should not, in short, assume that all economists, or even all adherents to an economic approach to moral regulation,
teach or were students at the University of Chicago.

There is nonetheless good reason to pay attention to the theorists associated with the Chicago school of economics. In taking ideas about rational-choice egoism to degrees rarely contemplated before, these thinkers
have about them the air of a revolutionary movement. (There are, in this
context, many similarities between the Chicago school approach and most
forms of Marxism. Both assign priority to economic motives and tend toward structural functionalism; they share similar conclusions with respect
to certain theoretical matters—for example, that government regulation is
done in the interests of those presumably being regulated; and, as I will
argue shortly, the Marxist theory of false consciousness and the Chicago
school notion of optimality are basically the same idea.)[12] As revolution-
aries, Chicago school adherents are the first thinkers to give us some idea
about how moral obligations would be structured if capitalism develops to
the point where economic relations are no longer softened by ties of trust
and solidarity in civil society.

Chicago school theorists insist that the tools of economic analysis can be used not just to decide whether production should be increased or wages decreased, but in every kind of decision-making situation. Thus we have been told (either by Chicago school theorists or by others writing in the same spirit) that marriage is not so much about love as about supply and demand as regulated through markets for spouses; immigration could be much better controlled by selling the right to resettle in the United States instead of by feeble efforts at enforcement of borders; laws prohibiting usury restrict credit for those who need it most; people should have the right to sell their body parts, after they are dead, to any willing buyer; corruption speeds up service and is therefore a rational option when lines are long; the best solution to the problems of surrogate mothering is to allow parties to contract freely on the market with no government regulation; and a man commits suicide "when the total discounted lifetime utility remaining to him reaches zero." [13] From the perspective of the Chicago school, there is no behavior that is *not* interpretable as economic, however altruistic, emotional, disinterested, and compassionate it may seem to others.

The hypothesis that all behavior is motivated primarily by economic factors is revolutionary precisely because relations in civil society—based on such motives as love, a willingness to let others go first, and respect for tradition—have generally been viewed as constraints on people's selfish instincts. (That is why families and communities have traditionally had more moral stature than have markets.) In rejecting that understanding, advocates of pure laissez-faire often adopt a certain "naughty boy" tone, as if morality were of concern only to sissies—another point of similarity with Marxism. [14] Thus economists and moral philosophers influenced by laissez-faire perspectives have argued over whether blackmail ought to be legal because it represents only "the receipt of money in exchange for the service of not publicizing certain information" or have concluded that "someone writing a book, whose research comes across information about another person which would help sales if included in the book, may charge another who desires that this information be kept secret . . . for refraining from including the information in the book." [15] In a similar manner, concerns about insider trading on Wall Street or the practice of hostile takeovers are approached not in terms of right and wrong but as questions of risk and information: we ought to be concerned about insider trading practices, according to one economist, not because "excessive resources are sucked into bribing officials . . . but because so few" are; according to another, arbitragers receive high pay because the information they acquire is so risky to obtain.[16]

"Tough-mindedness" toward moral issues is generally defended on realistic grounds, based on the argument that the economist, rather than ethically justifying people's behavior, is really only scientifically describing it. Yet the economic approach does have a moral dimension, being characterized by an insistence that moral obligations to others can be satisfied only by first satisfying obligations to the self.[17] One could illustrate the particular approach to moral obligation contained in the new economics with any of the above examples, but one other, because it deals with the problem of intergenerational moral responsibility that will be a major theme in the chapters that follow, seems particularly relevant. Suppose you have worked hard, experienced a bit of luck, and managed to accumulate a small fortune. Knowing that no amount of money can buy immortality, you have to decide how to distribute your fortune among your six children. You have three girls: should you treat them equally with the boys? One of your children is lazy and irresponsible: should he get a share equal to the others? Another has always been your favorite: shouldn't you encourage his talents by leaving him more? What makes questions of this sort interesting is that when the children receive the money, you yourself will be dead. Do you therefore have an "interest" in how the money is distributed?

If the social sciences were sciences like biology or physics, they would approach these questions empirically. How, they would want to know, do people make decisions about their obligations to the next generation? We have a good deal of empirical information on this subject: for example, although daughters can face discrimination, people tend to divide their fortunes equally among their children, using a kind of commonsense morality that enables them to avoid difficult issues like whose behavior is to be encouraged and whose punished.[18] But the social sciences are not just descriptive—they are also exercises in moral philosophy. And so it has proven impossible to resist asking a further question: how *should* people bequeath their fortunes? Economists have an answer: self-interest ought to follow us into the grave.

One recent study of these issues by a team of economists offers the hypothesis that people leave money in order to influence "strategically" the behavior of the recipients. Yet as we have seen, the empirical evidence on the matter seems to lean the other way. These economists respond by making three points. First, such nondiscriminatory patterns of bequeathing contradict "altruistic" theories fully as much as they do "economistic" theories. Second, some counterevidence does support the strategic theory of bequeathing. And third (and most crucially for the present discussion), evidence of nondiscriminatory bequeathing "establishes that, for reasons not captured in our model, parents do not manipulate their children 'optimally.'"[19]

The concept of optimality transforms the economic approach from a descriptive science to an exercise in moral reasoning. People, it is alleged, will always act in a rational way when they possess full information. Therefore, if they do not act the way a rational model of behavior predicts they will, their aberrance must be due to an information failure, an inability to make the "optimal" decision. Scientifically, the concept of optimality makes no sense, for it introduces nonfalsifiable propositions into methodology; one can never *not* find rational conduct when such a handy way to explain away discrepancies is present.

To illustrate, consider Timothy Hannan's study of bank robbers. Hannan argues that bank robbers will not strike if bank security precautions are strong enough to deter them. Yet in a study he cites, only 6 percent of robbers knew of police procedures in the area in which they robbed, 82 percent did not know if the money was marked, and 59 percent did not know if the bank had a camera. He concluded that such ignorance was not "optimal" for the robber and that a rational bank robber would obtain such information to be more successful.[20] It would seem that the concept of "optimality" is to the Chicago school what false consciousness is to the Marxist, a catchall that enables the theory to be preserved regardless of empirical evidence to the contrary.

If the notion of optimality makes little sense scientifically, it makes a great deal of sense morally. By upholding an ideal standard against which actual behavior can be found wanting, the notion of optimality asserts the primacy of what ought to be over the reality of what is. In the theorists of the Chicago school of economics, therefore, we find a combative style and mode of argument that is generally associated with moral fervor. There is a challenge in this literature: seemingly altruistic behavior, such as that explored in Richard Titmuss's study of blood donation, is addressed instead with the tools of rational self-interest.[21] Despite the mathematical models, exuberance pervades the literature: political economists apply their models to all kinds of fascinating situations, such as dueling, symbols and clan names, blackmail, plea bargaining, quackery, photocopying, the conditions of academic life, and the deeds of Adolf Eichmann.[22] There is, finally, aggressiveness in this literature, as if its participants were, in fact, at war. (Not surprisingly, rational-choice theorists also think they can explain war.)[23]

If the Chicago school theorists are fighting a war, the enemy, it would seem, is sociology, which for most economists is the discipline least committed to the assumption of rational choice (even though, as I will discuss in Chapter 7, rational-choice theory has gained popularity in contemporary sociology). Gary Becker, for example, allows room for the other social sciences—including sociology—but only if they accept the terrain established by economics.[24] Jack Hirshleifer speaks of the "expanding domain" of economics.[25] Reuven Brenner goes further. He asks whether economics is an "imperialist" science and answers that, because it contains superior predictive ability, it indeed is. Brenner concludes that the efforts of the Chicago school to colonize the other social sciences by using the techniques of economics is not some passing fancy but may be a permanent shift in the hegemony of the social sciences.[26] Science does not generally arouse such passion; only a moral vision can generate a literature so lively. Surely Donald N. McCloskey is correct in arguing that one finds in the Chicago school, especially in the "Kipling of the economic empire, Gary Becker," a form of rhetoric, even of literature, complete with conventions, metaphor, and symbolism. Of this literature McCloskey notes (as is true of all literature): "It is no use complaining that we didn't *mean* to introduce moral premises. We do."[27]

In the days of Adam Smith, moral philosophers addressed questions of economics. Under the impetus of the Chicago school, economists are now addressing issues of moral philosophy. Not all Chicago school theorists see themselves as engaged in moral reasoning. Milton Friedman, for example, is among those who, following in the tradition of positive economics, argues that the role of the economist is not to examine the ethical question of what people's wants ought to be, but instead to develop mechanisms that allow those wants to be maximized—irrespective of what they are.[28] The whole problem of ethics and morality, Gordon Tullock has similarly argued, could be solved if we just developed an academic division of labor: sociologists, psychologists, and political scientists could concern themselves with how preferences are formed, leaving economists free to determine "the likely outcome of the interaction of individuals attempting to maximize their preference functions in a society where it is not possible for everyone to have everything he wants."[29]

This formulation, however, is not especially satisfactory, because ends and means are not so radically distinct; to choose efficiency or rationality as the means is already to make a judgment about the kinds of ends sought.[30] More recently, Chicago school theorists have begun to recognize that positive economics is not enough. If we believe that ultimately there is no accounting for tastes, then we run the risk of value relativism, of failing to examine where the deep structure of preferences begins. George Stigler and Gary Becker recognize the danger of value relativism to their theory and, quite appropriately (given assumptions of their theory), challenge it. All tastes must ultimately be subject to economic analysis, they argue, including tastes shaped by seemingly nonrational behavior such as addiction or fashion, for otherwise the tools of economics would have no special claim over the tools of the other social sciences.[31] In other words, economics cannot be an imperial science unless, like all forms of imperialism, it is also a moral vision, one that asserts the primacy of certain fundamental values—in this case the value of maximum freedom in making choices— over others. That people ought to have as much choice as possible, and that they ought to be given the means to realize their choices in as many areas of their lives as possible, are not scientific but moral objectives.[32]

When the focus of inquiry shifts from an empirical examination of hypotheses to assertions about the nature of wants, the criteria by which arguments are evaluated change as well. Prediction (or even logical rigor) becomes less meaningful than alternative visions of a model of man, a sense of who we are and why we come together with others to fulfill our needs. That such visions differ so widely may explain why debates over rational-choice theory and whether it can serve as a model for all the social sciences, not just economics, tend to be so passionate. When neither religion, tradition, nor literature is capable of serving as a common moral language, it may be that the one moral code all modern people can understand is self-interest. If social scientists are secular priests, Chicago school economists have become missionaries. They have an idea about how the world works. This idea seems to apply in some areas of life. It therefore follows, they believe, that it ought to apply in all.

Markets and Social Constraint

The moral energy that inspires the Chicago school and contributes to its impressive vigor surely stems from the collective sense of its members that they are trying to expand the realm of human freedom.[33] Yet because, in their view, the only serious threat to freedom can come from government, they are, unlike the thinkers of the Scottish Enlightenment, insensitive to the idea that if freedom is a product of civil society, it can be destroyed by the market as well as by the state. If all behavior is viewed as self-interested, then all relationships are instrumental. If we cannot escape rational calculation, the realm of what Smith called *necessitudo* is once again expanded, only now it is the necessity to act out of rational self-interest in everything we do, rather than the necessity imposed by arbitrary political power, that has the potential to threaten the autonomy of civil society. There can be no "natural sympathy" in a world without civil society, and there cannot exist, as a result, social relationships that are worthwhile simply because they are what they are, with no thought given to what they mean in terms of personal gain.

Chicago school theorists do not, of course, directly discuss the nature and character of civil society; indeed, they never even use the term. That they nonetheless manage to indicate their hostility to the idea of a realm of autonomy into which the calculating mentality of the market should not be permitted to enter is illustrated by the notion of compartmentalization. "The heart of my argument," Gary Becker has written, "is that human behavior is not compartmentalized, sometimes based on maximizing, sometimes not, sometimes motivated by stable preferences, sometimes by volatile ones, sometimes resulting in an optimal accumulation, sometimes not."[34] Can we really believe, Richard Posner asks, that "the individual's decisional processes are so rigidly compartmentalized that he will act rationally in making some trivial purchase but irrationally when deciding whether to go to law school or get married or evade income taxes or have three children rather than two or prosecute a lawsuit"?[35] From the viewpoint of these theorists, human beings are presumed always to act in the same way. No area remains outside the scope of the market, for there is only one compartment in social life: the one defined by self-interested action.

How far Chicago school theorists are willing to take their arguments against compartmentalization can be illustrated by Elizabeth Landes and Richard Posner's argument for a free market in babies. At the present time, they suggest, revulsion against the buying and selling of babies, combined with ineffective legal efforts to regulate such activities, has caused a massive number of social problems: irregularities in adoption procedures, dismal foster care, a scarcity of white babies and a surplus of black babies, and excessive abortion. If women were allowed to sell their babies on the market, abortions would decrease because it would be economically feasible for (especially poor) women to carry their babies to term and then sell them: "The emphasis placed by critics on the social costs of a free market in babies blurs what would probably be the greatest long term effect of legalizing the baby market: inducing women who have unintentionally become pregnant to put up the child for adoption rather than raise it themselves or have an abortion." Foster care would be unnecessary, or at least only a last resort, because the demand for and supply of babies would reach equilibrium. Problems of racial discrimination would be taken care of by the market, for blacks would buy black babies and whites would buy white ones: "Were baby prices quoted as prices of soybean futures were quoted, a racial ranking of these prices would be evident, with white baby prices higher than nonwhite baby prices." Baby breeding would be encouraged, but such activity would be of limited importance: "Baby selling may seem logically and inevitably to lead to baby breeding. . . . However, so long as the market for eugenically bred babies did not extend beyond infertile couples and those with serious genetic disorders, the impact of a free baby market on the genetic composition and distribution of the human race at large would be small." In short, Landes and Posner argue that direct moral restraints on the exchange of babies are ineffective regulators; encouraging people's rational action through the market would do a superior job in solving many of the existing problems that social workers and sociologists have failed to solve.[36]

Landes and Posner's article, like so much of the Chicago school oeuvre, reads as if its authors were deliberately flouting conventional morality in asserting the strength of their new vision. (It also contains a Swiftian sense of irony, but that is presumably unintentional.) By choosing babies as the subject of their analysis, they no doubt wanted to emphasize their objection to sentimentalism, to the idea that there are precious things that are not possible commodities or that do not have economic value. They could hardly have picked a more appropriate example, for to most people the relationship between parents and children is the very definition of civil society: an intimate realm in which caring will serve as a relief from the demands of self-interest reinforced in the economy.

The objection to compartmentalization is thus an objection to the notion that people will develop different moral rules appropriate to different spheres of conduct. Since the meaning of civil society lies precisely in the fact that it establishes realms of intimacy, trust, caring, and autonomy that *are* different from the larger world of politics and economics, to abolish compartments in favor of one moral model is to abolish civil society. That prospect is what makes the theory of the Chicago school so controversial. Few doubt that economics is a powerful tool, that it has an appropriate place in society, that there ought to be markets that organize some aspects of life, and that encouraging rationality and self-interest can be an appropriate moral guide in some of what we are called upon to do. But to break down *all* compartments so that only rational choice remains is another matter entirely.

Many of those advocating such a course recognize how unprecedented their proposals are. Gary Becker could never be accused of misunderstanding Adam Smith, for he points out how often Smith refused to extend the logic of self-interest into noneconomic, especially political, matters. In contrast to Smith, who strove to delineate different realms with different moral rules, Becker believes that market assumptions are "applicable to all human behavior, be it behavior involving money prices or imputed shadow prices, repeated or infrequent decisions, large or minor decisions, emotional or mechanical ends, rich or poor persons, men or women, adults or children, brilliant or stupid persons, patients or therapists, businessmen or politicians, teachers or students." The assumptions of the market posit individuals as utility maximizers who operate from a stable set of preferences and obtain satisfaction in a market equilibrium with others. If used "relentlessly and unflinchingly," Becker writes, such assumptions provide "a valuable unified framework for understanding *all* human behavior," yielding insights "for understanding behavior that has long been sought by and eluded Bentham, Comte, Marx and others."[37]

If, as Gary Becker claims, Smith was an insufficient Smithian, other market enthusiasts seem to feel that Bentham was not Benthamian enough. The utilitarian calculus Bentham invented was supposed to solve many sticky problems of ethical and moral theory by reducing them to individual decisions about pleasure and pain; for this reason, utilitarianism has generally been criticized by moral philosophers for its insensitivity to the moral and ethical issues that have long dominated Western discourse.[38] To the pure theorists of the market, however, Bentham is an inappropriate guide because his philosophy has *too much* moral content. Richard Posner sees no contradiction in the fact that many leading Benthamites, especially John Stuart Mill, could switch to a socialistic philosophy once they deduced that a market system was not maximizing pleasure and minimizing pain. Pleasure, pain, and happiness, key terms in the utilitarian calculus, are value-laden terms, Posner argues, containing the totalitarian implication that one can determine for another what is pleasure. This constraint could be eliminated if we substituted for utilitarianism a different set of calculations, which Posner calls "wealth maximization." Any action that increases the wealth of a society is morally grounded, and any action that detracts from the maximization of wealth is ethically dubious. For Posner, then, the problem with utilitarianism is that it does not respect individualism *enough*: "the pursuit of wealth, based as it is on the model of voluntary market transaction, involves greater respect for individual choice than in classical utilitarianism."[39] Rarely before has the notion that fulfilling one's obligations to oneself is sufficient to fulfill one's obligations to society been so strongly articulated.

Chicago school economics thus represents what could be called a second generation of marketplace enthusiasts. The first generation, from Adam Smith through (perhaps) Herbert Spencer, were pluralists who accepted what Michael Walzer has called "separate spheres";[40] in their theories, as I have argued, morality provided a framework within which economic activity would take place. For the second, more monistic, generation of market enthusiasts, there is only one sphere, the economic. Its fundamental assumption that people seek to maximize their self-interest applies to all behavior, *even when markets do not exist*. Richard Posner, for example, has argued that judges, faced with a decision in which no way of calculating costs and benefits exists, should nonetheless create what he calls a "hypothetical-market approach" to guide their decisions.[41] There is in his view no separate sphere of justice. Indeed, there are no separate spheres at all, not even one for markets, if we understand those as physical places where people socialize as well as buy and sell. In the second generation of capitalist justification there is only *the* market, a mental process through which people calculate what is advantageous to them and what is not.

However theoretical and abstract the writings of the Chicago school of economics are, they illustrate what would happen if the realm of civil society were to disappear—in this case, under pressure not from the state but from the market. A world without civil society is a coercive, not a libertarian world, because it would destroy the noninstrumental ties between individuals that make freedom possible. Why, for example, do societies prevent the buying and selling of babies—or, for that matter, depending on the society, the running of nursing homes for a profit, advertising on television, the selling of blood, or the ability to avoid military service through payment?

The answer to this question lies, to paraphrase Oliver Wendell Holmes's comment on the law, not in logic, but in the social experience that shapes our lives. Modern people live under conditions in which ties of family, community, and friendship are weakening under the impetus of the market, as I will argue in the two chapters that follow. If we knew that civil society were secure—that we could expect that friends would live in the same places they grew up, that families would rarely divorce, that voluntarism and charity were strongly ingrained obligations—we might not worry so much about the intrusion of the market. But we know that these realms of intimacy and community are threatened; we seek to compartmentalize, therefore, for that is the only way to prevent civil society from being weakened further. Compartmentalization, in that sense, represents our recognition of the gift of society, our understanding that some things are too valuable to be associated with value. Hence it is not that people are by nature too "good" to sell their own children—make them desperate enough and they might even contemplate eating them. Rather, we create social rules to restrict the freedom of a few to buy and sell as they please in order to protect everyone else from buying and selling.

Michael Walzer calls these efforts to prevent the intrusions of the market into civil society "blocked exchanges," and he presents us with a fairly comprehensive list of what they are, including the selling of human beings themselves, political power, criminal justice, freedom of speech, marriage rights, exemptions from military service, divine grace, and "trades of last resort."[42] (That some of the items on Walzer's list have been put up for sale, such as police protection, which is increasingly private, or justice, which is increasingly corrupted, indicates how vulnerable civil society is under modern conditions.) Compartmentalization, it would seem, is necessary for freedom; only by isolating the most sacred of our common possessions can we be sure that we can keep them. To eliminate this ability to compartmentalize is not to increase our freedom but to subject us to obedience to rules over which we have little control. This is why Walzer, always judicious in his choice of language, can write that "a radically laissez-faire economy would be like a totalitarian state, invading every other sphere, dominating every other distributive process. It would transform every social good into a commodity. This is market imperialism."[43]

Because they seek the abolition of civil society, Chicago school theorists illustrate not the dangers that follow when people are given too much freedom, but the vulnerability of a realm of freedom to a realm of coercive authority.[44] A pure market society becomes, in Charles Lindblom's appropriate metaphor, a prison.[45] To the degree that a society chooses to organize all its affairs, not just its economic ones, by the logic of the market, to that degree would be created a society of nonautonomous individuals, unable to decide how they should live, though retaining, insofar as the market will allow them, the right to decide where.

Situated Freedom

Economists, strategic theorists, and even an occasional novelist have been fascinated with a game called "the prisoner's dilemma."[46] This game envisions a situation in which two people arrested for a jointly committed crime are held in different cells. Each is told that if he blames the other, he will go free. If each one acts out of self-interest and testifies against the other, however, both will wind up worse off. For any given player, therefore, the dilemma is whether to pursue self-interest or seek cooperation. The former avenue can mean big winnings but also big losses. The latter rewards both players, but in lesser amounts.

One question that the prisoner's-dilemma game addresses is whether people are better off when they make decisions based on what they think is in their own interest or instead try to take other people's points of view into their moral accounting. Robert Axelrod, a political scientist, demonstrated one answer to this question through the deceptively brilliant device of asking prominent economists and game theorists to enter a prisoner's-dilemma tournament themselves.[47] The program that won the first round, submitted by Anatol Rapaport, was called "Tit for Tat." The strategy involved deliberately losing the first round of the game and then simply repeating the other player's moves indefinitely. At some point the opponent receives a signal that communication is expected and returns the moves of the first player. Once cooperation is established, both players benefit more than they would under any alternative strategy. When Axelrod submitted a request for a second round in the tournament, informing all applicants that "Tit for Tat" had won the first time, the same strategy won again, even though some players attempted deliberately to beat it.

Reflecting on the results of his research, Axelrod argued that cooperation can produce more rational results than the more conflictual strategy of relying on self-interest. His results have been interpreted as suggesting that it is possible to resolve conflict without having to resort to all-out violence. No doubt this is a correct interpretation, but another conclusion also follows from his experiment. Suppose, for example, that a Chicago school theorist were invited to play in this tournament.[48] Would his submission, in accord with the theories of the school, base each move on the logic of self-interest? If so, would it fare well? It turns out that one of those who responded to Axelrod's initial invitation was Gordon Tullock, who, while not at Chicago, is a fairly extreme exponent of the idea that rational self-interest can be used to explain noneconomic behavior. Tullock did in fact submit a strategy based on optimizing self-interest: it finished next to last, barely beating out random responses.[49]

What seems clear from this experiment is that in any given situation there are two different ways to think about freedom. Those who followed Rapaport's winning strategy operated out of a situated understanding of their freedom. "This is where I am," they were saying, "in this game now with this potential opponent also in the game. I can deny the reality of my opponent and act as if my motives were the only ones that mattered, but if I do that, my freedom is reduced because he will act in the same way. If I instead recognize the reality of interdependence as the defining situation for my action, I can increase my freedom, but only by considering the point of view of others in making my decisions." Tullock, in contrast, operated from a conception of freedom which demands that the agent ignore the actual situation and make choices based on an a priori rule, in this case the rule that one try to maximize self-interest. His understanding of freedom seems to work by the rules of logic and clear thinking, but when applied to a specific situation it led only to frustration.

Modern people do not live in the tightly bound world of unalterable ties that characterized traditional society, but they do live in situations nonetheless. When people make decisions, they tend to look not to a mathematical formula to determine what is to their best advantage, but to what others do, to what they have traditionally done, or to what they think others think they ought to do. As with the prisoner's-dilemma game, a theory of moral obligation can either ask people to recognize the situations in which they find themselves and to develop their moral rules accordingly, or it can insist that they act out of principles that deny the limits imposed by situations. Modern people usually find themselves in three situations in particular: they live in time; they occupy space; and the rules that define their interaction are the product of a specific culture. Chicago school economics is premised on an effort to escape the limits imposed by all three of these givens.

Because we can do only a finite number of things at any one time, it is not difficult to conclude that economics, which is concerned with scarcity, can study the allocation of time just as well as any other good for which demand exceeds supply.[50] Clearly, in that sense, time has always been money. But time is also a constraint, a limit imposed on human activity by the fact that people need time to sleep, to vary their routines, and even, in a variety of circumstances, to wait. Because time imposes limits on what we can do, it plays havoc with assumptions about perfectly rational economic behavior. Wages, for example, tend to be determined by how long one has worked for a firm, not by one's contribution to the output of that firm.[51] Schemes to organize factories and offices to operate around the clock invariably fall victim to higher rates of absenteeism and turnover than occur in more "normal" nine-to-five work.[52] Invariably, more hospital "emergencies" take place on Mondays than on Sundays, and not even induced labor can explain why so many more babies allow themselves to be born on workdays than on weekends.[53]

Although time is money, therefore, not *all* time is, if for no other reason than that the number of hours in a day is limited while the amount of money available to society is not. Both biology and society guarantee that there will always be some time that is protected against the emergence of twenty-four-hour rational maximizers. Rather than accepting situations defined by time, however, theorists associated with the Chicago school resist all such constraints; from their perspective, there is no real distinction between time spent in economic activities, as generally understood, and all other time, such as weekends or periods spent sleeping—the latter are simply less associated with utility.[54] Yet because time is situational, any effort to maximize one person's time at the expense of another's means that neither of them can sleep. To live *in* time rather than *against* time requires shared rules that determine its distribution, rules that presuppose cooperation over time. Thus Axelrod discovered that when players viewed the prisoner's-dilemma game as a one-time-only event, they tried to act out of pure self-interest; but when they recognized that they would be playing the same opponent over and over again, they agreed to the rules of "Tit for Tat."[55]

There exists, in all societies, a commonsense understanding of moral obligation that warns people of the dangers of trying to escape the constraints imposed by time. To put the matter another way, people are often willing to wait. Yet why would one wait, when it is as clear to that person as it is to a Chicago school theorist that not waiting often has monetary advantages? We wait because we expect that most others will also wait. (People are generally willing to let one or two persons jump a line, but they recognize, often through acts of spontaneous collective definitions of the situation, that past a certain point the line breaks down.)[56] Waiting, in short, depends on the existence of the expectations of trust and solidarity that characterize civil society; through trust, as Niklas Luhmann has written, an individual "binds his future-in-the-present to his present-in-the-future."[57] Only when people have some sense that they share a common fate with others will they be willing to wait, even if their common fate is as minimal as entering a theater. (This is why societies always have implicit or explicit waiting rules, as I shall call them in Chapter 9—priorities that determine who gets what when.)

When people wait, they often do so in a specific place. Space is, like time, either a defining feature of the situation we are in or something from which premises of rational conduct demand we escape. Perhaps because of its link to civil society, contemporary sociology tends toward the former approach. People who examine the symbols created through mutual interaction are spatially oriented, because some physical place—what Erving Goffman called a "stage"—is necessary before people can work together to create their social realities. The very lines that people wait in form somewhere: at movie theaters, unemployment centers, or bus stops. These queues contain their own cultures, their own rules, their own dynamics. They bring together people who have something in common and put them in a situation conducive to the ritualistic expression of shared norms and interests. These factors may explain why people sometimes wait in line even when they do not have to; in his study of Australian rules–football queues, Leon Mann found that people will line up twenty-four hours in advance of the match even though they could buy tickets two hours beforehand without problem. Because the queue is a small-scale society, "lining up to get tickets for the event . . . almost becomes an end in itself, with its own intrinsic rewards and satisfactions."[58] In a similar way, auctions, which to an economist are abstract mental processes through which prices are established, are viewed by sociologists as lived experiences, located in specific regions of the country and even in particular halls and auditoriums, where generally like-minded individuals come together to define value through a process of social negotiation.[59]

In contrast to the sociological view that specific spaces contribute to the definition of group identity, the economic point of view tends to stress that people cannot appreciate a specific place for sentimental, emotional, or social reasons when rational calculation leads them to put a price on what that space, as a commodity, is worth to them.[60] Clean air and good architecture, both qualities associated with specific spaces, are, according to some economic theories, valuable only to the degree that they can be

translated into monetarily quantifiable benefits.[61] It therefore follows that
if ties to a particular place, rooted in family life or love of community, interfere with an individual's ability to act by rational choice, that individual
will move; thus migration, which can be so disruptive of social ties, is "a
means of promoting efficient resource allocation."[62] Similarly, "consumer
voters," as they have been called, will choose a place to live based on how
local services meet their preestablished preferences.[63]

The early political economists, Donald Lowe has written, contributed
to the idea that a sense of space (and time) could be liberated from the
limits imposed by stagnant societies.[64] Yet liberation from space, like liberation from time, can have unexpected consequences. The whole point of
liberating space was to create an opening within which different interests
could flourish. Yet when space is valuable only because of the price into
which it can be converted, it can have no meaning outside its costs and
benefits. Without compartments in life, without emotional ties to specific
places, without restraints on the mobility of labor and capital, all space becomes indistinguishable, valuable not because of its inherent symbolic
meaning, but only because others consider it worthwhile purchasing.
Space, which was brought into calculations of political economy by the
eighteenth-century theorists, is factored out again by late-twentieth-
century adherents of the Chicago school of economics. (To protect space
or, more correctly, specific spaces against the market, societies need what
I call "entrance and exit rules," which will also be further discussed in
Chapter 9.)

A third feature of situated reality for most people is culture. People do
not think of themselves as decision makers located outside the categories
that define their similarities with others; indeed, they tend to understand
their identity primarily as a cultural one, as representative of a group that
has a shared language, common symbols, certain sacred practices, and a
history. Culture, by definition, can never be universal; it is a form of compartmentalization, a way of differentiating one group from another. The
assumption of rational choice, by contrast, is put forward as cross-cultural,
applicable to all people in all places at all times, even though, as Kwang-
kuo Hwang has pointed out, models of economic man are of little help in
deciphering rules of social interaction in non-Western societies.[65] Not surprisingly, therefore, the University of Chicago tradition in economics is
hostile to culture, viewing it as an obstacle to the ability of people to make
their decisions as rationally as possible. From its point of view, culture is
an impediment to freedom. Like separate compartments, or indeed like
time and space, it ought to be broken down.

One will not find in the writings of the Chicago school of economics an explicit theory of culture, even though some thinkers, such as Richard Posner, have tried their hand at understanding the rules of "primitive" society.[66] But just as its hostility toward compartmentalization can be read as a distrust of civil society, the attitudes toward culture contained in contemporary theories of the market are revealed by discussions on another matter entirely: the assumption of stable preferences. Preferences, after all, come from culture. Since we cannot, at least without great frustration, prefer what we do not know exists, our preferences are shaped by the social world in which we live. Any theory of preferences is a theory of culture, and any theory of culture is a statement about preferences.

Economists associated with the Chicago tradition assume that individual preferences are not whimsical but reflect some consistent internal structure. Although many economists take pains to point out that the assumption of stable preferences is only an assumption, that their use of the concept is not meant to describe real behavior, the vehemence with which the assumption is asserted indicates a certain reluctance to abandon the idea that people's behavior is in fact predictable. In that sense, the assumption of stable preferences is more than just a fine point of methodology; it contains a model of man, a theory about the kinds of persons that certain economists believe should exist if the world is to become a more understandable place. To envision a society with stable preferences that are presumably shaped by "human nature" or basic acquisitive drives is not to transcend culture but to express the values of a society where culture is already weak and unable satisfactorily to bind. Since people already know what they prefer, they have no need to turn to institutions, traditions, other people, literature, or even television advertising, which might reveal new preferences.

In few other areas are the differences between Chicago school economics and most forms of sociology sharper than in that concerning the stability of preferences. Sociologists often begin with the assumption that, in the absence of social interaction with others, one can never know what one's own preferences are. In Harold Garfinkel's world, for example, we view individuals so complex that they can assume nothing; not even their sexual-preference schedules, as we see in his treatment of the transvestite Agnes, are fixed. All our preferences, even those one would assume to be determined by biology, change as we present ourselves to the world around us.[67] If Agnes is not sure whether she is a man or a woman, how can anyone be certain whether he prefers washing machines or blenders, much less know what is moral or just? Because we do not know who we are, let alone what we prefer, we have to interact with others to find out. Making demands on others is a way of making demands on ourselves. We cannot know what we want unless we know what other people want.

The world according to Garfinkel (and also to Erving Goffman) is a world in which reality and appearance never seem to coincide. Exactly the opposite could be said of theories of stable preference: there, appearance and reality are always the same. Consequently, the world of Chicago school economic theory is, for all its libertinism and radical secularism, a world without melody or frivolity. It would be enormously difficult to imagine great novels being written about people with stable preferences, for they would undergo no *Bildung,* either as a result of their internal moral development or of their confrontation with society. A world of stable preferences would be one in which there was no language, no persuasion, no history, no art, and no meaning. Strip away man's capacity, indeed his willingness, to interact with others and so alter their preferences (and therefore take the risk that they will alter his) and the ability of people to develop thickly textured lives is also stripped away. Such sterility may be why, despite theories of rational choice and their arguments to the contrary, most people accept the limits defined by culture. Not only are these bounds enormously difficult to resist, but they also make freedom, or any other value, possible by giving it a name and establishing rules for its use.

Because Chicago school theorists paint a picture of individuals struggling to liberate themselves from situations defined by time, space, and culture, there is in their work a touch of the Nietzschean *Übermensch.* The image of Ulysses at the mast, used to illustrate some of the problems of rational-choice theory, is appropriate, not only because Ulysses must bind himself in order not to respond to the sirens, but also because Ulysses is an epic hero who has escaped the circumstances of bounded life.[68] This promise of freedom from the ties of situation is what gives Chicago school economic theory its appeal, but it is also a major source of its difficulty as a moral theory for modern society. Freedom in an interdependent world, as Charles Taylor has argued, is not an abstract right, but a product of circumstance and context. Unlike pure individualism, which leads to a self that "is characterless, and hence without defined purpose, however much this is hidden by such seemingly positive terms as 'rationality' or 'creativity,'" the concept of situated freedom, as Taylor calls it, understands free activity "as grounded in the *acceptance* of our defining situation."[69]

It ought, therefore, to be clear why Gordon Tullock, who followed a strategy of pure self-interest, continually lost in the prisoner's-dilemma tournament to Anatol Rapaport, who accepted that the situation required taking the point of view of the other into account. Even though the prisoner's-dilemma game involves only two people and modern societies involve the interaction of enormous numbers, we nonetheless all find ourselves in situations where the pursuit of rational self-interest lessens people's ability to protect time, preserve space, and utilize their cultural tools. Civil society—concrete relations located in specific times, places, and cultures—allows people to define who they are.

Quasi-Modernity

Gary Becker, Richard Posner, and other enthusiasts for the market find it puzzling that people do not apply rational choice to everything they do. Yet, they seem to feel, given time, information, the right inducements, and the freedom to calculate what is and is not in his own interest, modern man will be able to dispense with old-fashioned moral restraints and, for the first time in human history, live purely by his own efforts. He has the possibility of becoming rich, but, even more important, he is modern. He ought, therefore, to be happy.

Yet unlike the optimistic welcoming of modernity one finds in the work of Adam Smith and his philosophical contemporaries, the world of Chicago school theory is not a happy one. Struggling to liberate ourselves from time, space, and culture, we are too busy to be satisfied.[70] We are engaged in a desperate struggle to be rational, even while recognizing that the more rational we are, the less fulfilled we seem to be. We are free in everything we do except defining, with others, who we are—yet that one exception, to our surprise, turns out, in a society characterized by the need to work together with others, to be the very definition of freedom. Bourgeois man without bourgeois society can enhance his wealth or self-interest, but he loses his ability to negotiate his way through the complex moral difficulties that modernity brings in its wake. He is logical in everything he does, but, as E. M. Forster concluded in *Howard's End*, "one's hope was in the weakness of logic."[71]

The promise of economic rationality is that, by following their own self-interest, individuals will automatically contribute to the social goal of a coordinated division of labor. There is an obvious need, with the modern condition so complicated, to believe that invisible hands, self-interested behaviors, and unanticipated consequences will do for society as a whole what they once seemed to do for markets, that is, coordinate diverse behaviors into a harmonious whole. One can understand the appeal—social coordination seems less abusable when made less visible. Put coordination out of sight; sublimate the collectivity through the actions of the individual; transform the irrational by emphasizing the rational. Let me keep my own and I will become, without ever being conscious of it, my brother's keeper. Scale down the moral demands, lower the ethical horizon, and bring people's behavior more in accord with how they are, not how they should be. Rather than being an affirmative manifesto of progress, reliance on the market under modern conditions is a message of resignation, an admission that the problems of complexity in society are so enormous that they can never be approached directly.

By eliminating from its moral vision a place to which people can go to escape the demands of rational choice, the Chicago school of economics reveals that the concept of moral agency associated with civil society is as essential to twentieth-century life as it was to the conditions in which Adam Smith wrote. We may want to believe that we can live without having to consider the needs of others when we act, but the moment we extend the dynamics of self-maximizing behavior to all areas of life we begin to realize our dependency on what others do. By denying the moral complexity that follows from the need to take account of others, economic models make fewer demands on the moral capacity that people, as social creatures, are capable of possessing. The price we pay for using these models is that, in denying the social in favor of the natural, we lose the very modernity they once gave us.

At this stage in their development, Western liberal democracies have by and large settled their accounts with nature. What they need is not a moral code first developed when the natural world threatened the social, but instead a moral code that incorporates the understanding of society and how it works which the past centuries have given us. We may have been wise, given the negative record of some of the experiments with collectivization in the twentieth century, to keep our faith in the promise of the market. But irrationality is not solved by calling it rationality. Coordination is not made easier by calling it freedom. Abuses of power are not curbed by redefining them as morally permissible. People do not satisfy their responsibilities to one another by thinking only of their responsibility to themselves. Economic man, so modern in his freedom, is only quasi-modern in his obligations; he is responsible for his own fate but, to the degree that he follows economic models of economic choice, has little sense of how to treat others. To create a society as modern as the individuals who compose it, we must look beyond rules that emphasize self-interest to rules that enable people to take account of who they are and who they want to be.

TWO

Markets and Intimate Obligations

The Reach of the Market

In the writings of the Chicago school of economics we have been presented with an outline of what can only be called a "second bourgeois revolution."[1] For early theorists of capitalism, especially Adam Smith, selfishness was a virtue, to be sure, but only if restricted to the realm of economic exchange. Not only the theory but also to some degree the practice of capitalism retained a distaste for the notion that the principles that organized the marketplace could be relied on to organize society as a whole.[2] No such apologetic tone characterizes the theorists of the second bourgeois revolution. If completely free choice is good enough for the economy, they are saying, it ought to be good enough for everything else.

The ideas of the Chicago school of economics can, if one so chooses, be dismissed as the latest in a series of somewhat bizarre cults that from time to time inflict their passion on otherwise sober academics. It is certainly the case that articles published in obscure academic journals, in which mathematical symbols have slowly risen in proportion to English words, are not likely to spur major transformations in society. Yet social science can not only influence but also foreshadow society. In their own peculiar way, Chicago school theorists have recognized trends that for American society (and perhaps a few others) raise new and complex moral dilemmas.

These trends involve not merely the increasing popularity of laissez-faire economic instincts and the public policies that follow from them. Lately, especially in the United States, government regulation of the economy has weakened, organized labor has become less able to restrict business prerogatives, and international competition has made the market more attractive than at any time since the 1930s. But in addition to the economic changes so visible in the United States, in recent years reliance on the market to structure choices made in civil society has grown markedly. In many ways this latter development is more revolutionary than the former, for although Americans have traditionally preferred the market to the state in the economic sector, in the intimate sector of society neither family life nor community relations were ever expected, throughout most of American history, to be organized by the logic of self-interest. Americans found in the family, in community spirit, in the voluntary group, and in principles of altruistic charity a self-image that stood in sharp contrast to the materialism of their economic life. If the notions of the Chicago school of economics—most especially the idea that no compartments exist to protect intimate and community life from the penetration of the market—foreshadow what is taking place in society, the moral implications for the United States are great indeed. We owe ourselves a closer empirical examination of the degree to which the boundary between civil society and the market has weakened in the one society in the world where, it is generally agreed, the market has worked wonders.

Private Families

Americans have generally viewed families as entities that ought to be at least partly protected from the reach of pure market forces. Of course, a good deal of romanticization is associated with this sentiment, since economic factors have always influenced family life in the United States, as everywhere else. Yet despite the fact that the family sector and the market sector have never existed in complete isolation from each other, the degree to which they have begun to interpenetrate in recent years does seem to represent a new stage in their mutual evolution.

Statistically speaking, the most striking indication of how far the logic of the market can penetrate into civil society is the change in the nature of the family brought about by increased adult (and even some nonadult) involvement in the labor market. Since men have worked for a wage for some time, this change inevitably involves women. In 1940, 14.7 percent of married women (with a husband present) were in the labor force; this statistic increased year by year, to 30.5 percent in 1960, 40.8 percent in 1970, 50.7 percent in 1980, and 54.2 percent in 1985 (see figure 1). Certainly, as historians and sociologists have pointed out, women have always worked.[3]

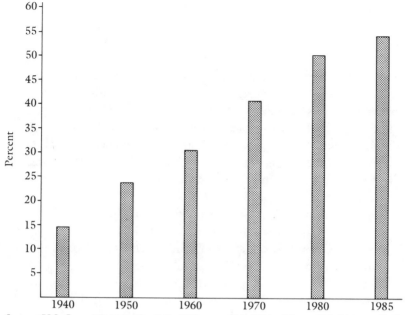

Source: U.S. Census Bureau, *Statistical Abstract of the United States* (Washington, D.C.: Government Printing Office, 1985), p 398; (1987), p 383.

Figure 1. Married Women (with Husband Present) in the Labor Force, United States, 1940–85

But they never worked, at least to this degree, by market principles. The primary form of women's work in nineteenth-century France and England was domestic service, that is, not in their own home but in someone else's home. Moreover, women did not take possession of their wage to dispose of as they wished until the twentieth century; before then they worked, as Louise Tilly and Joan Scott put it, "in the interest of the family economy" and, as a result, seemed "almost like an internal backwater of pre-industrial values within the working class family."[4] The post–World War II development, then, in which large numbers of women work in the market on a market basis, is "not a continuation, but a departure from, the earlier patterns."[5]

There are a myriad of reasons for the fact of working women. The most important, because it affects the most women, is that women have been forced to work. Increasing rates of divorce have combined with the structure of the welfare system to impose work discipline on poor women; the "feminization of poverty" is thus both cause and consequence of the intervention of the labor market into women's lives.[6] Moreover, for those not quite poor but hardly rich, a second income has become an economic necessity. As Paul Blumberg has documented, in the postwar period median family income rose sharply, from (in 1978 dollars) $8,848 in 1947 to $17,640 in 1978, a trend that, not unexpectedly, almost exactly parallels the increasing number of women in the labor force. Yet that rise has slowed considerably in the years since 1978 (see figure 2). When the effect of being raised into a higher tax bracket is taken into account, the median family income in 1979 was less than in 1969, even though more women were working.[7] For families at the margin of the middle class, and increasingly for middle-class families as well, in short, women are working so that the family can, at best, remain in the same place.

Not all of the increase in female labor force participation, however, can be explained by women's being forced to work. In a study of the choices women make between work and family, Kathleen Gerson found that fragility of marriage and domestic isolation were as important in women's deciding to go to work as strictly economic reasons.[8] For many of the women she interviewed, work appeared more as a pull than a push up the economic ladder. Among middle-class women particularly, the desire to work reflects the heritage of the woman's movement and the drive toward equality of the 1960s and 1970s; no longer content to remain home, women work for self-esteem, for greater decision-making authority within their families, and for security in the event of divorce.

As Gerson's research makes clear, the weakening of the boundary between family and the market has real benefits, especially for women. These benefits are so important, moreover, that most people, including this author, believe that we should not, even if we could, "go back" to the family structure of the 1950s. (In the "traditional" family, an artificial division of labor in which fathers were responsible for income and mothers for nurturance—by absolving the father of responsibility for the children and the mother of responsibility for the family's finances—stunted almost everyone.) Yet one ought also to recognize that, along with the greater freedom of choice associated with market intervention into the family, it is more likely that considerations of self-interest associated with the economy will serve as moral codes within the family than that the family will serve as a moral world capable of influencing behavior in the economy. This moral logic of self-interested rational calculation is reflected in such areas as family size, arrangements for child care, patterns of marriage and divorce, and relations among grandparents, children, and grandchildren, all of which,

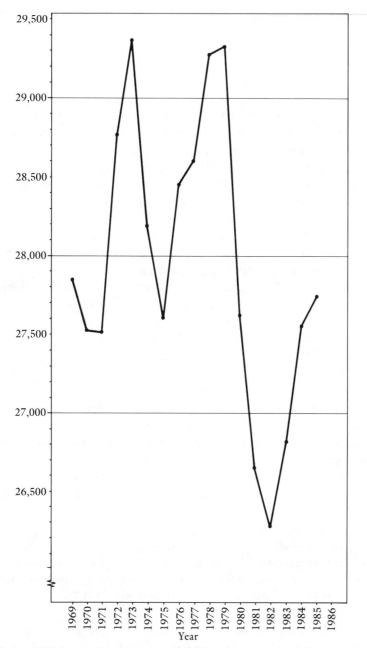

Source: U.S. Census Bureau, *Current Population Reports. Consumer Income, Series P=60. Money Income and Poverty Status of Families and Persons in U.S.* (Washington, D.C.: Government Printing Office, 1987).

Figure 2. Median Family Income, United States, 1969–85 (1985 dollars)

when combined, do seem to indicate a far greater reliance on the market as a moral code in the intimate sphere of society than existed previously.

Family size is one of the first factors to be affected. The entry of women into the work force coincided with technological improvements in birth control, making it possible for a greater number of women to engage in rational calculation with respect to pregnancy.[9] For some women, especially those committed to a time-occupying career, postponement of pregnancy, even to the point of impossibility, was not uncommon.[10] For those who wanted both work and children, single-child families became the sound compromise position.[11] As a result, fertility rates tended to go down as female participation in the labor force went up.[12]

Any number of children, even one, needs full-time care. The ways in which children are brought up also tend to be increasingly affected by the logic of the market, especially among the middle class. In working-class families, where "the emphasis is on help, cooperation, and solidarity with a wide range of kin,"[13] there is greater reliance on relatives to watch children than among professional and managerial workers.[14] In black communities in particular, grandparents are still a much-relied-upon source of support for child care.[15] Among middle-class families, by contrast, which put "strong emphasis upon the self-sufficiency and solidarity of the nuclear family against all other kinship ties and groupings," child-care needs tend to be contracted out in the market.[16] As Gerson discovered in her research, "reluctant mothers" did not "seek help from relatives or friends unless it was voluntarily offered." Afraid of the obligations that such ties would entail, "paid child-care arrangements were overwhelmingly favored by the group."[17] The career mobility needed for success in the corporate world makes impractical any kind of child care except hired help. Rosanna Hertz puts it this way:

For many dual-career couples, the location of the worksite takes them away from close networks of extended kin; career demands may require leaving the neighborhood and often the city where their family resides. . . . Many couples believe that their income is or ought to be sufficient to enable them to arrange childcare without incurring financial or, more important, familial indebtedness.[18]

Marriage itself has, like childrearing, become oriented increasingly along marketlike principles of exchange. As Andrew Cherlin has pointed out, "the generation that came of age after World War II differed from generations before or since in its pattern of marrying, divorcing, and childbearing."[19] Those born around 1920, Cherlin discovered, married earlier, had more children, and stayed married longer than those born around

1950. For the 1920s couples, in contrast to the generation that followed, marriage ties were more binding than the kinds of self-interested relations found in markets. As with working women, couples who established the dominant social tone of the 1940s and 1950s were the statistical exception, not those who came later; late marriage, for example, is far more common historically than early marriage, and remarriage was as common in earlier times as it is now, if much more often because of the death of a spouse than divorce.

Searching for an explanation of why an earlier generation opted for more binding ties, Cherlin cites the work of Glen Elder, Jr., who investigated the experiences of the Great Depression on those who grew up in its aftermath.[20] Elder's research demonstrates the importance of economic conditions outside the family to the choices that take place within it. Male children who experienced the Great Depression, for example, achieved more later in life than those who were unaffected by it, perhaps because of the searing economic insecurity they suffered.[21] Women of the Great Depression developed strong attachments to the marriage bond.[22] Even though the depression caused enormous stress on marriages, those unions that already had strong bonds tended to be strengthened even more.[23] One possible conclusion from this research is that those who experience most directly economic vulnerability to the market are less likely to structure their moral choices around market notions of free entry, rational choice, and quick turnover. This concept may also help explain why working-class and minority families, who are also extremely vulnerable to the market economically, rely more on traditions of reciprocity and dependency on kin than middle-class families.[24]

For the generation whose formative years were spent not during depression but during historically unprecedented prosperity, inexperience with the downside of the market may help explain their greater willingness to leave marriages more quickly. Two-income families have clearly raised more people into prosperity, but at the same time pressures from the market make marriages more precarious. As Blumstein and Schwartz put it, "In today's world, work and home life are more separate than ever, with work demanding much or all of a person's energy. The relationship may too easily become a secondary aspect of the individual's life. Work-centered people may not really want the relationship to go under, but if no one is serving as its advocate, the things that made a couple's life together special may be lost."[25] Whether or not increasing divorce rates can be directly attributable to market pressures, it is not so much the extent of divorce but rather *how* people get divorced in the United States that reveals how the decision-making logic of the market has penetrated the reality of family life.

As Lenore Weitzman has pointed out, ease of divorce has "shifted the focus of the legal process from moral questions of fault and responsibility to economic issues of ability to pay and financial need." Alimony may have been demeaning, but at least, in contrast to no-fault divorce, it was based on a theory of reciprocity, in which the wife's contribution to a husband's career was recognized. Equal division of property sounds fine in theory, but since men earn more money because they have a career (to which the wife often directly contributes), decisions to divide property equally "free men from the responsibilities they retained under the old system, [and] 'free' women primarily from the security that system provided."[26]

No-fault divorce, it would seem, is to marriage what laissez-faire is to economic policy, an effort by the state not to intervene in a matter of social significance. Also like laissez-faire, it is based on individualistic assumptions. New divorce laws, to continue with Weitzman's account, "alter the traditional legal view of marriage as a partnership by rewarding individual achievement rather than investment in the family partnership." While the laws are meant to apply to divorce cases at hand, they also affect behavior in marriage in the future, since they contain "incentives for investing in oneself, maintaining one's separate identity, and being self-sufficient."[27]

If husbands and wives loosen their ties, the effects will be felt by their children as well. Half of today's children will experience the breakup of their parents' marriage (or their own) during their lives.[28] One study of extremely affluent and mobile families north of San Francisco discovered that children still felt the pain of their parents' divorce five years later.[29] Although most children of divorce may well recover within two years, as has been argued,[30] children of divorce nearly always lose contact with the nonresident parent over time (or continue a relationship at so superficial a level that it involves what has been called "a ritual form of childhood").[31] There seems little doubt that when marriage ties were stronger, so were ties to the generation that came after, and likewise that as marriage becomes more individualistic, so do questions of responsibility to children.

Since the income of divorced women will go down while men's will increase, where do these women turn for support, especially women with children? Many turn to the generation that came before: their own parents. How contemporary grandparents and grandchildren treat their responsibilities to each other is the theme of Arthur Kornhaber's recent work. "A great many grandparents have given up emotional attachments to their grandchildren," he writes. "They have . . . , in effect, turned their backs on an entire generation." The result, he feels, is "a new social contract," the effects of which "have sheared apart the three-generational family and critically weakened the emotional underpinnings of the nuclear family."[32]

There is reason to believe that Kornhaber's conclusions are excessively dramatic. For one thing, ties along the female line across three generations remain strong in America.[33] Moreover, the whole thrust of Kornhaber's thesis has been challenged by Andrew Cherlin and Frank Furstenberg, who argue that because ties between grandparents and grandchildren are more subject to choice, they are more rooted in affection. Yet Cherlin and Furstenberg's informants do tend to confirm that Kornhaber is touching on important developments, for most of them wanted to experience the joys of casual interaction with (particularly young) grandchildren but also wished to avoid the responsibility of serious emotional ties. "Your children are your principal; your grandchildren are your interest," two members of Cherlin and Furstenberg's sample told them independently.[34] What is interesting about this comment is not so much the choice of an economic metaphor as it is that the accumulation of principal requires hard work and delayed gratification, as the early Protestants realized, while the accumulation of interest is passive and, from some points of view, even decadent.

Because so many American grandparents respect what Cherlin and Furstenberg call the "norm of noninterference"—laissez-faire rhetoric can be applied not only to families about to break apart but also to those staying together—ruptures have developed in the three-generational family unit as the market has come to serve as a metaphor for ties in the intimate realm. It is not surprising, therefore, that Cherlin and Furstenberg found that American grandparents "strive to be their grandchildren's pals rather than their bosses," "concentrate on those relationships that promise the greatest emotional return on their investments of time and effort," "do not play a major role in the rearing of their grandchildren," "do not directly transmit values to their grandchildren," and have, in short, "been swept up in the same social changes that have altered the other major family relationships—wife and husband, parent and child."[35]

Families in America have by no means disappeared, but they have, it would seem, been considerably changed. In a wide variety of family functions—ranging from the decision whether to enter the labor force to how many children to have to who should watch them to how relations within the three-generational family should be structured—the market has become a more important guide to choices made in one realm of civil society, that of the family. Marriages are more frequent and do not last as long; romance gives way to the hard realities of two-income families; time is always too short, friends too busy, and relatives preoccupied with other things.[36] Few like to, but people find themselves having fewer children and turning to the market for help in raising them. These developments reveal a picture of what can be called the private family, a tie that binds, to be sure, but one that does not bind so tightly that it can override a tendency of its members to ask what their family can do for them, not what they can do for their family. Individualism—which in, say, Hegel's philosophy would be countered by the demands of family—has become an increasingly important part of the way the modern family functions.

It is by no means inappropriate, therefore, that family relations have become one of the major areas in which economic theorists of the Chicago school have applied their tools,[37] nor that some sociologists have been, at least to some degree, attracted to the resulting models.[38] Yet when calculations of self-interest do become more relevant to moral decision-making in the intimate sphere of society, we ought to recall the findings of three psychologists in a study of American values:

When, finally, individual happiness becomes the criterion by which all things are measured, when the ability to withstand, strength of character, position in a community, the good of the group, exemplary and responsible adult behavior, and/or the welfare of one's children are all subjugated to individual happiness and "self-realization," then social arrangements weaken. And the calculus assumes a market quality: all things are measured by hedonic coinage.[39]

The effects of a more privatized family, in short, can be felt not only in the family itself but also in the society around it. Thus when ties in the intimate realm weaken, ties in the somewhat more distant realm of community can be expected to weaken as well.

Community and the Market

Community, Kai Erikson has written, is "the most sociological of all topics."[40] It is the basis for the distinction between *Gemeinschaft* and *Gesellschaft,* the ingredient presumed to be missing in nearly all studies of the instrumental rationality of modern life and the empirical locus of the distinctive contribution of American sociology. Yet despite a near consensus around the notion that modernity undermines community (including Marx, Weber, Tönnies, Durkheim, Simmel, Park, Wirth, Nisbet, and Parsons), contemporary sociologists and historians have found a surprising amount of community to have persisted in American life, not only in small towns[41] but even at the very center of the metropolis (particularly in working-class, minority, and ethnically homogenous areas).[42]

Although many have claimed that community need not necessarily decline as modernity advances, the concept of community is, at least to some degree, in tension with one of modernity's major instruments: the market.[43] "A community," Thomas Bender has written, "involves a limited number of people in a somewhat restricted social space or network held together by shared understandings and a sense of obligations"; thus, for community to exist there must preexist "a network of social relations marked by mutuality and emotional bonds." Community ties, consequently, are quite different than market ties. The former are intimate, reciprocal, and sympathetic, while the latter tend to be impersonal, rational, temporary, and instrumental. Americans have fought hard to hold on to community values because they understood that the growth of purely instrumental economic relationships would destroy the quality of their local societies. Their residence and their locality, in other words, would serve for them as a protection against a market over which they otherwise would have no control. "Market and community became alternative and competing patterns of order."[44]

In their effort to draw a distinction between community and the market, Americans possessed one overwhelming advantage. Land in the United States was so plentiful that not even the most ingenious capitalist could figure out a way to commodify it. By its very nature, land is difficult to organize by market principles, for markets are generally best at organizing mobile things, like commodities or human labor. As Peter Wolf has pointed out, "There is no central marketplace in real estate. The object of the transaction cannot be moved. Its value is so dependent on location that a distinct marketplace is irrelevant. Real estate is thus by nature more dependent on local people, local knowledge, and local deals than most other types of investment."[45] Precisely because real-estate organization was local rather than national, culturally and symbolically the notion that land should never be subject to the absolute logic of market priorities retained its power well into the second half of the twentieth century.

Even a generation as late as the one that came of age during the Great Depression and World War II—which, as we have seen, did not structure

internal family life according to market principles—was able to protect itself against the full effects of the market in its choice of residence as well.
For many Americans of that generation, the G.I. bill offered home mortgages at below-market rates, enabling them to afford the new, and relatively inexpensive, housing that was being built in the 1950s. Income-tax
policies were the single greatest subsidy in the postwar housing market.[46]
Not only was land subsidized, but so were building costs, as government
support for research into prefabrication helped develop aluminum clap-
boards, predecorated gypsum-board ceilings, plywood paneling, and other
staples of postwar housing.[47] Finally, even the money that people borrowed to pay for their houses was not lent to them on market principles;
fixed-rate mortgages, for example, absolved an entire generation from inflation for thirty years. Even working-class people, who are often the most
exposed to the market, were, in their housing choices, protected to some
degree against it. David Harvey has shown how in Baltimore "the white
ethnic areas are dominated by homeownership which is financed mainly by
small community-based savings and loan associations which operate without a strong profit orientation and really do offer a community service"[48]
and has pointed out how such savings and loan associations once made
"use of detailed local knowledge about both housing and people," before
giving way to national banks more interested in straightforward considerations of profit and loss.[49]

Given this protection against the market, it is not surprising that even in
urban areas community in America came to be defined in terms of social
networks and subgroup ties. Claude Fischer's extensive research into urban networks indicates that modern people living in cities are not isolated,
alone, and schizophrenic, as many critics of modernity alleged they would
be. Fischer demonstrates that even in the largest of cities, Americans have
extensive contacts with friends and workplace acquaintances. Cities ex-
emplify what he calls "more voluntary and modern kinds of associations,"
founded not on kin and tradition, but instead on "political alliance, cultural tastes, sexual proclivity, common handicap, and so on."[50] It is even
possible to argue, as Mark Granovetter has, that such "weak" ties actually
contribute to "strong" societies, because they "are indispensable to individuals' opportunities and to their integration into communities."[51] An
entire generation of urban sociologists in America has shown that the
negative view of the modern city upheld by Louis Wirth is by no means
accurate.

The problem is whether this positive American sense of community,
like the American image of the family, can survive the penetration of mar-

ket logic into civil society. Granovetter's argument about the strength of weak ties, because it is based on new opportunities, assumes favorable economic and social conditions (mobility, for example, presupposes continued economic growth). Similarly, Fischer's research into the social life of American urban residents was undertaken under economic conditions that were unusually positive. Americans could protect community because, in many ways, the market had not yet penetrated it. Community, in other words, even when strongest, is still potentially vulnerable to economic transformations. As Fischer points out,

kinship has always been the essential interpersonal glue of society; friendships can be seen as luxuries people develop in times of security, affluence, and freedom. One wonders about how strong unexercised kin ties will be in times of social trauma. If economic collapse, war, mass migration, or some other catastrophe struck northern California, could these people, particularly the city-dwellers, rely on their otherwise inactive kinship relations for survival?[52]

In some ways, the crisis that Fischer discusses did happen, and northern California was one of the first places it occurred; but it was not an economic collapse that caused the crisis, but an economic boom. Liberated by national banking, instant communication, geographic mobility, increasing scarcity, and capitalist ingenuity from local roots, housing in America became a dynamic investment, one so profitable that it led, for the first time, to the introduction of market principles into real estate, thereby transforming the whole meaning of community in America.

Rapidly increasing housing prices (between 1976 and 1984, the median price for existing housing rose from $38,000 to $72,000, and for new housing from roughly $40,000 to $80,000)[53] have been the single most important economic reality facing Americans over the past decade. To purchase increasingly expensive homes, Americans assumed higher levels of debt. Despite a generation's experience that in any month one week's salary should go to housing, homeowning costs, which before 1980 rarely exceeded 15 percent of the owner's income, increased to 42 percent by 1982, before leveling off at 33 percent a few years later.[54] (When combined with consumer installment debt, total debt in 1986, as figure 3 indicates, had grown dramatically over a decade.) In order to afford high levels of debt, many Americans began to experiment with new financial techniques that tied them directly to money markets of various kinds: when introduced in 1981, variable-rate mortgages accounted for 28 percent of all mortgages, and increased to as high as 70 percent in the years thereafter;[55] likewise second mortgages increased from roughly $10 billion in 1987 to $55 billion

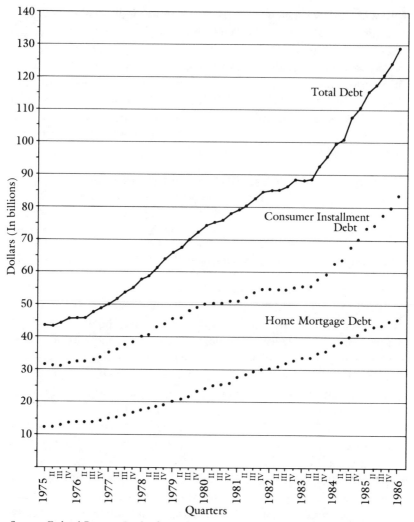

Source: Federal Reserve Bank of New York, *Quarterly Review* (Summer 1986), 16.

Figure 3. Estimated Home Mortgage and Consumer Installment Debt Service Payments, United States, 1975–86

in 1985.[56] These years saw as well the introduction of an active secondary mortgage market, so that homeowners often did not know who actually possessed their mortgage note. Even the subsidy provided by federal tax policies changed, as a major tax reform in 1986 decreased the share of housing costs paid by the government. The only surprise in all this was how long, in the development of this one capitalist society, it took before capitalism came to organize the real-estate market.

The results of the introduction of market principles into real estate—in which decisions about where and how to live are made under conditions of scarcity, both in land itself and in the money used to build on it—are predictable. Homeownership itself became more of an impossibility; although homeowners rose from 44 percent of American families in 1940 to 66 percent in 1980, this figure decreased to 63.8 percent in 1986, a decline that one government agency called "the first sustained drop in home ownership since the modern collection of data began in 1940."[57] The percentage of defaults on mortgages for one- to four-unit residential housing more than doubled between 1978 and 1983–84.[58] Moreover, the dollar amount of properties repossessed, as measured by the Federal Savings and Loan Insurance Corporation, increased from $797.4 million in December 1979 to $7.7 billion in 1985. A wall of protection between community and the market no longer seems to exist.

The changes brought about in people's relationship to the land on which they lived (and the built structures within which they lived) took place, and in no small measure were also due, to the exposure of American cities to a world-capitalist market from which they had once been more insulated. "The future of a city can never be deduced from its own internal potential trajectory," Harvey Molotch and John Logan have written, "but rather how it is institutionally integrated into the international system through which production and rent are organized."[59] While not a crisis in the sense of the Great Depression, the experience of full vulnerability to a national and international market, without support from strong ties of kin and neighborhood, creates for Americans a unique situation. Will Americans still form healthy networks, create vibrant subcommunities, join voluntary associations, help their neighbors when in trouble, support social services, and take pride in their place when place is defined by the market and no longer by community? Because the intervention of the market into the community is so recent, answers to these questions must necessarily be fragmentary. But some evidence exists that the nature of community life in America will change as market logic prevails.

As both national and international markets penetrate into urban life, some cities will become richer while others will become poorer. Interestingly enough, the moral consequences of both processes are similar. Wealthy cities like San Francisco experience a building boom, often called Manhattanization, that seems to their residents cold and unfeeling.[60] Poor cities like Elizabeth, New Jersey, instead of bemoaning the loss of industry in favor of insurance, bemoan the loss of industry in favor of nothing. There too, however, distrust and a complete lack of community solidarity once more replaced tightly bounded social codes.[61] Cities in America seem either on the way up or on the way down; in either case, they no longer appear to their residents as places in which social ties between individuals remain strong.

A parallel situation has taken place in rural areas, which in the past decade have been subject to unusually sharp swings in economic fortune. Both "boomtowns" and "busttowns" are places where suspicion, divorce, alienation, and distrust tend to increase. The energy crisis of the 1970s, by driving up the price of imported oil, brought a boomtown mentality to such states as Colorado, Oklahoma, Texas, and Louisiana. While rapid economic growth had many positive consequences, there were negative ones as well. Young people were especially alienated from the economic boom; not only did rates of antisocial behavior increase, but "boomtown's youth" did not experience rapid growth as either liberating or beneficial.[62] Although crime itself did not increase, fear of crime and suspiciousness toward strangers did.[63] Economic growth brought about an increase in off-farm employment in rural areas, which, at least in the case of families without strong traditions in farming, caused strong marital tensions.[64] Even those sociologists who felt that the negative consequences of boomtown growth had been exaggerated still found social problems: "The boomtown phenomenon does not disrupt actual informal ties, but it does diminish the effectiveness of facilities that support informal ties such as friendliness and community spirit."[65]

Booms tend to be followed by busts. The group of Americans that in recent years faced the full force of an economic bust are the same Americans that have been most exempt from the dictates of the market: American farmers. Not only has the federal government subsidized crop prices, but in their communities farmers borrowed money from local bankers who could be flexible in terms of repayment, and they developed cooperative relations of trust with other farmers, pledging to help each other out when times were bad. As the effects of a real market hit American agriculture, the moral nature of rural life began to change. The economic stress associated with farm depression caused personal stress in marriages, as people blamed each other for the problems they faced.[66] As was the case with boomtowns, rural poverty increased homicide, suicide, and divorce.[67] Mortgage foreclosures and repossessions, as in urban and suburban areas, increased measurably. The percentage of farmers in the Department of Agriculture's bank-lending area who went into bankruptcy rose from 0.75 percent in 1982 to 4.2 percent in 1986, while the rate of legal foreclosure increased from 18.1 percent of all farms that went out of business to 26.3 percent.[68] "Although anomie, implying a total breakdown of community, is far too strong a term," a leading expert on rural America wrote, "there appears to be widespread rural malaise and an unfilled potential for rural community development."[69]

These changes in the nature of the rural community have been exacerbated by the new social relations that have developed between bankers and farmers. Bank deregulation led to the closing of many local banks and their replacement by branches of national banks. Not unexpectedly, independent banks had been more likely to lend to smaller farmers and to be flexible in repayment schedules, while national banks insisted on making the farmer's decisions for him, including decisions about conservation and what to plant.[70] The consequences of such functionally rational decision-making on communities that had always operated otherwise have been vividly captured by journalists and novelists. Andrew Malcolm, who covered the farm crisis for the *New York Times*, wrote:

There was less trust in communities once held together by nods and handshakes. Now storeowners, longtime friends, asked for payment up front, or a letter from the bank guaranteeing payment come harvest. The bank . . . sent out computer-printed warnings to folks who'd never missed a payment, and were proud of it, just to be sure they wouldn't think of such a thing now. . . . The unprinted message in all of this was unmistakable: suspicion and fear were being unleashed.[71]

Rural areas have always had pride of place in the American moral imagination. Those who not only lived on the land but also worked on it for their livelihood would truly be moral. Their possession of land and their ability to apply to it their capacity to work anchored their existence in an otherwise unstable world. Only thus anchored could the farmer secure community, working together with like-minded others in ties of trust and local loyalty. When America became an urban and industrial nation, this link between morality and the land might have been permanently severed—except for the invention of the suburb.

In postwar America, the suburban home became the very definition of moral identity. Definitions of the self, as well as presentations to others, took place primarily through living arrangements.[72] As Constance Perin has emphasized, questions involving land use, no matter how economic, are also moral in nature: they "name cultural and social categories and define what are believed to be the correct relationships among them."[73] Americans, Perin argues, possess an implicit notion of a "ladder of life," in which progress through a series of predetermined steps results in the reward of single-family homeownership. In this way, social time and social space are linked, for passage through time guarantees possession of desired space. When the system works properly—that is, when people obey rituals of deference in youth in order to be rewarded with transition to a higher status when older—all is well with the world. At the end of the process, American homeowners become home sellers, realizing the profit that has accumulated in their one major investment and therefore prepared to spend their retirement years in comfort. The suburb, as the theater in which this moral drama took place, became the alternative to the brutal world of the market. Not a place for self-interest and the war-of-all-against-all, the suburb embodied friendliness, voluntarism, and community spirit. As Herbert Gans has emphasized, *class* was once a dirty word in American suburbia.[74]

This entire moral life cycle, it turns out, was premised on a housing market that never really worked as a market. It assumed that housing prices would always increase, when in real markets prices go down as well as up. It assumed that one would hold on to a house long enough to pay off the mortgage, when in real markets commodities are frequently bought and sold. It assumed that one had solidaristic relations with one's neighbors, since all would be experiencing the same rites of passage simultaneously. None of these assumptions were able to survive the introduction of real markets into American beliefs about community. Far more young people will never be able to buy a house, no matter how dedicated they may be to the rules of the game. Those who do will live in them for even shorter periods than already mobile previous generations as "trading up" becomes more common and long-term financial planning more uncertain. When a seemingly "natural" life cycle is broken by realities of income and class, it is no wonder that the notion of the suburb as a refuge from the harsh realities of money declines; in contrast to the silence about class found by Gans a generation ago, Mark Baldassare in a more recent investigation found suburbanites who could hardly talk of anything else. Contemporary suburbanites, he discovered, tend to be pessimistic, distrustful, unwilling to tax themselves to pay for services, and hostile toward newcomers.[75]

As with the family, the weakening of the compartment between the market and civil society often means that the moral logic of self-interest takes precedence over the moral logic of altruism and community service. Journalistic accounts covering the suburbs north of New York City discuss how rising housing prices and longer commuting times have made severe inroads into working-class enclaves and how as that takes place volunteer fire companies and other such nonmarket social practices no longer can recruit enough participants.[76] (In general, according to the only study available, volunteer firemen are white, married, small-town residents with generally a high school education, all of which suggests that they will, indeed, be unlikely to survive the entry of marketplace considerations into community.)[77] American suburbs were once thought of as strong cultures; indeed, a common story of American life in the 1950s was that in the suburbs conformity and group ties were so strong as to be stultifying. Now, under conditions of rising property values, the suburbs may be becoming so individualistic as to be anomic.

Although many of the transformations experienced by Americans as the market penetrates ideals about community are disruptive, the picture is obviously not entirely negative. The small community, which so emphasized moral life, was also stultifying and repressive. The bright lights of the city are difficult to shun, especially for people committed to cosmopolitan values. Mobility, for modern people, is as necessary as connectedness—and the market places a premium on mobility. Just as the entry of women into the labor market helped to destroy the inequities of the "traditional" family, the introduction of market rationality into community has had positive effects, such as the revitalization of older neighborhoods. Moreover, markets, at least in theory, like to remove "artificial" obstacles, and at least some of the progress made in America in breaking down racial and religious barriers is due to the triumph of the market, even if it substitutes income barriers in their place.

It is not the role of the market in decisions involving community that is really at issue, but its scope. From playing relatively little role in determining how Americans shall live, the market has come to play a very great role indeed. The somewhat abstract idea associated with urban economists inspired by the Chicago school—that space ought not to place emotional or traditional obstacles in the way of purely rational calculation—has begun to be more than a hypothetical possibility for many Americans. This development, moreover, has come simultaneously with the changes in family life discussed above. Because of this link between family and community, the introduction of market principles into both—at roughly the same time and applying to roughly the same generation—creates a double squeeze on people's expectations. The community, like the family, may be able to overcome these tensions and remain intact. Yet whatever happens in the future, the penetration by the market into community indicates a weakening of civil society that will be difficult to counteract.

The Market and the Common Life

One reason why Americans put so much faith in the idea of community is that a society organized by the market does not place a premium on public things. For Americans in search of a common life to counterbalance the effects of individualism, no institution was more public than the school. If there were a trinity of American inspirational stories, education would take its place alongside family and community as a place where public morality and virtue could flourish. "Whereas the United States was late and unenthusiastic . . . about the creation of modern welfare state policies, it was early and enthusiastic about the creation of modern public schools," Ira Katznelson and Margaret Weir have written.[78] Given their attachment to the common school, Americans were quick to establish boundaries around schooling to prevent the market—always viewed as efficient, rarely as moral—from coming in.

Thanks to the efforts of a generation of "revisionist" historians, we now know that nineteenth-century economic elites viewed educational reform as a method of reinforcing capitalist class relations at a time of industrial transition.[79] The discovery of economic motives behind mass education in the United States helps correct a previous picture that emphasized moral and religious fervor as the main inspiration for those movements, but it would be a mistake to ignore moral motives entirely.[80] Early common-school advocates, as David Tyack and Elizabeth Hansot have pointed out, were motivated by their moralistic and redemptive commitment to Protestantism.[81] Agents of educational change "were actors whose authority was more moral than official. . . . What held such individuals together, in this 19th-century conception of the polity, was not the coercive or normative power of the state but their common consciousness of the laws of God and the demands of rational human order."[82] Even when, in the early years of the twentieth century, American schooling began to be organized along professional, scientific, and managerial lines, reformers still had something more in mind than a narrow fitting of unskilled workers to skilled work. For them professionalism was, however self-serving, also an ideology that emphasized service to the public good.

TABLE I. *Private School Enrollments, United States, 1965–83*

	Total Number					Percentage Change
	1965–66	1970–71	1975–76	1980–81	1982–83	1965–83
Catholic schools	5,574,354	4,361,007	3,363,979	3,106,378	3,027,312	−46
Non-Catholic schools	795,453	1,004,408	1,228,370	1,748,568	2,277,729	+186
Total	6,369,807	5,365,415	4,592,349	4,764,946	5,305,041	−17

Source. Bruce S. Cooper, "The Changing Universe of U.S. Private Schools" (Institute for Research on Educational Finance and Governance, Stanford University, November 1985), 25.

As is the case with families and communities, the boundary between schooling as representative of community values and the market with its emphasis on self-interest has begun to break down. One indication of the declining commitment to public education is, of course, private education. Private schools have always existed in America alongside the public ones, and numerous signs indicate that their use is expanding. A dropoff in attendance at Catholic schools has been more than met by an increase in attendance at just about every other kind of private school. One researcher estimated the increase in non-Catholic private-school enrollment between 1965 and 1983 at 186 percent (see table 1).

It is not hard to find reasons for this change in Americans' commitment to public schools. Three sociologists have argued that private schooling provides greater future economic advantages than public schooling.[83] Although their data have been strongly criticized on methodological grounds,[84] the advantages of private over public schooling in America are indeed not only economic but also cultural, as an increasing number of parents know.[85] Private schools provide high school seniors with much better advice on college than do public schools, for example.[86] This may well be because public schools are characterized by legal/rational authority relationships, while private schools rely more on consensus.[87] If, in short, it is expected that people will make rational choices about schooling, it is clear which type of school, if they can afford it, they will choose. Cooper's conclusion that "parents may be treating both the private and public schools as a kind of 'educational marketplace'" seems the only realistic one.[88] (This increase in private-school attendance cannot, of course, be attributed to marketplace calculation alone; fundamentalists, for example, show extremely high rates of private-school switching, but this is for religious and moral reasons, not economic.) [89]

Recognizing changes such as these, some economists and public policy advocates have urged that educational vouchers, which would enable people to purchase private schooling with public dollars, be formally adopted in the United States. This idea has never caught on, though; Americans remain leery of allowing the market to intervene *directly* in the one aspect of their common life they hold most dear.[90] Indirect market intervention, however, is another matter entirely. Americans who can afford to do so tend to "buy" their public school by buying their house. Suburbanization has perhaps done more to destroy the ideal of common schooling than any other factor in American life. As Katznelson and Weir point out, "the geography of the American urban system has changed in ways that have made the hegemony of the market over the public schools nearly complete."[91] If increasing attendance in private schools is combined with movement to the suburbs, in which higher school taxes become the purchase price of quasi-private education, then public schools, instead of countering the effects of the market, become the market choice for those priced out of other markets.

The market affects not only where one goes to school but also how. Just as women have been entering the labor market in ever greater numbers, so have students. It is not homework but paid work that shapes the moral consciousness of American students. "A Study of High Schools," a project cosponsored by the National Association of Secondary School Principals and the Commission on Educational Issues of the National Association of Independent Schools, emphasized the incredible demands on students' time, due in part to the fact that most high school students work while attending school.[92] A "High School and Beyond" survey taken in 1980 estimated that 75 percent of the boys and 68 percent of the girls between sixteen and eighteen years of age were in the work force.[93] Young people have always worked in America; what is new is that now *students* work. Two psychologists, Ellen Greenberger and Laurence Steinberg, have examined in detail the implications of teenage work on schooling. Interestingly enough, they found that many students do not work because they are driven by economic need; moreover, they do not turn their salary over to their parents (though minority students still do).[94] High school students work to have more to spend, a surprisingly large percentage of it on what would be considered "luxury" items.[95] As "A Study of High Schools" puts the matter, "With so many opportunities competing for their attention, it is no wonder that many students—and their teachers, whose time is precious for similar reasons—regard school as just another part-time job."[96]

Working is often thought to be good for young people because it encourages independence and maturity. But this point of view, Greenberger and Steinberg argue, ignores the kinds of work available for most American teenagers.

Whereas work at one time served a valuable educational purpose for young people, performed an essential economic service to the family and community, and facilitated the development of relationships between young people and nonfamilial adults, during the past one hundred years early work experience has declined in its educational value, in its economic significance, and in the degree to which it fosters meaningful intergenerational contact.[97]

The decline of the educational value of teenage work, Greenberger and Steinberg continue, has intensified greatly in the past twenty-five years. During that time "old" styles of work, such as factory jobs or farm work, declined precipitously, while "new" styles of work, essentially service-sector jobs, increased just as dramatically. Indeed, only two jobs—in merchandising and food service—account for nearly half the jobs held by teenagers. Teenagers, especially including students, fill a particular niche in the national market: they work when other people eat dinner. Moreover, Greenberger and Steinberg found that such service-sector jobs do not prepare young people for adult work, do not contribute to intergenerational solidarity, and tend to harm performance in school. American teenagers reach adulthood knowing far more about how the market works than they do about history (or, for that matter, sociology).

Since marketplace considerations affect where and how children in America go to school, it should come as no surprise to discover that they have also become a metaphor for describing what takes place *in* the school. "A Study of High Schools" concluded that American high schools are best compared to shopping malls: students are buyers, and fickle ones at that, whereas teachers view themselves as sellers, often of commodities that the buyers would rather avoid. "The shopping mall high school cares more about consumption than about what is consumed." In contrast to an older image of the school, one rooted in compulsory-attendance laws, discipline-oriented teachers, and a standard curriculum, the contemporary American high school is committed to the notion of freedom of choice, which is often proudly seen as a "distinct virtue."[98]

The moral consequences of the shopping mall high school are not dissimilar from those of shopping malls themselves, for which moral sprawl is as good a term as any. "Our job is not to teach morality," one teacher told Arthur Powell and his colleagues, while another claimed, "I don't think it's good for me to impose my values on the class."[99] The stories the research team heard in a variety of American high schools confirmed the point. If lockers were vandalized, staff were quick to blame it on the lockers, not the vandalizers. Moral sanctions against improper behavior such as cheating were weak. Even when students did something blatantly wrong, staff tended to be divided on how to respond. That students might consider themselves responsible for their appearance seemed a foreign notion indeed. No moral value was attached to mastery of a subject. Faculty members were individualistic, having few meetings and few interests in common. A refusal to establish standards applied even to academic matters; teachers were quite often unprepared to draw the line between passing and failing performance. In the American high school, this study concluded, consumers have sovereignty, anything can be purchased, and, as in most laissez-faire situations, there are no coercive sanctions capable of saying no.

Many of these changes in the nature of American schooling were the result of movements to reform an older system that not only emphasized morality too much, but emphasized only one kind of morality. The early Protestant morality of American schools was anything but tolerant and enlightened; as late as 1939, a Pennsylvania teacher was fired because she worked after school in a tavern owned by her husband.[100] In a similar manner, professionalism, the ideology that replaced moral protestantism, was tied up with the interests of a class that viewed education as part of an instrumental design to rationalize a social order in which that class prospered. In contrast to the morality of a specific class or a specific religion, there is something to be said for a greater market role in individual choice in schooling, just as there is in families and communities. But it is also difficult to deny that privatization in a matter as socially important as schooling represents a step away from the notion of a republic as a group of people who share civic values in common, including the values that shape their growth and development.

Schooling is not the only common service being organized increasingly by market principles: one can see similar trends with regard to prisons, refuse collection, data processing, sewerage, bus system operations, vehicle towing, day care, child welfare services, hospitalization, ambulance services, fire protection, resource recovery, and cancer research.[101] Given the power of the market—helped along by the ingenuity of economists who believe in its virtues—there is, theoretically speaking, no service that could not be privatized. Even national defense and road building, generally viewed as quintessential "public goods," are not immune: at least one thinker committed to the market has proposed the privatization of defense services,[102] and two other economists have argued that new technologies— such as sensors built into cars to record highway usage—can enable private companies to undertake road building on a for-profit basis.[103]

The question, evidently, is not whether common services can be turned over to private operators; they can. Rather, the question is whether they should be. Privatization is an important trend because it raises the implicit question of whether people have any common stake in the provision of the services that define their society. If they do not, then the term used to describe all this activity, *deregulation,* is an appropriate one, for regulation is at the heart of the social fabric. If deregulation is carried to its logical extreme, it is difficult to imagine exactly what aspects of civil society would remain.

In the Absence of Civil Society

It is possible, given the passions that moral debates can arouse, that my point in this chapter may be lost. I am not arguing that in the United States such intimate sectors as the family and the community have been completely colonized by the logic of self-interest; the notion of a "second bourgeois revolution" remains more of a wish associated with Chicago school theorists than a reality describing American life. There still exists in the United States strong support for social security, extensive medical help for the elderly, and communities that have neither gone bust nor exploded; many families are characterized by strong ties of love and caring; people still assume responsibility for aged parents; the idea of educational vouchers has never taken hold. Nor does it follow that the kinds of trends described in this chapter will continue; nearly all trends in America seem at some point to reverse themselves, and talk of a rekindling of altruism and community spirit in the United States can be heard.[104]

At the same time, while the United States does not resemble the picture the Chicago school of economics painted of a society with no compartments between the market and civil society, aspects of that picture are more of a reality today than, say, twenty years ago.[105] It is as if we can contrast distinct life courses associated with two different generations in recent American experience. An older generation, fearful of the economic insecurity it felt when young, took refuge from the economy in civil society. Long marriages, whether satisfying or not, were combined with relatively stable communities and a commitment to the expansion of the public sector, all to create a system in which people could to some degree rely on one another for support. For a younger generation, by contrast, the market, rather than something against which individuals would be protected by civil society, has become more of a model by which relations in civil society can themselves be shaped. Marriage and childbearing are shaped increasingly by considerations of self-interest; communities are organized more by the logic of buying and selling than by principles of solidarity; and services, when no longer satisfactory publicly, are increasingly purchased privately. In a way unprecedented in the American experience, the market has become attractive in not only the economic sphere, but in the moral and social spheres as well. That trend may explain why, according to an intensive study of Americans' attitudes about themselves, a shift occurred between 1957 and 1976 "from normative concepts of morality to more individuated and morally neutral bases of self-conception." [106]

Perhaps the fairest way to conclude the discussion is to suggest that in the United States the market substitutes for a conception of civil society that no longer exists. Convinced—often correctly—that older forms of morality constrain them unjustifiably, Americans look for something better. An idealistic strain in American culture often leads reformers toward moral codes based on solidarity, reciprocity, and loyalty that seem compelling in comparison to the restrictions of the older morality and hold open a vision of future possibility. This has been the case in each of the areas discussed in this chapter, since challenges to the old morality have generally been launched by people who considered themselves to the left: in the women's movement, gentrification, and school reform, for example. Yet so weak has civil society become in the shadow of the market that when institutionalized change does take place, only the market remains to fall back on as a guide to moral obligations. That new moral obligations are created that are at least as problematic, if in a different way, than the old does not mean that Americans are rushing out and embracing the market because they are fundamentally selfish. It suggests instead that they face excruciating dilemmas. It is not easy to decide to continue with a career when your children would prefer you at home, to hire an illegal Peruvian immigrant to watch your children, to commit yourself to variable mortgage rates for thirty years, or to abandon public services for private.

Americans are not so much narcissistic as they are caught between competing moral codes, only one of which, they are convinced, will enable them to enjoy the irresistible benefits of modernity. The market, in other words, neither forces its will on unsuspecting dupes nor is eagerly embraced by selfish egoists. It is there. Not much else is. And it seems to offer the least problematic option for many good people.

The question, then, is not why the market is so strong in America, but why civil society has become so weak. An articulate notion of civil society never developed in the United States because in many ways America already was a civil society and so never needed to develop any theory about how it would work. The small town, the voluntary association, the spirit of the people—these aspects of how Americans viewed themselves contained such an emphasis on trust, friendship, and community that people simply assumed they would always be there. To the degree that these virtues were threatened at all, they seemed to be threatened by the state; to protect civil society, therefore, Americans often erected barricades in the wrong place. Suspicious of government, they did not realize until too late that the things they took for granted could be as easily destroyed by economic calculation as by political authority. Having in a sense been given the gift of society when young, Americans took it as a right rather than the remarkable present it was. If Americans now are to protect the remaining realms of intimacy and community against the market, they will have to create, through conscious deliberation, the kinds of ties of civil society that they once assumed God or nature would automatically provide.

THREE

Markets and Distant Obligations

Intimacy and Distance

For every social theorist who talks about the decline of the family, the community, and other warm, cozy things, there will always be another to remind us either that these things have not declined at all or that they were never as wonderful as their lamenters insist and we ought just as well to bid them good riddance. One version of this argument, insofar as it concerns problems of moral obligation, runs as follows. Modern liberal democrats, it claims, have important obligations to strangers and hypothetical others such as future generations. Since civil society is the realm of the personal, the intimate, and the local, strong obligations to those we love will in fact make it *more* difficult to consider the needs of strangers. We are better off, therefore, relying on impersonal mechanisms of moral obligation such as the market (or, for that matter, the state) because they are the best methods of insuring that those we do not know, but on whose actions we nonetheless depend, will receive the same kind of consideration as those we do.

This is a powerful argument, and, as I will try to show later in this book, it especially makes sense in understanding the moral logic of the welfare state. But it clearly applies to the market as well. If a businessman harms his wife and children by working long hours and is forced to fire trusted employees in order to increase his profits yet as a result of these actions contributes to economic growth that provides jobs and material benefits for future generations, who is to say that he has not, even without conscious intent, satisfied moral obligations to others? There will, in other words, always be some tension between intimate and distant obligations, and the question is never whether the former ought to take precedence over the latter or vice versa, but rather how the two can be brought into some kind of balance.

Yet for all its concern with equilibria, the market is not necessarily the best instrument for keeping precarious matters in balance. Markets are generally praised because they coordinate things indirectly and without conscious planning. As Thomas Schelling has taken the lead in pointing out, however, markets are often responsible for logjams when they encourage people to act in ways that, in the absence of market mechanisms, they would not have acted in the first place.[1] If we take the examples of traffic jams and residential patterns analyzed by Schelling as metaphors for the general problem of moral interdependence in modern liberal democracies, we are likely to find that indirectness and unconsciousness are not the best ways to balance obligations in the intimate sector with those to strangers and hypothetical others. I will try to demonstrate this point with respect to the United States by considering three ways by which modern liberal democrats are asked to consider the needs of distant others: by intergenerational transfers, which require people to think hypothetically about their obligations in time; by patterns of charitable giving and voluntarism, which express obligations altruistically to strangers; and by the degree to which culture establishes restraints on individual desires for the sake of living together with anonymous others.

Generations and the Social Order

Obligations between generations are not completely synonymous with obligations to distant strangers: when we provide for the elderly we do so in part by giving care to our own parents; when we provide for the very young we do so in part by giving care to our own children. Yet intergenerational moral obligations illustrate the general problem of organizing relations among distant others nonetheless. Obligations to the young and the old are obligations to others who, even if we know them, tend to be inherently dependent. They therefore can be taken as symbolic of all the kinds of dependency that exist in modern society. If the most visibly dependent elements of the population are not well cared for, it is difficult to imagine that others who think of themselves as independent—but who, because they are modern, are dependent on everyone else anyway—will be well cared for as well.

To examine the effects of greater reliance on the moral code of the market with regard to people distant in time from us, therefore, we must look first at the future prospects of those who are children today. To the degree that reliance on the market, especially in the economic sector of society, produces new wealth, its effects on future generations are positive, particularly for those in a position to take advantage of the new economic opportunities thus created. But we can identify three ways in which the needs of generations that will reach maturity after the present one are harmed by a weakening of the boundary between the market and civil society. One is an increase in the number of children who will grow up in poverty; the second is a weakening of the family as a support system, in ways harmful to children of all social classes; and the third is an emphasis on present consumption and gratification that encourages cynicism about the future.

The number of families below the poverty line in America rose dramatically in the early 1980s, the very years when Americans turned away from government in favor of the market. Although in recent years that trend has leveled off, the child poverty rate toward the end of the 1980s was the highest it had been since the early 1960s, despite a relatively well functioning economy (see table 2).[2] In 1983, 40 percent of the poor people in America were children, and 13.8 million American children lived in poor families.[3] Moreover, as these trends began to penetrate public consciousness, Americans remained reluctant to tax themselves in order to help the poor among them. As W. Norton Grubb and Marvin Lazerson put it, "In contrast to the deep love we feel and express in private, we lack any sense of 'public love' for children, and we are unwilling to make any public commitments to them except when we believe the commitments will pay off."[4]

Of all children, moreover, those who are poorest are most likely to feel the effects of the weakening of moral ties in the intimate realm of society. Many of the trends that have weakened family bonds, such as divorce, working-woman heads of families, and the difficulties of relying on kin for child care, will, demographers project, continue over the next few decades, even if at a lower rate.[5] Each trend will make it that much more difficult for poor children to escape from poverty. Between 1960 and 1980, the number of female-headed families tripled.[6] As a result, in Martha Hill's words, "most children now have mothers who are balancing child-rearing and market work responsibilities, many with no father present to assist in fulfilling these responsibilities."[7]

One likely consequence of increased child poverty will be a focus on survival in the present without consideration of consequences for the future. Phyllis Moen, Edward Kain, and Glen Elder point out:

TABLE 2.   *Families Below the Poverty Line, United States, 1969–85*

	Total Number (in millions)	Percentage of Population	Percentage Change	Threshold Income (in dollars)
1969	24.3	12.2	4.3	3,743
1970	25.4	13.0	5.1	3,968
1971	25.6	13.0	0	4,137
1972	24.5	12.0	−4.0	4,275
1973	23.0	11.0	−6.1	4,540
1974	25.0	11.5	5.6	5,038
1975	25.9	12.5	10.7	5,500
1976	25.0	12.0	−3.6	5,815
1977	24.7	11.6	−1.2	6,191
1978	24.5	11.4	0	6,662
1979	26.1	11.6	2.5	7,412
1980	29.3	13.0	12.3	8,414
1981	31.8	14.0	7.4	9,287
1982	34.4	15.2	8.1	9,862
1983	35.3	15.2	0	10,178
1984	33.7	14.4	−.8	10,609
1985	33.1	14.0	−1.8	10,989

Source. U.S. Census Bureau, *Current Population Reports. Consumer Income, Series P-60. Characteristics of the Population Below the Poverty Level, 1970–1986* (Washington, D.C.: Government Printing Office, 1987).

Family responses to economic distress are generally directed to immediate needs, with an eye toward specific, short-range consequences. As elements of strategies for economic survival, parental decisions are mostly geared to the short term. But what may be functional in the short run for the family unit may inadvertently have disastrous consequences for the lives of children. *It is these indirect and unanticipated outcomes that may, in fact, have the greatest significance for the life prospects of children.*[8]

American families, in other words, will increasingly live in two separate time frames. They will decide whether to pay for dental care, preventive medicine, or education based on present needs, not future potential. To the degree that they opt to live in the present—since the market leaves them little choice—an increasing number of parents will find themselves playing God, taking risks with their children's lives and praying that the risks are worth it.

Uncertain prospects face not only poor children in America. "Families at every economic level are increasingly unsure of what the future holds— for themselves and for their children," Moen, Kain, and Elder continue.[9] Under increasing financial pressure to pay for more expensive homes with higher mortgage rates, an increasing number of middle-class American families are finding themselves unable to save for their children's college education. In the absence of direct government grants-in-aid, the amounts taken out in student loans, once thought of as a middle-class supplement, not only tripled (in constant dollars) between 1975 and 1985 but were relied on by an ever greater number of borrowers. A study sponsored by the Joint Economic Committee of the U.S. Congress, while obviously unable to ascertain whether such heavy indebtedness will alter career choices and family size in the long run, pointed out that "there are clear signs that in-debtedness is likely to continue on its upward course" and noted that "students *cannot* know what the real burden of the debt they are assuming will be."[10] A reversal of intergenerational obligation seems to be taking place: those born around 1920 often deprived themselves so that their children could go to college; those born around 1970 will deprive themselves as adults, not to pay for their children's education in the future, but to pay back their own education in the past.

As the pressures put on the family by the market intensify, children and young people in all social classes are less likely to find parents with the time and energy to respond to their special needs. The emotional (and nutritional) consequences have already begun to worry child specialists. Rituals that incorporate children into family bonds, such as the family meal, have increasingly become a thing of the past. "Food relationships," two experts have written, "seem minimal, fleeting, and superficial."[11] The Kettering Commission on Youth spoke of a generation of young people "never having had the opportunity to care for a child or an elderly person, never having had to be with someone who was lonely, disconsolate, sick, or dying."[12]

Not unaware of the present generation's weakening sense of obligation to them, younger people have begun to act as if their future is quite problematic. Between 1960 and 1980, the suicide rate among young people in the United States doubled, about as dramatic a sign one can have of severe anticipations of the future.[13] (Teenage suicide might have surprised Durkheim, for, as he pointed out, suicide is rare among children.[14] Since teenage suicide is neither egoistic—many teenagers do not yet have a fully developed ego—nor altruistic—it is hardly an act of duty—it would seem to be an ideal type of anomic suicide.) Not a single rate of what are generally taken to be indicators of social disintegration—from crime to drugs to passivity—failed to increase among American youth in the past decade.[15] Eighty percent of American youths in 1980 could not name one foreign head of state, although, it should be added, adult recognition of basic political facts in America is not all that much higher.[16] A surprisingly large number of students were found to be believers in creationism, extraterrestrial life, and other notions that were supposed to disappear with modernity.[17] American youths, it seems fair to say, are not being especially well prepared to take seriously their membership obligations in the adult society they will join.[18]

Most of the attitudes toward social life we associate with the market are being passed on to a new generation. It is not that youth has become "immoral"; on most moral issues excluding those of sexual behavior, such as whether lying or cheating is justified, 1980s students were not significantly different in their responses than earlier generations of students.[19] Rather, students today seem much more attracted to educational patterns and career choices that will give them immediate payoffs in market terms. Thus surveys conducted annually by the American Council on Education have discovered a significant decrease in altruistic feelings among college students in the 1980s: the number of students who felt that being well off financially was an essential life goal increased between 1967 and 1987 from 45 percent to over 70 percent, while those who wanted to develop a meaningful philosophy of life decreased from 84 percent to 40 percent. Similarly, careers in education dropped to extremely low levels before starting a slow rise again in 1984, while business careers have consistently increased in number since 1973.[20] There seems little doubt that American youths have become more concerned with themselves and less concerned with the needs of others.

It is evident that not all the changes in young people's outlook and behavior can be traced to a greater reliance on marketplace principles in the intimate sphere of society. It is also true, furthermore, that a concern with the alleged immorality of youth has been a theme throughout American history. Yet despite the caveats, there have taken place changes of sufficient magnitude to conclude that reliance on the market as a moral code does not leave an especially positive legacy for future generations. For all those who may benefit economically from a loosening of the moral ties of civil society, there are many who do not. Moreover, something seems amiss in the social and moral prospects of all children, not just those living in poverty. The weakening of the boundary between civil society and the market allows little room for the symbolic ways by which present generations transfer obligations to future generations. Pessimism about the future, increases in antisocial acts such as suicide and crime, and a tendency to serve the self to the exclusion of others testify to the difficulty of considering obligations as abstract as those to future generations when present decisions are guided ever more by considerations of self-interest.

Just as a greater reliance on the moral code of the market makes sacrifices for future generations more problematic, it also suggests that present generations will be less likely to recognize that their good fortune was the result of sacrifices made by earlier ones. This is not to suggest that those who are now in retirement face a future of increasing poverty. Especially in material terms, older people in America have it better at the end of the 1980s than ever before. Indeed, the meaning of old age in the United States has been almost completely transformed, with many elderly people living longer and better than anyone could have imagined a generation ago. To the degree that the improvement in their condition is a product of the rapid increase in the stock market during the 1980s, market reliance has meant obvious benefits for those living on pensions. Much the same can be said for improvements in health care, the possibilities of warm-weather retirement, and other aspects of old age in the United States. We have, especially in contrast to previous periods, taken good care to satisfy our obligations toward those who came before us.

Yet in moral as opposed to material terms, the extension of the market into the intimate realm of civil society does have serious consequences for the lives of our elders, because the family is still the largest provider of support and care.[21] Proximity to children is an important prerequisite of care, yet grandparents and their children live farther away from each other than ever before. As Andrew Cherlin and Frank Furstenberg put it, "Grandparents are at the mercy of their children's mobility."[22] (Surprisingly, Cherlin and Furstenberg discuss only children who move away from their parents, not, in this age of Sunbelt retirement communities, parents who move away from their children.) Smaller families decrease the number of children available to support the elderly. Divorce, moreover, complicates the question of who is responsible to whom.[23] Under the impact of such changes, parents, like their children, look less to the future, although positive feelings about the future still underlie a willingness to provide care.[24] Friendship networks and ties of reciprocity can help substitute for weakening family ties, yet these aspects of civil society are also in decline as the market is relied on to organize real estate to an unprecedented degree.[25]

Such demographic changes, in Pamela Doty's words, "are likely to decrease the availability of informal family supports in the future."[26] The same tie between a weak sense of obligation in the intimate realm and a failure to recognize obligations in the distant realm that affects children in America, in other words, also affects the elderly.

Increasingly unsure that their families will be able to care for them and extremely distrustful of politicians at a time of cost cutting, older Americans have responded by forming interest groups and lobbying, quite successfully, for benefits.[27] In so doing, however, they tend to reinforce the idea that each generation is a special interest, whose primary responsibility is to look after its own.[28] As a result, talk of "intergenerational inequity" has become more frequent in the United States.[29] Anxious to protect the benefits they have won, the elderly often become politically unsympathetic to the needs of those who will themselves be elderly in the future. At the same time, a large number of recently married Americans, about to start families of their own under conditions of uncertainty about the future, instead of recognizing that their prosperity is the product of sacrifices made by older Americans when they were young, have begun to ask whether older Americans have it too easy. Thus polling data assembled by Daniel Yankelovich in the late 1970s indicated that parents not only expect to sacrifice less for their children but will also expect less from their offspring when they themselves go into retirement: the proportion of Americans who believed that "children do not have an obligation to their parents regardless of what their parents have done for them" was 67 percent.[30]

For all the success the market has shown in improving the material conditions of many, but by no means all, elderly people, it has at the same time confused our sense of what the young owe the elderly and what the elderly owe the young. The material success of the elderly in the United States contributes to their "modernization," to the triumph of such market-associated values as individualism. Symbolized by retirement communities in warm-weather areas which exclude families with young children or by the quest for perfect health regardless of the costs to the rest of the society, the elderly often find themselves cut off from other generations; in a certain sense, they live outside those aspects of the life course inevitably associated with aging. As Daniel Callahan has put it, "There can be no community at all, much less community among the generations, without some sacrifice of an unlimited quest for individualistic pleasure on the part of the old."[31] It is as if the same cynicism toward the future that is now developing among the young is matched by a cynicism toward the past on the part of older generations. In many ways, the fact that the elderly can live by the same moral rules as everyone else is a positive development, yet, like the very rich, the elderly are in fact different from everyone else. It is not discrimination, but simple common moral sense, that leads us to organize our relations with them by different moral rules than apply to individuals better situated to maximize self-interest in interaction with others.

If we take ties between the generations as symbolic of people's ability to be responsible for the needs of hypothetical and distant others, reliance on the market, as the American experience indicates, becomes increasingly problematic. Because of improved technology and health care, infants live to adulthood and the elderly live to an age that would only seem miraculous to previous generations. Yet it is not just that our obligations have expanded over time that is important; it is also that we have greater *awareness* of how these obligations ought to affect what we do. As Annette Baier puts the matter:

We are especially self-conscious members of the cross-generational community, aware both of how much, and how much more than previous generations, we benefit from the investment of earlier generations and of the extent to which we may determine the fate of future generations. Such self-consciousness has its costs in added obligations.[32]

It is questionable whether the moral principles of the market constitute the best way to represent this self-consciousness of intergenerational dependency. The very features that make markets so effective in the economic sector—indirection, spontaneity, and the ability to take advantage of unforeseen consequences—are not features that make for adequate recognition of the debts that all generations owe one another. Because the social fabric is vertical as well as horizontal, reliance on the market to account for intergenerational obligations takes inadequate recognition of what can only be called "the social limits to time."[33]

The Fate of the Third Sector

Ever since Tocqueville, Americans have prided themselves on their voluntary organizations. So important is the idea of voluntarism in America that it is often called "the third sector," sitting alongside the market and the state. The third sector includes charity, not-for-profit corporations, volunteer fire companies and ambulance services, museums and cultural institutions, hospitals, religious activities, public libraries, community organizations, blood donation centers, the Red Cross, the Peace Corps, and any other effort characterized by community spirit and altruism.[34] The Filer Commission on Private Philanthropy has estimated that one out of every ten Americans is employed in the third sector.[35]

The third sector is continually being rediscovered because it serves as a symbol of obligations to strangers. When we agree to donate time or to give to charity of our own free will, it is because we recognize that others whom we do not know are dependent on the choices we make. Although they are sometimes conflated, therefore, voluntarism and the market are quite different moral codes. One is based on sacrifice and puts the interest of the collective before that of the individual. The other is rooted in distrust and pleasure maximization and puts the interest of the individual before that of the collective.[36] Today, greater reliance on the moral code of the market in families and communities raises the question of whether Americans are as committed to the third sector as they have been in the past.

If asked about their attitudes toward voluntarism in surveys, Americans say they believe as much as ever in the ethic of the third sector. For example, data collected and published by the Independent Sector (a merger of the National Council on Philanthropy and the Council of National Voluntary Organizations) indicate not only that a large number of Americans (more than half) volunteer in one effort or another but also that the rate of voluntarism increased by over 20 percent from 1984 to 1985.[37] It is obvious that the idea of voluntarism is still powerful in American society, no matter how preoccupied Americans have become with their private selves.

Moreover, if positive feelings toward the voluntary sector increased, so have contributions to charity. A number of major empirical studies have measured the degree to which Americans give to charity, and most come to similar conclusions.[38] (Table 3, containing data collected by economist Ralph Nelson for the American Association of Fund Raising Councils, presents the most reliable as well as most representative figures.) First, the highest rates of charitable giving in recent years took place in the years immediately after World War II, when, as I argued in Chapter 2, the pressures of the market were lower than before or since. From this peak, rates of charitable giving began to fall, reaching a low point sometime during the 1970s. Beginning in the 1980s, however, government cutbacks in social programs sharply reduced the amount of funds available for the American version of the welfare state, and in consequence Americans began to increase the amounts they gave to charity.[39] (A variety of volunteer organi-

TABLE 3.   *Individual Giving, United States, 1960–85 (in billions of dollars)*

	Gift Amount	Personal Income	Gift Amount as Percentage of Income	Gift Amount in 1985 Dollars
1960	9.60	409.4	2.24	35.10
1961	9.50	426.0	2.23	34.38
1962	9.89	453.2	2.18	35.40
1963	10.86	476.3	2.28	38.41
1964	11.19	510.2	2.19	39.06
1965	11.82	552.0	2.14	40.56
1966	12.44	600.8	2.07	41.51
1967	13.41	644.5	2.08	43.49
1968	14.75	707.2	2.09	45.91
1969	15.93	772.9	2.06	47.05
1970	16.19	831.8	1.95	45.16
1971	17.64	894.0	1.97	47.16
1972	19.37	981.6	1.97	50.13
1973	20.53	1,101.7	1.86	50.02
1974	21.60	1,210.1	1.79	47.43
1975	23.53	1,313.4	1.79	47.34
1976	26.32	1,451.4	1.81	50.06
1977	29.55	1,607.5	1.84	52.80
1978	32.10	1,812.4	1.77	53.28
1979	36.59	2,034.0	1.80	54.58
1980	40.71	2,258.5	1.80	53.49
1981	46.42	2,520.9	1.84	55.26
1982	48.52	2,670.8	1.82	54.43
1983	53.54	2,836.4	1.89	58.19
1984	60.66	3,111.9	1.95	63.23
1985	66.06	3,294.2	2.01	66.06

Source. American Association of Fund Raising Councils, *Giving USA: Estimates of Philanthropic Giving in 1985 and the Trends They Show* (New York, 1986), 10, 15.

zations, including Hadassah and the National Association of Women's Clubs, report increasing membership in the early 1980s as well, which reverses an earlier decline.)[40] These latter developments in particular insure that the present period, characterized as it is by faith in the market, will not be characterized by greater private niggardliness—although, as Alan

Pifer of the Carnegie Foundation has written, the notion that private do-nations could make up for government programs "is, frankly, ridiculous to someone who is well informed about the entire field of philanthropy."[41]

Despite the fact that reliance on the market as a moral code has not harmed the moral logic of the third sector overall, there is at least some reason to think that it might in the future. As is the case with intergenera-tional moral obligations, people are more likely to volunteer and to give to charity—thereby recognizing their obligations to distant strangers—when family and community relations in the intimate sector of society are strong. A survey undertaken by the Survey Research Center of the University of Michigan for the Filer Commission indicated that married people give more to charity than single people, small-town residents more than ur-banites, and old people more than young.[42] Thus, although gross data in-dicate that people give as much to charity as ever, closer analysis reveals that ties of help from kin and neighbors have declined in America, even as ties of help at the workplace have increased.[43] Perhaps the most significant caveat in an otherwise optimistic picture about third-sector obligations is the fact that young people, who tend to give less to charity, also tend to volunteer less: the Independent Sector data showed an 11 percent drop in volunteer rates for Americans aged eighteen to twenty-four.[44] This decline, moreover, can be directly traced to greater market intervention in families: the added burden of student loans has been cited by the director of the Inde-pendent Sector as one cause of a declining commitment to voluntarism.[45]

Another obvious change in the intimate level of society that affects a willingness to express obligations to distant others is the entry of women into the labor market. In the United States, the giving of time rather than money has traditionally reflected a sexual division of labor, in which men worked for income and women devoted time to community and charitable concerns.[46] As women begin to work, their ability to participate in volun-tary organizations declines.[47] At least one study found that between 1974 and 1980 women's participation in voluntary associations declined signifi-cantly, a trend that has also been noted in such areas as religious work.[48] Moreover, when working women do volunteer, they tend to join associa-tions that have instrumental rather than expressive purposes, that is, orga-nizations with less of a direct service orientation.[49] Although one side to the women's movement of the 1970s was to encourage voluntarism in the form of women's self-help groups, birth counseling centers, and other in-novations very much in the Tocquevillean tradition of American life, it also seems inevitable that the drive for equality in wages and working condi-tions between women and men, however justifiable on its own terms, will significantly crimp a long-standing tendency for American women to express moral difference by participating in charitable activities out of a sense of obligation to the community.[50]

As these trends in family structure suggest, the problem is more one of time than of money. Because of greater family income resulting from two wage-earners, lower federal taxes, and an economic recovery, many families had more disposable income in the early 1980s. Yet giving time and attention to community is in many ways more important for strengthening the social bond between strangers than is giving money. As people work longer hours, they may be substituting higher monetary contributions for the time that is no longer at their disposal. Thus, if we consider the rates at which people offer something other than money, we find a decline as the market becomes a more important force in American life. Figures compiled by the Red Cross indicate that between 1972 and 1984, activities that require more than the giving of money, such as chapter formation, the joining of community volunteers, or student participation in school programs, have decreased (see figure 4).

Although corporate contributions to charity do not reflect the same tensions between intimate and distant obligations, greater reliance on the market ought to have consequences in this area as well. As with attitudes toward voluntarism and rates of private charitable giving, corporate contributions to charities increased in the first half of the 1980s. Data assembled by the American Association of Fund Raising Councils show that these increases in fact raised the level of corporate giving to the highest it has been since 1960 (see table 4). Such corporate generosity of course has its self-interested side, since firms, unlike individuals, give money not out of a feeling of personal obligation to strangers but instead to identify potential markets.[51] Moreover, since corporations account for only about 5 percent of charitable giving in America, the increase that did take place in the early 1980s in no way matched the concurrent decline in public funding. Salamon and Abramson estimated that private giving would have had to increase by 30 to 40 percent a year between 1981 and 1985 to make up for the cutbacks proposed in Ronald Reagan's first budget,[52] yet the largest one-year increase in corporate giving, between 1983 and 1984, was 16 percent.[53] Still, no one was forcing corporations to give more, and in that sense higher profits in the private sector do not necessarily produce lower donations in the charitable sector.

Whether that pattern will continue in the future, however, is also problematic. Because corporate donations are dependent on profits, they can easily decrease as economic conditions change—a trend that has in fact

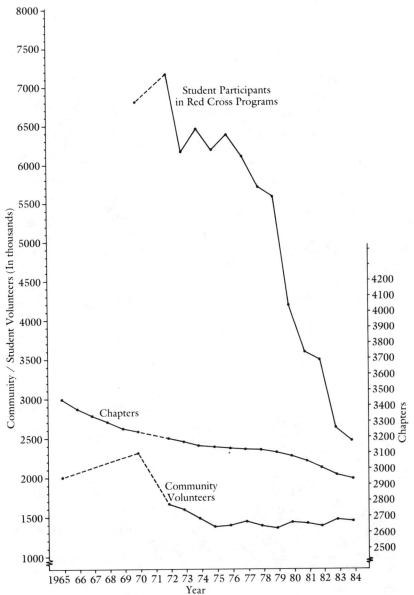

Note: 1971 data not available.
Source: U.S. Census Bureau, *Statistical Abstracts of the United States:* 1970, 307; 1976, 322; 1980, 363; 1984, 399; 1986, 384.

Figure 4. American Red Cross, Chapters and Volunteers, 1965–84

TABLE 4. *Corporate Giving, United States, 1960–85 (in billions of dollars)*

	Gift Amount	Pretax Net Income	Gift Amount as Percentage of Income	Gift Amount in 1985 Dollars
1960	0.482	49.8	0.97	1.762
1961	0.512	49.7	1.03	1.853
1962	0.595	55.0	1.08	2.130
1963	0.657	59.6	1.10	2.324
1964	0.729	66.5	1.10	2.545
1965	0.785	77.2	1.02	2.694
1966	0.805	83.0	0.97	2.686
1967	0.830	79.7	1.04	2.692
1968	1.005	88.5	1.13	3.128
1969	1.005	86.7	1.22	2.968
1970	0.797	75.4	1.05	2.222
1971	0.865	86.6	0.99	2.313
1972	1.009	100.6	1.00	2.611
1973	1.174	125.6	0.93	2.860
1974	1.200	136.7	0.87	2.635
1975	1.202	132.1	0.90	2.418
1976	1.487	166.3	0.89	2.828
1977	1.791	194.7	0.92	3.200
1978	2.084	229.1	0.91	3.459
1979	2.288	252.7	0.91	3.413
1980	2.359	234.6	1.01	3.100
1981	2.514	221.2	1.14	2.993
1982	2.906	165.5	1.76	3.260
1983	3.300	203.2	1.62	3.586
1984	3.800	235.7	1.61	3.961
1985	4.300	226.8	1.89	4.300

Source. American Association of Fund Raising Councils, *Giving USA: Estimates of Philanthropic Giving in 1985 and the Trends They Show* (New York, 1986), 33, 39.

already begun to happen. In 1986, the Conference Board in its annual survey noted a 2.5 percent decrease in corporate giving over the previous year. Even the figures of the American Association of Fund Raising Councils, which tend to portray higher rates of giving, indicated only a modest increase in 1986. According to William Woodside, executive chairman of Primerica Corporation (once known as American Can), a new breed of manager has already taken over American industry, one that thinks "it becomes positively un-American to look at anything except their own bottom line." These people may not agree with T. Boone Pickens's observation that "company giving has to be related to the company's interests; not be a gift to the ballet because my wife likes ballet." Yet when leveraged buyouts, insider trading scandals, and hostile takeovers characterize the corporate world, business giving for charitable purposes will likely decline.[54]

Much, although by no means all, of the evidence assembled here does *not* support my thesis that greater reliance on the market will harm one form by which we express obligations to distant others, that is, voluntarism and private charity. In the first half-decade of the 1980s at least, Americans, although preoccupied with material considerations, did not contribute less to charity or show less willingness to volunteer. Yet a nagging sense that this fact does not tell the whole story makes me reluctant to conclude that the matter is settled. In matters concerning private charity, a weakening of the boundary between the intimate realm and the market has already led to people's being less able to donate time to others and will likely, given present trends, produce problems for charitable contributions in the future. In matters concerning corporate charity, trends already indicate, because of increased economic competition and a more market-oriented sense of moral obligation, declines in the amounts that will be forthcoming.

We might therefore give the last word, not, of course, to Tocqueville, but to two contemporary French visitors, both of whom wanted to find the world of Tocqueville still in existence but, unhappily, did not. The anthropologist Hervé Varenne, who lived for a year in a small town in Wisconsin, was determined not to preach to Americans about their society as so many Europeans tend to do. Because one cannot live in a small town in America without becoming involved in the Farm Bureau Federation—or so Varenne thought—he began attending meetings. "The times I was present," he wrote, "no substantial issues arose and the meetings were poorly attended." Moreover, he found that this had been the pattern for some time. "The people who came were the original founders, now in their sixties to eighties. No young adults attended the meetings." Hence, "discussion was weak, superficial, uninvolved. The leader had to force and cajole people into taking positions, something that they did only after ensuring that unanimity would not be destroyed by their decision." The lessons taught at such meetings are far removed from Tocqueville's ideas about a virtuous citizenry.[55]

Similarly Michel Crozier, despite his great respect for the United States, was frightened by the change that had taken place in the country between his first visit in 1946 and a subsequent one in 1980. America was, in his view, a long way from Tocqueville's hoped-for "free schools" of civic virtue:

The United States today is no longer the America Tocqueville described. Its voluntary associations have ceased to be the mainstay of a democracy constantly on the move but are now simply a means of self-defense for various interests (which, though perfectly ethical, are still parochial in nature). This breakdown of community structures is what has made America a country full of anxiety, and periodically shaken by reactionary crusades.[56]

Voluntarism and charity, it seems fair to conclude, are still strongly encouraged virtues, and they still play an important role in American life. There are reasons, though, for worrying that future trends will not be so positive if the market continues to grow as a moral code for individual decision-making.

Loosely Bounded Culture and the Market

Modern liberal democrats are able to live together with strangers because their choices are to some degree organized by culture. When cultures work well, they do so by uniting members of a group around a set of common stories that define their identity. In most cases these stories emphasize the need for some kind of restraint on individual desires so that meeting obligations to others becomes as important as satisfying the needs of the self. Even in societies where religious traditions are weak, secular stories— Washington's honesty, Lincoln's humility—allow the transmission of moral rules by emphasizing trust, probity, solidarity, and other virtues that enable people to live in something other than a Hobbesian world. Culture, in short, like intergenerational obligations or the third sector, ties together distant strangers who would otherwise not recognize their mutual interdependence and gives them a stake in what others do.

Culture in America, especially when compared to more ethnically homogeneous societies, is not especially strong in its binding capacity. As Richard Merelman has pointed out, American culture is uncomfortable with bipolar dichotomies, strict standards, and sharp boundaries. It is not a Durkheimian morality standing above utilitarian individualism with disapproving powers, but rather an all-forgiving, undemanding, and affirming mechanism of reinforcement. Strong cultures dichotomize and, in the tension that results, unite. Weak cultures unify and, in the harmony that results, leave differences unresolved.[57] Culturally speaking, Americans tend to be unbound to begin with.

In recent years, there has been considerable discussion in the United States as to whether an already weak culture has not become even weaker. One does not need to be a preacher, or even a member of the Moral Majority, to recognize that the stories associated with Washington and Lincoln seem to have little to do with how Americans lead their lives in the late twentieth century. In the early 1980s, Americans were exposed to presidential aides who routinely broke laws; Wall Street brokers who traded on inside information; fundamentalist religious figures who engaged in dubious moral enterprises; defense contractors who thought first of their company's bottom line and only later of the national security; and interest groups whose concerns extended no further than their own self-interest, no matter how damaging to the social fabric as a whole. A general lament that more and more Americans think of themselves first and of their obligations to society only later, if at all, has become the stuff of conventional wisdom.

Is the conventional wisdom correct? Popular sentiment nearly always believes morality to be in decline and yearns for the "good old days," when people were honest and law-abiding. In the absence of any controlled experiments to measure whether honesty and trust have in fact atrophied, such sentiments can and should be dismissed as hopelessly nostalgic. It is therefore of particular interest that—in what can only be described as life imitating sociology—an experiment not even Harold Garfinkel could have invented for testing the strength of tacit understandings of the social bond took place, purely by accident, in Columbus, Ohio, on 22 November 1987, when the doors of an armored truck opened on Interstate Highway 71, spilling hundred-dollar bills all over the road. Did passing motorists, Lincoln-like, carry the bills back to the rightful owner, perhaps in expectations of praise or even a small reward? On the contrary, it seems, Bonnie-and-Clyde-like, that they not only kept the money they found but were praised in the public imagination for doing so.[58] (Likewise, the fact that one of the figures involved in the Watergate scandal, Jeb Stuart Magruder, was later hired to discover the moral lessons that followed from this incident indicates either a tremendous capacity for forgiveness or a serious confusion about what morality means.)[59] One can interpret the results of this fortuitous experiment in any number of ways, but surely one interpretation ought to be that rules of moral obligation to anonymous others are enforced either by cultural standards or not at all.

If it is difficult to know whether the moral stories that give strangers a stake in the actions of others are weakening in influence, it is even more difficult to know whether such a weakening might be attributed to greater reliance on the market and its moral code in the intimate realm of civil society. The grounds for thinking that this probably is the case should be obvious. One attraction of the market as a moral code is that, unlike strong cultural ties, it emphasizes the immediate fulfillment of individual needs and desires. As a result, and not surprisingly, a certain tension has always existed between culture and the market. One binds, the other unwinds. One is individualistic (if more in theory than in practice), the other collectivistic. One thinks of the present, the other of the past and the future. One seeks change, the other stability. Goods, as Mary Douglas and Baron Isherwood have shown, can be surrounded by the trappings of culture, but as we saw in the discussion of the Chicago school of economics in Chapter I, culture imposes limits, and markets have a way of overcoming those limits.[60]

Will greater reliance on the market's moral code in the intimate sphere of society weaken culturally defined obligations to distant others? It is impossible to say for sure. We can, however, find suggestive evidence in one corner of American life: advertising, the cultural industry with the greatest impact on popular perceptions in the United States today. Ironically this industry, before it came to be organized by market principles, was better able to tell stories that defined a common identity—even if those stories were those of the market—than it does now that the market increasingly regulates its internal dynamics.

Industries do not structure themselves according to the logic of the market overnight. Methods of production are often born in households or in small firms that operate by rules emphasizing intimacy and close personal contacts. Nonmarket methods of producing for the market have in fact been fairly common in Western experience: apprenticeship, family ties (still important in many ethnic communities), trusteeships, partnerships, and even early corporations were organized by an emphasis on personal responsibility rather than impersonal calculations of pure self-interest.[61] Advertising, like many industries, was not originally organized by market principles. Attracted to advertising as an arena to exercise a craft, the men who started the industry in the United States believed, however myopically, in a kind of cultural uplift. Advertising for them was a profession organized by a guild, not a free market in both labor and sales. Such marketplace principles as ease of entry and exit, weak customer loyalty, and ruthless competition were not as important as paternalism and gentleman's agreements. As Jackson Lears has shown, moreover, early advertising men believed that they were guardians of the public taste, not of business ends, leading campaigns for truth and sincerity, which their own advertisements were undermining.[62] A generation later, advertising men, even while paving the way toward a modern, consumption-oriented, capitalist society, were, in Roland Marchand's view, continually shocked at the gullibility of the very public they were trying to influence, as if greed and acquisition, rather than being essential moral features of capitalism, were somehow unseemly.[63]

From a craft American advertising has developed in the past twenty years into a form of enterprise organized to an unusually strong degree on market principles. As was the case with families, communities, and schools, it is surprising how late the market came to be relied on to organize advertising as a form of cultural production. Not until the 1950s and 1960s were employees recruited from all sectors of society and not just from WASP enclaves as before. Because they were labor-intensive, advertising agencies began to enter and exit the market with ease. Turnover among staff became more rapid than in any other industry; George Lois, once a "hot property" on Madison Avenue, quit Papert Koening Lois, started Lois Holland Calloway, quit that agency, joined another firm as president, was fired, and then started Lois Pitts Gershon—all within only a few years.[64]

By the 1970s, customers of the advertising industry were beginning to respond to increased marketplace logic. Rather than keeping their accounts with a single firm, they began to move their accounts rapidly from one agency to another. Agencies went public in an effort to raise cash (and then were often bought back by their previous owners). Mergers increased dramatically. Toward the end of the 1970s government regulatory agencies began to allow direct comparisons of competing products (a practice formerly banned by companies themselves as part of gentleman's agreements). International competition hit the advertising agencies in the 1980s as some of the most famous U.S. advertising firms were bought and sold by foreign companies, while new challengers, such as the British firm of Sachi and Sachi, began to dominate a world advertising market. Meanwhile at home, advertising took what seemed to be the last logical step; instead of interrupting programs—in this case, children's programs—with ads, it took control of the program itself, turning the whole show into a carefully designed product campaign.[65]

"The advertising profession," Merelman has written, "is composed of many small firms which compete with each other in a classical free market. Advertising agencies resemble corner grocery stores in a medium-sized city more than they resemble either the three commercial television networks for whom they design commercials or the corporations for whom they labor."[66] As it came increasingly to be organized by a new moral logic, the advertising industry no longer resembled an exclusive club of like-minded *artistes*. A new economic logic, in turn, affected the production of stories in the industry. The messages transmitted by advertisers began to depart from those emphasizing what Alex Kroll of Young and Rubicam called "the vibes you get in a screening room [or] . . . peer applause" in favor of what he calls "consumer take-away . . . the cold, gritty eye of the marketplace."[67]

Roland Marchand's rendering of the great parables of American advertising—the stories purveyed in the 1920s and 1930s—suggests that to the extent the advertising industry is *not* organized by the logic of the market, the greater its ability to tell the story of the market, for, in its early days, advertising was full of wonder toward capitalism and its potential to create a material utopia.[68] It was the set of gentleman's agreements and exclusivity, the feeling of belonging to a special club, that enabled the advertising industry to develop and deliver its message. In the intensely competitive environment of contemporary advertising, by contrast, nothing is taboo so long as it sells. Indeed, given the constant need for novelty in saturated advertising outlets, the more outrageous and morally offensive an advertising campaign is, the more likely it will be to call attention to the product being promoted. Not surprisingly, therefore, the advertising industry will even utilize anticapitalist themes if they help to sell the client's goods. In contrast to the great parables of capitalist growth that characterized American advertising fifty years ago, Michael Schudson's examination of more contemporary ads led him to this conclusion: "If capitalism is a system promoting private ownership, these ads are oddly anticapitalist or noncapitalist, honoring traditions of social solidarity like family, kinship, and friendship that at least in principal are in conflict with the logic of the market."[69]

Twenty years ago radical critics of advertising worried that people were being bombarded with so many messages supporting the capitalist way of life that their ability to develop their own opinions was seriously threatened.[70] At the present time, advertising illustrates another fear altogether: when culture-producing institutions are organized by the logic of the market, it is not the reproduction of any one set of cultural ideas that seems problematic, but the inability of these institutions to produce any cultural ideas at all. The debate between the advertising industry and its critics once centered on whether people shaped culture or culture shaped people. What seems to matter more, however, is the texture of the culture and the character of the people that are shaped. As advertising becomes more driven by a pure market logic, both the culture and the individuals affected by it are changed.

Culture, as we know from Clifford Geertz and other anthropologists, is an interpretative phenomenon, a way of telling stories.[71] For Americans, advertising is one of the primary means of storytelling. Yet as advertising becomes ever more organized according to the logic of the market, something happens to the stories. They thin out, become less ambiguous, more repetitious. Reluctant to offend any constituency, advertising searches for common themes; as Merelman puts it, it "fiercely condenses the mythic message in time and space."[72] Advertising, increasingly underinterpretative, involves itself with what Varda Leymore calls, not mythic, but "a degenerated form of myth," one always searching for the "exhaustive common denominator."[73]

The thinning of cultural experience that has occurred as advertising has become more oriented to marketplace demands would matter less if individuals had other places to turn for their stories. The problem is that liberal societies organized by the market are not strong on storytelling. As Stanley Hauerwas writes, "Ironically, the most coercive aspect of the liberal account of the world is that we are free to make up our own story. The story that liberalism teaches is that we have no story, and as a result we fail to notice how deeply that story determines our lives."[74] The story of capitalism was at least a story. Its passing, and the failure of its opponents to substitute a satisfactory alternative story, leave Americans with fewer common symbols that make sense of the society they inhabit.

We can, then, identify grounds for concluding that weakening moral ties in the intimate realm of society will contribute to a weakening of those forms of obligations to distant others that are expressed through culture. This is not merely to state that stories are more likely to be meaningful and to inculcate moral lessons when taught by parents to children or in similar intimate situations, though it is probably true that weakened family ties—such as the lack of contact between grandparents and grandchildren—have contributed to what David Gutmann calls "deculturation."[75] It is also to state that even when stories are told and retold as part of an industry designed to get people to buy things, they will be less morally binding when the industry itself comes less to resemble the moral world of civil society. To the extent that personal feelings and a sense of professional pride no longer mitigate against an "anything goes so long as it makes money" attitude, the messages of advertising will take on the same coloration as the methods by which they are produced. If advertising is one of the major forms of cultural production in America, cultural understandings are less likely to insist that collective recognitions of obligations to others ought to take precedence over the fulfillment of immediate desires.

The Market and the Social Fabric

Ever since Charles Dickens, stories about the penetration of the warmth of families and communities by the hard-heartedness of greed and self-interest have brought tears to the eye. Yet while bonds in the intimate realm of civil society do offer comfort and security, relations to strangers and hypothetical others are, in many ways, more important. Society can only reproduce itself when people are capable of identifying with those they do not know and, in all likelihood, will never come to know. We cannot have families to love and communities to appreciate unless we first have societies that require us to consider the needs of nonintimate others.

Our dependence on strangers and hypothetical others, and their dependence on us, ought to mean that we are best off relying on the moral codes of markets and states, since both, in contrast to the moral codes of civil society, emphasize impersonality and anonymity. It is surely for this reason that the market and the state play such major roles in structuring the moral obligations of modern liberal democrats. Yet if the experience of recent American life is any indication, reliance on the market to structure distant moral rules does not work as promised. By examining three ways by which we are called on to express obligations to distant others—intergenerational dependency, generalized altruism, and ties of culture—I have tried to show that the penetration of market logic into civil society in fact tends to weaken our sense of obligation to those with whom our fates are impersonally connected.

The moral principle of the market, that our primary obligation is to ourselves, fits intergenerational dependency poorly. It is surely more "rational" for one generation to transfer the costs of its debts to another, just as it is "irrational" to put money into social security funds when one may well have no opportunity to collect in the end. Furthermore, the ability of any particular generation to make rational choices is premised on the "irrational" conduct of the one that came before, since it was their sacrifice

that helped make possible our fortune.[76] The impatience with time manifested in the theories of the Chicago school of economics does have its
real-life counterpart in both an unwillingness to wait so that future generations might benefit and a lack of appreciation for the fact that the capacity to make rational choices depends on the altruistic deeds of previous
generations.

Even theories of moral obligation that avoid the problems of basing individual motivation on egoistic self-interest have difficulty expressing why
generations are interdependent, so long as they make individual calculations of interest their main assumption. In *A Theory of Justice*, for example,
John Rawls admits that "the veil of ignorance fails to secure the desired
result" when justice between generations is at issue. He argues that since
people in what he calls the original position cannot know which generation they will be part of, they will establish rules fair to all generations that
come after (a practice that is unjust to the first generation, as Rawls acknowledges). Yet by adding to this articulation the qualification that "a
generation cares for its immediate descendants, as fathers, say, care for
their sons," Rawls recognizes that, contrary to his general insistence on
moral rules that are impersonal and weakly motivated, intergenerational
obligations are a special case, in which affection and loyalty, even love,
ought to play a role.[77]

If it is true, as Karl Mannheim once wrote, that "as far as generations
are concerned, the task of sketching the layout of the problem undoubtedly falls to sociology," it may be because the ties between generations are
a matter of moral intuition, social common sense, and obligatory notions
of reciprocity, all of which are part of what used to be called civil society.[78]
It is simply no longer sufficient to quote Joseph Addison's aphorism that
"We are always doing something for Posterity, but I would fain see Posterity do something for us" and so dismiss the issue.[79] Indeed, few philosophers have dismissed the issue as thoroughly as Thomas Schwartz,
who argues that we have no obligations at all to the generations that will
come after us.[80] To develop satisfactory rules of intergenerational moral responsibility, modern liberal democrats would in all likelihood be better off
trying to protect the institutions of civil society rather than relying on a
moral code that often cannot see beyond the present generation.

A similar conclusion can be drawn concerning those obligations embodied in general altruism to strangers. It is obvious that altruism is an
important aspect of the social order; even Chicago school economists consider it important enough to theorize extensively about.[81] Sociologists and

anthropologists have also been interested in the "gift relationship," viewing altruistic behavior as the expression of the forms of solidarity that make society work.[82] There is something quaint about this literature that conjures up images of necklaces being passed around in ever-widening chains. Yet in large-scale, bureaucratic, and capitalist societies, where most interactions are between strangers, direct giving, as in the case of organ transplants, is still a social need.[83] Indeed, the more complex and anonymous societies become, the *greater* the need for people to give to each other. No one can enjoy a park unless others give the gift of keeping the park free of crime. When wage restraint characterizes wage negotiations, the gift of freedom from inflation is granted. When strikes are kept to a minimum, everyone enjoys the gift of less social disruption. Employers who do not fire workers when times are rough give the rest of society the gift of not having to pay, through taxes, the costs of unemployment.

Despite its emphasis on satisfaction and a utilitarian preference for the avoidance of pain, reliance on the market involves just as much sacrifice and gift giving as any other form of moral obligation. If workers accept lower pay or higher productivity as necessary to spur reindustrialization, they give to their employers the gift of higher profits. Deregulate airlines, and a predictable number of people will give the gift of life so that a social value called competition may be enhanced. When public land is turned over to the private sector, those who once received the gift of nature renounce their treasure so that others can use it for personal benefit. Scratch a believer in self-interest, and a philosopher of sacrifice—someone else's sacrifice—bleeds.

The question, then, is how different moral codes come to recognize and value the many small gifts of everyday life that reinforce the social order. The problem with reliance on the market as a moral code is that it fails to give moral credit to those whose sacrifices enable others to consider themselves freely choosing agents. By concentrating on the good news that we can improve our position, rather than the not-so-good, but socially necessary, news that we might consider the welfare of others as our direct concern, the market leaves us with no way to appreciate disinterest. Traditions of charity and voluntarism, by contrast, because they are premised on the idea that giving has moral and social rewards, symbolize the many ways in which the fates of strangers in modern society are interwoven, ways that become even more intricately bound as societies become more complex. If rates of charitable giving and voluntarism continue to increase in the United States, despite a greater trend toward reliance on the market in the intimate sphere of society, there is no need to worry about this problem. But if I am correct in suggesting that the penetration of moral codes emphasizing self-interest into families and communities will, over time, weaken a sense of obligation to anonymous others, then the economic approach will once again fail the moral difficulties of modernity.

Finally, the indirection offered by the market fails to respond to the challenge of linking people's fates together through culture. Reliance on the market, as the example of advertising shows, loosens cultural ties, thereby impoverishing moral codes that emphasize restraint and replacing them with codes that, by placing no value on anything, encourage a sense that everything is morally permissible. Advertising men, like public-opinion technicians and manufacturers of frivolous goods, respond that they are only giving people what they want. This is true: the market is a fantastically sensitive device for responding to changes in preference. But that is also what makes it problematic as a moral code organizing obligations among strangers. Responsiveness to distant others is hard work; it demands that we distance ourselves from the siren call of immediate desire.

One way this distancing has traditionally been accomplished is by insisting on culture so refined in its sensibility that ordinary people can merely stand in passive awe. Hence, the weakness of culture in America is often lamented by those of a conservative bent who would like to see the stories of another time preserved as if in aspic.[84] Yet cultural weakness ought to worry not only those committed to aristocratic values, but those committed to democratic values as well. Culture is equally problematic when, instead of the audience never being consulted, it is consulted all the time. Liberal democrats need to keep their instincts and their culture in a state of tension; neither must be allowed to rule over the other. Traditional forms of high culture leave liberal democrats little scope for participation. But culture organized by the moral code of the market leaves them little room for restraint. The demanding work of developing stories that join people together in mutual obligations will not come about if we rely on the market to structure the ways in which stories are told and retold; rather, only strong ties in civil society that insist on our participation in hearing and transmitting those stories will allow us to define and reinforce our rules of obligation to distant others.

Although few would doubt that the market's ability to produce economic growth today will meet obligations to generations tomorrow, reliance on the market does not solve the problem of balancing obligations in the intimate sphere of society with those toward distant others. Distrustful of compartmentalization, inclined toward expansion, resentful of the limits imposed by time, space, and culture, the market is a poor instrument for sensitizing individuals to the complexities and paradoxes of moral obligations under modern conditions. We are more likely to meet those demands, as I will argue later in this book, when we learn through our relations in civil society the social practices that enable us to empathize with others, even with strangers and future generations. To meet the complexities of modernity, we are better off extending inward moral obligations outward, rather than outward moral obligations inward.

State

FOUR

The State as a Moral Agent

Political Science as Moral Theory

However Americans structure moral obligations, most modern liberal democrats do not rely on the market to establish the rules that guide their interdependence; they look instead to the state. When people consider their debts and legacies to past and future generations, when they want to acknowledge their ties to others around them, when they try to develop rules for sharing the things they have in common, they tend to reach, almost automatically, for laws and bureaucratic regulations. Governments may be as uncomfortable in recognizing the inherently moral nature of the decisions they make as political scientists have been in recognizing the inherently moral nature of their subject matter, but both, in concerning themselves with public policy, are involved with how modern liberal democrats regulate their moral relations with one another. As Theodore Lowi succinctly puts it, "Despite what social science may say, politics is morality."[1]

Reliance on government to organize rules of obligation to others is the starting point for various efforts at developing a political approach to moral regulation. Instead of suggesting that one can fulfill one's obligations to others by first satisfying one's obligations to oneself, the political approach stresses the need for some authoritative instrument capable of providing the direction and steering necessary to account for the needs of all. What has traditionally made the state seem capable of acting as a moral agent is the supposition that while individuals have interests, the actions of governments can rest on *dis*interest. Because markets celebrate interest—indeed, because they view the pursuit of interests as the only realistic substitute for the no-longer-viable pursuit of such aristocratic practices as virtue—the defense of the state as a moral agent and, consequently, the political approach to moral obligation were once associated with the political right. Conservatives, in Kenneth Dyson's words, "had . . . in common a pessimistic conception of human nature, above all a fear of the anarchy and destruction that could follow from the 'self-interested' individual who was detached from the bonds of a well-ordered society."[2]

Whatever else may be said of them—that, for example, they were elitist, patriarchal, and antidemocratic, all of which are true—conservative theories of the state rarely lacked a concern with the relationship between morality and politics. Even when the state was viewed as *Machtstaat* rather than *Rechtstaat,* an emphasis on the ethical nature of politics was central to conservative thought.[3] Political conservatism of this organic kind, however, could not survive the transition to modernity. As Albert Hirschman has put it, "The possibility of mutual gain emerged from the expected working of interest *in politics,* quite some time before it became a matter of doctrine in economics."[4] As self-interest in economics and liberalism in politics swept through eighteenth- and nineteenth-century thought, conservative theorists of the state either held fast to fixed principles that most people no longer followed or—at first reluctantly, later enthusiastically—joined in the celebration of an individualism they had once condemned.

Liberal principles now have a near monopoly among political theorists of modernity. Western liberal democracies, as their name implies, are characterized by respect for the idea that individuals themselves have the freedom to determine what they ought to do. This has been a momentous development in the Western world's political history, and nearly all to the good, but nonetheless it has one serious problem: if everyone is free to act as he or she chooses, what exists to insure that people will recognize their obligations to one another? I will argue in this chapter that for most of its history liberalism did not need to answer this question. A liberal theory of politics was linked to a conservative theory of society. By simply assuming that liberal citizens were tied together morally by tradition, culture, religion, family, and locality, liberal theory was able to emphasize the benefits to be gained by the free exercise of political rights, since society could always be counted on to cement the moral obligations that politics neglected.

In contemporary liberalism, by contrast, the assumption that strong social obligations make possible weak political ties is harder to maintain. As the moral world associated with civil society comes to be taken less and less for granted, liberalism moves in two directions: either toward a reliance on economic models of politics (in which it is assumed that rules of self-interest can bring about appropriate results without civil society playing a role) or into a defense of the state (as the only agent capable of serving as a surrogate for moral ties of civil society that are no longer especially binding). While the former approach has attracted a good deal of attention in contemporary liberal thinking, manifested in such developments as "public choice" theory and, to a lesser degree, the political philosophy of John Rawls, the latter has had far more currency in practice, for it forms the core idea of the welfare state. The welfare state brings to the surface the unanswered question in liberal theory—who is responsible for others when people are expected primarily to be responsible for themselves?—and then provides an answer: government will assume the task of protecting the moral order that makes society possible. The political approach to moral obligation, once associated with the right, has, with the development of the welfare state, come increasingly to be associated with the left.

Reliance on government to strengthen a sense of moral obligation is, in the minds of most modern liberal democrats (and certainly in the mind of this author), a substantial improvement over reliance on the market. Particularly when it concerns meeting obligations to distant and hypothetical others, the welfare state has increased a general recognition of the interdependence of fates that characterize social life in modern society. Yet the welfare state works best when it builds on and strengthens already-existing social ties. When government is relied on to furnish rules of moral obligation, will it weaken the very social ties that make government possible in the first place? How one answers this question will determine one's position with respect to the political approach to moral regulation. If one concludes that government is capable of serving as a substitute for the moral ties in civil society once associated with family and locality, the welfare state must be judged a great success. But if the assumption by government of moral responsibility is seen as subtracting from a sense of personal responsibility for the fate of others once associated with the intimate realm of society, the problems of the political approach to moral obligation begin to seem more serious.

The Marriage of Liberalism and Sociology

Early liberal political theory struggled valiantly with the problem of how citizens could be at once individuals possessing rights and members of a community obligated to others. Despite various (and important) differences in emphasis, the early liberal thinkers usually invoked a theory of contract; people enter voluntarily into relationships with government (or each other) and are therefore bound to it (or them). Even since David Hume's criticism of contract theory—how can a promise be made the basis of a social and philosophical order, Hume asked, when the very notion of a promise presupposes such an order?—philosophers, political theorists, and sociologists have had their doubts that consent, especially the tacit consent of generations living long after the social contract was signed, could serve as an adequate theory of political obligation.[5]

In recent years, the liberal theory of obligation has come under unusually strong criticism. John Dunn, while noting the attractiveness of liberal theory, writes that "there seems every reason to doubt the possibility of a comprehensive and coherent *modern* philosophy of liberalism."[6] A. John Simmons, after reviewing the arguments within the liberal tradition about tacit consent, natural duties, gratitude, and fairness, concludes that liberalism "cannot offer a convincing general account of our political bonds" and that "citizens generally have no special political bonds which require that they obey and support the government of their countries of residence."[7] Carole Pateman, on different grounds, finds that "the problem of political obligation is *insoluble* unless political theory and practice moves outside the confines of liberal categories and assumptions. The modern problem of political obligation arose with liberalism, but liberalism cannot provide a solution."[8]

Early liberal thinkers could not, it is true, justify a moral order within the terms of liberalism; but the point is, they did not even try. Unlike some contemporary thinkers who try to find in government a place within which moral obligations can be inscribed, seventeenth- and eighteenth-century liberals located the source of the moral order in society instead. Early liberalism assumed a sharp distinction between state and society: only if the latter were strong could the former be allowed to be weak. The same understanding of civil society that tempered the effects of self-interest in economic theory also provided the basis for the social contract in liberal political theory. Liberal theory, in other words, was not completely a *political* theory; there existed a sociological component to liberalism, without which little in the theory could make sense.

Not all liberals can be described as contractarians. Liberalism has attracted not only those inclined toward rules based on reason and logical rigor, but also those, such as Benjamin Constant or William Wordsworth, influenced by romanticism and feeling.[9] While admittedly a sociological influence is more likely to show itself among the latter than the former, it is important to realize that even among those early liberals most committed to pure contractarian principles, a sociological component was never absent. No thinker in the liberal tradition, to take the extreme case, was more radically individualistic in his assumptions than Thomas Hobbes. Gregory Kavka sees in Hobbes's political theory a notion of political obligation so relentlessly modern that, with a few corrections, it can be used to develop rational models of game-theoretical choice.[10] Yet even Hobbes possessed something of a sociological theory, or at least a social-psychological one. Men leave the state of nature, he wrote, because among the laws of nature is "complaesance, that is to say, that every man strive to accommodate himselfe to the rest."[11] Moreover, there are in Hobbes's social psychology a surprisingly large number of motivations (such as reputation, gratitude, envy, honor, dignity, shame, pity, emulation, admiration, jealousy, ambition, offense, displeasure, contempt, and lust) that rely on others for their realization.[12] We may not like them, but we recognize real social creatures, not abstract mental calculators, living in Hobbes's state of nature.

For John Locke, the social and moral background within which liberal assumptions made sense—but outside of which they would be disastrous—was provided by religion. Locke shared a well-understood tradition of religious cosmology with the thinkers of his time that was so important, as Dunn has argued, that he would never think to analyze it in his writings. This religious order establishes the preconditions that make it possible for individuals to be individuals. As Dunn puts it, "Men exercise claims over other men. They also exercise claims over non-human nature, both animate and inanimate. They have responsibilities, too, in the exercise of either of these—responsibilities to God in both cases and thus derivatively, in the case of claims over men, to other men."[13] Within such a cosmology, individualism is not nearly as radical as it seems; the realm to which it applies, after all, is a relatively small one: everything that is left over after God has done his divine work. Because of Locke's understanding of Christianity, Sheldon Wolin writes, "a society based on the consent of each of the members implied that each was a moral agent fully capable of understanding the moral postulates on which society rested."[14]

Individualism was not, for the early liberal thinkers, an end in itself. True, bourgeois society would unleash individuals to realize their self-interest, but this was not because individuals were "inherently" self-interested. If anything, people were viewed as driven by passions, for which individualism would be the corrective. Thus it was possible to believe, as we know from Hirschman's investigations into these issues, that the world of business and commerce, while driven by self-interest, would also be a realm of harmony (*doux commerce*) because individualism would be less antisocial than what it replaced.[15] Individualism was valued because it would contribute to a realm of authenticity, which stood in sharp contrast to the intrigue, gossip, and artificiality of court society.[16] One could be a free individual only within civil society; a man completely without social ties, because he was a slave to his passions, could never be free. Only in civil society could one be civilized.

There has thus long existed a relationship both intimate and estranged between sociology and liberalism. For one thing, they begin with different first premises. From the one tradition stemmed the idea that, as Anthony Arblaster puts it, "the individual must choose his values for himself, and construct his own morality."[17] From the other came the notion that society creates the need for a morality that precedes the individual and gives meaning to his existence. These differences could, however, be resolved through the concept of civil society. Civil society enabled eighteenth-century liberals like Ferguson, Hume, and Smith to add a sociological dimension to their work, just as a more modern understanding of civil society enabled the sociological theorist Durkheim to add a liberal dimension to his. For all their differences, liberalism and sociology needed each other.[18] Even Jeremy Bentham, who so often serves as the foil for sociology's own self-conceptions, was, as Charles Camic has pointed out, capable of saying that "it is desirable that on every occasion the course taken by every man's conduct should be in the highest degree conducive to the welfare of the greatest number of those sensitive beings in whose welfare it exercises any influence."[19]

So long as liberalism and sociology coexisted, even if uneasily, the inherent problems of each could be overcome. For sociology, the acceptance of liberalism was an introduction into modernity, about which it was otherwise ambivalent. For liberalism, the willingness to accept sociology meant that the full consequences of a purely individualistic understanding of the world could be postponed. By the end of the nineteenth century, the link between liberalism and sociology became more explicit than ever before. In England, liberal thinkers such as T. H. Green, Henry Sidgwick, and their followers rejected laissez-faire, from within essentially liberal premises, as incapable of generating a satisfactory account of moral and ethical obligations.[20] L. T. Hobhouse saw himself as a professional sociologist (although his efforts in that direction are no longer taken seriously), even as he tried to formulate a satisfactory liberal political theory.[21] Much the same was the case in the United States, where sociology was linked to traditions of social reform and Protestant evangelical redemption.[22] The marriage between sociology and liberalism, in short, led to the introduction of the modern welfare state and its emphasis on obligations to all—embodied, most illustratively, in T. H. Marshall's oxymoronic term *social citizenship*.[23]

Even though late-nineteenth- and early-twentieth-century liberals laid the groundwork for thinking about welfare, they were not prepared to argue that all matters involving the common welfare ought to be regulated by the state. Critical of the market yet suspicious of reliance on government, most of these thinkers hoped to stress the importance of civil society in opposition to the state. This they did through the theory of pluralism. The key concept that allowed the tempering of liberal individualism for the sake of obligation to others became the group. "A nation can be maintained only if, between the state and the individual, there is intercalated a whole series of secondary groups," Emile Durkheim wrote in *The Division of Labor in Society*.[24] Durkheim, who in his writings was so hostile to individualism and the notion of economic man, could turn around and identify himself as a liberal believing in individualism only through his commitment to some form of pluralism.

The discovery of the group enabled Durkheim to combine his belief in morality with his commitment to modernity. Throughout his writings, Durkheim worried about the corrosive effects of liberal individualism. Anomie or normlessness, he said, faced those atomistic individuals who were cut off from others. Intermediate groups, lying between a purely individualistic market and a coercive and distant state, enabled modern individuals to avoid an anomic fate. Through the concept of a group, liberalism and sociology could maintain their relationship. Durkheim's views were therefore quite similar to many of the prominent British liberals of his day. Harold Laski, for example, argued that groups should be conceived of as persons, a point of view he later rejected, while G.D.H. Cole went so far as to speak of a "group soul."[25] Thus the group became civil society in modern dress.

It was not just intimate groups such as families and local communities that were capable of tempering the effects of pure liberal individualism. Guild socialists of the early twentieth century looked to labor unions to play the same role. As the century progressed, professional associations, schools, and even business organizations were viewed favorably by pluralist thinkers, because each stood midway between the state and the individual. Organizations and institutions in the social realm were seen as alternatives to mass society: they could "socialize" individuals, thereby softening and deflecting demands on public authority before these reached the elite; conversely, the demands of the elite would be transmitted through intermediate associations down to individuals, losing their sharp, authoritative edge in the process.[26]

Sociology was thus essential to liberal theory because civil society (or its functional equivalent, the group) provided the moral dimension that liberalism lacked. Through their social ties liberal citizens, who were otherwise individualistic, would operate in a moral order that made their individualism tolerable. Sociology, in that sense, was the missing ingredient in an otherwise unworkable liberal theory of obligation. The ties that linked people together could grow out of friendship, gratitude, personal knowledge, groups, informal networks, deference, loyalty, obedience, and conformity, but whatever the motivations that led people to recognize their moral obligations to others, the concept that solved the riddles that liberal theory could not answer within its own framework was nearly always sociological and rarely liberal.

By mid–twentieth century, liberalism and sociology had become even more entangled. Confronting a world of large organizations, bureaucratic states, economic planning, and challenge from communism and fascism, liberalism, instead of being a theory of individualism, began to show an "addiction towards social conformity," to use Wolin's apt phrase.[27] Appalled at the consequences of individual action in a collective society, liberalism as a theory of pure individualism seemed to have reached a dead end. The dominant partner in the marriage between liberalism and sociology, to the shock of both parties, turned out to be sociology. Individualism, if post–World War II American political science was any indication, was the one thing that liberalism no longer seemed to tolerate.

Collective Anomie

Political theory plays increasingly less of a role in the debate over approaches to moral obligations in modern society, while political science plays increasingly more—for all its recent preoccupation with objectivity and scientific technique. This is especially true of those American political scientists who, in the years after World War II, looked back to Durkheim's France and Laski's England and tried to bring the theory of pluralism up to date within an American context.

Although the leading pluralists of the early postwar period were liberal in their political sympathies (appreciating capitalism as an economic system and individualism as a fundamental good), the essence of their approach to political regulation was the development of models of the political system that constrained individual self-interest and channeled it in safe directions in order to insure the stability of the overall society. Even sociology was not anti-individualistic enough for them; to understand American politics, they turned to anthropology, the discipline most compatible with a view that culture, not individuals, shapes reality. If an anthropologist sensitive to symbols and ritualistic behavior and an economist searching for rational political conduct modeled on the market both examined how political scientists described the conditions of political life in the United States from the 1930s until sometime in the recent past, the anthropologist would have stood in more familiar territory.

Anthropology was often explicitly used to understand the operation of national political institutions. David B. Truman's *The Governmental Process* borrowed from such writers as Clyde Kluckhorn, Ruth Benedict, Emile Durkheim, Ralph Linton, and Karl Polanyi; Truman attributed the success of interest-group democracy to certain unwritten "rules of the game," defined as "norms, values, expectations" the violation of which "normally will weaken a group's cohesion, reduce its status in the community, and expose it to the claims of other groups."[28] Similarly, Donald R. Matthews devoted an entire chapter in a book on the U.S. Senate to what he called "folkways" such as reciprocity, apprenticeship, courtesy, and institutional patriotism, all based on something other than self-interest.[29] Of all political institutions, the Senate was the most like a "club." In it, unquenched desire for power was checked by the necessity to wait one's turn for a committee assignment; seniority institutionalized a criterion of distributional justice based not on individual rational choice, but on institutional needs.[30] Bureaucratic policy making was undertaken through relationships of "clientelism" (a term borrowed from peasant communities, not modern urban life), in which, whatever the formal mechanisms of politics, informal negotiations between like-minded partners was the rule, not conflict between antagonists.[31]

At the same time, politics at the individual level was not, according to the pluralists, the product of rational self-interest calculated by isolated individuals. Political machines in urban areas, to take one example, were seen as premised on traditions of solidarity and group loyalty: while the standard text on the subject describes them as "interested only in making and distributing income—mainly money—to those who run it and work for it,"[32] other writers have found the political machines to represent a "moral force" teaching "standards of right and wrong that can guide practical decisions—that can be manifested in the smallest things—in the ways in which people bring up their children and treat their neighbors, or the manner in which they generally deal with the interests of others."[33] Voters, candidates, even activists similarly entered the political system to express social needs and community norms.[34] By serving as "supplier[s] of cues by which the individual may evaluate the elements of politics," parties assured stability in the political system.[35] Trust in that system and in the candidates who served it was taken for granted, even though trust is difficult to find when relationships are strictly instrumental.[36] When the single most prestigious group of political scientists in America sought a term that would mark the distinctive characteristic of successful Western democracies (of which the United States was presumed to be a model), they turned again to anthropology: political "culture" was the buzzword of 1960s political science.[37]

The world of American pluralism was safe and secure. There was no need to be anxious about the corrosive effects of liberal individualism, because groups—from the family all the way to that group to end all groups, the state—took care of collective needs. As long as such a world existed in theory, the liberal problem of moral obligation did not have to be faced: true, our political ties to others were weak, for that is what made us liberal, but our group ties to one another were strong, for that is what made us pluralists. By borrowing an approach to moral obligation from sociology and anthropology, political scientists were able (at least until the 1960s) to avoid the question of whether individuals whose only links were political rather than social could satisfactorily regulate their interactions. When the break came, when sociology and liberalism finally divorced from each other, it was because the sociological assumptions that pluralist writers made about group behavior could not survive the actual way that groups operated in the modern state.

Groups, thinkers like Durkheim had hoped, would serve as the corrective to anomie. But groups can perform that role only if a distinction exists between state and society, one in which groups, by remaining part of society rather than turning to the state, act as individuals' collective conscience. What Durkheim (and pluralist political scientists in America) failed to anticipate was that groups could become attached to the state itself, divorcing themselves from society in the process. In contrast to Durkheim's hopes, groups in modern liberal democracies became too important to remain private. As Lowi in particular has emphasized, modern liberalism is not individualistic but collectivistic; groups compete for the favors bestowed by the state. "Interest-group liberalism," as Lowi calls it in *The End of Liberalism,* in effect changes the moral rules of liberal society.

As the political benefits of the modern state increase, groups organize to fight for them; but in so doing they make impossible the sociological practices that the early liberals saw as tempering the implications of liberalism. Interest groups do not have passions that need to be tempered by interests; they have only interests. Individuals can create bonds of loyalty and personal obligation, but groups cannot. Individuals enter into contracts; groups can be conceived of only as forming alliances. It is possible, as sociological liberals like George Herbert Mead pointed out, for individuals to develop a social self by putting themselves in the position of others, but groups commit institutional suicide if they try to act that way. A society of individuals seems possible, for individuals are capable of having a collective conscience; a society of interest groups seems impossible, for groups do not know guilt. Individuals, in a word, because they are social, can have moral obligations, while groups, because they are organizations, cannot.[38]

As interest groups seek to maximize their advantages over other groups in order to obtain benefits from government, behavior undertaken without regard for its effects on others becomes not just routine, but expected. Durkheim's solution to anomie is instead a cause; groups, rather than absorbing private egos into the collectivity, collectivize anomie, transforming it from an attribute of individuals to an attribute of organizations. Collective anomie threatens a return to Hobbes's war against all, but with a difference. For Hobbes the necessity for sovereign authority stemmed from forces over which people had little control, produced as they were by nature or by scarcity; because individuals were by nature selfish, they needed a sovereign to regulate them. For modern interest-group liberals, though, it is our institutions, not our nature, that demand we distrust one another. We are not responding to constraints in our environment; rather, we are creating those constraints in our very actions. Under conditions of interest-group liberalism, because we have a sovereign institution called the state that exists without an alternative morality rooted in civil society, we have continually to recreate selfishness in our actions with one another.

The notion that sociological and anthropological practices could restrain self-interest in favor of collective norms no longer seemed realistic when the state came to play so large a role in regulating interest-group conflicts. As if recognizing new political realities, American political science, so recently pluralist, began to shift to a point of view emphasizing how self-interest—at the governmental, group, and individual levels—operates unconstrained by moral obligations to others. Political machines, for example, which had been understood as based on solidaristic principles, were now viewed as in decline, replaced by administrative agencies that negotiated with interest-group representatives.[39] Political parties, which had expressed ties of tradition and the group, were undermined by independent voting and shifting loyalties.[40] Rather than taking their voting cues from others around them, citizens began to judge politicians in the light of rational choices; if elected officials did not stimulate the economy, they would be punished in the voting booth.[41] Candidates were now understood to rely increasingly on political consultants, whose only responsibility was to the person who hired them, not to any unwritten rules of the game.[42] Public opinion was organized by a "marketplace for ideas," but that market, like all markets, isolated individuals in the formation of their opinions.[43] Society, more than ever before, seemed to drop out of politics, leaving only individuals and states behind.

Because groups in civil society that once restrained individual self-interest have begun to break down, political scientists now increasingly view government as operating by a moral code that emphasizes individual rational choice. Informal networking in Congress gives way to technical staff experts who do not share traditions of reciprocity and mutual understanding with those with whom they negotiate.[44] Political scientists talk of the "rampant individualism" in institutions like the Senate which have abused the "collegial process"[45] or emphasize the impact of the "me decade" on the House of Representatives.[46] Samuel Kernell expresses the changes in one sentence when he writes that Washington, D.C., "is a community governed less by leaders and more by the requirements of independent egocentric actors."[47] Even bureaucratic clientelism was affected by these developments. At first liberal efforts at social regulation brought government into more activities; when the reaction set in, conservative efforts at deregulation began to remove it. Yet these two trends, so different in many ways, had one thing in common: instead of the administrative process being viewed as adjudicated by like-minded interests, both trends are characterized by a litigious model of administrative politics based on the assumption that interest groups and bureaucrats respond primarily out of self-interest as they understand it.[48]

The American political-science literature illustrates the consequences for the political approach to moral regulation when social ties no longer prevent actors from acting in a purely liberal fashion. A situation in which large-scale organizations press government to satisfy their immediate demands irrespective of the social consequences is completely foreign to the moral universe of early liberal political theory. Then the morality of civil society was assumed to make liberal politics possible; now the rules of liberal self-interest make moral obligation impossible. When sociology and liberalism were forced to part ways, liberal thinkers had to return to the question they had long been excused from considering: who is responsible for others if each actor in the liberal world is concerned primarily with his own interest?

The answer was provided by one of the most important books dealing with groups in the modern state, Mancur Olson's *The Logic of Collective Action*. Olson painted a remarkable picture of how, in a world without sociology, a theory of liberal individualism inevitably becomes a defense of coercive authority. The nature of the groups in Olson's portrait stands in direct opposition to that envisioned by the early pluralist thinkers. For them, groups would "socialize" individuals into their obligations to one another. The members of Olson's groups, in contrast, do not act out of sentiment, loyalty, passion, or belongingness: they join groups only to obtain the rewards that groups can offer, and since the benefits groups provide are collective goods, they will obtain those benefits whether they participate in the affairs of the group or not. Thus, since every member receives the same benefit, even if one risks her life in a picket line, a second gives twenty hours a week of his free time after work, and a third stays home and watches football, the last is acting the most rationally.

So long as participation in the affairs of a group is not expected, the paradox of the "free rider" does not pose any particular problem of social coordination. In a modern society, however, everyone is affected to some degree by the actions of everyone else. Even if direct participation in the collective life of the society is not encouraged, some form of indirect participation is always necessary. How, under such conditions, is participation to be organized? Because the free-rider option is so tempting to rationally calculating individuals, people will not advance their collective objectives

unless there is coercion to force them to do, or unless some separate incentive, distinctive from the achievement of the common or group interest, is offered. . . . If the state, with all of the emotional resources at its command, cannot finance its most basic and vital activities without resort to compulsion, it would seem that large private organizations might also have difficulty in getting the individuals in the groups whose interests they attempt to advance to make the necessary contributions voluntarily.[49]

If Olson is correct, obligations to others cannot be satisfied, when each actor has no moral ties to others, without some form of coercion.

Liberalism, which before was a minimalist theory of the state, has, if this picture is correct, become instead a minimalist theory of society. Government could be weak, according to classical liberal theory, only because society was strong. In contemporary versions of liberal theory, the opposite has occurred: society has become so weak that government, by necessity, has become strong. No longer is a liberal theory of the state linked to a conservative theory of society; in Olson's world, *all* motivations, wherever located, are individualistic. The notion that people might carve out a realm of social existence to be organized by moral rules emphasizing trust and solidarity is as foreign to liberal theorists like Olson as that "compartmentalization" is to the self-interested calculators envisioned by the Chicago school of economics. Politics without society, in a word, threatens both: politics cannot exist because all behavior between individuals and government is reduced to an economic quest for self-interest, while society is rendered impossible because no moral ties between individuals exist to soften a Hobbesian struggle over resources.

A Republic of the Head

The disappearance of civil society from the liberal theory of politics creates an awkward problem. If individual actors are not tied together by sentiments, culture, reciprocity, and other features familiar to any sociologist, the only agency capable of providing moral guidelines would, from Olson's analysis, appear to be coercive authority. Yet many liberals retain a bias against state intervention. Consequently one important trend in contemporary liberal theories of politics is to search for substitutes for government, a search that can succeed only by finding other institutions that share with government some coercive capacity.

The variant of contemporary liberal theory that best illustrates the futile search for an alternative to government regulation is "public-choice theory," the most complete effort to extend market principles from the eco-

nomic sector of society to the political. That this by now enormous literature is normative I take to be beyond question, for inherent in all of it is a
standard not only of how people allegedly *do* act but of how they *should* act
as well.[50] Nor is it my intention to criticize this literature, for everything I
could say about it has already been said, even thirty years ago before the
public-choice approach became so widespread:

> Man is not just an animal who, unlike the others, is provident and calculating. . . .
> How men see themselves . . . is intimately connected with their mental images of
> the community; they are not mere competitors, however benevolent, in a market
> for the supply of personal wants; they are members of society, and their hopes and
> feelings, both for themselves and others, would not be what they are apart from
> group loyalties. They see themselves having rights and duties, as moral beings, be-
> cause they have some conception of a social world with parts for themselves and
> others to play in it.[51]

I turn instead directly to the writers in this tradition, for they illustrate why
the state—or whatever one chooses to call it—is the only alternative to the
social ties of civil society if all individuals think first of themselves.

Most, though by no means all, public-choice theorists are politically
sympathetic to a weak state. Indeed, they take the notion of a voluntary
contract that has always existed in liberal theory and make it the basis of all
interaction—illustrated, for example, by transaction-cost economics, the
minimalist principles of political consent associated with writers like James
Buchanan and Gordon Tullock, or William Riker's efforts to demonstrate
that various paradoxes of voting cast suspicion on any populistic notions
of a general will.[52] Yet unlike early liberal theorists, who assumed that society would provide the strong ties that made a weak state possible, public-
choice theorists share assumptions about human nature that make it impossible for individual rational actors to act out of sociological motives.
How, then, is the social contract enforced if all rational actors will seek not
to have it enforced? The only answer to this question is to create a coercive
authority that, for all intents and purposes, acts like a state without being
called one.

The fascination with coercive authority that we find in extreme versions
of public-choice individualism can be seen in the work of James Buchanan.
If all individuals act rationally to further their self-interest, it stands to reason that they would want to use the public treasury to line their own
pockets. And if all politicians responded to those demands, the result
would be fiscal bankruptcy. Responding to this dilemma, Buchanan, to-

gether with Gordon Tullock, called in an early work for "enlightened self-interest" on the part of pressure groups, since they could never be expected to "exercise sufficient self-restraint, given existing rules."[53] As if recognizing that such a call was premised on the existence of norms in civil society that his own theory denied could exist, Buchanan later argued that because "budgets cannot be left adrift in the sea of democratic politics," the rules of politics would have to be changed.[54] The argument was brought to its logical conclusion when Buchanan realized that only a new constitution, one that placed monetary matters completely outside public choice, could guarantee a stable currency.[55] Buchanan trusts rules more than he does people: "Good games," as he and Geoffrey Brennan put it, "depend on good rules more than they depend on good players."[56] The problem, as I argue in Chapter 8, is that the players—and no one else—make the rules. By advocating an inflexible constitution, that part of government most difficult to change by democratic procedures, Buchanan becomes, in an important sense, more statist than the Keynesians and welfare-state politicians he criticizes.

The application of transaction-cost economics to firms and hierarchies reveals a similar bias toward strong authority. As long ago as 1937 R. H. Coase, in his classic article on the theory of the firm, recognized that the logic of self-interest for organizations in the external world—called the market—could not apply to the decision-making structure within the organization.[57] Because theories of rational egoism assume that everyone operates out of self-interest, relations within a firm are marked by "transaction costs" in which freely calculating actors demand something in return for their participation. To followers of transaction-cost economics, individuals within organizations do not restrain their interests, give favors, or act from a concern for the common good. Thus hierarchical authority, the direct opposite of the presumed voluntarism in the external market, is necessary so that the firm can manage its internal relations efficiently. Only through hierarchy can we "prevent agents from engaging in dysfunctional pursuit of local goals," writes Oliver Williamson. Since it is important to regard "the business firm as a governance structure rather than as a production function," transaction-cost economics demands that we "supplant the fiction of economic man" and develop "an elementary appreciation for 'human nature as we know it.'"[58] Organizations, it would seem, can be free only if individuals live in chains. Once again, rational-choice liberalism cannot solve the problem of obligations to others when civil society is weak, except by creating some form of "governance structure" that can compel obedience.

The moral philosophy of John Rawls also sheds light on what happens to liberal political theory when it is no longer attached to a conservative theory of society. Unlike public-choice theorists, John Rawls does not believe that rational action should be the basis of all human activity. "The ideal market process and the ideal legislative procedure," he writes, "are different in crucial respects. They are designed to achieve distinct ends, the first leading to efficiency, the latter if possible to justice."[59] In Rawls's version of liberal theory, individual actors are not egoists; indeed Rawlsian principles are generally viewed as leading to a defense of the welfare state, not of the free market. But Rawls, like public-choice theorists, assigns no role to civil society in his moral theory. Consequently he, like them (if at a more elevated level), leans toward a substitute for the coercive capacity of the state: the notion of obligation as a duty stripped of voluntary motivations.

Rawls argues that morality passes through three stages: authority, association, and principle. In the first stage, which is associated with childhood, we simply accept our moral rules from our superiors because we cannot judge them ourselves. Having learned discipline this way, we are prepared to move on to the morality learned through association with others. Rawls here develops ideas remarkably similar to those of Talcott Parsons: "The morality of association includes a large number of ideals each defined in ways suitable for the respective status or role."[60] Thus, so long as we exist at the level of the morality of association, Rawls has a point of view that, like Parsons's, is based on a functionalist reading of Durkheim:

Since the arrangements of an association are recognized to be just (and in the more complex roles the principles of justice are understood and serve to define the ideal appropriately), thereby insuring that all of its members benefit and know that they benefit from its activities, the conduct of others in doing their part is taken to be to the advantage of each.[61]

Had Rawls stopped at this point, he would have been in the grand tradition of liberalism, relying on conformist sociology to soften atomistic individualism. (See Chapter 7 for more on this point.) But the morality of association is a passing phase, one that prepares people for "the ideal of just human consideration"—a morality of principle.[62] (Rawls is strongly influenced by Lawrence Kohlberg's idea that morality passes through certain stages with an implicit ranking.)[63] Through our associations, Rawls argues, people learn the importance of purely abstract deontological principles of justice. We make decisions in the original position in order to create moral rules that enable us, in a well-ordered society, to return to that position for our morality: "The appropriateness of moral sentiments to our nature is determined by the principles that would be consented to in the original position."[64]

Rawls presents an elaborate, even eloquent, statement of what a just society would resemble. Love of the principles of justice would serve as the basis for human cooperation. We would live in a social union, and unlike the situation in pure laissez-faire, our fates would be interdependent. There would, in a well-ordered society, exist a division of labor, community, sociability, reciprocity, history, and culture. Yet unlike eighteenth-century theories of civil society, Rawls's theory of morality contains little or no sociology to provide the glue of moral obligation. It is far better, according to Rawls, to feel guilty that we violated a principle than that we violated a friendship.[65] Trust, loyalty, friendship, love—these are "contingencies" or "accidental circumstances of our world"; moral considerations are therefore not to be premised on "the well-being and approval of particular interests and groups, but are shaped by a conception of right chosen irrespective of these contingencies." Conscience, which in Durkheim's view makes society possible, is according to Rawls something "oppressive" that a just society will help us to "suffer much less from."[66] People, in the Rawlsian republic, do not love other men and women: they love humankind instead. Rational people are not even allowed the quality of envy in Rawls's original position, even though they are in Hobbes's state of nature.[67] Rawls's moral vision is one in which we are all tied together by our common intellectual respect for the rules of justice. This is a republic of the head, not the heart.

By relentlessly downplaying a sociological dimension to his theory Rawls develops an understanding of moral obligation which he shares with Lawrence Kohlberg, an understanding that, in the words of Carol Gilligan, is "formal and abstract" rather than "contextual and narrative."[68] Liberal society in this portrait may be just, but it has no richness of interpretative meaning, no collection of stories, traditions, and practices which, because they are imperfect and ambiguous, allow real human beings to create a morality for themselves out of the textures of their interactions with others.[69] Facing the momentous questions posed by Plato's noble lie or Dostoevsky's Grand Inquisitor, Rawls relies on a secular and rational notion of moral order: "Conceptions of justice must be justified by the conditions of our life as we know it or not at all."[70] Modern people are tied to one another, but in a completely impersonal way—as Michael Sandel puts it, "not [as] egoists, but [as] strangers, sometimes benevolent." The republic according to Rawls, Sandel has argued, is cold and unfriendly: "Unlike classical Greek and medieval Christian conceptions, the universe of the deontological ethic is a place devoid of inherent meaning, a world 'disenchanted' in Max Weber's phrase, a world without an objective moral order."[71]

In a world where people raise children, live in communities, and value friendships, a moral theory that demands rational cognition to the degree that Rawls's does is little help and may well be a burden. It teaches people to distrust what will help them most—their personal attachments to those they know—and value what will help them least—abstract principles that, for all their philosophical brilliance, are a poor guide to the moral dilemmas of everyday life. By upholding a world of perfect thinkers, it has little of relevance to say to imperfect doers. Having sacrificed their affective and known bonds for abstract principles, and having yielded their capacity to empathize and interpret in favor of a capacity to reflect, how would such principled individuals govern their moral obligations in a thoroughly secularized society?

According to Rawls, political obligation is a concept that applies only to legislators and people of privilege; everyone else has, not obligations, but natural duties. Duties, unlike obligations, "apply to us without regard for our voluntary acts." Surprisingly for a thinker within the liberal contract tradition, Rawls strips from the notion of duty (which, after all, applies to most people in the society) any voluntary choice whatsoever:

Thus if the basic structure of society is just, or as just as it is reasonable to expect in the circumstances, everyone has a natural duty to do his part in the existing scheme. Each is bound to these institutions independent of his voluntary acts, performative or otherwise. Thus even though the principles of natural duty are derived from a contractarian point of view, they do not presuppose an act of consent, express or tacit, or indeed any voluntary act, in order to apply.

Rawls argues that people who acknowledge "the natural duty of justice" avoid the need for "a greater reliance on the coercive powers of the sovereign."[72] In short, authority is inside of us telling us what not to do instead of outside of us doing the same thing. Although Rawls offers a passionate defense of civil disobedience and is clearly more humanitarian than public-choice theorists, the implications of his approach indicate that liberalism without sociology treads on ground hostile to the very emphasis on voluntarism with which liberalism began.[73]

The opposition between individual freedom and state authority that guides so much of contemporary liberal political theory is, as both public-choice theory and Rawlsian liberalism show, a false opposition: civil society, not the individual, is a better alternative to government in modern society. Although believers in laissez-faire complain that the state has grown at the expense of individuals, and advocates of a stronger state sometimes bemoan individualism, the truth is that the decline of obligations once associated with civil society strengthens both individualism *and* governmental authority. On the one hand liberal theory without society leads individuals and organizations to view the state as an agency that can satisfy their desires, and to be quite insistent when they feel it does not. On the other hand the state, in the absence of civil society, has grown to meet those needs, expanding into areas of policy that were once considered outside its purview. As Hegel first argued, the growth of liberal individualism and the expansion of the state occurred together. It is unclear which is more problematic: complete anarchy or complete authority. In contemporary liberal theory, they actually seem like two versions of the same fate.

Moral Neutrality and Social Democracy

Not all political scientists, theorists, and activists are satisfied with an approach to moral regulation that calls for an authoritative solution to the moral dilemmas of modernity but only reluctantly find that solution in government. Instead of looking to some model of individual rational choice as a substitute for a civil society that no longer works, one can instead rely unapologetically on government to carry out the moral tasks that civil society once played in liberal theory. Although it is anything but fashionable to defend the state as a moral agent, two examples are particularly relevant to the problems of moral regulation in modern liberal democracy. One is a form of conservatism that, unlike rational-choice theory, distrusts the market and supports state intervention in moral matters. The other is a social-democratic understanding of the welfare state that justifies government as the only agency in modern society capable of insuring the maintenance of moral obligations between individuals.

An example of a conservative defense of government as the necessary protector of morality can be seen in the writings of political scientist Lawrence Mead. "A 'free' political culture," he writes, "is the characteristic, not of a society still close to the state of nature . . . , but of one already far removed from it by dense, reliable networks of mutual expectations." Mead argues, following Tocqueville, that only when people exist in strong civil societies with well-defined codes of moral obligation can a good society be realized. For Mead, however, civil society is a thing of the past. Over the course of a generation or so, Americans have become "less able to take care of themselves and respect the rights of others."[74] It has therefore become imperative that Americans be made to feel more responsible for their sense of moral obligation.

Mead understands morality in conservative terms, as adherence to rules of conduct shaped by tradition and respect for authority. From that perspective, civil society is *not* what it used to be, since modernity unquestionably lessens the hold of patriarchal families or hierarchical social institutions. Unable to see the turmoil of modernity as an opportunity for incorporating the views of moral agents into the operation of moral rules, however, Mead has little choice but to call for state intervention in the moral sphere. Pondering the lack of success of welfare programs, Mead implicitly endorses a proposal by former Representative Martha Griffiths to force welfare recipients to work "if necessary under the threat of taking their children away."[75] If Chicago school economists think about letting mothers sell their babies, some contemporary conservatives think about taking them away; without a sociological understanding of economics and politics, it would seem, one can do everything with children except raise them. (This issue is not merely academic; the right of the state to take babies away from their families, as we will see in the next chapters, became a major political issue in Scandinavia.)

Mead should be admired for his intellectual honesty in facing up to the need for moral regulation, not only in contrast to those who call themselves conservative but rely almost entirely on the market, but also in contrast to tendencies on the left toward moral neutrality in politics. The explicit moralism of his way of thinking at least recognizes that modern liberal democrats do have obligations to one another. Yet Mead illustrates the inherent problems of relying on government to supply a sense of obligation no longer present in society, for in the end obligation can be achieved only at the price of democracy and self-realization. More likely, however, it will not be achieved at all; if families and communities have already failed to develop a capacity for recognizing the mutual interweaving of fates, states will hardly be more successful.

Social democracy, like Mead's emphasis on obligation, also began with a moral dimension: the welfare state received its inspiration from Christian and humanitarian emphases on moral responsibility.[76] Some concern with notions of a moral community inspired most of the important theorists of the modern welfare state. Thinkers like Richard Titmuss, for example, argued that the welfare state symbolized the art of giving and thus created a moral environment within which governments could strengthen ties among individuals.[77] Similarly, T. H. Marshall's concept of "social citizenship" combined elements of both sociology and politics. Social citizenship was neither a kinship bond associated with traditional society nor a materialistic bond associated with capitalism; it requires, he wrote, "a bond of a different kind, a direct sense of community membership based on loyalty to a civilization which is a common possession."[78]

Yet even though social democracy and the welfare state were inspired by moral ideals, their advocates soon grew suspicious of civil society as a place in which they could be developed. Distrustful of localism, private charity, "small is beautiful" attitudes, and even, on occasion, families, social democrats are quick to point out—in the words of Gösta Rehn, one of the contemporary architects of the Swedish welfare state—that "networks organized on the basis of local or group solidarity alone will inevitably leave many out in the cold."[79] As the concern for equality of conditions and universal access to benefits became a major feature of welfare state thinking, government became the primary tool to realize these goals and moral language something of an anachronism. The passage of the moral world of civil society, from the point of view of many social democrats, was a sign of progress. If conservatives like Lawrence Mead long for civil society but, in its absence, endorse government as a moral agent, social democratic defenders of the welfare state, if not enthusiastically, then certainly with little reluctance, come to the conclusion that government is a preferable moral regulator to any other available option.

As the inheritor of the political approach to moral regulation, the modern welfare state faces a paradox: whereas contemporary liberals are uncomfortable with an explicit discussion of moral issues, contemporary governments are actively intervening ever more directly into moral matters. Liberals ought to be committed, Ronald Dworkin has argued, to "official neutrality amongst theories of what is valuable in life."[80] (Or, as Bruce

Ackerman puts it, it is a "hard truth" that "there is no moral meaning hidden in the bowels of the universe.")[81] Government in modern societies tends to follow such advice, concerned less with results than with procedures, balancing claims without judging the claims themselves, acting, in short, as a referee between different interests in society without, at least in theory, having an interest of its own. In the United States, for example, the New Deal marked a major transition toward a better life for most people, yet in "shifting the grounds of democracy from ethical to technical considerations," to quote Russell Hanson, it left a moral vacuum at the heart of American politics,

for it then became apparent that this rise of a conception of democracy that looks neither to the past nor to the future signified the relative decline of all ethical conceptions of democracy, regardless of their specific moral content. Henceforth, the meaning and legitimacy of democracy in America was linked to economic performance and the abundance of consumer goods, rather than moral achievement.[82]

Yet while anxious not to become involved in moral discussion, the modern state, especially the modern welfare state, assumes responsibility for raising children, taking care of the elderly, insuring that the disadvantaged are looked after, and establishing the rules by which people's fates are interlinked. Modern welfare states are, more than ever before, engaged in the business of regulating moral obligation, even in the absence of a moral language by which to do so. "When the economy becomes the polity," Sheldon Wolin has written, "*citizen* and *community* become subversive words in the vocabulary of the new political philosophy."[83] Without a moral language shaped by community, one rooted in ties in civil society that give people a sense of personal stake in the affairs of others, how can we be sure that the welfare state's greatest accomplishment—its sense of caring—will be preserved?

There is little doubt that government does a fairly good job of providing material things, that its ability to transfer funds from the wealthy to the poor can create greater equality in society. But whether government can act as a giver of care, especially those forms of care we associate with families and communities, is another matter entirely. As government becomes more involved in activities once believed to be the proper realm of families and local communities, Max Weber's prophetic warning not to introduce the salvation of souls into politics needs reinterpretation. Since government is a primary moral actor in any case, the question is no longer whether this should be so, but instead whether government has the right to seek the same monopoly over morality that it has assumed over the control of violence. It is at least possible that ever greater state intervention in civil society may ultimately have the same consequences as the weakening of the boundary between civil society and the market: a world without strong caring relations among people who are close can harm the capacity of people to take responsibility for unknown distant others.

In order to examine the relationship among the welfare state, civil society, and moral obligations, it is useful to turn away from the United States, where reliance on government to organize the moral order is haphazard and reluctant. The most appropriate place to look to instead is Scandinavia. The Scandinavian societies are far more willing than those in North America to rely on government to insure that their citizens meet their moral obligations to others. Indeed, many Americans look with a certain envy at Scandinavia on the grounds that experiences there prove the possibility of socialism.[84] Whether these countries are in fact socialist or not, they undoubtedly illustrate not only the advantages, but also the problems, of relying on a political approach to moral regulation. Few can object to the conclusion of Stein Ringen, a Norwegian political scientist, that the Scandinavian societies illustrate the "possibility of politics," the notion of "seeking to attack social inequalities via legislative and administrative measures of a piecemeal kind."[85]

To argue that the Scandinavian societies best illustrate in practice the dilemmas of liberal theory described here in theory is not to claim that these countries rely so much on the state that there is no longer any room for society, or even sociology. We are—not only in Scandinavia, but everywhere in the world—a long way from a purely liberal society in which government regulation becomes a substitute for ties in civil society that no longer exist. In Scandinavia in particular, social solidarity and norm-driven behavior are a very important part of social life. (The various Scandinavian terms for society—the Swedish *samhälle,* for instance, or the Danish *samfund*—emphasize, more than does the English term, the collective, or *Gemeinschaft,* aspects of the social order.) Moreover, the Scandinavian societies have been unusually successful at creating, for most of their citizens, something very close to the "good life." An effort by Richard Estes of the University of Pennsylvania to measure this good life—based on indicators ranging from vulnerability to natural disaster to cultural diversity, the status of women, and welfare benefits—lists Denmark as the most desirable society in the world to live in, with Norway second and Sweden not far behind.[86]

A further examination of the moral consequences of the Scandinavian welfare state is called for not because it has proved a failure, but instead because it has been such a great success. Just as Americans appreciate and have benefited from the market, Scandinavians have appreciated and benefited from the state. Yet it is also true that the welfare state in Scandinavia has developed in a way never anticipated by its founders. Rather than engaging in the business of transferring money from the wealthy to the poor, the welfare state has increasingly been occupied with the building of institutions designed to satisfy moral obligations once associated with civil society. Just as in the United States the market has begun to cross the border with civil society, in Scandinavia the state has begun to cross that border from the other direction. It is because state intervention in civil society has progressed further in Scandinavia than anywhere else in the world that new and awkward questions about moral responsibility in modern society need to be addressed in a Scandinavian context. Liberal political theory, even at its best, has in recent years had difficulty recognizing a role for moral obligations and intimate social ties. It remains to be seen whether liberal political practice—even at *its* best—has encountered difficulties of the same kind.

FIVE

Welfare States and Moral Regulation

A Scandinavian Success

Success stories in twentieth-century politics have been all too few, but the Scandinavian welfare states certainly count among them. It is difficult to think of societies where principles of solidarity and a recognition of obligations to strangers have been more embedded than in Sweden, Denmark, and Norway. (Iceland, although part of an entity called Norden, and Finland, although geographically, if not linguistically, tied to the rest of Scandinavia, will not be considered here.) At a time when other countries use the state to wage wars or even exterminate whole races, the Scandinavians use it to encourage a sense of moral obligation. That is something to be proud of, and most Scandinavians are.

An increasing reliance on government to express the rules by which people are obligated to one another is an undeniable fact of recent Scandinavian experience. In 1960, public expenditures as a percentage of gross domestic product (GDP) were 25 percent in Denmark, 31 percent in Sweden, and 30 percent in Norway. Two decades later they were close to or had exceeded 50 percent; only Holland was in the same class as Sweden and Denmark in terms of total amount of public spending, and no other country in the world saw government grow at such a rate during those years as those two. (Norway's increase in public outlays, although smaller, was still quite high comparatively speaking.) Compared to the United States, where public expenditure as a percentage of GDP in 1982 was 10 percent higher than in 1960, in Sweden and Denmark it was 36 percent higher.[1]

Also unlike the United States, the great bulk of this money was used not for defense or interest on the public debt, but for welfare state activities that, in one way or another, express a sense of obligation to others. In Norway, where the welfare state is less developed than in Sweden and Denmark, an effort to break down the spending increase since 1950 into its component parts revealed that welfare expenditures rose, while all other categories (except the miscellaneous category) decreased.[2] Most welfare state programs have, as a result, become more generous; real social security expenditures, one of the largest items in the budget, increased by 124 percent in Norway, 111 percent in Sweden, and 88 percent in Denmark between 1970 and 1980.[3] The welfare state has grown to a size, and at a rate, never imagined by its founders.[4]

For these reasons, the Scandinavian welfare states are the best places to turn to examine empirically the consequences for civil society of a greater reliance on the political approach to moral obligation. (Important differences distinguish the Scandinavian countries; these will be discussed as we go along. My point here is that, especially in comparison with the United States, there is a "Scandinavian" approach to moral obligation that overrides local differences.) The strength of the welfare state—indeed, the accomplishment that makes the welfare state the great success story of modern liberal democracy—is its recognition that the living conditions of people who are strangers to us are nonetheless our business. The problem is whether this success comes at the cost of weakening social and moral ties in civil society, especially in families and communities. If it is true that people are more likely to learn a sense of obligation to others through the social practices they develop in the intimate sphere of society, and in that way also learn of their personal responsibility to distant and hypothetical others, the welfare state can bring in its wake an unanticipated problem: when government assumes moral responsibility for others, people are less likely to do so themselves.

Public Families

A major task of the welfare state has always been to provide for people who could not provide for themselves. Since most people live in families, the aid they received from government—in the form of old-age pensions, welfare benefits, or medical care—created a connection between the family and the state that has existed for some time. In its early formulation the welfare state borrowed the language of the family; it was, according to the

Swedish leader Per Albin Hansson in the 1920s, a *folkhem,* or people's home. "In a good home," Hansson noted, "equality, consideration, cooperation, and helpfulness are the guiding rules."[5]

Considered in a material sense, the consequences of the welfare state for the family have been extremely positive. By removing families from the vagaries of the market, by protecting workers against arbitrary firings, by contributing to economic growth, by creating equality in society as a whole and thereby reducing stress, and by (in later years) making it easier for women to work in order to add to family income, the welfare state in Scandinavia raised a large number of families out of the realm of need and into the middle class.[6] Given the success of various programs of social support in Scandinavia, it is self-evident to argue that "the family supports the welfare state, and the welfare state needs the family."[7] Yet recent changes, both in the family and in the state, raise the question of whether these realms are not really distinct, with implications for how people balance their obligations in the intimate sphere with those in the distant.

In the early days of the welfare state, government programs primarily emphasized transfer payments: shifts in income from one part of the population to another. With respect to families, child allowances—cash payments paid to parents on the birth of each child—are the most representative type of transfer payment. Particulars vary from country to country, but Scandinavian child-support systems tend to be divided into ordinary payments on the one hand, available to all families until the child reaches the age of sixteen, and special supplements to single women or handicapped children on the other.[8] (The Swedish system also includes support for educational study, which can last until the age of twenty.) During the 1970s, child allowances in general decreased in all the Scandinavian countries. To some extent this was because of a falling birthrate, but it was also because of public policies that broke the principle of universalism—such as means testing in Denmark in 1977 and 1981 or the 1982 Norwegian decision to stop support in the month the child reaches sixteen rather than continuing the entire calendar year. (The latter decision was due in part to the fact that expenditures on child allowances in Norway, which had increased 300 percent at the end of the 1960s, began to increase again in 1979–80.)[9]

Yet if direct payments to families in the form of child allowances decreased, overall government expenditures for the family increased during this period. At their highest point, expenditures on family programs represented only 3 to 5 percent of the gross national product (GNP)— small in comparison to large-expenditure items such as social security, but

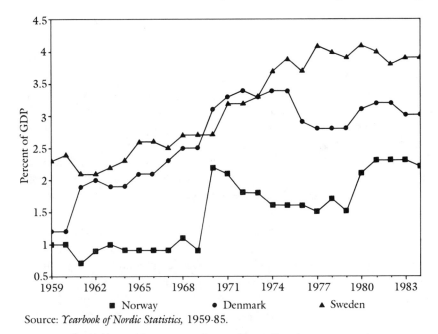

■ Norway   ● Denmark   ▲ Sweden

Source: *Yearbook of Nordic Statistics,* 1959-85.

Figure 5. Family Welfare Expenditures, Scandinavia, 1959–84 (as percentage of GDP)

still representing a substantial increase (in Sweden, a doubling) over a twenty-year period (see figure 5). Much of the explanation for why general family expenditures increased while child allowances decreased lies in a greater reliance on newer kinds of programs that changed the *character* of the relationship between the family and the welfare state. Instead of being based on the principle that the obligation of government was to transfer money from those who needed it less to those who needed it more, these programs emphasized the principle that government could build the institutions and carry out the services that the family itself had once provided.

Of course, government has always provided services for families, the most important of which is education. Unlike in the United States, where the market has become far more involved in the business of schooling, education remains an overwhelming public priority in Scandinavia. Sweden actively discourages private schools in any form; Norway, while it also relies extensively on public schools, does recognize some areas—such as religion or training in specific trades—where private schools are appropriate.[10] Of the three countries, Denmark is the only one that actually encourages private schools: 10 percent of school-age children attended private schools there in the late 1980s, up from 5.2 percent a decade before.[11] Yet even in Denmark the state plays a role, because the government pays up to 85 percent of costs of sending a child to private school.

What has changed in the past two decades with respect to schooling is not the public commitment to education itself, but rather an increasing reliance on government to provide after-school programs—in marked contrast to the United States with its latchkey children. An extensive range of institutions exists for watching children in the late afternoon, and demand for such programs is growing: a 1980 use study showed that approximately 16 percent of Swedish and Danish children relied on such after-school centers, and by 1984 that figure had risen to 30 percent.[12] Besides the wide range of activities offered by after-school programs, many organizations that once had a more private character, such as sports clubs, are now increasingly supported by public funds.[13] Youth in Scandinavia, in short, have a good deal of contact with the state, not only when they are in school but even after school is over. As a Norwegian writer puts it, youth has become more "organized" in this part of the world.[14]

A second indication of an increasing reliance on government in the family sphere in Scandinavia is the greater use of foster homes, institutions, and other methods for coping with problem children. A strong ideological component of the Scandinavian welfare state involves the idea that social problems can be passed on from parents to children and that government intervention is required to break the vicious cycle of inheritance.[15] When there is a problem in the child's immediate environment—such as alcohol or drug abuse, poverty, violence, or a mother unable to cope—it is expected that the state will play an interventionist role. In general, that role has grown. The number of children under preventive care in Norway increased from about 2,000 in 1965 to over 5,200 in 1984, while in Denmark between 1970 and 1980 the number of children placed in foster homes increased by 400 percent.[16] In 1974, 16,884 Swedish children were voluntarily placed in foster homes, and 9,960 involuntarily; by 1981, the proportions had shifted dramatically, as 12,378 children were involuntarily placed and 9,483 voluntarily.[17] Sweden, as a result, developed a world reputation as the home of a "child Gulag." In 1983, for example, the German magazine *Der Spiegel* ran a story on Sweden saying that "nowhere else has the state become so totalitarian as in this country."[18] A 1982 change in the law, however, helped bring the rate down;[19] now, on a per capita basis, Denmark has more children "outside the home"—both voluntarily and involuntarily—than Sweden.[20]

No one doubts that it is better for children in extremely problematic circumstances to be moved. The problem is who makes the decisions and how. In the Scandinavian countries, social workers and other therapeutic professionals have developed a preventive approach to these matters; for example, the expert testimony of psychologists is generally relied on to decide whether children should go to foster homes (or, in divorce cases, which parent should get custody) to an unusually high degree.[21] Often basing their decisions on statistical tendencies and the hypotheses generated from these tendencies, social-welfare professionals feel that by knowing which kinds of families are likely to have the most problems, authorities can step in before the trouble starts. Thus, according to three Swedish social workers, circumstances such as alcoholism can have "a destructive influence on the child *even when specific acts of abuse [do] not occur.*"[22] Scandinavian societies in this sense resemble what Jürgen Habermas has called a *therapeutocracy,* in which professional expertise comes increasingly to substitute for family autonomy.[23]

Far and away the biggest component of the increase in government's role in providing services once assigned to the family, however, is the decision to finance and build a nationwide system for the provision of public day care, especially in Denmark and Sweden. The figures compiled in table 5 indicate that in all three Scandinavian countries, the number of children in public day care has doubled, or in some cases tripled, from the mid-1970s to the mid-1980s. (The gap between Denmark and Sweden on the one hand and Denmark and Norway on the other is even greater than these figures indicate, since in Norway more older children are in public day care part time than full time.)[24] Yet in spite of these increases, public day care is far from universal, since only in Denmark, and then only for older children, does the utilization rate account for more than 50 percent of all children.

Various efforts to examine reliance on public day-care institutions indicate that demand for them exceeds supply and that if more were to be built, more would be used. Danes lead Scandinavia in this respect. In 1985, only 5 percent of Danish children under the age of six were being raised full time by their mothers at home, while 55 percent were in public day care, 21 percent were in private day care, and between 3 and 5 percent were being watched by working parents on shifts, mothers on pregnancy leave, unemployed members of the labor force, or parents who worked at home.[25] (The first figure is somewhat deceptive, since women can be in the labor market and still be home full time with their children, what with maternity leaves, shift work, and work at home.)[26] In Sweden, by comparison, a 1980

TABLE 5.   *Places in Day-Care Institutions, Scandinavia, 1975–84*

	0–2 Years		3–6 Years	
	Number of Places	Percentage of Total in Institutions	Number of Places	Percentage of Total in Institutions
Denmark				
1975	22,264	10	93,374	32
1978	22,963	12	105,553	36
1981	26,957	15	123,410	42
1984	28,466	18	122,219	51
Norway				
1975	4,296	2	26,183	10
1978	6,179	4	55,161	23
1981	8,605	6	74,328	35
1984	10,008	7	84,435	41
Sweden				
1976	18,998	6	46,964	12
1978	25,181	10	75,442	19
1981	37,074	13	102,721	26
1984	47,103	17	126,143	33

Source. Nordic Statistical Secretariat, *Social tryghed i de Nordiske lande* (Copenhagen: NSS, 1986), 89.

study showed that 43 percent of children up to six years of age remained at home with one parent, while 30 percent went to public institutions, 14 percent went to private day care, and the rest were provided for with other solutions; 19 percent of children who qualified for public day care could not obtain it.[27]

In the area of family welfare, especially with the commitment to public day care, we can see the emergence of what can be called a "new" welfare state, which, unlike the older one with its reliance on transfer payments, is much more directly involved in the regulation of moral obligations in civil society. Some sense of this shift in the character of the welfare state is provided by figure 6. In the mid-1960s, day-care facilities absorbed approximately 2 percent of all welfare state expenditures for families in Norway and Denmark, while child-care allowances constituted approximately half. By the 1980s, the balance had shifted considerably. Now (with Norway again the exception) day-care expenditures absorb close to half the family welfare expenditures, while the family allowance proportion has fallen to less than 20 percent. The new welfare state represents an important change in the relationship between government and the moral order as the state

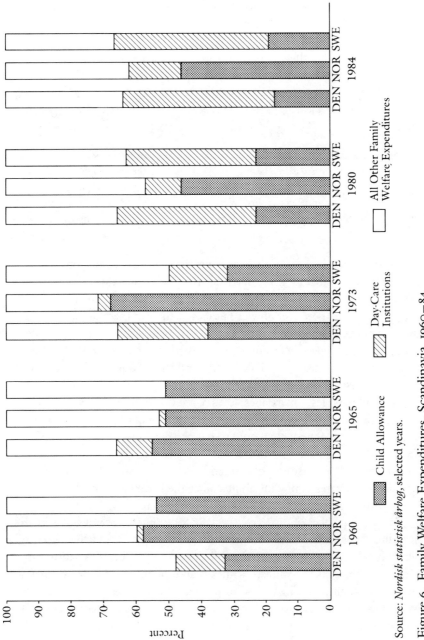

Source: *Nordisk statistisk årbog*, selected years.

Figure 6. Family Welfare Expenditures, Scandinavia, 1960–84

has come to play a far more direct role as a surrogate parent, making important and difficult decisions such as how children should be raised or which children ought no longer to live with their parents.

At the same time that changes in the welfare state have had a more direct effect on families, changes in the family have had a more direct effect on the welfare state. Statistically speaking, the Scandinavian countries have among the world's lowest rates of family stability, with Sweden as the extreme case.

Sweden is a society where the traditional family does not have a strong position. By international comparison, the marriage rate is low, the frequency of informal cohabitation high, and average household size small. The rate of family break-ups, the average age of mothers at first birth, the rate of children born outside of wedlock, the rate of single-parent families, and the rate of gainful employment are all high.[28]

All these trends have been increasing in Scandinavia. A study of the Danish family and how it changed between 1975 and 1985 indicated that young people, especially boys, were twice as likely to leave home at a young age; that there were fewer families with young children; and that the percentage of children born out of marriage increased (although more children had two people raising them).[29] As this last point indicates, high divorce rates (the divorce rate doubled in all three countries between the 1960s and 1980)[30] do not necessarily mean more single parents: the percentage of "paperless" marriages, as they are called here, doubled in Norway between 1977 and 1984; in Denmark, 23 percent of cohabiting couples in 1986 were unmarried, compared to 9.6 percent in 1974; and in Sweden, 46 percent of the children born in 1984 were to parents who were not legally married.[31] Yet because cohabitation is so extensive, the divorce rate actually understates family instability, since the breakup of many relatively long-term relationships is not included in the figure.

The consequences of divorce, especially for women, are not as severe in Scandinavia as in the United States. A Danish study found that women were often better off in new partnerships than in their former relationship. Moreover, their social contacts with kin and neighbors did not decrease after divorce, although in around 10 percent of cases there were problems with loneliness and isolation.[32] Still, divorce does weaken relations in civil society: people who were once intimate, of course, have less contact with each other, and when they do, they experience difficult emotional problems; serious consequences for health and longevity are associated with divorce; and the children of divorced parents find themselves in awkward, and often lonely, situations.[33] While such trends are similar, if somewhat more extreme, to trends throughout the West and in that sense cannot be attributed to the growth of the welfare state per se, it also seems clear that the welfare state makes divorce somewhat easier to obtain and weather (by providing day care for the children, for example) and then seems the most appropriate mechanism for resolving the problems created by divorce (such as providing extra funds for newly divorced women).

As the state grows and families weaken, it becomes more difficult to remain hopeful that state intervention will not significantly alter the character of the institutions in civil society. Certainly the "traditional" family, in which the wife stays home and raises the children while the husband works (a tradition that is, in fact, the historical exception), has been changed significantly by the welfare state. The results from studies of low-income maintenance experiments in Seattle and Denver—where greater financial help to women increased the rate of family breakup—are applicable to women at all income levels in Scandinavia.[34] The important question is not whether the nuclear family has declined, but what is in the process of replacing it.

In Scandinavia something is emerging that can be called a public family, in contrast to the emergence of a private family in the United States. A dramatic increase in the percentage of women entering the labor force has occurred in Scandinavia, as elsewhere; in Norway, whereas in 1965 14 percent of women with small children were in the work force (full and part time), by 1986 that figure stood at 69 percent.[35] The great bulk of this new work involves civil service jobs that carry out the functions once performed by private families. In Norway, 66 percent of social workers, 93 percent of nurses, and 98 percent of home helpers are women.[36] Of the growth in the labor force that took place in Denmark between 1960 and 1981 owing to the entrance of women, 25 percent was in day-care institutions and old-age homes, 12 percent in hospitals, and 27 percent in schools.[37]

Socializing the young and caring for the sick, viewed traditionally as women's work, are still women's work, but now they are carried out for a government wage rather than within a family setting. Within a twenty-five-year period, women have jumped from the family sector over the market sector to a direct, and often difficult, relationship with the state sector—as dramatic, if not more dramatic, a development as the transformation of men from peasants to workers two hundred years ago.[38] It is in this sense that we can speak of the public family in Scandinavia. The distribution of sex roles has not greatly changed in Scandinavia (gender-defined work has probably been more thoroughly transformed in the United States), but their character has changed greatly: they have become "nationalized," in the sense that the Scandinavian welfare states organize through taxation and public services activities for all of society that were once undertaken more intimately and privately.

Many positive things can be said about the public family, especially that it has incorporated into T. H. Marshall's concept of social citizenship the rights of wives and mothers.[39] But because the family symbolizes to such a great extent the moral relations of civil society, its character is inevitably too intimate and emotional to be well regulated by government. The notion of a "people's home"—with which the welfare state began and to which a great deal of attention is once again being paid—seems increasingly problematic.[40] A people's home suggests that the caring which characterizes the intimate sector ought also to characterize the public sector; as Hansson put it in 1928, the rules of the home, when extended to society as a whole, "will mean the dispersal of the social barriers that now divide the citizens."[41] But the term raises as well the opposite possibility: if commitments in the home weaken, so will commitments to the people (I will explore this subject in Chapter 6). Home, in short, is where "the people" ought not to be, at least not on a permanent basis; it is rather the place where specific people seek to strengthen their moral ties to other specific people. This is not to say that the penetration of the welfare state into civil society is a mistake; there are many cases when state intervention in the home is justified. But it is to say that the moral issues involved in the new welfare state are more serious than at first was realized. The Scandinavian welfare states, which express so well a sense of obligation to distant strangers, are beginning to make it more difficult to express a sense of obligation to those with whom one shares family ties. The irony of this development may be that as intimate ties weaken, so will distant ones, thus undermining the very moral strengths the welfare state has shown.

Social Networks and the Welfare State

Johan Borgen, a Norwegian novelist, wrote of his childhood: "Good people lived in our street, people who knew one another and greeted one another—in a way it was each person's security in a society that was already facing hidden threats from outside."[42] In Scandinavia, the experience of farm life, village sociability, and regular church attendance is only a generation removed; older residents of the dense housing complexes in

Oslo and Stockholm were born into an entirely different world. Few wish to return to that world (although Borgen, when he read his memoir on Norwegian radio, did attract a huge audience). The point is, rather, that social changes which may have taken a century to take hold in other places occurred within one lifetime here.

Of modernity's trinity—urbanization, industrialization, and bureaucratization—the first two came late to Scandinavia. Sweden, the most industrially advanced of the three Scandinavian countries, was still primarily agrarian as late as 1900, and even its early industry was decentralized throughout the country in milltowns. Forty years later, as Gösta Esping-Andersen puts it, "Sweden had become the epitome of the Marxist polarized class society."[43] Although the changes that have taken place in Denmark and Norway are not as dramatic as in Sweden, there they are even more recent. "Between 1960 and 1980," Natalie Rogoff Ramsøy notes, "two-thirds of all the smallholdings in Norway (that is, farms with no more than 12.5 acres under cultivation) went out of production"; moreover, from 1930 to 1980 the number of self-employed persons decreased 45 percent, while the number of people employed for a wage increased 122 percent.[44] In Denmark it was not until 1958 that as many people were employed in industry as in farming, and by 1970 agricultural employment had decreased until it accounted for only 10.8 percent of all jobs; twice as many people worked in the professions as on farms.[45]

The "great transformation" was not only more rapid and more recent in Scandinavia than in Great Britain or the United States, but it was also, and to a much greater degree, led by the state rather than the market. Fundamental moral questions, such as where and how people ought to live, were answered by relying on government. From 1931 to 1960, the urban population of Sweden increased from 38 percent of the total to 73 percent, in part because of public policies designed to reshape the map of Sweden.[46] The question of where to house these new urban residents faced Social Democratic governments, which developed what they called the *miljonprogamm:* a plan to build one and a half million new apartments between 1960 and 1975.[47] Such plans succeeded: by 1980, well over half the housing in Sweden had been built in the previous thirty years.[48] (Only war-devastated West Germany built more housing in this period.) In Norway, as Rogoff Ramsøy has pointed out, housing and similar social services were also developed by administrative logic:

The trend toward practicing economies of scale extended far beyond the limits of the productive economy. . . . The same principle was applied to local administration and to the transformation of the primary school system. A considerable amount of Norway's postwar urban housing was built in the form of large projects following principles of industrial organization.[49]

(Denmark, by contrast, encourages more private housing than, especially, Sweden, and its cities are characterized more by suburban patterns familiar to Americans than by large-scale apartment complexes.)[50]

The situation in Scandinavia is both similar to and different from that in the United States. In America, as I argued in Chapter 2, a strong reliance on voluntary associations, traditions of local autonomy, kinship networks, tax subsidies, and other practices delayed the entry of marketplace principles into real-estate transactions for a surprisingly long time. In Scandinavia, changes in the moral dynamics of local communities are just as recent. Some sense of how dramatic these changes in the character of civil society have been can be gained from table 6, showing information based on a sample of five thousand Danes interviewed in both 1976 and 1986. The intimate world of a Dane born in 1910 is radically different from that of one born in 1950: the former was likely to have been raised in a rural area with a tight-knit and large family, presumably (although we have no direct data on this) in frequent contact with other similar families in the same locality, whereas the latter was likely raised in a smaller, more unstable family in a more urban area. The difference with the United States, of course, is that in Scandinavia it is not the relatively late arrival of the market that has changed the character of civil society, but the relatively late arrival of government.

The major question posed by changes of this magnitude is whether they cause a weakening of social ties and informal networks similar to that caused by the growth of the market as a moral code in the United States. Bent Rold Andersen argues that they have:

Weakened social networks, a phenomenon widespread in the Western world, cause fewer conflicts in the welfare state, where the public sector readily takes over. Like a vicious circle, this itself tends to speed up the dissolution of networks and thereby extends the public sector ever more. This flexibility, this ease of response, has become a threat to the welfare state itself.[51]

Andersen's view has been strongly challenged, especially by Stein Ringen and Gösta Rehn, both of whom argue that the welfare state has in fact strengthened informal networks and social ties.[52] All three, however, may be correct.

Ringen and Rehn rely on a series of studies undertaken by the Institute for Social Research of the University of Stockholm. Surveys of the Swed-

TABLE 6. *Relations in Civil Society, Denmark, 1906–86 (in percents)*

Date of Birth	Father Farmer or Farm Worker	Working Mother Outside Home	Five or More Siblings	Parents Divorced/ Separated
1906–10	42	8	45	2
1911–20	39	9	40	2
1921–30	34	15	34	5
1931–40	34	18	23	7
1941–50	23	23	14	6
1951–60	16	26	11	13

Source. Figures assembled from Erik Jørgen Hansen, *Danskernes levevilkår* (Copenhagen: Hans Reitzels, 1986), 68; and Erik Jørgen Hansen, *Generationer og livsforløb i Danmark* (Copenhagen: Hans Reitzels, 1988), 51.

ish population in three separate years—1968, 1974, and 1981—were conducted to discover, among other things, the amount of contact people had with friends and relatives. These data show, almost without exception, increases in the number of social contacts over this thirteen-year period. For example, the number of people who visited relatives regularly increased from 28.1 to 31.0 percent of the total sample, and the number that visited friends increased from 29.8 to 39.9 percent. Measuring the same phenomenon in the reverse way, the Swedish studies showed that isolation has decreased: the number of people who had very few contacts with relatives dropped from 15.8 to 11.9 percent of the total, while the figures involving friends decreased from 9.8 to 5.8 percent.[53] Material published after Ringen's book appeared confirms his point. Although the number of Swedes living alone has grown, social contacts showed little significant difference between 1981 and 1986, and in some cases even increased.[54] The appropriate conclusion to be drawn from this material is that, especially in comparison to societies that rely on the market, there is no reason why reliance on the state has to be accompanied by isolation and alienation for the majority of citizens.

Yet the number of contacts people have says little about what they expect from one another. That question is better answered through community studies, which explore the nature of the social contacts between people at the local level. One such study, based on the social-network analysis techniques developed by North American sociologists such as Claude

Fischer and Barry Wellman, had results in Sweden quite similar to those discovered in the United States. Working-class people had fewer ties to others than middle-class people, but the ties they did have were much stronger and involved relying on others for help. Among middle-class civil servants, by contrast, ties between individuals were more geographically spread out and specialized, characteristic of "weak ties" that, according to Mark Granovetter, have their own kind of strength.[55] A similar study, conducted in a medium-sized Danish city in Jutland and a Copenhagen suburb, revealed that while large numbers of people would ask others for help in the form of advice or to "give a hand" with moving, very few were willing to ask people from their networks for more ongoing assistance, such as picking up or watching children, shopping, or cooking. Moreover, significant numbers of people had no real desire for greater help from their social contacts.[56]

One possible conclusion to be drawn from all this research is that the social trends associated with the welfare state both strengthen and weaken community ties simultaneously. (Whether the welfare state actually causes these trends is beyond the ability of this observer, and most likely any observer, to determine.) By contributing to social prosperity, these trends, as Ringen and Rehn emphasize, increase leisure time and expand the social horizons of the beneficiaries. At the same time, by raising working-class families into the middle class, they contribute to the geographic and social mobility that undermines solidaristic neighborhood patterns; help to create networks of civil servants that can provide necessary services more efficiently, but also more impersonally, than friends; and cause new housing to be built, the very practicality of which improves the material conditions of many families but also contributes to a certain anonymity. Ties between neighbors and friends, in short, expand and contract at one and the same time.

The trends associated with the welfare state do not abolish community, but, as with the family, they do alter its character. Obviously the family still exists: people still get married, have children, and experience daily life through their families. In turning some of the functions of the family over to government, Scandinavian societies have strengthened some of its aspects, especially its level of economic support, but weakened others, especially its ability to serve as a source of moral rules. In a similar way, the rapid urban development and extensive social programs of the welfare state do not eliminate the frequency of contacts with others; informal networks, for example, can still be relied on to solve some of the social problems handled by the welfare state.[57] In general, however, such contacts express a sense more of sociability than of moral obligation.

That moral ties in civil society may have weakened in Scandinavia, even while social ties have been strengthened, is indicated by rates of crime, alcohol consumption, and, to a lesser degree, suicide, all of which tend to garner a good deal of attention when these societies are discussed. One should interpret these statistics with some care. Sweden, for example, does not have—as most people believe it to—the world's highest suicide rate: that honor belongs to Hungary. Nor is a dramatic increase in alcoholism all that uncommon: every Western society has experienced an increase since World War II, and in Sweden the rise in alcohol consumption follows almost exactly the rise in disposable income. Yet one cannot ignore such trends, for ever since Durkheim, the notion that the strength of civil society can be measured indirectly through behavior patterns indicating weak social networks has become something of a commonplace.

What should concern us most is not the number of suicides in Scandinavia relative to other countries—a difference that might be explained by, for example, the weather—but instead the increase in suicides in this part of the world when the weather is held drearily constant. (Actually, in all the Scandinavian countries suicides are less frequent in December and February and more frequent in May and August.)[58] Such an increase— ironically, given its reputation—is not true of Sweden, where the suicide rate declined from 22.3 per 100,000 people in 1970 to 18.2 in 1985.[59] The other two countries, however, experienced a significant increase. In Norway the suicide rate, though it remained at roughly the same level from 1951 to 1970, began to increase substantially after 1970.[60] A similar pattern holds for Denmark, where the total number of suicides increased from 931 in 1960 to 1,484 in 1983 before leveling off in the past few years.[61] If Durkheim was correct that suicide is symptomatic of declining social solidarity, then the increase that has taken place over the past twenty years is at least partial cause for believing that the moral ties of civil society are less strong than they once were.

A similarly dramatic rise can be detected in yet another indirect measure of the strength of civil society: the rate of consumption of dangerous substances. As with suicide, Scandinavians are known as hard drinkers, but again, what is of importance is the increase that can be measured over time. All three Scandinavian countries have relatively similar patterns. In general, the consumption of hard liquor has decreased, in part because of stricter regulation, whereas the consumption of wine and beer increased sixfold between the 1950s and the 1980s.[62] These trends have been accompanied, again as elsewhere in the West, with increases in tobacco consumption and narcotics use.[63] There is, of course, much debate about what this increase in alcohol consumption means, since even with recent increases it is at about the same level it was in the nineteenth century. Yet the visible rise in the number of derelicts on the streets of Stockholm, Oslo, and Copenhagen says something about the weakness of ties in civil society, even if exactly what it says is open to dispute.

Finally, a sharp rise in crime has taken place in all three Scandinavian countries over the past twenty years. In 1970, 47 murders were reported in Denmark, 6 in Norway, and 218 in Sweden; ten years later the numbers were 236, 31, and 394, respectively. Assaults also increased, if not at quite the same rate.[64] But perhaps the most illustrative statistics in this context are those for breaking and entering, for it is relatively petty crimes of this sort that most break down the kinds of trust and mutual help networks of civil society. As figure 7 indicates, these rates have nearly quadrupled in Denmark and Sweden. Behind such figures lies a change in the nature of the civil society: less trust, greater fear of involvement, and a dramatic increase in the use of bicycle locks.

What is perhaps most important to emphasize about all these figures is not that each, by itself, represents a weakening of the social fabric; in comparative terms, Scandinavia is certainly not characterized by normlessness. (Indeed, the opposite charge—excessive conformity—is the one most often leveled against these countries.) Rather, each category is related to the others, suggesting that all together they measure the extent to which a group exists, whose size is difficult to determine, that is not part of the welfare state's success story. People who commit suicide, for example, are far more likely than people in the general population to suffer from problems of alcoholism; and excessive use of alcohol in turn contributes to violence against others.[65] They are also likely to be, in classic Durkheimian fashion, unmarried, residents of large cities, and without siblings or friends, as one Norwegian study concluded.[66] (Similarly, Danes who attempted suicide were three times more likely to live alone than members of the general population, and those who succeeded were four times more likely to.)[67] These interrelationships suggest that while social contacts and networks are still healthy among those who benefit from the welfare state, they are weaker than ever among those who, for whatever reason, are alienated from its way of functioning.[68]

Such a conclusion is reinforced by an examination of the relationship

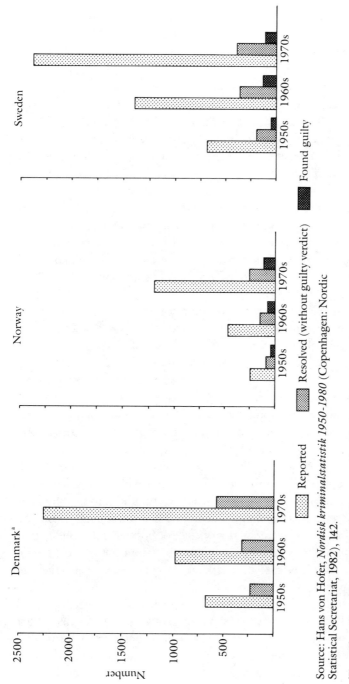

Source: Hans von Hofer, *Nordisk kriminalstatistik 1950-1980* (Copenhagen: Nordic Statistical Secretariat, 1982), 142.

[a]Figures for guilty verdicts and resolved verdicts are combined for Denmark.

Figure 7. Breaking and Entering, Scandinavia, 1950–80 (from reporting to sanctioning, per 100,000 population 15–67 years of age)

between income level and social isolation under the welfare state. Social research in Scandinavia has long emphasized a concern with reducing the effects of inequality. Consequently, the populations of these societies are routinely divided into various "social groups" measuring such characteristics as income, political resources, and other indicators of unequal social status. In a recent Danish study of the quality of life, all five social groups reported less isolation over time; the number of people who felt that there was no one they could talk to or that they were too often alone even though they did not want to be decreased between 1976 and 1986, thereby confirming the point that the welfare state does not lead to isolation and weak networks. But the most interesting fact that has emerged from this breakdown of social contacts by social class was not that working-class people have fewer contacts than middle-class people, although they do; it was that the only group in the entire population whose degree of loneliness and social alienation has increased, and often at significant rates, was that which could not be categorized as a distinct social group at all.[69]

There is, in conclusion, one way in which higher suicide or alcohol consumption rates, if interpreted with caution, seem to indicate a weakening of moral obligations in civil society in Scandinavia. Strong moral ties in civil society can help to soften the fall of those unable to function in a modern political and economic system. When these ties weaken, they add to the isolation and marginalization of those already isolated and marginalized. The welfare state, because it relies on government to strengthen the social bond, places a premium on the mobilization of political resources. For that reason, its primary moral commitment is to those who share a political definition as citizens, not those who share a social definition as generalized brothers or sisters. Scandinavian societies have broadened the concept of citizenship to an unusually wide, but still not all-inclusive, degree. Hence, for all those who are brought in to the functions of the welfare state, there will always be some who are left out. Reliance on government instead of the moral ties of civil society to express obligations between people improves the social conditions of most but worsens the lot of those who, already worse off, lack the resources to operate effectively in a system organized around political rules.

When we try to answer the question of whether community and social ties have weakened as the welfare state has grown, we find evidence that can support almost any response. A reasonable conclusion might be that both the social trends associated with the welfare state and, to an undeterminable degree, the welfare state itself have altered the character of everyday life, moving it from informal reliance on what Gösta Esping-Andersen and Walter Korpi call "kinship and community altruism" toward what they call "the strength of entitlements to welfare based on social citizenship." As a consequence, we can agree with them that in this part of the world "the principles of the welfare state are pushed further into civil society than is internationally common."[70]

The notion of social citizenship embodies all the strengths and weaknesses of a political approach to moral regulation. Citizens, even social citizens, have rights. People who live in civil society have obligations. The replacement of one language by the other implies a movement from society to politics, from a recognition that we owe things to one another because we share certain understandings to a recognition that we can expect things from others because we vote and belong to an organized political community. This is not a problem if one believes, as Helga Hernes does, that "although the institutional balance between state and society in Scandinavian social democracies has quite clearly gone in favor of the state, there is . . . an awareness of the dangers of alienation that has resulted in important participatory reforms at all levels, involving individuals in their functionally limited corporate roles."[71] But if one shares a Weberian distrust of government, even of benevolent and participatory ones, a political approach to moral regulation, by thinning out the moral texture of civil society, does seem to contribute to a sense that moral obligations can be satisfied without the active participation of individuals as moral agents.

From Welfare *State to Welfare* State

Created by working-class men at a time of economic insecurity, the welfare state brought into being a new kind of society, characterized by a commitment to full employment, the provision by government of services deemed essential to the realization of a better life (such as medicine and education), and a system of transfer payments designed to promote the general goal of rough equality between social classes. So impressive has been the overall performance of the Scandinavian welfare states that we tend to forget how recently they were constructed. As Esping-Andersen and Korpi point out, the "Scandinavian model" is almost entirely a post–World War II phenomenon.[72]

Just as the Scandinavian welfare state itself is a recent phenomenon, even more recent is the emergence of a "new" welfare state emphasizing the construction of institutions designed to carry out tasks once assigned to civil society. (The commitment to the building of public day-care centers, for example, stems only from 1970.) If the old welfare state, in the course of the 1980s, has stopped growing and is instead entering a period of consolidation, the new welfare state is growing more rapidly than ever.[73] If it continues to grow at the pace it has, we can expect that by the year 2000 Scandinavia will again have created a new social experiment. Unlike the earlier version, this welfare state will be one in which both men and women work while their children are cared for in public institutions. (It may also be the case, as a Norwegian projection points out, that women will come to dominate the public sector as men flee to the private sector.)[74] At the same time, the industrial working class will continue to shrink and the middle class will not only grow but also, to a greater degree than ever before, avail itself of the benefits of the welfare state. Finally, public policy will not only protect against economic insecurity but also try to secure the good life for as many as possible. These societies, in short, will continue to be caring ones, but the caring will increasingly be carried out by therapeutic professionals in institutions and less by immediate kin, neighbors, and social networks. Moral obligation will, in that sense, be more public than ever before: government, to an unprecedented degree, will be involved in the structuring both of obligations to distant others and of obligations to intimates.

What is taking place in Scandinavia, in short, is the replacement of the *welfare* state by the welfare *state*. Instead of familial and community relations creating a sense of responsibility for the welfare of others, which the state enforces as a matter of last resort, the state is becoming the primary moral agent in society, seeking to express, as best as it can, a sense of responsibility for the welfare of those who no longer have much power in civil society. The emergence of the new welfare state has helped to create an atmosphere of uncertainty about future directions. That uncertainty can be understood neither politically, for the welfare state is still very popular,[75] nor economically, for it has not faced, at least to this point, an unsolvable economic crisis.[76] It is, rather, moral in nature. In everyday life it takes the form of tax avoidance, distrust of authority, and, in the words of former Danish social minister Bent Rold Andersen, a feeling that "the Nordic governments, in their steady expansion of the public sector, have overrated the willingness of individual citizens to contribute their share to the communal pot."[77] Among academics and social scientists, it usually takes a conservative form, with the argument that the welfare state has become "heartless" and tends to weaken families and private charity.[78] (Leftist intellectuals, who in the 1960s were critical of the welfare state, now tend to defend it and to call for its extension; feminist thinkers, similarly, while often ambivalent, generally find the programs of the welfare state to their liking.)[79] At no time since World War II has concern over the moral consequences of state intervention been as strong in Scandinavia as during the past few years.

There are, in particular, two essentially moral issues that the new welfare state has been unable to address satisfactorily. The first involves the dilemmas of the public family. Early notions of the welfare state were premised on the idea that men would work and women would stay home, thereby making unnecessary (to be more correct, unthinkable) the idea of government substituting for one critical ingredient of civil society—the family. As one Danish historian has put it, "While the working class movement strongly stressed a struggle over the old society's patriarchy and patriarchal relations in production and the public society, it was completely silent about patriarchal relations in the workers' own families."[80] Now that the rates at which women work for a wage are higher in Scandinavia than in most other countries, reliance on government to carry out tasks of social reproduction fills the gap between the society that existed a generation ago and the one that exists now.

As many feminists have correctly argued, the bulk of welfare work has traditionally been invisible and unpaid, performed by women within the family.[81] The entry of women into the labor market on the one hand and the growth of a new welfare state on the other make the invisible a public policy and the unpaid a civil service career. This represents progress: women are freer, workers are less easily exploited, contributions are recognized, and the problems of destructive families are corrected. Yet when the state is responsible for social reproduction, the family cannot be as responsible, despite the best efforts of many families. One can therefore admire the frankness of someone who argues that in the face of all these problems, our best hope is to accept the reality of Goffmanesque "total" institutions for carrying out these tasks and to try to make them as humane as possible.[82]

That we may have to turn our moral responsibilities over to institutions, no matter how reformable they may prove to be, acknowledges, however, why the new welfare state, for all its benefits, treads on slippery moral ground. Day care provides an illustrative example. Surely any two-income couple is grateful to be able to deliver their small children to a day-care center before going to work. And most people recognize that, despite cutbacks and staffing problems, day-care centers try to be caring places.[83]

Yet when small children spend the greatest number of their waking hours being watched by public employees—who have their own children, their own rights, and their own wage to consider—moral dilemmas easily arise. What is in the best interests of parents, especially two working parents, is not always in the best interests of children (see Chapter 6 for more on this theme). While parents generally like the system of public day care, they would prefer different kinds of work arrangements that would allow them more time with their children—and reduce their feelings of guilt.[84]

It is, in short, possible to have two full-time-employed partners, state-financed day-care institutions, and well-functioning families, but not all three at once. Yet most people want, and feel entitled to, all three. One response to such a dilemma is not to choose among the three goals, but to juggle. Each of the Scandinavian societies juggles in a different way: in Norway, public day care is relied on far less than in the other two countries, and friends, neighbors, and grandparents are relied on more; Sweden has a very large amount (second only to Norway among the industrialized countries) of part-time work for women, which, in combination with paid maternity leaves, substantially reduces the number of small infants in public day care; and Danes, who tend to be more libertarian than Norwegians and Swedes, solve the problem by somehow finding a way to pick up their children by 3:30 P.M.[85] Yet such juggling does not resolve the moral guilt that people, especially women, feel. No matter how publicly articulated the ideal is that raising children is a social responsibility which can be carried out by the state, many women still feel that the responsibility is their own. The result has been described by Natalie Rogoff Ramsøy:

Women today suffer from a role squeeze—an incompatibility between their family and other obligations. Recent surveys document the problems that result. Married women with young children have far less time at their disposal than any other group in the population, and they also exceed all others in psychosomatic symptoms—sleeplessness, nervousness, depression, use of tranquilizers, etc.[86]

As a substitute for the family, it would seem, government is a second-best solution. Given other goals—the most important of which is greater sexual equality in the workplace—state intervention in civil society becomes a necessary, but not completely satisfactory, response.

A similar set of moral problems follows from a second difficult dilemma: the degree to which the new welfare state, instead of transferring funds from the rich to the poor, becomes a subsidy for the middle class. The original goal of the welfare state was to alter the rules of distributive justice in society by reducing the barriers between social classes. As Esping-Andersen and Korpi have argued, a political strategy designed to represent only the interests of the working class could never hope to succeed. In order to appeal to middle-class voters, Social Democratic parties developed notions of universality in the distribution of benefits. Benefits were no longer a matter of charity but a right, comparable to the property rights historically enjoyed by the rich.[87] The popularity of Social Democratic governments in the 1960s and early 1970s was due to the political success of universal programs financed by seemingly endless economic growth.

The very success of the welfare state in raising more people into the middle class has, however, changed its moral equilibrium. Unlike the egalitarian thrust associated with the first welfare state, which used the powers of government to level income differences between classes, the new welfare state increasingly begins to provide disproportionate benefits to the middle class. (This is true not just of Scandinavia, but of other societies as well.)[88] To some degree, this change in the distributional effects of welfare programs is directly attributable to the fact that the new welfare state, unlike the old, builds institutions to carry out tasks of moral obligation once associated with civil society. For one thing, a large number of people elevated to the middle class are themselves public employees working in the labor-intensive area of service delivery. As they begin to exceed the number of people employed in the private sector, they develop a double claim on the welfare state as both providers and users: "In Scandinavia, the producers and clients of the welfare state together make up between 40 and 50 per cent of the electorate."[89]

In addition, the political dynamics of service delivery are quite different from those of transfer payments. It is, administratively speaking, relatively easy to universalize a cash payment, since all it involves is sending out a check in the mail to everyone. When government provides a service, by contrast, those who are most likely to benefit are those organized to take advantage of it. In the field of day care, where the ideal of universal access would come close to bankrupting society, selectivity had to be introduced, and the selectivity, not unexpectedly, shows a class bias: working-class women are more likely to stay home with their children or, when they work, to rely on relatives or hire other mothers (often paid for, and regulated, by the state).[90] Furthermore, when cutbacks become necessary, it is more difficult to cut back institutions with highly articulate middle-class clients and constituencies. The idea of universality, which made perfect sense when the primary task of the welfare state was to redistribute income, becomes an impossible goal (and can only contribute to cynicism toward the welfare state's objectives) when society is better off.

As opposed to transfer payments, which represent a "vertical" redistributive effect from the rich to the poor, institutions such as day-care services tend to benefit the middle class and therefore represent a "horizontal" shift from one part of the middle class to another. This may help to explain why no legitimacy crisis faces the welfare state. It may also help to explain why the tax revolt against the welfare state has fizzled (the welfare backlash parties in Norway and Denmark, after a period of decline, are now as strong as ever, but their focus is as much on immigration as on taxation), since it was only a matter of time before the middle class discovered that, for all the tax burden imposed by the welfare state, the advantages in policy were considerable. Hence, white-collar workers in Norway have begun to polarize in their attitudes toward the welfare state, with those who work in the private sector more against it and those in the public sector more for it.[91] In Denmark, the number of lower-paid civil servants who supported the parties to the left of the Social Democrats nearly doubled, between 1971 and 1984, going from 14 to 26 percent of the vote.[92] Even in Sweden, where working-class solidarity for the welfare state is strongest, other income groups clearly recognize an interest in government provisions.[93]

The middle-class bias that follows when the welfare state intervenes in activities once carried out by civil society undermines the logic of solidarity that made the welfare state such a powerful idea in the first place. Esping-Andersen in particular has emphasized that the moral power of the welfare state comes from the "decommodification" logic it introduces by universalizing benefits.[94] Yet if reliance on institutions, as opposed to transfer payments, is inevitably selective, the result is to *re*commodify what government has to offer. The new welfare state increasingly enables middle-class people to buy the labor of others who will perform their moral obligations for them. That is not only a far cry from what the welfare state was originally designed to do, but it also raises the uncomfortable question of whether subsidizing middle-class life-styles can generate the same kind of consensus and moral solidarity once associated with creating greater social equality.

The Scandinavian welfare states have for over half a century been premised on the assumption that the state could act as the moral conscience of society. It is remarkable how long that assumption has been maintained, and certainly many people think it can continue to be so maintained indefinitely. Yet it is also the case that in Scandinavia society has acted as the moral conscience of the state. Ties of political consensus, strong moral traditions associated with Lutheranism, solidaristic ideologies growing out of social and political movements, and common moral lessons taught by the family have long worked to insure that state intervention would occur within generally accepted boundaries. In particular, government intervention took place primarily within the economic sector of society, and its major forms—even in Sweden, where reliance on the state was strongest—were indirect. (Sweden did not consider nationalizing private companies until the 1970s, and it remains reluctant to regulate private industry; indeed, in many ways direct government regulation of industry is more directly enforced in the United States than in Sweden.)[95]

Unlike the situation in the United States, where the entry of the market into civil society was heralded by Chicago school theorists before it happened in practice, in Scandinavia the boundary between the state and civil society was increasingly crossed in practice without anyone thinking about it in theory. As the Scandinavian welfare states approach the year 2000, the precarious balance between state and society that made the older welfare state work so well is becoming harder to maintain. Families and communities, instead of contributing to the articulation of moral understandings that soften political regulation, are themselves increasingly organized according to political rules. Notions of solidarity and a consensus around the principle of equality, which made sense when governmental intervention was indirect, are turning into a defense of the interests of those classes who benefit primarily from the new services the welfare state offers, as interest groups become passionate about defending the programs that benefit them but less concerned about the programs that benefit others. Nearly everyone laments the increase in antisocial behavior associated not only with criminality, but also with everyday rule-breaking and moral shortcut-taking. The international outlook and humanitarian instincts long associated with Scandinavia are put under strain as a result of increased immigration. Surely not all these changes can be attributed to a greater reliance on politics as a way of organizing moral rules, but at the same time, such a reliance does make it more difficult for the Scandinavian societies to protect traditions of consensus and solidarity—for which state intervention can be a helpful, but never complete, substitute.

The concept of welfare, Erik Allardt has written, contains three elements: *having,* defined as the realization of both physical needs such as good health and long life and material needs such as sufficient income;

being, defined as individual identity and the possession of enough political resources to realize this identity; and *loving,* defined as "needs of solidarity, companionship, or, above all, participation in a network of social relations, in which people think about and pay attention to one another."[96] The question posed by the new welfare state is whether a weakening of loving will affect having and being. One way to find out is to examine the implications of greater state intervention in the intimate sphere of society on the same measures of moral obligation to distant strangers used earlier with respect to the market: intergenerational transfers, ties to others expressed through altruism and charity, and the webs of social existence defined by common possession of cultural symbols. If there is a moral problem with the new welfare state, it will show up precisely where the older one was strongest: in the sense of solidarity people feel toward those they do not know and probably never will.

SIX

States and Distant Obligations

The Social Democratic Generation: Before and After

One of the most important questions we can ask about the Scandinavian welfare states, in both their earlier and their more recent forms, is how they sustain a sense of obligation across generations. This question is particularly appropriate in Scandinavia, because there the social-democratic movement that created the modern welfare state is itself a generational phenomenon:[1] shaped by the experience of the Great Depression, social-democratic voters possess distinctive attitudes emphasizing equality and economic security.[2]

There is certainly good reason for this generation to be proud of its accomplishments. The welfare state has created what Swedish demographers call a "golden generation": an entire cohort of people whose conditions of material life have improved as a result of government programs.[3] Those who were born between 1920 and 1930 are today unusually well off. Their children have left home, their pay is high thanks to seniority rules, and they can expect generous pensions when they retire. The combination of all these factors gives them enough disposable income to come about as close to the good life as is possible in any Western liberal democracy. Yet what is true of the golden generation is not necessarily true of all generations in Scandinavia. The problems that follow from reliance on the state as a moral code are more likely to appear among people who are both younger and older than the golden generation itself.

Political approaches to moral obligation tend to be as oriented to the needs of the present generation as economic approaches, if for different reasons. Whereas the market discourages sacrifice for future generations in exchange for maximal satisfaction now, the state organizes moral obligation by mobilizing political resources, a practice that tends to slight the needs of those, especially the very young, who have fewer resources at their disposal. In that sense, reliance on the state as a guide to intergenerational obligations produces results in Scandinavia not dissimilar to those produced in the United States by reliance on the market. The economic security and material achievements of the welfare state have created a positive legacy for future generations, but at the same time they have, to some degree, contributed as well to a weakened moral commitment to those generations.

The situation facing young people in Scandinavia parallels in significant ways the situation facing young people in the United States. Declining fertility rates (what Alva Myrdal has graphically called a "birth strike"), pessimism about the future, youth unemployment, increased rates of crime and drug addiction among the young, and a sense that the "youth revolt" which began in the 1960s has turned sour are all common themes in discussions about Scandinavian youth.[4] Despite the success of the welfare state, consequently, specialists on youth problems speak in terms quite familiar to their American colleagues. Ivar Frønes, for example, views attitudes toward children as representing direct consumption rather than investments in the future, while Inger Koch-Nielsen, in a study of future prospects for children in Scandinavia, talks about "a ticking bomb in the development of society."[5] The feeling has been best expressed by Frønes: after World War II, he said, it was "youth [that] would build the country. Now youth has become synonymous with problems."[6]

The very young in Scandinavia today are being raised completely unlike any previous generation. "Growing up postmodern," as the Swedish psychologist Lars Dencik puts it, involves living with adults, one of whom is likely not to be one's biological parent; having step-siblings as often as one has siblings, and having fewer of the latter in any case; spending most of the day, from a relatively early age until the start of school, in a public daycare institution; experiencing generally low levels of contact with friends and neighbors; maturing extremely quickly, and developing a series of capacities that stress self-control and self-mastery.[7] One question raised by these patterns is whether the accomplishments of the new welfare state—its achievement of greater equality between the sexes and its emphasis on rights rather than responsibilities—come at the cost of exposing children to new ways of growing up the future consequences of which are uncertain.

Such a question is generally asked at the point where the postmodern family overlaps with the new welfare state: the public day-care center. A series of efforts have been made in Scandinavia to determine the consequences for children of public day care. The most positive results were found by Bengt-Erik Andersson, who, in conjunction with an international group of social psychologists, conducted a longitudinal study of 119 Swedish children from age one through age eight. While many of his findings revealed that participation in public day care had neither a positive nor a negative long-term effect, either in the development of academic skills or in psychological measures such as self-confidence, Andersson did discover that age of entry into the public day-care system seemed to be a consistent predictor of success later on: the earlier a child began, the better the later academic success.[8]

Andersson's findings were contrary to the conclusions of many child psychologists, especially those influenced by the "object relations" school of psychoanalysis who stress the need for early and permanent contact between parents and children. (They were also contrary to the proposals of the Swedish Social Democratic party, which argue for eighteen months paid maternity leave.) They are, however, consistent with other studies that show positive results from the experience of public child care, emphasizing, for example, the autonomy that children can learn or the value of day-care centers to bring children into contact with other children from a wider variety of backgrounds, including differing ages, than would have been possible if they had been brought up at home.[9] From studies such as these one can conclude, as both Andersson and Dencik do, that a good deal of the guilt experienced by parents when they utilize public day care is unnecessary. But there are reasons, many of them not quantifiable through statistical research, to believe that such a conclusion is not justified.

One reason is that Andersson's research stresses the importance of "good" day care, but not all public day care is good. Various problems plague the day-care sector in Scandinavia, the most important of which are the notoriously frequent turnover of personnel in day-care institutions and the fact that children in day care spend little time together with the immediate family.[10] This latter problem, moreover, is compounded by the fact that small children in the Scandinavian countries, because of the general weakness of civil society, have relatively little contact with friends and relatives outside their immediate family network.[11] Such factors may explain why other studies have found serious emotional problems associated with public day care: some, for example, found that young infants were particularly disturbed by their entry into a new environment, even if such feelings tended to pass with time, while others, not only in Scandinavia but elsewhere as well, have concluded that children in public day care tend to be more aggressive.[12] Once-optimistic views about public day care—which assumed that, in Birthe Kyng's words, children would be "more self-sufficient, that is, more independent of support from adults, less shy than children raised at home, and more open in peer-group relations"—are increasingly being replaced with the neutral notion simply that public day care does no harm.[13]

Denmark relies on public day care to a greater degree than any other country in the world. It is therefore worth pointing out that a Danish national commission on the status of children, in a report issued in 1981, warned of a "closed children's world" cut off from adult life.[14] Responding to that report, the National Association of School Psychologists also investigated what many have called "the new children's character" in Scandinavia and concluded, among other things, that

it is becoming more common that children who are beginning school are anti-social, loud, and confused. They are uncertain, unhappy, and badly in need of contact. They do not have the awareness that early beginners in school once had, and they are lacking moral conceptions. They have no respect for elders and are untrained in using their body and their hands. Many are passive or aggressive, and they do not understand ordinary reprimands.[15]

This notion of a "new children's character" must be interpreted with some caution, for, as Kyng points out, it applies to all children, not just those who attended day care while young.[16] (It has also been suggested, by a therapist who works extensively with small children in Denmark, that the proper term ought to be a "new parent's character," since it is the parents whose behavior has changed, more than the children.)[17] Still, findings such as these suggest that the public family does involve an element of moral gambling with the future.

There can be little doubt that many children are served well by public day care, especially in contrast to the United States and the haphazard effects there of reliance on the market. If the American and Scandinavian approaches to raising children were the only ways possible, the needs of future generations would, at least in this observer's opinion, be better served by the latter. Nor is there any doubt that even if public day care is organized more according to the needs of the parents than of the children, more productive and content parents make for happier children. Yet nonetheless, there is reason to listen when Scandinavian parents express guilt about their children. As nearly all studies of public day care suggest, every child has different needs, and individual parents are usually in the best position to know what the specific needs of their children are. Public provision of day care has undoubtedly made the Scandinavian state, as Helga Hernes puts it, "woman friendly."[18] Whether the new welfare state is "child friendly" remains undetermined.

In contrast to the situation with the very young, the response of the welfare state to the very old, at least in recent years, has not been one of building institutions to carry out tasks once associated with civil society. Rather, public policy toward the elderly has changed from an effort to provide nursing homes and other forms of institutional care to one emphasizing "community care" for the elderly, such as service centers that assist older people during the day, housing complexes for the elderly with special provisions for their needs, and extensive home-help coverage. This pattern has been clearest in Sweden, which historically has had the greatest commitment to institutionalized care: in 1970 the number of places in institutions for the elderly in Sweden was three times that of Norway and twice that of Denmark, although by 1980 the differences among the three Scandinavian countries had begun to even out.[19] Projections for the future, moreover, indicate that decreasing institutionalization in Sweden combined with the building of nursing homes in the United States (often under private sponsorship) will equalize the pattern between these two countries, otherwise so different, within a decade.[20]

Deinstitutionalization reflects one of those rare meetings of the mind between political ideologies: it satisfies the right, because it is the cheapest solution, and it satisfies at least some on the left because it is more humane. Consequently, little support for routinized institutionalization for the elderly remains in Scandinavia. Even when older people are so sick that they must depend completely on institutional care, old-age homes still require families and social networks to complement what they can offer.[21] The trend against building institutions for the aged, then, represents something of a shift in welfare state thinking, for the goal in this area of public policy is not to supplant civil society but to strengthen it—although in so doing, such a policy exposes itself to criticism from a social-democratic perspective, which stresses that only government delivery of services can approximate the goals of universality and relatively equal access.[22]

The significant question posed by these reforms is not whether, as ways of encouraging moral obligation in the intimate sector, they are a good idea, for they are, but whether civil society is strong enough to support them. Because so many other aspects of the new welfare state in Scandinavia use government as a substitute for the moral ties of civil society, greater reliance on family or community help can mean turning to sources of moral support which themselves have been weakened.[23] Consequently, for all the improvements in the material, physical, and even social conditions of the elderly that have taken place in Scandinavia in recent years, the webs of interdependence between the elderly and other generations have weakened in ways not dissimilar to those in the United States.[24]

An informal system of caregiving based on the family assumes that families can accept the burden. That assumption becomes harder to maintain when the family has been transformed as much as Scandinavian families have been in the past quarter century. Single people, whether they have never married or are divorced, experience more strain in caring for their parents than do married people.[25] Similarly, the two-income family often has less time to take care of the elderly.[26] Furthermore, the past twenty years have seen dramatic changes in the household structure of the elderly: the percentage of those living either alone or just with their spouse has increased in all three countries, whereas the percentage of those living with their children or with others has decreased (see figure 8). The cross-generational family unit living together no longer exists, at least not in any great numbers.

Changes in family structure carry many positive results. Older people now have the means to be independent of their children, and they clearly like it that way.[27] As in the United States, grandparents prefer what has been called "intimacy at a distance"; [28] the ideal situation for them is one where they can maintain their independence but still live close enough to be with their families occasionally. (Visiting across generations, not surprisingly, increases as co-residence between generations decreases.) [29] Moreover, the desire of the elderly to be independent of younger generations is reciprocated by a desire on the part of younger people to be independent of their elders.[30] Caring for the old is enormously difficult work that requires personal self-sacrifice and can create almost unbearable strain, especially for women, who, to a much greater degree than men, tend to take on these responsibilities.[31] It has for example been found that in Scandinavia older men are far less likely to care for a sick wife than are older women to care for a sick husband.[32] Similarly, when a spouse of either sex dies, the role of caregiver is assumed by daughters, rarely by sons.[33] Just as the wel-

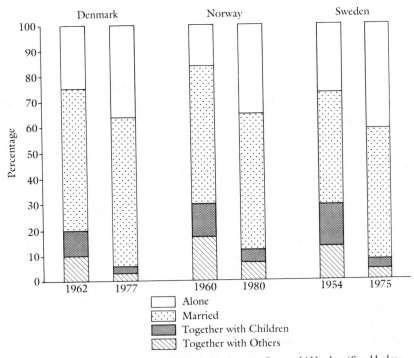

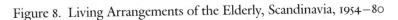

Source: Svein Olav Daatland and Gerdt Sundström, *Gammal i Norden,* (Stockholm: Initiatives for Service and Housing Sectors for the Elderly Project, 1985) 42, 108.

Figure 8. Living Arrangements of the Elderly, Scandinavia, 1954–80

fare state has reduced the burden on women of caring for children, it has also reduced the significant burden of caring for the elderly.

Some demographers and social scientists argue that independence from family ties—ties that can be emotionally destructive—represent a positive gain for the elderly.[34] Yet a good deal of recent research has also shown that older people thrive best when they can count on informal help from social networks, including the family.[35] Clearly some kind of balance between public and intimate caring is required: the question is whether a political approach to moral obligation can provide it. To some degree it can; Scandinavian programs for the elderly are among the best in the world (and are often cited by Americans as models for treating responsibilities to older generations).[36] Yet because political approaches to moral obligation tend to emphasize the interests of various groups who are struggling for benefits from the state, a weakening sense of moral obligation toward the elderly can be detected in Scandinavia. Younger people, for example, show less willingness to support programs for the elderly, while, at least in some circumstances, programs for the elderly have been sacrificed as part of interest-group politics to the needs of parents of small children.[37] (In Denmark between 1977 and 1987, expenditures on day care increased 77 percent, whereas those for nursing homes increased 48 percent, home helpers for the elderly 56 percent, and community care 38 percent.)[38]

Community networks among the elderly are not relied on as much as family networks; one Norwegian study found that government services first, and families second, were more important as sources of care than were friends in the immediate environment.[39] To the degree that reforms in the provision of services to the elderly try to rely more on local networks and ties, they often show mixed results at best. It is difficult for local ties to supplement government programs because government programs for so long served to supplement local ties. The progrowth policies of postwar Social Democratic parties—which often put a premium on the geographic mobility of labor, as in Sweden, or on the construction of new housing projects that depleted older neighborhoods and towns, as in both Sweden and Norway—weakened the kinds of long-standing friendships on which older people can rely. In a study of intergenerational mobility, Gunhild Hammarström discovered that moral solidarity across generations in Sweden had not decreased over time and in some ways had increased, but the extent of such solidarity was dependent on stable communities, irrespective of whether they were urban or rural.[40] Geographic and social mobility pay greater economic rewards than they do moral rewards, at least insofar as intergenerational obligations are concerned.

Whether the housing projects of the postwar period can provide their own sources of social support for the elderly is doubtful. One study in Denmark did find that when the elderly move to a new housing development, they tend to maintain the friends they had before and, especially if they are already active, to make new friends in their new situation.[41] More common, however, is the experience in Norway, where the government attempted to design community solidarity into new housing projects for the elderly. Among the first residents, ties of reciprocity did enable people to call on each other for help, but as the population aged and health problems increased, the reciprocal system broke down. Ties of civil society among old people, researchers discovered ten years later, were simply not strong enough to be sustained.[42] It would seem that the pattern among the elderly with respect to civil society is similar to the pattern in Scandinavia as a whole discussed in the previous chapter: informal networks exist, but they cannot be relied on to any significant degree for caring. Older people, especially those without children, feel sorely the lack of friends with whom personal problems can be discussed.[43]

As elsewhere in the world, problems of generational interdependence will become even more complex in the future because of greater longevity. The Scandinavian societies lead the world in life expectancy. Parents and children can now expect to have fifty years of life overlap. Grandchildren and grandparents (and, of course, great-grandparents and great-grandchildren) will have opportunities to know one another better and longer. It is likely that in the near future Scandinavian societies will experience as a common occurrence two generations of retirees in the same family (and likewise, as Kari Wærness has pointed out, two generations of widows).[44] The very success of the Scandinavian welfare states in prolonging life and contributing to its material satisfactions, even among the oldest members of the population, will to some degree be lost if trends in its development contribute to what Bent Rold Andersen has described as a segregation of generations, leading to "the knowledge and experiences which they share . . . becoming less common, to the disadvantage of all but mostly the old."[45]

The welfare state, it would seem, has reached the point at which it becomes difficult to achieve equality among present generations without taking steps with implications for future generations that cannot be determined and for previous generations that are problematic. No one in Scandinavia seems to have solved the problem of how to combine two contrasting goals, each laudable in itself: on the one hand, an extension of citizenship rights in the present, reflected especially in support for women to enter careers and achieve equality with men; and on the other, reliance on the family and community to supplement institutional care for both the very young and the very old. Both goals can be met, but they require the use of common sense and everyday moral sentiments rather than an insistence on political rules disproportionately stressing the rights won by present generations. A reliance on government to satisfy obligations to the old and the young is a precondition for modernity, but it also becomes morally complicated when it replaces, rather than supplements, care for individual children and elderly. Taking care of the young and the old is no doubt demanding and burdensome, but it is also one of the only ways we have to understand personally the vertical nature of the social fabric.

The Welfare State and Social Obligations

Understanding more about the invisible ties of moral obligation that make society possible has always been part of the sociological mission, as exemplified in the study by Richard Titmuss of British and American blood donation patterns.[46] Yet the spirit of voluntaristic altruism that Titmuss so praised mixes uneasily with a political approach to moral regulation, for the latter, especially in a Scandinavian context, views charitable giving and voluntarism through unfriendly eyes—as threats, and niggardly ones at that, to the idea that social benefits ought to be a right guaranteed by government and delivered to all rather than a feeling dependent on individual whim. The replacement of private charity with universal access to benefits and rights guaranteed by government surely represents a strengthening of a sense of obligation to people unknown to us. But it also potentially means that if in some ultimate sense the responsibility for the care of strangers belongs to government, then it no longer belongs to us.

It is not the case, as some critics of the welfare state have charged, that because the role of government is so extensive, people in Scandinavia no longer care to donate their time and energy to others. As a result of the welfare state people have more free time, and as the studies of social networks cited in the previous chapter indicate, they often use their time in cooperative activities with others. One of those activities involves voluntarism: participation in community organizations, sports activities, scouting and other similar groups, political movements, and even private social-welfare activities. Research conducted in both Denmark and Sweden indicates that voluntarism is alive and well in Scandinavia. In Denmark, for example, only a small portion of the population was found to have engaged in traditional social work—the welfare state does that—but, depending on definitions, anywhere from 25 to 44 percent of the adult population was engaged in voluntary activities of one sort or another.[47] Swedes use their free time in many ways, including private-consumption activities such as watching television or repairing their homes, but around 40 percent of them participate in public activities such as organized sports or cultural events.[48] Moreover, such participation in voluntary activities has grown over the past decade.[49]

Nor is it the case that private charity has disappeared from the welfare state. In Sweden to be sure, where private charity is discouraged, relatively few examples exist of organizations in the area between the state and the market (called in recent publications of the Swedish Finance Ministry "border organizations," a newly coined term).[50] Even though new self-help-type organizations have appeared in the 1980s—in the realm of day care, for example—these tend to be small and localized. Such is not the case in the other two Scandinavian countries. In Norway, a study conducted in the city of Bergen found private organizations active in such areas as pensions, mother's help, aid to the handicapped, help for the sick, international solidarity, and many other areas.[51] In Denmark, an examination of 115 voluntary organizations indicated that they still play a major, if invisible, role in social welfare, leading social workers and social theorists to begin a debate over the nature of what has been called the "third network" of private charitable organizations and the role they ought to play "between the market and the state."[52]

Private charitable organizations surely do have a role to play, even in societies where the welfare state is highly developed. To illustrate, consider the experience of one such organization, a Danish charity called Mothers' Help. As a result of the horrendous conditions that faced poor, young, single women who became pregnant, private charitable efforts to help them were a feature of Danish life since the turn of the century.[53] These efforts were coordinated in 1939 when an earlier generation of Danish feminists, acting often out of a spirit of noblesse oblige ("hat ladies," as they are called in Danish), founded Mothers' Help.[54] The aim of the organization was to provide legal and social advice, economic support, educational funding, services for infants, and institutions to care for the single mothers both during their pregnancy and for the period immediately after childbirth. Between 1939 and 1973, the total number of women who used the charity increased more than tenfold, from 3,342 to 44,158.[55]

As is often the case in matters of social help, conservatives preferred that initiatives such as this be in private hands ("I don't believe in the Good Samaritan when he becomes a civil servant," one conservative member of parliament said when Mothers' Help was founded),[56] while Social Democrats thought it ought to come under direction of the state. The latter route was taken in 1976 under a new social assistance law developed—ironically, given some of his later statements about the weakness of social networks in the welfare state—by Social Minister Bent Rold Andersen. In return for greater governmental resources for unwed mothers, the new law abolished Mothers' Help, incorporating it into the state. The idea behind the reform was that, instead of having many different needs met by many different agencies, people who relied on government for social support should be able to see only one social worker or agency to help them with all their problems. The reform was typical welfare-state policy: sensible, rational, and efficient.

In 1983, a new generation of feminists—upset by the cutbacks in social services supported by a conservative government—refounded Mothers' Help. Thriving on the spirit of the feminist movement, the new voluntary organization flourished. Proud of its independence, it existed almost entirely on grants from foundations and contributions from individuals, with the exception of some funds from the Common Market and from the Danish lottery system.[57] Yet because the organization flourished, the question of public support immediately came up again; a 1987 evaluation, for example, suggested that since Mothers' Help had been able to accomplish so much with "free labor power," it ought to receive more direct public support.[58] Combined with the usual problems that face voluntary organizations—administrative difficulties, personality conflicts, disagreements between volunteers and paid staff—it seemed inevitable that Mothers' Help would once again have a high public subsidy.

As this example indicates, an organization that begins voluntarily will either meet a need or it will not. If it does not, it goes out of business. If it does, the state will play a far more active role, sometimes by taking the organization over, more commonly by financing it.[59] Governmental subsidies to private organizations vary from year to year and from organization to organization. Table 7 contrasts the share of the budget that comes from voluntary contributions with the share that comes from state subsidies for nine Scandinavian charitable organizations: the Red Cross, Save the Children, and the emergency relief organizations associated with the established Lutheran church in all three countries. In general, between one-quarter and one-half of the money is from public subsidies. Moreover, the public share has increased over the course of the 1980s: in only one case was the share of the budget from voluntary donations higher in 1986 than in 1980; similarly, in only one case was the share of the budget from government sources smaller in 1980 than in 1986. Because of the degree of public subsidy, the terms *private* or *voluntary* with regard to social organizations take on a different meaning in Scandinavia than in the United States.

As the state comes to play a greater role in subsidizing private charitable organizations, will individuals feel less of an obligation to give time and money to charitable and voluntary causes? Of the three Scandinavian countries, Denmark offers the best answer to this question, for it is the one that relies most on private organizations in the social-welfare sector. Two general indicators of a sense of voluntary obligation to strangers are Titmuss's own example, blood donations (since only Denmark among the

TABLE 7. *Voluntary Contributions and State Subsidy, Selected Scandinavian Charities, 1980–86 (as percentage of budget)*

	Denmark		Norway		Sweden	
	Voluntary	Govern-mental	Voluntary	Govern-mental	Voluntary	Govern-mental
Save the Children						
1980	40.1	4.2	43.0	25.4	NA	NA
1981	35.0	5.2	44.0	33.0	NA	NA
1982	16.3	2.3	45.6	22.1	55.4	23.1
1983	20.9	12.6	50.6	34.3	45.1	31.7
1984	NA	NA	43.8	45.7	48.8	29.2
1985	NA	NA	33.1	52.1	52.0	22.5
1986	NA	NA	41.0	48.0	50.2	26.9
Red Cross						
1980	51.2	17.3	0.0[a]	0.0	32.6	38.0
1981	35.5	26.9	0.0	0.0	31.7	37.1
1982	31.3	31.1	0.0	0.0	41.3	36.9
1983	NA	NA	0.0	0.0	NA	NA
1984	32.2	26.1	30.1	23.7	40.4	39.0
1985	22.4	21.7	30.6	0.0	33.5	46.7
1986	10.8	16.1	29.2	0.0	22.9	48.8
Lutheran Church Aid						
1980	33.4	34.2	59.2	40.5	48.6	13.5
1981	25.2	46.7	45.7	53.0	48.6	14.4
1982	23.0	43.6	43.0	44.4	40.6	23.7
1983	20.0	44.4	28.0	58.7	40.6	22.8
1984	30.8	41.6	33.4	58.5	NA	NA
1985	21.5	39.2	26.0	68.7	68.9	20.6
1986	21.1	42.7	42.1	43.4	68.3	24.0

[a]The Norwegian Red Cross is mostly supported through a national lottery system.

Sources. Denmark: Dansk Røde Kors, *Årsberetninger,* 1980–86; Dansk Red Barnet, *Årsberetninger,* 1980–86; Dansk Folkekirkens Nødhjælp, *Årsberetning,* 1980–86. Norway: Norsk Redd Barna, *Årsmelding og regnskap,* 1980–86; figures supplied by Norwegian Red Cross; Norsk Kirkens Nødhjelp, *Årsrapport,* 1980–86. Sweden: Svensk Rädda Barnen, *Barnen och vi,* 1980–86; Svensk Lutherhjälpen, *Årsbok,* 1980–86; Svensk Röda Korset, *Årsbok,* 1980–86.

Scandinavian countries relies completely on voluntarism for blood donations), and "home visits" sponsored by the Danish Red Cross.

There was a dramatic increase in the voluntary giving of blood over the fifty-year period 1932–1982 in Denmark, from 1,639 individual donors a year to almost 410,700.[60] This evidence indicates that the expansion of the welfare state can be accompanied by an increased personal sense of one's stake in society. Yet since 1982 the number of blood donors has not increased at anywhere near the same rate; in fact, it has even begun to fall, as

TABLE 8.   *Voluntary Activities, Denmark, 1976–86*

	Blood Donations		Home Visits	
	Total Number	Percentage of Population	Total Number	Percentage of Population (per 1,000)
1976	258,019[a]	5.09[a]	1,600	.3154
1977	363,657	7.13	2,000	.3931
1978	366,090	7.17	2,238	.4385
1979	376,596	7.35	1,300	.2541
1980	386,653	7.53	NA	NA
1981	389,594	7.60	NA	NA
1982	402,809	7.85	NA	NA
1983	410,700	8.02	NA	NA
1984	407,856	7.96	4,811	.9407
1985	396,585	7.74	4,449	.8703
1986	410,284	8.00	4,681	.9135

[a]1976 data based on only three-quarters because of an alteration in bookkeeping procedures.

Source. Data on blood donations are from Danmarks Frivillige Bloddonorer, *Årsberetning 1986;* data on home visits are supplied by the Danish Red Cross. Total population figures are from *Danmarks Statistisk Årbog,* relevant years.

table 8 illustrates. Similar patterns exist with respect to home visits: a dramatic increase followed in very recent years by a general leveling off. If the number of participants in voluntary charity is taken as an indication of moral obligation, the idea of voluntarily helping others has clearly not diminished in the welfare state, at least not in Denmark. Yet in terms of the rate of absolute increase, obligations to others are not growing as they did in the past.

It is, however, somewhat unfair to measure the strength of Scandinavians' sense of obligation to distant strangers by using examples of voluntary activities. The promise of the political approach to moral regulation is that government can do a better job of insuring obligations to others than can private charity. Since reliance on government represents a transfer of funds from some people to others through a system of taxation and public spending, a more meaningful test of people's feeling of obligation to perfect strangers ought to lie in their willingness to pay taxes. Any American reader of the last sentence may be skeptical—who is *ever* willing to pay

taxes? Yet Scandinavia is, on this point, quite different from the United States. Swedes are more likely not to be negative about their tax obligations and even, in terms of the benefits they receive, to be positive.[61] In Scandinavia much more than in the United States, the legitimacy of taxation is accepted, precisely because the welfare state promises to do a better job of using the money to meet the needs of others.

Scandinavian societies, because they rely so extensively on government to express citizens' moral obligations, have the world's highest taxation rates, over 50 percent of gross income in both Sweden and Denmark.[62] Whether such high rates will lead to tax avoidance and hence a weakened sense of obligation to others has been much debated in Scandinavia; the late Gunnar Heckscher, citing a claim by Gunnar Myrdal that Sweden is becoming a nation of tax dodgers, concluded that "the gap between legal and moral concepts is growing: tax dodging is undoubtedly illegal, but many Scandinavians refuse to regard it as immoral."[63] It is difficult to obtain precise empirical information on whether high taxation leads to tax avoidance, given that nonpayment of taxes is illegal. Evidence from Norway, however, suggests that as income increases, and hence the rate of taxation, people attempt (in legal ways) to stretch their deductions further. Between 1973 and 1979, for example, the deductions that people claimed increased—presumably as a result of higher taxes.[64] Public-opinion surveys for Norway also pointed in the same direction. Although the questions on tax avoidance differed between 1971 and 1980, making direct comparison impossible, 21 percent of the Norwegians surveyed in 1971 admitted that they avoided paying taxes, compared to 39 percent in 1980, while 60 percent in 1971 said that they would have liked to, compared to 64 percent in 1980.[65]

Further conclusions about obligations to others can be drawn, not from the overall rate of tax avoidance, but from an assessment of who tries to escape paying taxes and who does not. Women, according to Einar Øverbye's Norwegian study, seek to avoid tax obligations less than men. Yet both men and women between fifteen and twenty-four years old were in most cases twice as willing as those over sixty-five either to admit to tax avoidance or to say that they plan to avoid taxes, a development that foreshadows problems of moral obligation in the future.[66] The clearest finding is that tax compliance is related to class position. In Sweden, a 1970 study by Joachim Vogel found that wage-earners were less likely to agree that taxes were high enough to justify finding means to avoid them than those who owned their own businesses, a finding confirmed again, if to a weaker degree, in 1980–81.[67] In Norway, a more recent study showed that greater income was positively correlated with the wish to avoid paying taxes.[68]

What matters when it comes to tax avoidance is opportunity; those who can avoid paying taxes, will. This fact in turn suggests that in Scandinavia questions of tax obligation have less to do with a sense of obligation to others than with a utilitarian calculation of costs and benefits.[69] Vogel, for example, discovered that fear of being caught is the single most important reason for tax compliance in Sweden. Moreover, he found that people who felt that their friends were cheating on their taxes were more likely themselves to cheat on their taxes.[70] Beyond a certain point—and the problem always is that no one knows exactly where that point is—high tax rates do seem to encourage less of a sense of obligation to strangers and more of a sense that the perceived and actual costs of the new welfare state have made the free-rider option more attractive for those who can take advantage of it. In the Scandinavian welfare states the result is, as Pekka Kosonen puts it, a deemphasis on solidarity and a greater stress on individualism.[71]

Similar results are found when work done off the books—another form of tax evasion—is investigated. Here again, because the activities are illegal, hard data are hard to come by. While it is clear that Scandinavians are less likely to engage in illegal work than, say, Italians, most studies indicate that such activities are on the rise in all three countries. Gunnar Viby Mogensen, relying on survey data, concludes that between 1980 and 1984 the number of Danes engaged in illegal work increased from 8 percent to 13 percent of the population, with revenues amounting to around 4.5 percent of total income—figures that ought to be taken as a minimal indication of unreported work.[72] The underground economy, however, is probably stronger in Sweden than in Denmark; one estimate suggests that it now stands at between 12 and 25 percent of total income.[73] (Surveys in Norway, by contrast, found that the shadow sector diminished slightly in size between 1979 and 1983.)[74]

When investigators do not use survey data, they often rely on two other approaches to assess the extent of illegal work. One, called the currency-demand approach, tries to measure changes in the amount of money in circulation, on the assumption that illegal work is likely to be paid for in cash rather than by check or credit card.[75] The other approach, the causal approach, seeks to identify the cause of illegal economic activity and to identify its amount based on changes in the cause.[76] The figures produced by both approaches (see table 9) allow us to draw some tentative conclu-

TABLE 9. *Shadow Economy as Percentage of GNP, Selected Countries, 1960–80*

	Monetary-Demand Approach		Causal Approach	
	1960	1978–80	1960	1978
Austria	2	10	5	9
Belgium	—	21	5	12
Britain	—	7	5	8
Canada	—	11	5	9
Denmark	**4**	**9**	**4**	**12**
West Germany	2	11	4	9
Finland	—	—	3	8
France	—	7	5	9
Holland	—	—	8	10
Ireland	—	8	2	7
Italy	—	30	4	11
Japan	—	—	2	4
Norway	**2**	**11**	**4**	**9**
Spain	—	23	3	7
Sweden	**2**	**13**	**5**	**13**
Switzerland	1	7	1	4
United States	3	5	6	8

Source. The Economist, 19 September 1987, 22.

sions. First, although the two approaches yield varying results in many countries, that is not the case for the Scandinavian countries; we can therefore place some confidence in them. Second, they indicate that the shadow economy has in fact grown in Scandinavia. (It has elsewhere as well, though rarely by the same magnitude.) Sweden and Denmark rank among the world's leaders in illegal work, along with Italy, Spain, and Belgium, while Japan and Switzerland fall at the other end of the spectrum.

The figures in table 9 also point to a third conclusion with respect to shadow-sector work. The fact that in Italy the currency-demand approach shows a high figure and the causal approach a low one suggests that there the need for cash is the strongest motivation for entering the illegal labor market. To be sure, a monetary incentive for such work exists in Scandinavia as well; the average black-market transaction in Denmark costs about $100.[77] But the fact that the Scandinavian countries do not show up much higher in the currency-exchange approach than in the causal approach suggests that illegal work in Scandinavia is also the result of stringent government regulation. If it is illegal for a painter to paint his own house or for a farm family to consume more than one pig a year, then it is not surprising that people engage in illegal work not only as a way of gaining extra income, but also as a way simply of exchanging services. The largest sector of the shadow economy in Denmark is in building and construction, where, for example, a painter might do work on an electrician's house and vice versa.[78] Even the second-largest category, service delivery (consisting largely of a black market in day care), though done for extra cash, also contains an element of informality in that it allows women with children of their own to remain at home while still earning extra income.[79]

As with tax avoidance, participation in the illegal economy varies with one's position in society. The two groups most likely to pay their taxes— women and older people—are also least likely to engage in underground work.[80] Young men, the presumed major wage-earners of the future, are the most likely to avoid obligations to society. In contrast to the situation with tax avoidance, however, working-class people take far greater advantage of the market in illegal work than do salaried and self-employed people. If the wealthy purchase services off the books, it is the working class that sells them; in that sense, shadow-sector work is the poor man's form of tax avoidance. Together, tax avoidance and illegal or "black" work suggest that the number of people who carry out their obligations scrupulously may be approaching a minority in Scandinavia.

In many ways, the desire to escape heavy taxation reflects a preference for the obligations of civil society rather than those of the state; the exchange of services conducted in the Scandinavian underground economies is often among neighbors and kin. Yet taxation has assumed the importance it has in Scandinavia precisely because the distrust of private charity makes government almost the sole tender of obligations to others. The moral gamble of the welfare state follows directly from its moral monopoly. Having discouraged private charity and voluntarism with the argument that governmental provision is more reliable and more fair, the welfare state also monopolizes resistance to moral obligation: what in other societies might be viewed as a trend away from charitable giving in Scandinavia inevitably becomes resistance to taxation. At the same time that the welfare state extends care to more people and fulfills important obligations to strangers, it also encourages a cynicism toward social obligation, making what ought to be a sense of solidarity with others into a cat-and-mouse game against the authorities. High tax rates in Scandinavia encourage governmental responsibility for others; they do not, however, necessarily inspire a personal sense of altruism and a feeling of moral unity toward others with whom one's fate is always linked. In that sense, obligations toward others have been transformed into duties, weakening a personal stake in those obligations in the process.

Political Culture and the Welfare State

One of the more controversial debates in Scandinavia in recent years was initiated by a German, the poet and political essayist Hans Magnus Enzensberger. After a visit to Sweden in 1982, Enzensberger wrote a series of articles for *Dagens Nyheter* in which he complained that Swedes had given up their sense of freedom and personal autonomy in exchange for faith in a benevolent state. "Whether it is a question of using a 'hot line,' of alcoholism, of state planning or health care, of bringing up children or having their wages taxed, Swedish citizens are always prepared to come to the authorities innocently and full of trust, as if their benevolence were beyond question," he wrote. "It ought not be surprising," he added, "that the state's power has grown unopposed, creeping into all the cracks of daily life, regulating people's doings in a way without precedent in free societies."[81]

Enzensberger is certainly not the first non-Scandinavian to find too much authority in this part of the world; conservatives, especially of the free-market type, have done so for years.[82] To anyone at all sympathetic to the welfare state, the notion that Sweden is essentially an Eastern European country without lines, where individual freedom is constantly under attack by Big Brother, is absurd. Greater equality in Scandinavia has undoubtedly contributed to a decline in the ability of the very rich to lead lives of eccentricity, but for the overwhelming majority the welfare state has greatly expanded the scope of free choice.[83] Yet Enzensberger's remarks, while exaggerated, cannot be dismissed—and not only because he, unlike earlier critics, is on the left. As a poet, Enzensberger is talking about culture more than anything else, and in this sense he is correct: reliance on the state, like reliance on the market, makes more difficult the development of cultural practices that contribute to the narratives which give people a stake in the fate of others.

It is often forgotten, given the breadth of the welfare state, that reliance on government was not the only possible path to modernity in Scandinavia. Modern Danish culture has been shaped to a remarkable degree

by only one man, the poet and theologian N. F. S. Grundtvig. His emphasis on folk high schools that would combine practical and theoretical
knowledge with an ethical sense of personal responsibility and concern for
the fate of others provided an institutional basis for the modernization of
Denmark.[84] While Grundtvig himself is unique in Scandinavia—"In Sweden," Arne Ruth has written, "there is no similar cultural hero on whom
an analysis of the deeper layers of national identity could focus"[85]—his
emphasis on education and moral growth is not. In 1899, for example,
the Kooperative Förbundet (KF) was developed in Sweden as a consumer
federation based on principles hostile to both the market and the state.
At one level the cooperative movement was a business engaged in the
manufacture and sale of products to consumers; at another level it was
an ethical and moral movement with purposes primarily educational and
cultural. Consumers, according to a central ideological theme of the movement, needed to be able to take responsibility for themselves, a responsibility that the KF organized through training courses developed at its own
headquarters, the Vår Gård (Our Place).[86] The cooperative movement, furthermore, was only one kind of people's movement; turn-of-the-century
Sweden had others, in such areas as sports, nonestablishment religions
(primarily Methodists, Baptists, and the Salvation Army), and temperance. Even social democracy, which created the modern welfare state, began as a people's movement.[87]

As this last fact suggests, not all the founders of modern social democracy were convinced of the benefits of a completely political approach to
moral regulation, although some were: the Dane who created his country's
social insurance system, K. K. Steinicke, wrote in his autobiography that
he "never had anything like the same interest in politics as in legislation
and administration."[88] In Norway, what we today call the welfare state was
called by its founders the "social state," by which they meant an emphasis
on the use of government to improve the conditions of people in poverty,
not necessarily the use of government as a more general regulator of moral
obligations.[89] In Sweden, Gustav Möller, minister of social affairs in
1924–26 and 1932–51 and the most important builder of Sweden's system
of social insurance, viewed the state as symbolic of the old-order ruling
class. Bureaucrats were, in his view, conservative defenders of privilege
who would, if they could, undermine efforts to bring about greater equality for the working class. Distrustful of the state bureaucracy, Möller
sought to rely on local authorities rather than centralized power and tried
to build into the design of public policies some degree of personal respon-

sibility.[90] (Möller developed the idea of child allowances, which, as I discussed in Chapter 5, have in recent years been supplanted by newer institutional forms that take on much of the moral responsibility of families.)

In part because social democracy was a movement of enormous power and importance, its triumph during and after the Great Depression became one of those stories that gave people a sense of a common fate. What I called earlier in this chapter the "social-democratic generation" is characterized, not merely by material satisfaction, but also by a common sense of struggle and purpose. To this day, the solidarity that has motivated the building of the welfare state remains strong, particularly among those who recall the earlier years of working-class struggle. As Ruth has pointed out, the result of the success of social democracy was a change, "not only in the formal division of power, but in the moral quality of society as well."[91] Social democracy itself became a culture, complete with symbols, stories, and moral teachings.

Popular movements such as Grundtvigism, cooperativism, and early social democracy, because they contained moral alternatives to the market and the state, tended to emphasize individuals as being part of the culture in which they lived. To use modern social-scientific language, they viewed individuals not as consumers or voters with stable preferences, but as moral agents capable of personal and social growth. Much of this has changed as the state (and, to some degree, the market as well) came to play an ever greater role in organizing modern life in Scandinavia. The folk high schools associated with Grundtvig still exist, but they have become more integrated into society, losing some (just how much is a matter open to much debate) of their distinctive moral character in the process.[92] The cooperative movement, too, has fallen victim to the widening reach of both the market and the state as not only successful merchandising in the private sector but also the extension of the welfare state into educational policy have undermined early accomplishments.[93] Swedish educational policy is especially difficult to reconcile with the educational and cultural ideals of the cooperative movement, for it was in this area more than any other that the fears of men like Möller were realized: today education in Sweden remains under the control of boards that tend to be bureaucratically rigid and concerned chiefly with the promulgation of strict rules.[94]

Finally, social democracy itself can no longer inspire a sense that individuals belong together as sharers of a common fate. The economic and political stagnation of social democracy in the 1980s is a moral and cultural stagnation as well. The story of how the working class took political power and created a society based on principles of equality and solidarity no longer inspires the same sensibility it once did. Yet no other stories have developed to replace it. For Sweden, Ruth writes, "a fundamental problem for any movement seeking an alternative course is that there is no binding moral tradition behind the project of Swedish modernity." The constitution, he points out, is too recent. Religion plays little role in so secular a society. The peasantry no longer exists. Workers lead relatively comfortable bourgeois lives. Because "a plausible political alternative is nowhere in sight," the "Social Democrats have reappeared as the administrators of the fragments of collective destiny; their appeal, however, derives more from their perceived competence in holding growth stoppage and unemployment at bay in these troubled times than from any positive vision of the future." [95]

The market, as I argued in Chapter 3, tends to unbind cultural ties. Without the existence of common stories defining why individual instincts need to be restrained for the sake of living together with others, people who rely on the market for their moral code lose a sense of a shared fate. Reliance on the state makes escaping one's obligations to others far more difficult, but it too produces a similar kind of "deculturation." As tends to be true everywhere in Western liberal democracies, the stories that form a common culture thin out as people allow government to organize for them their obligations to others. It is in this sense that Enzensberger's comments about the reach of the state in Scandinavia should be understood. A political approach to moral regulation substitutes the sense of participation in a common struggle with administrative rationalization: it is, for most people, a great relief to know that the struggle is over, and an even greater relief to know that it has been won. But it is also impossible to ignore that, in winning, Scandinavians have begun to lose the art of defining for themselves what about their cultures links them together in webs of mutual obligation.

Personal Responsibility and Moral Energy

Although considerations of balance and style would make such a task appropriate, it has never been my intention in these chapters to argue that the market and the state are *equally* problematic in their organization of obligations to both intimate and distant others. In a few areas, my own political feelings to the contrary, the market does appear to do a superior job, most especially in the realm of private charity. But overall the Scandinavian welfare states are far more successful at organizing modern moral obligations than are market-oriented societies like the United States. In the welfare state there is better provision for the elderly and the young, government support for the socially needy can be counted on, and a sense of general social solidarity, although weakened, still exists.

My point, rather, is that the welfare state has in recent years been called to organize moral obligations in ways for which it is ill equipped. By intervening in civil society to an extent that no one could have anticipated, the "new" welfare state has paradoxically made the organization of obligations to distant strangers and hypothetical others more difficult. One common theme runs throughout the three areas discussed in this chapter. Whether it is a question of obligations to young and old, of private charity and voluntarism, or of cultural definitions regarding the collective project, the new welfare state, in assuming greater responsibilities, has led to a decline in a sense of individual moral responsibility that threatens the ability of Scandinavian societies to find new sources of moral energy.

Problems of personal responsibility in the new welfare state arise particularly with the young, with the generations to come. Economically, of course, the welfare state guarantees the young that they will never have to face the problems of insecurity which plague teenagers in the United States. Consequently, there tends to be less generational selfishness among young people in Scandinavia, but more of a sense of bewilderment and moral confusion. Generally unaware of the struggles that made the welfare state possible in the first place, often unfamiliar with a world in which insecurity was a common lot, teenagers in the welfare state often seem ill prepared to act as moral agents responsible for their own fate. They tend to assume, in other words, that when their parents are no longer responsible for them, government will be. As Bent Rold Andersen has written,

Increasing numbers of young people are going to the welfare office on their eighteenth birthday, arguing that, since the legal financial duties of their parents have ceased, it is now the obligation of the public to support them. . . . Many people do feel that the public has a responsibility toward these young people and would consider it immoral if the welfare offices refused to help.[96]

Although what Andersen writes is obviously not true of all young people in Scandinavia, he touches on an important point. It is not the moral failure of "welfare dependency" that is of concern but its opposite: a fascination with rights and benefits so finely tuned that the idea of *not* asking for a right to which one nevertheless is entitled rarely occurs. One of

182   *States and Distant Obligations*

the great successes of the welfare state has been the extension of the language of rights downward in age. Yet because an emphasis on rights blends so easily into the notion that someone else ought to assume responsibility for one's own decisions, future full members of society, in so quickly transforming themselves into rights bearers, contribute to the moral problems of the society they will eventually inherit.

Similarly, the distrust of private charity and voluntarism that has so characterized the growth of the welfare state is bound to have long-term social repercussions. It is often conservatives who concern themselves with the effects of the welfare state on generalized feelings of altruism toward strangers. Sweden's Gunnar Heckscher, for example, has written as follows:

One of the slogans of the advocates of the welfare state has been that "society is to blame," for poverty, delinquency, and many other ills. In the long run such attitudes have eroded individual responsibility. . . . The opposition to "charity" has had similar effects: suffering and need "should" be dealt with by the state and local authorities at the expense of the entirety of taxpayers, and as a consequence individual citizens/taxpayers believe that they are under no obligation to act. . . . Voluntary social work is frowned upon and has virtually disappeared, with some exceptions in the case of religious organizations, but the vacuum has not always been filled.[97]

But the same issue has been raised by thinkers on the left. Michael Walzer, for example, asks why socialists have been so afraid of the idea of voluntarism. "After all," he writes, "a great deal of socialist activity has been paid for by private contributions or made possible by voluntary labor for the cause. . . . Why should we become the defenders of the bureaucratic state?"[98]

Why indeed? In a society like the United States, where government support for the needy is minimal, private charity plays an important *material* role in assuming responsibility for the fate of anonymous others. In Scandinavia, where government support is extensive, the role of private charity and voluntarism fulfills an important *symbolic* role. As Walzer writes, "The act of giving is a good in itself; it builds a sense of solidarity and communal competence."[99] There has to be a point at which the welfare state is pronounced a success, a point, in other words, at which the most basic problems of inequality and need in society have been solved. At that point, a sense of altruism and voluntary obligation toward others ought to supplement what the welfare state does best. If this does not happen, then the welfare state will continue to find problems that only it can solve, relying on experts to identify the scope of the problems and, as a result, becoming an administrative substitute for the common conscience that people themselves ought to have.

Finally, a general sense that the state has taken over tasks once associated with cultural solidarity has also contributed to a declining feeling of personal responsibility. Because the state has come to be so heavily relied on in Scandinavia, it is easy to conclude—as Enzensberger did—that Scandinavians are in danger of losing their moral autonomy to government. This, however, is an incorrect interpretation of a correct problem. What is really taking place in Scandinavia with the intervention of government in so many areas of life is the *politicization* of cultural rules. The welfare state substitutes the notion of a right for the notion of an obligation. The language of rights, though positive with respect to individual freedom, is nonetheless limited with respect to social interdependence. As Ulrich K. Preuss has written, modern legal forms emphasizing rights are "disembedded" from the social order in ways similar to Karl Polanyi's analysis of markets. The growth of legal rules parallels the "dissolution of comprehensive social institutions and the distinctive institutionalization of economic, cultural, religious, familial . . . motives, interests, and interactions."[100] The political logic of the welfare state is vertical, emphasizing the relations between individuals (or the groups to which they belong) and the state; it is rarely horizontal, emphasizing the interrelationships between individuals (or groups) themselves. Whether individuals are sovereign and government their servant or the other way around is not as important, ultimately, as the fact that individuals and government—and not the cultural meanings existing between them—are the only forces in the equation that matter.

An inability to solve moral problems as it has been able to solve economic problems will always create difficulties for the Scandinavian welfare state. These societies have clearly, to use the words of Esping-Andersen and Korpi, "emancipated individuals from the traditional compulsion to work and save for a rainy day." But it is not true, as they continue, that "the old liberal dogmas of self-reliance and new liberal dogmas of 'help to self-help' have been replaced by a powerful commitment to collective social responsibility for the optimal welfare of citizens."[101] These dogmas have been replaced instead by *governmental* responsibility, by reliance on the state to organize rules of moral obligation among both strangers and those in the intimate environment of civil society. If government were the only collective authority that mattered, there would be nothing more to say on the subject. Yet it is precisely because society itself is also a source of collective authority that the story of the welfare state has not ended. By overcoming economic scarcity, the welfare state has made possible a new sense of moral obligation. By replacing economics with politics rather than a social commitment based on personal responsibility, however, it finds itself unable to complete the project it began.

Society

SEVEN

Sociology Without Society

Beyond Political Economy

It is not difficult to understand why markets and states have become the preferred moral codes for modern liberal democrats. When societies make provision for individuals to maximize their self-interest in economic activities, benefits in growth follow that flow to (nearly) everyone—a reality that even some of the world's most committed socialist countries have been forced to acknowledge. Yet when societies also require that common citizenship obligations be recognized, states play an essential role—a reality that even some of the world's most committed capitalist countries have also been forced to recognize.

Some positive benefits follow even when both markets and states spill over the borders of economics and politics and begin to organize the moral rules associated with civil society. In the United States, increasing reliance on the moral rules of the market within families and communities has contributed to greater individual choice, especially for women, and has also broken patterns of racial segregation in local areas. In Scandinavia, few doubt that the intervention of the new welfare state into the family has not had positive results, especially again for women, but also to some degree for children and the elderly. Markets and states are inevitably associated with modernity, and few would take the moral risk of dismissing either outright.

Yet despite such advantages, there are, as I have argued throughout this book, ways in which neither the market nor the state has lived up to the promise of modernity. When markets and states increase in power at the expense of civil society between them, they create new moral dilemmas even while seeming to solve older ones. The position of present generations is strengthened at the expense of those before and after, either because of the market's emphasis on rational choice or because of the state's receptivity to interest-group politics. Ties between anonymous others expressed through voluntarism and charity can weaken, either because they are sacrificed to the market's emphasis on egoism or because of the state's assumption of impersonal responsibility. Finally, culture—understood as symbols and stories that give strangers a stake in what others do—tends to thin out, vulnerable to both the organization of cultural production by the market and the replacement of cultural ties by political ones that emphasize rights. When it comes to the difficult business of balancing obligations in the intimate sphere of society with those in the distant sphere, excessive reliance on either the market or the state is too much of a good thing.

There is a need in modern liberal democracies, no matter how committed they may be to either the market or the state (or both), to develop a third way of thinking about moral obligation. If the social sciences are moral theories in disguise, sociology lays claim to all those obligations that are inspired neither by a rational quest after self-interest nor by a fear of coercive external authority. Sociology, in short, has its own turf in the intellectual division of labor called the social sciences. Liberal democrats need a sociological approach to moral obligation to remind themselves of the fragility of the gift that makes them modern—of how they themselves, through the social practices they develop together with others, create the moral rules by which they will be governed and which give them, as a result, some sense of a personal stake in what happens to other people.

In spite of the need for a sociological approach to moral obligation, sociology has become the poor step-sibling of economics and politics in modern liberal democracies. Just as markets and states have become the primary ways in which modern liberal democrats organize their moral relations to one another, the social sciences associated with each—economics and political science—have become the dominant ways of thinking about modernity. When the two are combined, political economy, because it exists where the market and the state meet, appears to be the most realistic means for understanding both individual decisions and collective structures in modern society. Yet even political economy cannot explain everything there is to explain about modernity, including political and economic matters themselves.

Sociology's historical concern with trust, altruism, and empathy is, from the perspective of political economy, often considered naive, if not irrelevant. Yet all societies, no matter how tough-minded their institutions, operate successfully because some people trust others, because conformity tempers individualism, because some are willing to let others be free riders, and because not all people press their rights simultaneously. The secret of success for those political economies that work best often lies in neither politics nor economics.[1] In recent years, it has been recognized that countries with relatively low inflation and high productivity, such as Japan, Austria, and West Germany, receive economic benefits from the existence of strong social and cultural ties: loyalty to the firm, fewer accidents, and greater wage restraint, to name but a few. Such recognition puts a dent into theories premised on a simple choice between market and state. Group loyalty can be a more important factor in discouraging inflation or encouraging economic growth than new technologies or Keynesian macroeconomic policies.

In addition, in any modern society behavior will exist that cannot be explained either by models of rational self-interest or by enforced collective obligations. Even though the market now organizes more activities in civil society, people still agree to serve on committees, run for local office, watch other people's children, contribute lavishly to potluck dinners, clean up their neighborhoods, restrain their wage demands, honor one another, observe traditions, have and raise children, return books to libraries, share facilities, marry for love, serve on juries, refuse bribes, fasten their seat belts, let others pass on the highway, give to charities, donate blood, serve larger portions, tip strangers they never expect to see again, pay back debts, offer refuge, help friends, and volunteer for dirty and difficult jobs. Likewise, even though the welfare state now organizes many obligations to strangers collectively, some people still pay their taxes willingly, support volunteer efforts, rely on social networks, take care of their parents, and spend as much time with their children as they can. Civil society has certainly been trespassed upon by the market and the state, but it has not disappeared altogether.

Despite the continuing importance of areas clearly identifiable as sociological, recent attempts to understand modern liberal democracy—even those critical of the market and the state—have not recognized them. Charles Lindblom, for example, wrote a book called *Politics and Markets,* as if politics and markets were the only two choices we have; similarly, a book that attributes the success of Scandinavian social democracy to solidarity calls itself *Politics Against Markets,* as if solidarity were a totally political, and not also a social, concept.[2] In many ways more surprisingly, Albert

Hirschman's *Exit, Voice, and Loyalty,* one of the most genuinely inter-disciplinary books of recent years, is really concerned only with exit (the market's response to decline) and voice (the state's response); in later work, when Hirschman reflected on his book and the critical reaction to it, loyalty was dropped altogether.[3] Even Hirschman's work on shifting in-volvements, which charts how dissatisfaction with markets and states cre-ates cycles of increasing frustration in modern liberal democracies, does not address the possibility that those societies with a strong social code, one that is neither purely private nor purely public, manage to avoid the very cycles of disillusionment that Hirschman chronicles.[4]

Under the increasing hegemony of political economy, debates in the contemporary social sciences tend to emphasize either a rational-choice in-dividualism that conforms to the assumptions of the market or a struc-turalism that follows the assumptions of the state. As the work of numer-ous writers—Anthony Giddens, for example—has demonstrated, impor-tant matters are generally overlooked in this debate, no matter how fiercely it may rage.[5] Moreover, rational-choice assumptions and structuralist theo-ries are not as distinct as they may at first appear. Even the most rigorous advocates of pure rational egoism, such as Gary Becker, recognize the simi-larity of the market and social structure as regulatory mechanisms.[6] Like-wise, even a tradition like Marxism, which is generally viewed as struc-turalist, has affinities with theories of rational choice.[7] As many items, in short, are missing from the agenda of these debates as are included.

The recovery of sociology and its moral tradition is thus a necessary step if modern liberal democracies are to do a better job of managing their dis-contents. Sociology can offer to the moral complexity of modernity a dis-tinctive way of thinking about obligations to others. Markets and states have gotten people fairly far along the road to a better life, offering greater freedom on the one hand and a recognition of obligations to others on the other. But they have done so by taking real people living in specific social situations and removing them from the process by which morality is under-stood. It is the responsibility of a sociological approach to moral obliga-tion to put people back in.

Modernity or Morality?

It would be a mistake to believe that a sociological approach to moral obli-gation has been in decline in contemporary liberal democracies because the other social sciences, especially economics, have designs on its subject matter. On the contrary, rather than having been "colonized," sociology's problems stem from its own inability to decide exactly what its subject matter should be.

Many sociological theorists, especially in the classical period of the field's development, knew at least what their subject matter was *not*. For a writer like Durkheim, the sociological theorist most explicitly concerned with morality, both the market and the state were to be viewed with skepticism. The state, he wrote, "is too remote from individuals; its relation with them too external and intermittent to penetrate deeply into individual consciences and socialize them within. Where the state is the only environment in which men can live communal lives, they inevitably lose contact, become detached, and thus society disintegrates."[8] The market was even more alien to Durkheim's ideas about a moral social order. Unlike today's enthusiasts for the market, he put no value on the creation of wealth: "Too much wealth so easily becomes a source of immorality. Through the power wealth confers on us, it actually diminishes the power of things to oppose us." For Durkheim, economic and moral man were in opposition; utilitarianism and other defenses of the market were merely "apologies for a diseased state."[9] Markets cannot be trusted as a form of moral regulation in modern society, he wrote, because "the more one has, the more one wants. . . . To achieve any other result, the passions must first be limited. Only then can they be harmonized with the faculties and satisfied. But since the individual has no way of limiting them, this must be done by some force exterior to him."[10]

Yet for Durkheim, as well as for other thinkers in the sociological tradition such as Simmel or Mead, it was one thing to find markets and states wanting, but it was another thing entirely to find a satisfactory alternative. Civil society would seem to be the obvious choice, yet in putting forward civil society as a moral ideal, the sociological tradition immediately faced a difficult decision. On the one hand, if civil society was viewed as an organic community with strong social ties that were in the process of being destroyed by modernity, sociologists who accepted morality ran the risk of rejecting modernity. On the other hand, if they accepted large states and complex economies as the price to be paid for modernity, they ran the risk of rejecting morality. The sociological tradition was faced with a dilemma: both morality and modernity were important, yet each seemed to work at cross purposes to the other. To be modern was to be free from ties of community and tradition and to live instead with forms of regulation that were formal, specified, and impersonal, whereas to be moral was to live with common cultural values and strongly inscribed traditions that effectively denied democracy, individual self-development, and equality. In short, one could have either individual rights without binding moral codes or binding moral codes without individual rights.

The easiest response to such a dilemma was, of course, to choose one or the other. Ferdinand Tönnies knew what his choice would be. The moral order of *Gemeinschaft,* he wrote, "has its roots in family life and . . . its forms are in the main determined by the code of the folkways and mores," while under more modern conditions the moral order is "entirely a product and instrument of public opinion, which encompasses all relations arising out of contractual sociableness, contacts, and political intentions."[11] A moral sociology, therefore, led Tönnies to reject modernity in favor of traditional social bonds that expressed a more organic form of moral community. This way of thinking about morality has had some influence in sociology, including notably the urban sociology sparked by the University of Chicago in the 1920s. Yet extensive historical research has revealed that, in fact, a lost world of community was far from idyllic. In rejecting modernity, moreover, such a sociological approach to morality rejected as well the freedom and self-realization that come in modernity's wake.

This same difficulty faces contemporary thinkers who uphold the moral understandings of the past in the face of the changes wrought by modern economies and political systems.[12] Although it is true that the market has caused a weakening of the social bond, it is also true that the market represents progress over premarket forms of social organization that limit the capacity of individuals to realize their individual freedom. One can therefore defend the bourgeois family as the best protector of valuable moral rules, but only by adopting a certain skepticism toward one of modernity's most powerful and positive tendencies: the freedom of women to enter the larger world of economics and politics. (The best effort in presenting a justification of the bourgeois family that I know of, while wishing not to engage in "nostalgia or reactionary romanticism," still finds "destabilizing" the entry into the work force of women with small children.)[13] In a similar way, the modern state tends toward rules that are formalistic and bureaucratic, but it is also the most realistic protector of equality, as well as the primary line of defense against the market. Rejection of the state as a moral agent, consequently, especially the modern welfare state, carries with it the rejection of important social gains won only through struggle.

Most contemporary sociologists, it must be said, have recognized the dangers of such antimodern inclinations: Tönnies has inspired far fewer followers than Marx or Weber, both of whom sometimes expressed long-ings for a lost moral world but each of whom, in different ways, made their peace with modernizing tendencies. I therefore have little more to say about theorists who took this course, other than to repeat that my dis-agreements with them are essentially political—that is, I would seek to preserve, and then to improve on, the gains in freedom and collective obli-gation brought about by reliance on markets and states. Yet even as we recognize such gains, we must also be wary of the other direction, which in fact has plagued contemporary sociological theory more than *Gemein-schaft* longings. Because markets and states are the primary ways by which modern liberal democrats understand their obligations to one another, if sociology welcomes modernity uncritically, it risks sublimating a specifi-cally sociological understanding of moral obligation into either the as-sumptions of methodological individualism associated with the market or structuralism associated with the state.

Caught between its longing for a premodern form of organic commu-nity and its jealousy of the other social sciences, especially economics, which seem so rigorous and self-assured, sociology, despite its origins in moral theory and philosophy, has failed to develop as an adequate moral science. It is difficult to measure precisely the impact that social-scientific theories such as those of the Chicago school of economics or of the politi-cal philosophy of John Rawls have on the way individuals make their everyday decisions (academics often being given to exaggerating their in-fluence). Yet this much can be said: when individuals, uncomfortable with moral decisions rooted in either self-interest or enforced obligations, look to the social sciences (or to popularizations of their theories) for answers, they find something of a vacuum where sociology ought to be. Sociology, it would seem, has not lived up to the moral inspiration of its founders.[14]

Three Sociologists in Search of Society

There is not much society left in sociology, especially not in America. By clearly choosing modernity over morality, the great bulk of American socio-logical theorists since the 1930s have had to borrow, and ultimately shape their work by, models of moral obligation taken from the other social sci-ences, especially economics and political science. Three recent theorists who best illustrate this development are Peter Blau, who collapses sociology into economics; Morris Janowitz, who blends it into political science; and Talcott Parsons, who, in trying to protect the social, redefined it in a way that stripped it of its morally binding power, and consequently adopted, toward the end of his life, the political approach he once rejected.

Peter Blau's *Exchange and Power in Social Life* is one major contemporary attempt to use the insights of economics to shed light on social dynamics.[15] Although Blau himself has largely abandoned the effort, his book still stands as the best illustration of the advantages and disadvantages of an "economic" approach to society.[16] As such, it is invaluable as an exercise in moral philosophy, for it illustrates the difficulties of basing claims for moral social obligation on a theory of individual motivation.

For all its use of economic theory, Blau's book most resembles seventeenth- and eighteenth-century tracts on moral philosophy: it is a sort of *Poor Richard's Almanac* of contemporary sociology. The maxim that "men are anxious to receive social approval for their decisions and actions, for their opinions and suggestions," for example, is Blau's, not Benjamin Franklin's or Samuel Johnson's.[17] Throughout Blau's book run somewhat cynical quotations from Adam Smith's *Theory of Moral Sentiments,* La Rochefoucauld's *Maxims,* and works by Mandeville, Machiavelli, and de Jouvenel, as if these, and not George Homans or contemporary psychology, were its true inspiration. In *Exchange and Power in Social Life* we have a guide to the morally perplexed, a treatise on how people *should* interact with others, not just how they *do*. Unlike Adam Smith and other eighteenth-century moralists, however, the specific courses of action that Blau urges people to take are rooted, not in civil society, but in mass society.

Blau insists at many points in his book that his theory of social exchange is different from economics. In economic exchange people are contractually engaged to reciprocate, he notes, while in social exchange their obligations to one another are "unspecified." For this reason, Blau argues, social exchange breeds trust and so makes society possible. This slow building of trust uses "the self-interest of individuals to produce a differentiated social structure within which norms tend to develop that require individuals to set aside some of their personal interests for the sake of those of the collectivity."[18] It is clear that Blau's ideas about trust are quite different from those of the early political economists, such as Adam Smith. Smith, as I argued in Chapter 1, believed that exchange motivated purely by considerations of self-interest, no matter how appropriate it might be for economics, was inappropriate to sustain the moral relationships of civil society, because it lacked sympathy. Blau, in contrast, sees the entire social order as being no more than a by-product, a function, if you will, of self-interest.

Adam Smith argued that morality was guaranteed by an impartial spectator—a minimal morality, to be sure, but one requiring that at least one person does not act out of self-interest. Blau, however, cannot even establish a minimal Archimedean point for moral action, since everyone is motivated by the same self-interested decisional calculus as everyone else. No wonder, then, that in Blau's theory morality, like everything else, is valued not for itself, but for the functions it performs in society. Morality facilitates exchange:

> By adhering to . . . moral principles, individuals establish a good reputation, which stands them in good stead in subsequent social interaction. A good reputation in the community is like a high credit rating—for a respectable parent or a girl who is highly thought of as well as for a trustworthy businessman—which enables a person to obtain benefits that are not available to others. Conformity frequently entails sacrificing rewards that could be attained through direct exchange, but it brings other rewards indirectly.[19]

When morality is seen as something to be hoarded for future investment potential, its ability to regulate our passions so that we can contribute positively to society instead of only to ourselves is undermined. Not surprisingly, therefore, Blau's theory of moral obligation shares much more with Chicago school economic theorists than it does with Adam Smith. When Blau says that "men make charitable donations, not to earn the gratitude of the recipients, whom they never see, but to earn the approval of their peers who participate in the philanthropic campaign," he sounds like Gary Becker talking about the costs and benefits of investing in altruism. And just as the Chicago school theorists share many points of agreement with Marxism, Blau, like contemporary Marxists, argues that behind any action one will always find a hidden interest. "By assuming the moral obligation to be charitable to the poor, the upper class establishes a claim to moral righteousness and superiority, which ideologically justifies and fortifies its superior social status and power."[20]

Given these aspects of Blau's theory, it is not at first clear just what makes the social order possible. It cannot come from trust, since we trust one another only to the degree that our own interest is served; Blau specifically rejects the notion of a norm of reciprocity associated with Alvin Gouldner.[21] Nor can it come from a personal sense of moral obligation, since morality facilitates exchange rather than the other way around. It must, however, come from somewhere, and in Blau's theory it comes ultimately from a form of social conformity very characteristic of the 1950s.

Blau expects that shame, fear of disapproval, and a general inability on the part of weak individuals to resist mass social pressure will regulate people's social exchanges: "Social consensus defines beliefs as right or wrong. Although it is possible for men to maintain convictions in the face of contrary public opinion, it is most difficult to do so; and the more at odds a man's beliefs are with prevailing values, the more important it is for him to receive some social support to sustain them."[22] The pervasive fear of mass society that runs through social thought from Tocqueville to Ortega is here welcomed. A tyranny of the majority can be relied on to provide the basis for a moral order.

What gives Blau's understanding of moral obligation its particular tone is that fear of being different which was so characteristic of the Eisenhower years. Many of Blau's examples of social exchange, for example, concern dating, certainly an arena of some popular concern in the 1950s. But the example that best illustrates the role mass society plays in Blau's moral theory poses you as someone who has many times accepted favors from a neighbor and is then asked by that neighbor to lend him some tools. If you say no, it becomes more difficult for you ever to ask that neighbor for another favor. Furthermore, the neighbor will be reluctant to cooperate with you in the future. He may even tell others in the community about your moral failure, causing others to think less of you and you to feel extremely guilty. For all these reasons, you will be better off discharging your social obligation and responding to the request for a favor; the social disapproval that would follow from not doing so clearly costs more than the time and effort it would cost you to lend the neighbor the tools.[23] As this example illustrates, a world composed of sovereign calculating individuals turns out to be a world in which everyone is afraid of the disapproval of those around them.

Whether neighbors approved or disapproved of the individual choices of each other was more than a passing issue in the 1950s because of McCarthyism. Suppose that the rewards of interacting with your neighbor were plentiful: lively conversation, reciprocal exchange of favors, perhaps even sexual attraction. Then you discover that your neighbor wants you to sign a petition opposing Jim Crow laws in the South. What should you do? As a guide to a morally perplexing time, Blau's book offers some advice: find out if your neighbor is a real communist or only a person with progressive views.

The progressive neighbor is a man with whom one can discuss politics and whose opinions on various issues carry some weight. One is inclined to grant some of his points in the expectation that he will reciprocate and make concessions too. If his viewpoint is somewhat more extreme and less flexible, however, he is defined as a Red, and his arguments no longer have to be taken seriously, which averts the necessity of continually having to defend one's opinions against fundamental criticisms. When a person's social values put his beyond the pale, there is no basis for the give and take of debate.[24]

Mass society enters Blau's analysis through the shift to the passive voice ("he is defined as a Red"). Since social conformity defines the situation, the individual is relieved of moral responsibility for his or her actions. Suddenly, instead of individual calculation, society imposes itself, enforcing its own brand of constraint. But since Blau's theory is premised on psychological individualism, nothing in it can resist social intervention. As was the case with public-choice liberalism or the idea of the market discussed in previous chapters, an emphasis on individualism collapses into a defense of more coercive moral codes—in this case, social conformity rather than a strong state. Without a specific sociological approach to moral obligation, in short, a theory premised on methodological individualism winds up either with no collective authority at all or with collective authority so pervasive that no individualism remains.

The same kind of problem, if from a different direction, characterizes the theories of sociologists like Morris Janowitz, who substitute for a sociological approach to moral regulation notions emphasizing governmental authority. Despite his affiliation with the University of Chicago, Janowitz gives no credence to neoclassical economic theories, or to any sociological or political analysis based on their assumptions of rational choice. "Narrow economic self-interest," he has written, "does not account for the positive role citizenship played in the development of democratic political institutions and practices. Citizenship rests on some elements of group obligation." Janowitz, unlike Blau, is not only directly in the Durkheimian tradition of *Moral Education,* but his ideas about social control are also quite similar to eighteenth-century notions of civil society. Janowitz is an explicit moralist whose concern is with civic obligations, which he defines as "the contributions and sacrifices a citizen makes to keep the political system effective."[25] Janowitz has devoted the great bulk of his writing to furthering people's sense of moral obligation to the larger political structures in which they live.

There was a time, Janowitz argues, when moral duty was expressed through the idea of social control. Here social control does not mean, as it does in Blau, mass society imposing its will on the individual through legal or social coercion. Instead Janowitz—quite in the manner of Smith, Hume, and Ferguson—argues that the social sciences in general, and sociology in

particular, were organized around the notion that society was made possible when people regulated their own moral conduct through their interaction with others.[26] In his magnum opus, *The Last Half Century,* Janowitz
provides us with an invaluable intellectual history of a notion of social control that runs through all the social sciences, even economics. (Frank
Knight, for example, an originator of the Chicago school of economics,
combined a belief in the market with notions of self-restraint, according to
Janowitz, in sharp contrast to his contemporary intellectual heirs.)[27] Specifically, in this book Janowitz argues that during the past fifty years a series of interrelated developments have weakened the sense of moral obligation felt in Western societies, especially in the United States.

The breakdown of the kind of voluntary social control we associate
with civil society is, Janowitz contends, due to a number of factors. Primary group relations were undermined by bureaucratic intervention. Industrial relations relied too much on the conflicting self-interest of unions
and managers. Residential patterns dispersed local networks. A heavy emphasis on advertising and its resultant hedonism, combined with a tendency on the part of the news media to take an adversarial attitude toward
established authority, weakened discipline and obedience. The Supreme
Court paid too much attention to rights, too little to obligations. Schools
no longer taught civic obligation but emphasized value relativism. Nuclear
weapons undermined the need for mass armies with their need to teach
loyalty and discipline.[28] And even the welfare state confused people's ability to make moral choices, substituting notions of immediate gratification
for ties of personal loyalty.[29] Janowitz is anything but a liberal in economics or politics; the moral world of liberal individualism is, in his view (and,
as is probably obvious, in mine as well), seriously out of balance.

Janowitz's generally gloomy assessment poses one main question: what
can be done about the decline of a moral notion of social control? One
would think that if strongly inscribed codes of moral behavior did once
exist, compelling people to accept legitimate authority and discipline, the
best solution to the decline of social control would be to encourage people
to redevelop those codes. But it is apparently too late for civil society to
ever again play a role in strengthening the moral order. Having rejected
the *Gemeinschaft-Gesellschaft* distinction as oversimplified, Janowitz makes
it clear that he does not want to throw out the moral codes of modern
society, especially ones like the trend toward strong government. Here
again he resembles closely the Durkheim of *Moral Education.* For just as
Durkheim, for all his opposition to the state, wound up writing in defense

of the nation, albeit a very abstract and universal one,[30] Janowitz resolves his ambivalence and turns to the nation-state, but this time a very real and authoritative one, as his solution to moral decay. Janowitz does not trust modern people to find the source of social control in their voluntary interactions with others. Government will have to do it for them. Whereas Blau collapses problems of moral obligation into the market, Janowitz elevates them into the state.

Two examples can illustrate why Janowitz does not trust people to develop the internal social control they once, in his view, possessed. One has to do with crime. Janowitz argues, again from a Durkheimian perspective, that "criminality . . . is a direct measure of the moral climate of a society." In America, a combination of rising crime rates and efforts on the part of legal theorists and judges to redefine criminality has led to a "decline of the legitimacy of coercive sanctions," which in turn immediately raises the question of how society can reestablish moral order. To the degree that he provides an answer, Janowitz endorses (even if reluctantly) governmental authority. He reminds the reader that "the threat and use of force in the past have been essential for achieving social and political 'progress.'" Legitimate coercion, he feels, is necessary, but it can have unanticipated consequences. Realizing that the direction of his analysis is pushing him toward a defense of state power, however, he backtracks and calls the intellectual problems involved "baffling."[31]

A similar reluctance to rely on individual self-control, which forces him again to a defense of the state's authority, characterizes Janowitz's discussion of military obligation. Unlike Milton Friedman and other members of the Chicago school of economics, Janowitz is opposed to the idea of using economic incentives to attract an army. Because for him "the strongest test of citizen obligation is performance of military service in defense of the nation state," the decline of conscription that followed both from the aftershocks of Vietnam and from a general reliance on strategic theories of deterrence has serious negative consequences for social control. Janowitz hopes to correct the balance between rights and obligations, but he does not accordingly conclude that appeals to patriotism will bring about a sense of civic obligation. "A single-minded program of increasing civic education to reenforce patriotism is of little import," he writes; indeed, in his view "there can be no reconstruction of patriotism without a system of national service."[32] Because, no matter how constructed, some system of compulsory national service would involve governmental coercion, Janowitz, even while recognizing the complexity of the problems involved, is forced once again to rely on a political institution, not internal social control, to compel a morality that no longer exists.

The modern world, it would seem, has simply become too hedonistic and pleasure-seeking for Janowitz's taste, but, lost as we are, he cannot recommend that we find the correct and righteous path within ourselves. We instead need the discipline that only strong authority can impose on us to override our failure to perceive what it is in our long-term best interest. Janowitz, who describes himself politically as a social democrat, writes with an almost hopeless air of resignation: "My intellectual approach reflects the traditions of realism in political sociology in which I have been immersed for a lifetime and from which I cannot escape." [33] Such sociological realism leaves no place for the notion (also primarily associated with the University of Chicago Department of Sociology) that people create their own social realities, including the moral rules that bind them. Morris Janowitz—who, along with Edward Shils, is the most direct inheritor of the theory of civil society as it came from Europe to Chicago—is no longer willing to assign that theory much importance.

It is unfortunate that Janowitz is reluctant to rely on civil society as a source of moral regulation alternative to both the state and the market. For if morality is to come from the social activity of individuals, it can work only (at least in modern societies emphasizing self-development) if people are given a certain freedom to explore alternative avenues of moral growth. This Janowitz is unwilling to do. His notion of a strict and unforgiving morality leads him to condemn political and social movements—such as the women's movement or minorities' efforts to explore their heritage—as contributing to the breakdown of moral order. In his discussion of civic values in education, for example, he condemns efforts by educators to introduce realism into textbooks, describes the Vietnam generation as characterized by a "weakened sense of citizen obligation," expresses his dismay at black separatism, and writes of Mexican-Americans that they "are not likely to be profoundly influenced by an American type of civic education," preferring instead "the communalism of Mexico." [34] These are, to say the least, highly debatable propositions. Unable to recognize that these claims are moral ones (thereby raising the issue of whether society is willing to negotiate new standards of morality in cooperation with those that chafe under older definitions), Janowitz concludes by welcoming the centralization of authority characteristic of modernity while refusing to accept the notion of individual and group moral development that often comes with it. The result is not so much to reestablish a balance between rights and obligations so much as to ask for public quiescence so that the state can once again establish the conditions of moral order.

In collapsing a sociological approach to moral obligation into a political one, Janowitz flirts with a neo-Hobbesian defense of political authority that brings him close to some of the thinkers, like Lawrence Mead, discussed in Chapter 4. Yet sociology has often distinguished itself from political science by its *non*-Hobbesian roots. Talcott Parsons, for example, elevated a critique of the Hobbesian conception of social order to make it into a defining principle of contemporary sociological theory. Parsons takes the realm of society more seriously than either Blau or Janowitz, but when all is said and done even he, like them, is caught between individual voluntarism and governmental constraint, unable to locate society in his sociology.

Between the Great Depression and the rapid economic growth and social mobility of the late 1950s and early 1960s, America experienced a dizzying succession of changes, not only in its internal character but also in its relationship to the rest of the world. Americans' precrash notions of moral obligation—emphasizing voluntarism, localism, personal contact, family and kinship solidarity, and trust—were, in the course of economic and political centralization, rendered irrelevant. It was this sense of a moral crisis, described, for example, in the *Middletown* books of Helen and Robert Lynd, that gave Talcott Parsons a sense of mission for his sociology. Parsons, more than any other American sociologist, was caught up in explaining, in his own way, the dramatic passage from a world in which civil society played an important role to one in which states and markets came to dominate social life. One of his goals was to clarify for other social scientists how Americans, now increasingly normless, should act in the face of unprecedented social transformations.[35]

Parsons's search was for a specifically sociological theory, one that could not be reduced to psychological or cultural premises. The task of the social theorist, he said, is to find the "transformation formula" by which the need dispositions of the individual and the role expectations of the social structure can be reconciled.[36] Parsons rejected the idea, so central to marketplace theories, that there is no morality standing above and regulating the process of exchange. But he also rejected the cultural-anthropological idea that morality is a strict code which shapes individual motivations. Parsons looked for a morality more demanding than individualistic utilitarianism yet not as strict as Durkheimian solidarity. The key concepts of his theory, from the notion of action to the idea of pattern variables, follow from this quest.

Parsons identifies three kinds of evaluative action: instrumental, expressive, and moral. How do we know when to act morally rather than expressively or instrumentally? If we can act morally under certain conditions and instrumentally under others, why would anyone choose to act in a non-self-interested way? Parsons addresses such questions of moral theory as these through the concept of role performance. If we act in a role that values affectivity over affective neutrality, for example, the criteria we use to evaluate our moral obligations to others will differ (in the one case by responding as if other people were kin, in the other as if they were clients). If we act in a role that prefers collectivity-orientation to self-orientation, we know when self-interest must give way to solidaristic norms. The catalogue of pattern variables in Parsons's scheme represents a plurality of moral roles, each one taking moral obligation away from *both* individual choice and social constraint and giving it instead to the role.

This notion of a plurality of roles constitutes a moral theory of morality, a theory of why we act morally in some circumstances and not in others. Because moral standards are "standards in terms of which more particular evaluations are themselves evaluated," Parsons's early work was extremely relevant to a time when the old moral codes of localism and personal responsibility had broken down, but new ones—either of an unrestricted market or of a fully functioning welfare state—had not yet been established.[37] In this context it made sense to inscribe moral codes onto roles rather than individual or collective norms. For an insecure people, a role-specific morality relieved enormous sources of anxiety. Thus a professional could distance himself from his idealistic youth (choosing affective neutrality over affectivity), identify with cosmopolitan horizons (universalism over particularism), congratulate himself for his social mobility (achievement versus ascription), specialize (specificity over diffuseness), and yet all the while claim that he was not seeking personal gain (collectivity-orientation over self-orientation).

If the social structure is built on roles and institutions and not the other way round, what stands above the roles to insure that they can continue to "bind in" people's actions? Surprisingly, for a theorist so concerned with integration and consensus, Parsons has no satisfactory answer to this question. Reluctant as he was to draw on cultural definitions of moral conduct, he never assigned to the social system as a whole a goal or objective, having reserved that for the roles that compose it. Thus, if the pattern variables change, so do the moral codes associated with them, leaving no compelling reason why anyone should be bound by them. In this vein, Parsons saw modern medical practice as an "excellent opportunity to illustrate some of the interrelations of the principal elements of the social system which have been reviewed in more abstract terms."[38] Yet it is also an appropriate illustration of how his theory fails to explain why the morality associated with role performance should be binding, either on those who occupy the roles or on those whose behavior is to be sanctioned by them, when roles are in the process of change.

Medical practice was an area in which Americans were experiencing rapid changes in the years that Parsons wrote. The image of the country doctor who knows the personal history not only of his patients but also of their parents and children was being replaced by the anonymous "delivery" of health care as a "service." Neither patients nor doctors knew what their moral obligations were in this rapidly changing environment; both, to use Parsons's term, were undergoing "strain." Patients, Parsons tells us, were irrational. They did not use reason to evaluate their doctors but merely assumed that the local physician must be the best. They were laymen, incapable of understanding their own illnesses, let alone the financial and emotional stress that sickness often entails. Scientific medicine—all that is modern in health care—could prolong their lives and was a course that they rationally ought to choose, but their superstition, localism, and personal loyalty often prevented them from seeing what was clearly in their own best interest. Doctors were in a moral bind as well. They were idealists who believed that they could help people, but often there was little they could actually do. They invaded their patients' bodies, psyches, and balance sheets, yet they also needed distance from the emotional desires of the grateful recipients of their care. With every party to the modern medical relationship caught between competing moral codes, the whole system would seem unable to function. That it did at all is due to the moral rules inscribed in the roles that both patient and physician were called on to perform.

All six of the pattern variables that define the professional come to the aid of the confused and uncertain individuals caught in the intricacies of the modern doctor-patient relationship. Specialization gives the doctor expertise and the patient a reason for suppressing his or her own lay suspicions. Collectivity-orientation assures the patient that the doctor is not following the call of profit; thus the patient is more likely to believe what the doctor says. Affective neutrality rationalizes the doctor's brisk manner and need to pry, legitimating to the patient behavior that might otherwise seem immoral. All of this (and the three pattern variables not discussed here) creates trust, "the belief that the physician is trying his best to help the patient and that conversely the patient is 'cooperating' with him to the best of his ability."[39]

Thus, in something of a roundabout way, we come to the concept at the heart of a theory of civil society, that of trust. "Trust," Allan Silver has written, "is among the most recurrent themes in liberal thought."[40] Without trust, there can only be the Chicago school of economics or state intervention into civil society. Trust softens market relations—which is one reason why Adam Smith assigned it such importance in *The Theory of Moral Sentiments*. At the same time, trust dilutes the impact of Hobbesian authority: to the degree that people trust their leaders, the state has legitimacy and need not rely on force—which is why so much of liberal political theory has relied on sociology. For anyone attempting, as was Parsons, to develop an alternative to both the market and the state, trust can be expected to play a crucial role.[41] If doctor and patient do not trust each other, they would appear to have two ways to keep their relationship alive: one is to reduce it to a cash basis so that there is no mystification or emotional double-cross; the other is to have the state regulate it. In either case, trust would be sublimated out of civil society, into either politics or economics. Parsons hoped to avoid this sublimation by locating the moral basis of trust in the roles that the actors perform. But what if the roles change?

It is widely recognized that many of the features of Parsons's chapter on modern medical practice are time-bound. Because the professional role of doctors is defined by a collectivity-orientation, he argued, it is wrong for patients and doctors to "shop around." We now call that getting a second opinion, a practice that today is highly recommended. Yet in Parsons's scheme, a second opinion would be constituted as a violation of the patient's trust in the first doctor's opinion. Similarly, not only is there now generally believed to be a profit motive in medical care, but many policy proposals for health insurance rely on the profit motive as a form of regulation. Affective neutrality is hardly necessary to convince patients to undress in the doctor's office, as Parsons suggested; changing social definitions of nudity take care of that. The professional role of doctor (and the subservient role of patient) have changed enormously since Parsons wrote. And if roles change, morality must change too. But since Parsons inscribed trust onto roles that no longer exist, there is no independent basis for trust in his analysis. With the collapse of the consensus around which doctors and patients structured their obligations, people have no choice but to resort to monetized or authoritative regulations. For all the structural density of Parsons's scheme, it is ultimately based on an extremely fragile alternative to the state and the market: one little wind of change, and the whole thing crumbles.

Without a compelling reason to explain why voluntaristic action should lead to binding moral obligations, Parsons opts for sentiments not unlike the social conformity on which Peter Blau relied:

Attachment to common values means, motivationally considered, that the actors have common "sentiments" in support of the value patterns, which may be defined as meaning that conformity with the relevant expectations is treated as a "good thing" relatively independently of any specific instrumental "advantage" to be gained from such conformity, e.g., in the avoidance of negative sanctions.[42]

In this respect, Parsons sounds like all liberal theorists: an emphasis on voluntaristic individualism seems to lead directly to amoral selfishness and so is bound by an external, and rather authoritarian, checkpoint, in this case social pressures. (In Chapter 4 I tried to show how John Rawls, though he starts from completely different premises, joins Parsons in asserting the importance of a "morality of association," before he moves on to a "morality of principle.")

Parsons displayed a significant shift in emphasis in the years after World War II. As William Buxton shows, the McCarthy crisis and the challenge of the cold war led to "the politicization of Parsons"—namely, an effort to make his political sociology far more explicit than it had been in the theory of action and social structure.[43] Especially in his critical review of C. Wright Mills and his examination of voting behavior, Parsons began to focus on the polity as the subsystem most explicitly concerned with the task of binding. Power, he wrote, "involves a special problem of the *integration* of the system, including the binding of its units, individual and collective, to the necessary commitments."[44] While Parsons remained at all times a pluralist, his effort to locate a specific realm for the polity in his theoretical scheme was a clear outgrowth of his earlier failure to specify why obligations, in a voluntaristic formula, should ever be binding. In defining the polity as "the aspect of action concerned with the function of the collective pursuit of collective goals," he acknowledged that in reality the polity was not one subsystem equivalent to others (such as the economy) but, because modern societies were organized collectively, one that increasingly stood above the others, incorporating them within its role requirements.[45]

The whole point of Parsons's theoretical scheme was to develop an alternative to the automatic regulation of the market and the authoritarian potential of the state. This he failed to do. Parsons's specifically socio-logical conceptions of obligation, rooted in roles that were above the indi-vidual but below the state, were simultaneously too weak to encourage the individual to adhere to them and too strong to ground feelings of soli-darity and loyalty in voluntaristic action. A theory that began explicitly as a way to avoid the problems inherent in pure individualism and pure collec-tivism, because of its failure to anchor morality either in individual moral choices or in cultural patterns of constraint, reproduced the unsatisfactory treatment of moral obligations contained in both.

Sociological Ambivalence

Despite the collapse of the Parsonian consensus in the late 1960s and 1970s, contemporary sociological theorizing has been unable to go beyond the limits of thinkers like Blau, Janowitz, and Parsons. The "economic ap-proach" to sociology developed (and abandoned) by Peter Blau has en-joyed a substantial revival in contemporary sociology owing to the attrac-tiveness of rational-choice theory. Not only have economists of the Chicago school variety written about noneconomic areas within civil society such as the family, but sociologists too have begun to use rational choice theory to explore such quintessentially sociological themes as the nature of group loyalty and the problem of cooperation.[46] At the other end of the spec-trum, the political sociology of Morris Janowitz and the post–World War II Talcott Parsons has also enjoyed a rebirth. Efforts have been made to re-cover Parsonian structural-functionalism, albeit with important modifica-tions in the determinism of the Parsonian scheme, while the revival of neo-Marxist and neo-Weberian scholarship has led to a greater focus on the state in contemporary sociological theory.[47] In the absence of a theory of society, in other words, contemporary sociology is becoming political economy under another name. Despite recent forays into the classical moral tradition of sociology, the bulk of work done in the field is as far from the Durkheimian attempt to develop a distinctive moral science as ever.[48]

There is something ironic about sociology borrowing its subject matter from its sister social sciences. The attraction of an economic or political approach for sociology is the avoidance of having to look backward to an allegedly more moral community. Yet so doing is not all that different, in one important respect, from the direction taken by romantics like Tön-nies. According to those who choose morality over modernity, society is too good for the modern world; as a result, a specifically sociological understanding of moral obligation plays little part in understanding how it functions. Yet if sociological theorists choose modernity over morality, as do Blau, Janowitz, Parsons and their more contemporary followers, they borrow so much of their moral vision from either the individualism of the economic approach or the collective enforcement of obligations of the political approach that sociology becomes a minor branch of other major fields. Both the acceptance and the rejection of modernity lead sociology toward its own abolition. Sociology without society will be the fate of any attempt to formulate an approach toward moral regulation that without reservation either rejects or accepts both the market and the state.

One could, of course, view the gradual disappearance of a specifically sociological approach to moral obligation as a good thing. After all, what has been taking place in the social sciences is a genuinely interdisciplinary movement. The creative energy of much of contemporary social-scientific research lies in what Albert Hirschman calls "trespassing," an art at which Hirschman himself is a master. Subject matter no longer counts for much in identifying any individual social science discipline, for each has become more concerned with the purview of what used to be thought of as the others' proper domain. Nor is technique the primary differentiation, since increasingly the formal rigor of economics has drawn all the social sciences. What began in the eighteenth century as a unified endeavor may again become one in the twenty-first.

There are obvious benefits to this intermingling of the social sciences, yet from a moral, as opposed to a scientific, point of view something will be lost if sociology drops its search for a distinctive approach to the problem of moral regulation. Modern liberal democracy needs a way of thinking about moral obligations that expresses the same ambivalence about modernity that modern liberal democrats so often feel. What Robert Merton, in a different context, has called "sociological ambivalence" should be the defining characteristic of a sociological approach to moral obligation.[49] Unlike romantic, nostalgic longings for an earlier time, sociology ought to accept modernity and, with it, markets and states. But sociology ought also to accept them critically, by pointing out their limits and reminding people of the assumptions on which they are premised—something the theorists discussed in this chapter did not do.

It is important that this same ambivalence toward markets and states be carried over into an ambivalence toward civil society. Civil society should not be viewed, as it is by those who reject modernity, as a moral paradise of

the past. But neither should it be rejected out of hand in favor of rational choice on the one hand or the determining power of large-scale collective structures on the other. Civil society is indeed vulnerable to both the
state and the market, as I have argued to this point. But that means neither
that its disappearance is inevitable nor that it will be protected automatically and passively. It is possible for social ties to complement, and even
strengthen, the ties of the economic and political system, but only—as I
will argue in the remaining chapters—if people develop their own capacity
as moral agents and work actively and deliberately at protecting what is
social about themselves. Understood in this way, civil society is the proper
subject matter of sociology, but civil society viewed as the process by
which individuals construct together with others the social meanings
through which they interpret reality—including the reality of moral obligation itself.

Sociology, by retaining an ambivalence toward modernity, will possess
a distinctive temperament or style. Each of the social sciences has, in fact, a
style. What Donald McClosky has argued for economics—that it is a specific form of rhetoric—is also true of political science and sociology.[50] The
modern economic temperament, especially in the Chicago school of economics, is spunky, irreverent, and brash. Convinced that they have discovered the dirty little secret of modern society, the ubiquity of self-interest
behind the respectable bourgeois cloak of do-goodish rhetoric, Chicago
school theorists approach their subject avidly. Enthusiastic in their task,
respectful of one another's work, and distrustful of their antagonists in this
struggle for moral souls, their temperament is lodgelike in its ritualism and
bonding patterns. It is a distinctively New World tone, *arriviste* and impa-
tient, distrustful of settled customs, raw. Chicago—the natural location for
writers like Theodore Dreiser who also worked to strip the politeness
from bourgeois conventionality—is the perfect home for a temperament
so vigorous yet so lacking in nuance and irony.

In contrast, much of the defense of the state that one finds in the political approach to moral obligation, especially in the writings of Morris Janowitz, Samuel Huntington, and Lawrence Mead, is characterized by a tragic
vision of society. Its temperament is essentially puritanical, holding out a
vision of redemption in which people are expected to take responsibility
for their own actions but where it is recognized that, in the world we (un-
fortunately) live in, only discipline and authority can keep society functioning. High-minded, serious, worried—the distinctive temperament of
the political approach to moral regulation is as Bostonian (and therefore

Jamesian) as the economic is Midwestern (and therefore Dreiserian). Its temperament is reflective of a WASP elite in decline, a touch of noblesse oblige matched by a tinge of resentment that those who ought to be grateful for the elite's advice are not paying any attention.

The temperament of contemporary sociology, in contrast to both these approaches, ought to be marked by respect for ambiguity and a willingness to live with paradox. Sociology should be the liminal science, concerned as much with the outcasts of society as with either the older aristocracy or the newly rich. Its sense of the moral order ought therefore to be fluid, unlike the political approach, but not so fluid that, like the economic approach, it will be generally unable to locate institutions. Sociology should be less high-minded and serious than the political approach, reminding us that morality is not so strict and unforgiving that it stands ready to condemn all who do not meet its strictures. But it should also be far more morally conscious than the economic approach, reminding us that the individualism and freedom that markets give us carry with them a responsibility to be aware of the effects our actions have on others. The concerns of sociology should be with feelings and emotions rather than instincts and preferences (in this sense, it is not surprising that two of the most important works in contemporary sociology use the word *heart* in their titles).[51] Tending more to the literary and cultural than to the scientific and analytical, sociology has a style that emphasizes the expressive rather than the utilitarian strand of American culture—Ginsberg and Didion, these are its appropriate literary cousins. In short, the sociological temperament is neither Bostonian nor Midwestern; its essence, and much of its best work, is inspired by California and by the underside of New York.

Ambivalent toward its subject matter and ambiguous in its style, sociology would be best off retaining a certain awkwardness in its political perspective as well. Classical sociology was unsure of its political heritage, counting among its founders radicals like Marx as well as conservatives like Tocqueville. It is difficult to classify the politics of most of the major thinkers in the sociological tradition. Was Durkheim a conservative, a liberal, or even a radical?[52] Was Tönnies a reactionary or a reformer? Were Simmel and Weber apologists for capitalism, as Georg Lukács once argued, or among its foremost critics?[53] Sociology began as a debate between conservatives and radicals; it ignored, as best it could, most of the political positions in between.

In contemporary political debates, states and markets play the dominant role, with those who support the market on the right and those who support the state generally on the left. (There are occasions, as I will argue in the following chapters, where these positions reverse themselves.) By accepting and rejecting modernity simultaneously, contemporary sociology ought to be neither a form of the pure liberalism associated with the Chicago school of economics nor a form of the statism that many kinds of Marxism—from orthodox Leninism to orthodox Social Democracy—espouse. Between one approach that fails to recognize that what others do is my business and another that makes it my business without my having a say, it is not hard to conclude that in moral matters, neither those who call themselves conservative nor those who call themselves leftist have a way of balancing obligations both to the self and to others. Conservatives recognize obligations but distrust people; radicals identify with the people but rarely talk about moral obligation. Sociology, in this context, ought to be neither radical nor conservative, but both simultaneously. Politically speaking, sociology is essentially a dialogue between those on the right who distrust the market and those on the left who distrust the state. Its best practitioners today—like its best practitioners when it began—are those (including Daniel Bell, Alain Touraine, Robert Bellah, and Jürgen Habermas on my own personal list) who are difficult to pinpoint politically.

Sociology should be ambivalent as well about its methodology. Like the other social sciences, it cannot ignore the importance of empirical data and the power to prove a point through statistical analysis. But the rigorous models and abstract reasoning characteristic of the economic approach, and which are becoming increasingly popular in political science too, are inappropriate for an approach to moral obligation that would make real-life experience central to its understanding, simply because they have little to do with most real-life situations. There are other ways to avoid pure subjectivity than by using algebra. More concerned than the other social sciences with the passing of time, for example, sociology ought to place greater emphasis on history. More concerned with ties of culture that link the fates of strangers, it ought to rely on narrative and interpretative skills as well. Sociology should be the one approach to moral obligation where straight lines, perfect logic, mathematical proofs, and unambiguous results count less. Its methodology should be concerned with reminding everyone that behind every number stands a person.

Sociology, in conclusion, ought to be the guilty conscience of economics and politics, the one approach to moral regulation whose main message is that being modern imposes obligations on us as social beings, even as the other moral codes that contribute to our modernity tell us otherwise.

Sociology and society should be just a bit out of kilter, simultaneously old-fashioned and radical, behind and ahead, above and below. The task of sociology is not to make the engine of modernity run better but to complain about the cost of the fuel.

Given the paradoxes of modernity, there is little wrong, and perhaps a great deal right, with being ambivalent—especially when there is so much to be ambivalent about. Modern liberal democrats, as I argued in the Introduction, must respond to unprecedented moral demands at a time when the moral codes by which they live are exceptionally weak. When the problem of understanding obligations to family members and intimate others is equally as pressing as that of understanding obligations to strangers and future generations, perhaps the best way to begin is to be modest, tentative, even humble. Trying as they are to hold fast to both morality and modernity, liberal democrats do not need moralists to dictate the rules of moral obligation. What they need is an approach that, instead of insisting it has all the right answers, tries to locate a sense of moral obligation in common sense, ordinary emotions, and everyday life. The distinctive contribution of a sociological approach to morality, in other words, is not to tell people what they ought to do in situations of moral complexity, but rather to help individuals discover and apply for themselves the moral rules they already, as social beings, possess.

EIGHT

The Social Construction of Morality

Moral Selves

If modern liberal democrats are going to develop a different way of thinking about others, they must first develop a different way of thinking about themselves. Every moral theory is, after all, a theory of the self. When human agents are viewed as self-interested utility maximizers, we can be fairly certain that the theory's initial assumptions about the self will lead to certain moral positions—such as a belief in freedom of choice. Similarly, when individuals are viewed as inherently aggressive or short-sighted, a defense of governmental authority is likely to follow. In modern liberal democracies, as I have argued throughout this book, these two views of human agency have tended to dominate discussions of moral obligation, emphasizing either obligations to the self at the expense of others or obligations to others at the expense of the self.

An alternative view of moral agency already exists in the sociological tradition, not in the macro-tradition associated with Parsons, but in the micro-tradition associated with symbolic interactionism and phenomenology. (It exists in other fields as well, especially anthropology, social psychology, and, as we shall see, even economics.) From this literature it is possible to assemble a picture of agency in which individuals create their own moral rules through the social interactions they experience with others. In contrast to the moral codes embodied in markets and states, which tend to locate moral obligation in rules that are believed to be just, modern liberal democrats need a theory in which human agents are not only rule followers, but rule makers as well.

The social construction of morality is rooted in the assumption that individuals never act out of any one overriding motivation but respond to a plurality of varying circumstances.[1] Sometimes self-interest will determine their responses, even in matters concerning the family and community where they may not think self-interest the best possible option. Other times they will be moved by community spirit and considerations of altruism, even at the risk of considerable economic sacrifice. (As Virginia Held puts it, "Morality, which ought to guide us in all contexts, ought to guide us differently in different contexts.")[2] The number of possible sides to the self, Amitai Etzioni has pointed out, can be infinite, even though so many theorists, especially in economics, focus only on one side.[3]

Because modern individuals are social and not just natural creatures, they incorporate into the self a generalized sense of society by contemplating the effects of their actions on others, just as, in nearly everything they do, they assume that others will similarly incorporate into *their* actions the effects of living together. A sociological approach to moral obligation focuses neither on the individual standing outside of society nor on society as if it were not composed of individuals, but instead on the way individuals and society interact to make the moral order possible. The closest we can come to the notion of civil society as a living reality (without rejecting modern liberal democracy outright in favor of some older form of presumably moral community) is to recognize that it is only through the situations in which we come together with others that we develop the moral rules which make our interactions possible.

That individuals possess commonsense knowledge of what they expect of themselves and others—that, in other words, they create their own moral obligations in the circumstances of everyday life—we know from the experiments of Harold Garfinkel, which demonstrate the trust and shared understanding inherent in all social interaction.[4] A surprisingly large amount of "tacit knowledge" is embodied in every social situation, including knowledge of moral rules. While neither Garfinkel nor his mentor, Alfred Schutz, explored in great detail the source of these tacit understandings, they must, because they are expressed in language and other mutually understood symbols, be an aspect of culture. "Our everyday world," Schutz did write, "is, from the outset, an intersubjective world of culture."[5] A moral order exists in the intersubjective meanings we attach to the world around us. So much are moral and normative issues at the heart of everything we do that there is, as John Heritage suggests, no "time out" from the need to account for what we are doing and why.[6]

Garfinkel was reluctant to place too great an emphasis on culture because of his insistence on the need to turn Parsons inside out. That reluctance can be avoided, however, if culture is viewed not as a structure with its own logic but, to use Eugene Rochberg-Halton's term, as "the cultivation of meaning."[7] The meanings created by culture are not (as much of contemporary semiotics seems to claim they are) icons, a fixed part of a society's repertoire that can be interpreted only by specialists. Instead, they are part of a fluid process of everyday negotiation. As Rochberg-Halton puts it, "The self consists of a communicative dialogue of signs rooted in an environmental context and requiring cultivation for its emergence and continued growth."[8] Modern people are their own semioticians, decoding the signs around them so they will know what to do next.

In contrast to both structuralist and individualist theories of moral obligation, the social construction of morality envisions people as living in structures but possessing the capacity to bend those structures to their own needs as their situations change. Few writers in the social sciences have emphasized this dialectic between structure and antistructure as much as the anthropologist Victor Turner. Structure, he writes, has a "cognitive" quality, pointing toward "a set of classifications, a model for thinking about culture and nature and ordering one's public life." By contrast, what Turner calls "communitas" is existential in nature, emphasizing all those aspects of society that are "spontaneous, immediate, [and] concrete." Too much structure, and society becomes rigid, unable to accommodate new demands. Too much communitas, and the "material and organizational needs of human beings" cannot be met.[9] Society, it follows, is a process, not a thing, oscillating between rules that establish behavior and behavior that establishes rules.[10]

Just as modern people have political freedom but, as Randall Collins has argued, spend relatively little time thinking about politics, they also have moral freedom but do not spend every minute of every waking day thinking about morality.[11] Morality matters most during certain highlighted moments in the life course, which may be planned and intentional, like marriage, or sudden and spontaneous, like death or a political crisis. "At certain life crises," Turner writes, "such as adolescence, the attainment of elderhood, and death, varying in significance from culture to culture, the passage from one structural status to another may be accompanied by a strong sentiment of 'humankindness,' a sense of the generic social bond between all members of society."[12] These bracketed moments—"formal episodes," as Rom Harré and Paul Secord call them—make it possible for people to give account of what they are doing by reflecting on the moral consequences of their actions.[13] The social bond is reinforced through the kinds of symbols and rituals associated with such moments of moral intensity.

Because moral reflection tends to be episodic rather than continuous, it is not the case that to act as moral agents people need to be viewed, Rousseau-esque, as inherently moral in the absence of social constraints. Nor need we insist, in opposition to Rousseau and other utopians, that the individual self is genetically structured to follow the relentless laws of human nature determined by natural selection.[14] The moral self, as Drew Westen puts it, is "synthetic," representing a deliberately created way of reconciling the needs of the self with the needs of others.[15] The long debate in Western philosophy about the nature of human nature is, from the standpoint of the social construction of morality, misplaced.[16] It is not how we are in nature that matters. (Indeed, if anything, the social construction of morality shares with economic and political approaches to moral regulation a sense that individuals, if imagined in some kind of "natural" state, would not be inherently altruistic or cooperative. It is rather what we do with society that counts. People build institutions, organize rituals, create symbols, and engage in practices because they, unlike beings found in nature, have the power to determine how their relations with others will be organized.[17] Where the sociological approach to moral regulation parts company with the economic and the political is in the idea that society can control nature, instead of that nature or natural instincts foil the best intentions of society. People are neither inherently moral or immoral: they are merely torn between the desire to act selfishly to get what they want and the recognition that only society can prevent them from doing so.

Only one basic assumption lies behind this view of agents as able to make their own moral rules, and that is that people are, in the words of Harré and Secord, "capable of monitoring their own self-monitoring."[18] We are not social because we are moral; we are moral because we live together with others and therefore need periodically to account for who we are. Morality matters because we have reputations to protect, cooperative tasks to carry out, legacies to leave, others to love, and careers to follow. As Kathryn Pyne Addelson has argued, the concept of a career (defined by Erving Goffman as a "regular sequence of changes . . . in the person's self and in his framework of imagery for judging himself and others")[19] is relevant to discussions of moral obligation because individuals go through moral passages—such as an abortion—which help them make sense out of the situations in which they find themselves.[20] Morality thus understood is neither a fixed set of rules handed down unchanging by powerful structures nor something that is made up on the spot. It is a negotiated process through which individuals, by reflecting periodically on what they have done in the past, try to ascertain what they ought to do next.

To account for the contingent and the unexpected, moral rules need to be able to respond to situations that do not quite fit within the terms of already-existing moral rules. One reason why the micro-tradition in sociology is so often concerned with the outcasts of society—with institutionalized victims, as in Goffman's work, or the socially "deviant," as in the University of Chicago tradition and the writings of Howard Becker[21]—is this sense that morality as a socially constructed process requires that we pay attention to those who, because they are outside the framework of the "respectable," sharpen our understanding of moral rules.[22] The social construction of morality involves in particular a fascination with what Turner calls "liminality," the boundary between the accepted and the unaccepted, under the assumption that what is morally problematic today will alter the definition of what is morally permissible in the future. Just as for the individual morality occurs during episodes in the life course, for society as a whole moral questions are raised whenever an outcast group seeks entry, no matter what the reasons for its liminal status—social class, gender, sexual preference, geography, or color.

Because a sociological understanding of morality is located in the concrete situations of everyday life, the sociological theory of moral agency has a different perspective on matters of space than does, especially, much of economic theory. Since individuals can determine who they are only by interacting with people around them, they depend on spatial relations to establish their identity. As George Herbert Mead put it, "one has to be a member of a community to be a self."[23] Niklas Luhmann helps explain why: "Anyone who has been around for some time is . . . entangled with his self-presentation in a web of norms which he himself has helped to create, and from which he cannot withdraw without leaving part of himself behind."[24] For this reason, the "exit" option associated with the market is rarely available when civil society is strong, for to exit from the responsibilities of a situation is to exit from the very self that the situation defines. In this sense, exit serves organizational needs more than individual needs; the perpetual threat to organizations of people possibly leaving contributes to that "concentration of the mind" on the part of those who run the organizations, no doubt making them more concerned with economic efficiency.[25] (Exit also, as I will argue in the next chapter, lessens the sense of moral obligation on the part of those who stay, because they assume that others will eventually leave regardless.) But exiting pays few benefits to individuals, who, since they do not stay and try to alter their situation, experience no moral growth. To act in cognizance of the space one occupies, in other words, is to extend one's moral capacity. A liberal theory of obligation, however, because it so often "equates agency with exit," defines the good society (or organization, institution, or practice) as what it is not.[26]

Much the same is true for time. Moral agents must act in time, for it is only through a conception of time that individuals can acknowledge the permanence of the self. A moral self is an immortal self; it is a self that wishes to contribute to society even after the person who occupies the self is dead.[27] The desire to leave a legacy is perhaps most evident among those who self-consciously desire fame, such as athletes, musicians, or writers. Yet they possess in extreme form what all moral selves inherently possess: the need to project the self into the future in order to evaluate its performance in the present. We take the point of view not only of others with whom we share social space, but also of hypothetical others who have not yet been born. Only in this way can individuals take cognizance of the passage of time, a process that makes it possible for the self to mature.

Cognizance of space and time is at the heart of moral maturity. When we sacrifice for the sake of future generations or take into consideration the viewpoints of spatially situated others, we consider our obligations to our moral selves to be superior to any monetary or political advantage that might come from taking an easier option. This change of preference we undergo by exercising moral responsibility is called learning, and as Amy Gutmann has pointed out, learning is the weak point of many liberal theories of economics and politics.[28] Modern societies have a tremendous need to learn. It would be unproblematic, and also unuseful, to think about moral obligation if everyone (through, say, membership in the same ethnic or religious group) shared the same perspective on what they ought to do, for then—as Durkheim emphasized so often in *The Division of Labor in Society*—their sameness would guarantee their solidarity. In modern conditions of moral choice, however, the actions of others different from us do have an impact on what we can do, and everything we do has implications for those others. Thus, to give account to strangers culturally different from us, moral rules cannot remain forever the same: morality is a dynamic concept because, through learning, the self experiences growth.

Yet how can individuals grow when their preferences are assumed to be stable? The models of individual rational choice associated with theories of the market so often fail to give a satisfactory account of moral obligations because, as good as they are at measuring preferences, they fail to acknowledge preferences *about* preferences[29]—perspectives that are not given a chance for expression because the interpretative and communicative skills that people have as social beings are viewed as too cumbersome to be measured. In the concept of the self associated with the market, then, individuals are seen as intellectually capable of little more than consumption. Moreover, as Robert E. Lane has argued, because markets, by presenting "ready-made differentiations, . . . preference schedules, and budgets rather than ideologies . . . call for relatively little abstract thinking," consumption "can be negotiated with only modest cognitive capacity."[30] (Certain political processes, such as public-opinion polling, similarly fail to take into account complicated or ambiguous responses.)[31] Markets may expand the number of choices available, but all choices remain at the same level of moral complexity.

The social construction of morality is premised on the notion that in any given situation an individual will have many possible opinions, all of them associated with different degrees of moral complexity. Moments of moral intensity are more likely to elicit responses that are buried deeper in the self than are mere preferences; these responses are equivalent to what Bellah and his colleagues have called the "second language" of citizenship, which underlies immediate and easily formed opinion.[32] One way to characterize the difference between immediate preferences and more highly nuanced moral understanding is to use the distinction economists Samuel Bowles and Herbert Gintis make between choosing and learning. Choosing in the absence of a theory about learning, they point out, often leads to a situation in which people, to be free to choose, need to be compelled to learn, whether by patriarchal families or hierarchical schooling.[33] Moral learning, in this sense, is different from what the economist calls "full information." In the economic approach, the agent is like a vessel into which information is poured; some vessels are nearly empty, others are close to brimming over. However much information is poured in, the shape of the vessel remains constant. When people learn moral rules through interaction with strangers, by contrast, the vessel changes shape; it may even become emptier as more is poured in, because the knowledge gained has expanded the capacity to receive more knowledge. If modernity did not make Protean demands on us, requiring that we develop different moral rules for different contexts, the economists' view of information might be sufficient. That it is not is because we have the power not only to determine how much information we should have, but also to define just who we are.

A sociological approach to moral regulation, therefore, does not conclude that people will always make the most appropriate moral decisions simply because they are given the chance to do so. Indeed, in contrast to the democratically registered preferences associated with markets and public-opinion polls, such an approach insists that a preference expressed without a moment of passage or confrontation with a different point of view is an inadequate guide to moral obligation. The problem in modern liberal democracies is not that ordinary people do not have a say, but rather that it is so easy for them to say what they prefer without being forced to think through the consequences of their opinions for others. The harder it is to do something, the more it seems to mean morally. This is not an argument for making numerous rights which modern people take for granted, such as the right to express an opinion or purchase one commodity instead of another, less accessible. Yet it is, I would argue, a serious mistake for a society to confuse a political opinion or an economic choice, which costs little to express, with a moral position, which demands maturity and growth.

Modern society faces what I, if I were an economist, would call the "principle of increasing free-rider opportunity." Despite what Michel Foucault has written about surveillance, no eye gazes on us at all times, monitoring everything we do.[34] The opportunities to take moral shortcuts are enormous, and not everyone resists them. In traditional societies, where moral rules were shared by all, the problem of the free rider could be solved by group pressure, conformity, guilty consciences, unquestioned authority, and other mechanisms that forced obligation to the community. How, though, if everyone is free, are modern societies to protect themselves against the deleterious effects of too many free riders?

Short of an increase in governmental authority, the traditional Hobbesian solution to excessive individualism, the only answer to the problem of the free rider is moral growth. By combining a theory of learning with an emphasis on choosing we can conceive of the social construction of morality as what Alasdair MacIntyre has called a practice:

By a "practice" I am going to mean any coherent and complex form of socially established cooperative human activity through which goods internal to that form of activity are realized in the course of trying to achieve those standards of excellence which are appropriate to, and partially definitive of, that form of activity, with the result that human powers to achieve excellence, and human conceptions of the ends and goods involved, are systematically extended.[35]

MacIntyre uses chess to illustrate his point. Excellence in chess can bring status and even money, but also self-confidence and a feeling of having done something to the best of one's ability. If one cheats at chess, more money or fame may be forthcoming, but only at the cost of having cheated one's own capacity to feel that one has done one's best. The same can be said of society. Without the ability to learn through the practice of morality, the social order becomes impossible when the temptations to free-ridership are so great.

A third perspective on moral agency different from those of the market and the state, in short, allows us to view moral obligation as a socially constructed practice negotiated between learning agents capable of growth on the one hand and a culture capable of change on the other. If the cultural demands are too stringent, individuals sacrifice themselves for the collective good, producing, to be sure, a moral vision, but, as we saw in the discussion of Morris Janowitz in Chapter 7, one that is cramped in its view of human potential. If, in contrast, individuals can only choose and not learn, then they are constrained not by their society but, as the early work of Peter Blau demonstrates, by an acquisitive psychology which tells us that no matter how we might *want* individuals to act, self-interested is how they *do* act. Morality is more contextual than either culturally deterministic or individualistic theories want to allow. The moral self is, in Mitchell Aboulafia's phrase, both mediated and mediating.[36] We make the moral rules that make us: we are, in a word, what we do, and what we do is done together with others. We create our moral rules as we link our individual needs with the understanding we obtain from other people of what the consequences of our actions are likely to be.

Nonheroic Morality

The social construction of morality differs from two other ways of thinking about moral obligation which have little in common except that they both downplay the capacity of individuals to construct their own moral rules through social interaction with others. One is a Durkheimian effort to find the source of moral obligation in society; the other, associated mostly with analytic philosophy, economics, and psychology, attempts to find the source of moral obligation in individual choice.

No sociologist was more concerned with the problem of moral obligation than Durkheim. "We must discover," he wrote in his treatise on education, "those moral forces that men, down to the present time, have conceived of only under the form of religious allegories. We must disengage them from their symbols, so to speak, and find a way to make the child feel their reality without recourse to any mythological intermediary." But if people are free and rational individuals, making decisions for themselves, how can we expect them to act morally when morality itself is "a comprehensive system of prohibitions" whose object is "to limit the range within which individual behavior should and must normally occur"? Not only are moral codes stringent, but they are also demanding: they are "regular, they recur—always the same, uniformly, monotonously the same."[37] It is difficult to imagine that free people, not bound by religious ties, secular in their conception of obligation to one another, would choose to fulfill moral obligations if these obligations are so personally unrewarding.

As if recognizing that his sociological theory was caught between contradictory goals—rationally chosen individualism on the one hand and inscribed moral obligations to others on the other—Durkheim, as is well known, solved the problem by finding in society an alternative to the morality once taught by religion. Society, or what Durkheim often preferred to call civilization, represents "the highest form of the psychic life"; it "has a creative power which no other observable being can equal," being "the most powerful combination of physical and moral forces of which nature offers us an example."[38] Society is like the hero of an epic saga, possessing superhuman qualities at which ordinary mortals can only wonder. The Durkheimian insistence on social obligation, by reminding us of how fallible we are in the face of the heroism of our collective life, ironically absolves us from the need to act morally as individuals. Moral societies will counter the actions of amoral people. (Given the contradictory nature of his ideas, Durkheim never carried his point this far; in fact, he was enamored of Kantian strains of individualism. Still, it is difficult to ignore the implications of some of his more heroic statements about group and collective life.)

Moreover, Durkheim's approach to moral obligation is vulnerable to criticism from another direction. The problem is best captured by this statement: "History has established that except in abnormal cases, each society has in the main a morality suited to it, and that any other would not only be impossible but also fatal to the society which attempted to follow it."[39] Such moral relativism, which was carried forward by most forms of contemporary structural functionalism, left sociological approaches to morality without a baseline for moral judgment. As Derek Phillips argues, Durkheimianism and structural functionalism, taken to their logical conclusion, cannot tell us why the Germany of Hitler or the Cambodia of Pol Pot were immoral.[40]

In recent years an important revival of moral theory in philosophy and the social sciences has been taking place that departs from Durkheim's way of thinking about moral obligation. The trends are diverse, but nearly all this work has two things in common: they find the source of moral conduct in individuals, not society; and, to avoid moral relativism, they search for universal standards of justice that can be applied to all societies and all situations.

This moral revival is best seen in the work of psychologists and economists on the one hand and of analytic philosophers on the other. Psychologists, especially Piaget, Kohlberg, and Doob, have been seeking to increase our understanding of moral choice.[41] Even experimental psychologists, whose work has had the closest resemblance to natural science, are examining the conditions of prosocial behavior, altruism, and the nature of distributive justice.[42] In nearly all this work, but especially in Kohlberg's, a neo-Kantian concern with the rationality of the individual moral agent links the concerns of psychologists with those of such moral philosophers as John Rawls. This cross-fertilization between social science and moral philosophy can be seen in economics as well. Not only are some economists concerned with collective obligations and moral choice, but philosophers have also been influenced by economic models such as utilitarianism, rational-choice theory, and state-of-nature assumptions.[43]

Whatever the origin of this blending of social science and moral philosophy, one of its strongest features is a commitment to methodological individualism. In contrast to any emphasis on collective obligations, this way of thinking about moral obligation tends to argue that justice is furthered when individual choice is maximized; the social order, if considered at all, is judged to be moral when individuals act justly. Thus, for example, Leonard Doob investigates the social sciences to find answers to eight questions: what will I do? what can I do? what may I do? what must I do? what would the consequences be? what ought I to do? what shall I do? what did I do? All eight questions have as their subject the first person singular. Although Doob suggests that one can substitute the pronoun *we* for *I*, his work nonetheless carries a strong sense that morality is essentially a question of individual agents acting in a duty-bound way.

Also in contrast to Durkheimianism, the current revival of moral theory is especially preoccupied with the dangers of moral relativism. It is as if in thinking, for example, about a moral issue such as justice one can contrast a sociological approach with a philosophical one.[44] First, unlike the emphasis that sociologists place on situational circumstance, many contemporary philosophers seek to discover principles of morality or justice that are deemed to be "beyond subjectivity."[45] Second, as Allan Gewirth argues, morality from the viewpoint of contemporary analytic philosophy is independent of "ideals or institutional practices," while the focus of sociology tends to be institution-specific, with norms and values changing depending on the specific institutional context.[46] Third, in the analytic tradition moral rules create obligation by their intrinsic superiority alone; people are expected to obey them simply because they are just. Authority from a sociological perspective, by contrast, tends to be personal rather than impersonal; we receive our sense of obligation not from inside ourselves, but through our interaction with others. Finally, theories of moral obligation associated with neo-Kantian philosophy do not depend on social consensus: they are morally just whether people view them so or not. In sociology, however, thinkers from Durkheim to Parsons have viewed consensus as the sine qua non of the social order.

There is a great deal to be criticized in the Durkheimian approach to moral obligation, and it is no wonder that methodological individualism and universal criteria of justice have flourished. But these developments bring problems of their own. For one thing, methodological individualism has a heroic dimension quite similar to that of Durkheimianism, only now it is the individual moral agent, not society, that is asked to carry a superhuman burden. In both the economic literature celebrating individual choice and the writings of moral philosophers like John Rawls, the heroic quality of the individual lies in his ability to do what is right, irrespective of group pressure. Standing against society, the moral individual is a person of character, Max Weber's inward-seeking Protestant writ large. This heroic view of morality achieves perhaps its ultimate expression in Kohlberg's notion of moral hierarchies, which posits a final stage of moral choice so refined in its sensibility that the American constitutional system is only the fifth stage of a six-stage process (with actual citizens, and even many leaders, only at stage four).[47] In this perspective, logic, clear thinking, and reason are emphasized over sentiment, emotion, and intuition. Ordinary commonsense understandings count for little, and if, as David Gauthier writes, "the reader is tempted to object to some part of this view, on the ground that his moral intuitions are violated, then he should ask what weight such an objection can have, if morality is to fit within the domain of rational choice."[48]

Moreover, the search for universal moral principles associated with much of analytic moral philosophy comes at the cost of assumptions about human behavior that strip from individual agents the capacity to respond to specific circumstances.[49] This would not matter if the purpose of philosophical investigation were pure thought—logical clarity for the sake of logical clarity. Yet although philosophers often express this ideal, they also desire to offer moral advice to ordinary people on real issues of moral perplexity such as whether to have children, abortion, death, animal rights, nuclear weapons, the environment, and world hunger.[50] When principles rooted in universal criteria of justice are brought down to earth, real people do not always find the moral positions that follow all that helpful. For example, Derek Phillips—basing his arguments on the rigorous logic of Allan Gewirth, who attempted to derive principles of justice from the nature of inquiry itself—ends his discussion of the relationships between parents and children by stating that "the number of different life prospects or possibilities that a parent must foster is left open."[51] It is probably a sound conclusion, but it could as easily have been reached from common-sense experience as from universal principles.

A sociological approach to moral obligation in modern society must respond to the criticisms that have been correctly leveled at the Durkheimian approach. This task is made somewhat easier by the recent movement in philosophy away from a purely analytic tradition and toward an orientation that incorporates such classic sociological themes as the ambiguity (and socially determined nature) of language, the nature of real experience (as emphasized by American pragmatists such as John Dewey), exploration of how human beings make moral judgments, and, closest to the spirit of my own work, an understanding of the ways in which individuals act as makers of their own symbolic worlds.[52] Even a recent work within the Oxford analytic tradition itself deals with themes—such as how "socially defined and determined pursuits and activities" affect well-being—that at one time would have been considered outside that tradition.[53]

This movement away from both methodological individualism and the universal search for moral principles needs to be met at least halfway by sociologists, who should distance themselves from an entrenched Durkheimian position on morality in favor of greater autonomy for the individual agent and less emphasis on moral relativism. The possibility of doing so will be enhanced if sociologists, in paying more attention to their field's micro-tradition, understand moral obligation as being socially constructed. The social construction of morality offers a way of thinking about moral obligations that avoids the problems of Durkheimianism without leading to equally problematic methodological individualism and abstract judgmentalism.

In contrast to the latent structuralism in Durkheim and Parsons, which often leads to an undervaluation of the capacity of individuals to act as their own moral agents, an approach based on the micro-tradition in sociology sees individuals as capable of producing the realities with which they live. Yet it would be incorrect to turn around and suggest that the social construction of morality is based on principles associated with methodological individualism. Rather than positing that people's motivations are individual, and thereby ignoring the fact that in modern society reward systems are collective, this approach to morality emphasizes that individual growth and self-mastery can be achieved only through the collective reward of interaction. In the autonomy they have to create moral rules, individuals are not, as they are in individualistic theories, free to act unencumbered, for what gives them the ability to create moral understandings in the first place are all the things they share in common with others, from language to stories to practices to laws. Because morality is a socially constructed process, no individual, standing alone, can ever be moral—or immoral.

Furthermore, the idea of socially constructed morality is not nearly as vulnerable to the charge of moral relativism as is the Durkheimian tradition. If people make the moral rules that make them, then the standard for evaluating an institution, practice, or society itself is the degree of latitude it gives people to make their own moral rules. The test of an economic institution or practice is efficiency, which is why economists like the market. The test of a political institution is universality, which is why social democrats have relied on the state. The test of a social institution or a society has to be its contribution to moral practice. In short, a standard of moral propriety does lie outside the realm of any particular individual's subjective judgment: a morally just society is one whose institutions maximize the capacity of its members to contribute to the formation of the rules by which they will be governed. Dictatorial societies or rigidly hierarchical organizations cannot be said to have morally just rules when the context to which they apply is one that denies the possibility of moral agency in the first place.

Societies—or the intellectuals who speak for them—ought, in the spirit of Durkheim, to establish goals that mean more than the additive preferences of the individuals who compose the society. Likewise, it is the philosophers' duty to debate fundamental principles of the just and the good so that individuals will have a moral framework against which to judge their actions. Yet because all moral rules are ultimately designed for real people, to both of these activities should be added a recognition of the role played by individuals as builders of the rules by which they will regulate their moral relations. The problem with a Durkheimian reification of society is that the state has taken on the role of society; consequently, obedience to rules generated by a structure outside the realm of individual choice lessens the capacity of individuals to be personally and directly responsible for the fate of others. The problem with an economic or psychological reification of the individual is that the market organizes an ever greater number of individual choices, a process that similarly pays little attention to how individuals take the points of view of those with whom they share some fundamental characteristics. Individuals are not so heroic that they can choose what to do without conscience, guilt, conformity, and the need to be liked. Societies are not so heroic that they can always know what is best for the individuals that live within them.

When heroic approaches to moral obligation confront the real world of markets and states, disappointment of the moral philosophers in ordinary individuals for their failure to live up to the heroic goals established for them is the likely result. For all the emphasis on the importance of obligation (either to the collective called society or to the individual standing alone), underlying both the economic and the political approach to moral obligation is a sense that people cannot, finally, be entrusted with the serious business of knowing how to act in the interests of justice and morality. They must follow rules instead. In contrast to the social construction of morality, market- and state-driven theories of moral obligation—at least in their pure form—tend to view those rules as formulated not by people themselves, but by some authority standing above or outside them.

Rule Following, Rule Making

All the contemporary social-scientific approaches to moral obligation are committed to the notion that modernity requires rules that regulate people's interaction with one another. Where they differ is over the question of whether rules ought to guide choices or choices, rules. From the perspective of the social construction of morality, the self is viewed as a rule maker. The common assumption in both the economic and political approaches to moral obligation, by contrast, is that the self is a rule follower. Markets and states reach their limits as moral codes for modern liberal democrats because they assume that moral obligation lies in rules rather than in the people whose behavior they will govern.

Theorists of the market spend much time justifying freedom, but they rarely consider the nature of the self who is expected to be free. When they do, freedom often means not the freedom to choose moral rules, but only to choose between options shaped by rules that cannot be challenged. Because these higher rules—what Geoffrey Brennan and James Buchanan call "meta rules"[54]—are viewed as beyond human intervention, the individualistic conception of the social order does not emphasize the notion of people as builders of their own social rules; on the contrary, to quote F. A. Hayek, "the individual responses to particular circumstances will result in an overall order only if individuals obey such rules as will produce an order." Thus, every social order will contain elements that are outside the conscious control of the human agents that live within it: the social order, in short, "will often exist without having been deliberately created." The model of man in such theories, far from emphasizing the capacity of moral selves to make rules, comes close to assuming that people act by instinct and without thought.[55]

This rather limited view of the moral agent contained in the economic approach is shared by many who find the source of moral order not in individual choice, but in some form of political authority, such as bureaucratic regulation or law. As Lon Fuller puts it, "Just as man is restricted in what he can do by the limits imposed by physical nature, so also is he limited in the choices open to him in arranging the forms of his social life." Fuller uses a familiar distinction between the morality of aspiration and the morality of duty. The former, which we associate with the Greeks, emphasizes a person of character who struggles to be virtuous, whereas the latter "lays down the basic rules without which an ordered society is impossible." Since "there is no way by which the law can compel a man to live up to the excellences of which he is capable," legal morality (together with the economics of marginal utility) is best off restricting itself "with our efforts to make the best use of our short lives."[56] It is therefore not individuals that embody morality, but the law itself—much as in the idea that freedom is embodied in the market, not in the moral agents who enter it.

When rules are viewed as beyond the capacities of human agents to change, they make the business of satisfying obligations to the self and to others seemingly easier. Because actions that follow the logic of the market are often tinged with personal guilt and appear to be antisocial or in opposition to many religious ideals, the existence of agreed-upon economic rules—like belief in the existence of God in earlier times—creates a framework for deciding what is right. Having finally chosen what seems to be the most efficient course of action, we need not, so long as we follow the rules of the market, ponder also whether that course is proper. Similarly, when we turn over to government the regulation of social relations that were once outside its purview, we create a new set of rules within which to make decisions. We will follow certain procedures, agree that certain governmental agencies will have the final say, guarantee or restrict certain rights of access, and conform our behavior to the bureaucratic requirements generally demanded by government. One of the enormous advantages of allowing government to intervene in society is that once it establishes procedures, half of the difficulties of being modern are relieved: people can argue with each other over their share without having always to start from scratch.

Yet the ease of moral decision-making by fixed rules is deceptive, for the conditions of being modern inevitably raise the question of who made the rules in the first place. When everyone agreed that a supernatural being or an omnipotent head of state was the chief rule maker, it followed that people ought to be rule followers. But modernity destroyed that assumption. By asserting the principle of freedom, modernity holds out the possibility of a people free to decide the rules by which they will regulate their interaction. When man the toolmaker is supplanted by man the rule maker, any theory of moral obligation that does not allow at least some popular input to how rules are made will invariably cause frustration. Because "rule-regulated action does not imply rule-determined action," a focus on rules to the exclusion of the agents who make them will always tell only half the story of moral obligation in modern society.[57]

What follows from failing to recognize the sociological reality that people do create their rules as they go along, no matter how much they may seem to prefer to assign those rules to outside authorities, is illustrated by Brennan and Buchanan's analysis of constitutional rules. Brennan and Buchanan wish to create a constitution that protects us from the temptation to use government to regulate economic life. "Now it may be," they say, "that the rules are unclear, as they often are in social contexts." What to do? "Justice requires clarification of the rules and reconciliation of ambiguities."[58] Leaving aside the question of whether justice is best served by clarification or ambiguity (I will argue momentarily that it is usually best served by the latter), the task of interpreting rules inevitably falls to people—unless, of course, one assigns it to God, which Brennan and Buchanan emphatically do not. Since those who have the power to make rules have also the power to change them, insisting on a new constitution or a civic religion of restraint (the two solutions Brennan and Buchanan offer) is not going to produce the stability of rules that market theorists would like to establish.

No matter how great a society's reliance on the rules of the market, or how extensive the intervention of the rules of the state, people will always find a way to alter and interpret them. Market rules, for example, tend to be more ambiguous than many economists are willing to assume. Even securities markets, which are generally presumed to be anonymous and so hurried that they allow little time for personal relations, operate chiefly because social patterns and ties develop that enable the participants to conduct their business because they know and trust one another.[59] Similarly laws, which in theory are strictly written and applicable to unforeseen situations, are, like all texts, interpretable, their ideal universal applicability tempered in actuality by what Clifford Geertz has called a "to-know-a-city-is-to-know-its-streets" aspect.[60] Legal rules, then, whatever they are supposed to be, turn out to be ambiguous, situational, personal, and contingent (which is why people hire lawyers).[61] Simply put, no rules, at least in modern society, are completely external to the people who are ruled by them.

A sociological approach to moral regulation is needed to complement the rules of markets and states, for this approach is far more tolerant of the notion that individuals, in constructing their own moral rules through interactions with others, have a moral capacity given them by society to work with others to alter, rather than just accept, the rules by which they will be bound. Modern liberal democrats, to use the language of Duncan Kennedy, are governed not only by rules (which draw obligations as tightly as possible) but also by standards (which allow for discretion in how the rules are applied).[62] At least three reasons explain why modern liberal democrats, no matter how much they may at times appreciate the formality of strict rules, nonetheless transform those rules into standards when confronted with concrete cases: they want to take context into account; they want to assert the moral validity of particular claims; and they want to allow for ambiguity in resolving unexpected dilemmas.

In everyday life there are numerous occasions when people, in common-sense fashion, believe that circumstances and contexts ought to soften the implementation of moral rules. The market, for example, may demand that employees be fired when times are bad, but if an employer knows his em-ployees and has employed them for some time, specific circumstances sug-gest that the rules of the market not be followed. Similarly, legal regulation can impose drastic sentences for certain offenses, but the perpetrator's status—as young, married, female, or a first-time offender—will always be taken into account at sentencing time (as will considerations of race, lead-ing liberal theorists of the law not to want to consider context). No won-der that the belief in theory that rules should be universally applied is nearly always met in practice by a belief that exceptions should rule in individual cases.

Despite the fact that context and circumstances are often taken into ac-count in the practical application of rules, neither the theory of the market nor the liberal theory of law allows much room for contextual excep-tionalism. Personal contingency, for example, is, in the moral theory of states and markets, irrelevant or even antithetical to the proper operation of those theories' moral codes. Unlike the affective ties and community ex-pectations that signaled market transactions in earlier times, modern mar-ket rules do not demand of those who follow them that they have much in common—except, of course, their commitment to those rules. As Bren-nan and Buchanan put it, "There need be no shared objective in socio-political rules. Individuals are recognized to possess their own privately determined objectives, their own life plans, and these need not be common to all persons. In this setting, rules have the function of facilitating interac-tions among persons who may desire quite different things."[63] Legal regu-lations similarly put a premium on what Lon Fuller calls "formal rules of duty and entitlement" instead of on associations based on personal feel-ings, local knowledge, ties of blood, or other contingent factors.[64] And ad-ministrative bureaucracies act in a morally responsible manner not when they are empathic or willing to make exceptions based on unique circum-stances, but when they operate according to agreed-upon formal criteria of procedure.[65]

Correspondingly, individuals generally believe that the moral meaning of their activity is defined by the specific objectives that they seek. An orga-nization whose purpose is to fight cancer is viewed as existing on a higher moral plane than an industry that makes enormous profits from exploiting the elderly. Helping others in need, likewise, is morally preferable to buying junk bonds as a way of disposing of surplus cash. Faced with a bewildering number of choices, people look to moral codes to tell them which of their possible actions will contribute to some social or moral good.

Yet the moral codes of the market and the state often have difficulty responding to such questions. Since all situations are idiosyncratic, and therefore not comparable, the only way to develop rules that, in the interests of justice, will apply in universal fashion to all situations is to emphasize their procedural form. Much of contemporary moral theory therefore tends to be value-neutral with respect to purpose. The market does not make judgments on the things being distributed by its logic, whether these be prostitution services, education, health care, or life itself. In like manner, legal morality is, in Fuller's words, "over a wide range of issues, indifferent toward the substantive aims of law and is ready to serve a variety of such aims with equal efficacy."[66] Such approaches to moral decision-making share Lawrence Kohlberg's notion that the moral point of view is defined "in terms of the formal character of a moral judgement, method, or point of view, rather than in terms of its content."[67] (Even democracy itself, which if open to competing discussions of ultimate purpose can lead to paralysis and deadlock, can be justified, not according to the principles for which it stands, but according to the procedures it establishes for establishing those principles.)[68] The commonsense idea that what we do matters as much as, if not more than, how we do it is lost to the procedural approaches to morality embodied in so much contemporary economic and political theory. When we follow such rules, we lose our ability to judge social practices by their inherent moral content.

Finally, the rules associated with states and markets do not place a high premium on ambiguity.[69] Ambiguity is a marvelous invention when groups want to avoid situations in which one party's gain is automatically another's loss. Just as diplomats try to find ambiguous wordings in treaties so that all sides can claim to be winners, commonsense morality suggests solutions to difficult moral dilemmas that allow as many people as possible to retain their self-respect. (In this sense, total power and textual strictness go together. When one party seeks to assert power over another, it will generally do so by claiming that only one interpretation of a text is acceptable. This may be why authoritarian movements of the right insist that the Bible or the Constitution means literally what it says.) It may take great technical skill to design rules so that their application will be as precise as possible, but it also takes great skill, usually more of a social than a technical kind, to fudge precise results in favor of ambiguous applications that make the whole business of living together with others less tense.

The rules favored by markets and states favor precision over ambiguity. In markets, for example, establishing a price for a particular commodity often seems to settle questions about what it is worth—thereby eliminating ambiguity. (Surely one of the attractions of Chicago school economics is the idea that if we can establish a cost for time, or for voting, or for a life, we can reach some consensus on value, a dilemma that has plagued philosophers for thousands of years.) Similarly, the principle behind administrative law disfavors what Richard Stewart calls "vague, general, or ambiguous statutes," because if a delegation of power allows for discretion, then politics will take the place of law in deciding how resources are allocated. (That politics does this anyway is one reason why the "traditional model" of administrative law has been a failure.) [70] It is enormously difficult to admit the principle of ambiguity and still have law. Even a legal theorist as fascinated by developments in literary criticism and interpretative anthropology as Ronald Dworkin, who, in his words, "marched up a steep hill" to a hermeneutic interpretation of legal texts, marches back down again when confronted with the need for a theory of legal rules that is as specific as possible. [71]

Between them, the moral theory of the market and the moral theory of the state allow remarkably little scope for people to develop their own moral capacities. Markets and states combine to reduce the moral agent to being a mere chooser among alternatives rather than a shaper of the alternatives to be chosen. Both approaches assume that in the absence of strictly defined rules we might favor association over principle, situation over procedure, context over universality, morality over law, and flesh-and-blood over abstraction. Political and economic rules expand to the extent that we distrust our own sociability. Knowing that we will be moved by exceptions, aware that we are rarely strong enough to rise above context, afraid that we might listen to our hearts rather than our heads, we enact economic and political rules so that we need not worry about moral growth. Then, when faced with situations where we are forced to grow, we find that the rules in place are of no help to us, and it is not long before we invent ways to ignore them. Rules, in modern liberal democracy, have a heavy load to carry. They are substitutes for the civil society we are always in danger of losing.

Toward a Moral Sociology

Recognizing the dangers of subjectivity and relativism, sociologists are often reluctant to identify too closely with civil society, for they understand the particularism of its moral claims. Even Jürgen Habermas, the sociological theorist who has come closer than any other contemporary thinker to identifying the threats to the lifeworld posed by markets and states on either side, writes very much within the neo-Kantian tradition of searching after universal moral principles, taking out, in his moral philosophy, the human beings which social theory has already put back in.[72] Yet one way that sociologists can remain true to their historic concern with civil society, and at the same time not retreat into a romanticization of subjectivity and emotionalism, is by concentrating on an approach that emphasizes individuals as the creators of the moral rules by which they govern themselves.

Civil society, if understood as the place where people pause to reflect on the moral dilemmas they face, is necessary if individuals are to possess those capacities of agency that will enable them to make rules as well as follow them. Rather than implying a longing for a moral order of the past, civil society ought instead to serve as a metaphor for all those episodes and encounters that give modern liberal democrats the foundation for thinking through, in connection with others, the rules by which they will be governed. Families, communities, friendship networks, voluntary organizations, and social movements are to be valued not because they create havens in an otherwise heartless world, but because it can only be within the intimate realm, surrounded by those we know and for whom we care, that we learn the art of understanding the moral positions of others.

It is, as the pragmatic tradition in American philosophy emphasizes, through experience that we resolve demands which, in theory, often seem unresolvable. Moral obligation is a learned practice. If we do not exercise our capacities to act as moral agents, they will atrophy and we will lose them. Living with the contradictory moral impulses of modernity means a great deal of trial and error, imperfect moral decisions, hesitations, and uncertainties. The institutions and practices of civil society are a kind of trial heat for the even more difficult business of taking the perspective of future generations, responding to the needs of strangers, or learning to live within diverse cultures. We will best find the way to balance obligations in the intimate sphere with those to distant strangers, neither by registering our preferences without a moment of moral passage nor by allowing our preferences to be determined by adherence to rules established by collective authorities, but instead by keeping vibrant those aspects of the intimate world that enable us to dig a little deeper to find within ourselves what we ought to do.

In the face of rules that try to define as precisely as possible how people should act, sociologists ought to be concerned with the ways people themselves interpret and apply rules that appear abstract, formal, and universal. The situations of everyday life, the ethnographies of concrete communities and families, and the intensity of close observation—all of which serve to remind us of the importance of the intimate world—act as a check on the tendency of social scientists and philosophers to become so taken with the wisdom of their moral advice that they forget that it is real people, leading anything but heroic lives, who constitute the stuff of society. Sociology, therefore, rather than developing a rigorous and formal theoretical apparatus along the lines once taken by Talcott Parsons, ought to do what it always has done best: empathically to understand, through close observation, the ways in which people create their symbolic worlds. Of all the social sciences, except anthropology, sociology has been the one most concerned with the warp and woof of real life. It would be ironic if, at a time when the complexity of moral decision-making demands greater respect for the everyday capacities of individuals to use their social skills as moral actors, sociologists, somehow envious of the other social sciences with their "more modern" rigor and powers of abstraction, were to abandon the tradition of close observation that has been their most powerful contribution.

Sociology ought, in short, to give voice to ordinary people, struggling in the context of their lived realities to act as moral agents. This does not mean that sociologists are simply transmitters of the messages they receive from their subjects. When individuals talk with social scientists, especially when they talk in any moral depth, the process should be a moral passage for both of them, and in the best sociological work it generally is. Who can doubt, for example, that Kristin Luker or Jonathan Rieder learned something about the moral worlds of people—right-to-life activists or opponents of integrated neighborhoods—with whom they strongly disagreed?[73] (One hopes, although this is less clear, that the subjects of study learned something from the sociologists as well.) Sociology is not populism, an identification with the moral purity of the oppressed. It is a way of thinking about moral obligation, and it has moral obligations of its own. Sociologists deal with delicate materials: feelings, ethical sentiments, intimate relations. They are therefore responsible for taking those materials seriously, for neither reducing their findings to the expression of preferences nor assuming them to be attitudinal quirks that will be smoothed over by efficient methods of measuring public opinion.

Neither populism, then, nor sermonizing—whether this takes the form of warning individuals who live in capitalist societies of the evils of selfishness (the left-wing version of sermonizing) or of complaining about the moral flabbiness of welfare states (the right-wing version)—is appropriate to sociology. After all, neither the market nor the state could survive if everyone structured their decision making strictly according to a market- or state-driven logic. There will always be individuals who will not follow the urgings of the state or market, who will find their own solutions to the decisions they must make. A socially constructed morality is needed to tell them that rewards exist for taking personal responsibility for actions, such as doing one's best, being responsive to others in one's shared space, and taking the point of view of future generations. Modern liberal democrats always find ways to work around the rules that attempt to structure behavior. All they lack is an approach to moral obligation that tells them there are often valid reasons for doing so.

A sociological approach to moral regulation respects the commonsense rules that people create, with others, through moments of moral passage. In particular situations the cues of civil society will tell them that acting out of self-interest is appropriate, as Chicago school theorists claim is the case in all situations. But the opposite may apply as well. Against the penetration of the market into the realm of civil society, as has occurred in the United States, should be balanced the capacity of people to treat one another out of compassion and generosity. Moreover, some kinds of obligations to others can be best carried out by governments, just as sometimes, even though people have a right to claim rights granted them by the government, something tells them they ought not to. When the state comes to play as important a role in civil society as it has in Scandinavia, the capacity of individuals not to claim rights but to think instead about obligations is worth remembering.

No one said that modernity would be easy. If the rules that apply to the intimate realms of family and community are never extended to strangers, moral obligations become parochial and restrictive. Likewise, if the rules that apply to strangers and hypothetical others are applied to families and communities, moral obligations become cold and impersonal. It is understandable, given these difficulties, that people seek relief from the complexities of moral decision-making by turning to markets and states, both of which make modernity easier by asking people only to decide, not to decide *how* to decide. Yet excessive reliance on the rules of the market and the state create problems of their own. By encouraging a sense of possibility and progress, rules hold out the vision of freedom and choice, but then—in the name of universality, lack of ambiguity, procedure, formality, and impersonal administration—deny to people the freedom to make choices about the rules themselves. It is as if the train to modernity stops halfway down the line. To get to the final destination—assuming we still want to—we need to recognize individuals as the ultimate creators of the moral rules that govern them.

NINE

The Gift of Society

The Breakdown of the Moral Consensus

In the years after World War II, Western liberal democracies developed a common solution for their political and economic problems which linked government and the market together in what Claus Offe has called the Keynesian welfare state.[1] In a peculiar kind of way, political consensus seemed to generate moral consensus. So long as the Keynesian welfare state functioned, moral issues played little role in the public life of modern liberal democracies. Economic growth generated government surpluses, which in turn promised to provide for older people, take care of the dependent, and leave legacies to future generations. Between them, the market and the state made necessary neither guilty consciences nor sermons about obligation. It may not have been the end of ideology, but it might well have been the end of morality, at least as traditionally understood.

Just as the Keynesian welfare state has broken down as a political and economic compromise capable of containing the major conflicts in modern liberal democracies, so has the general consensus that moral issues ought to play little role in public life broken down as well. In the late 1970s, from both the right and the left, new issues came to the fore. Ecological consciousness, the peace movement, and feminism, on the one hand, and opposition to busing and abortion, support for prayer in schools, and hostility toward the teaching of evolution, on the other, began to dominate the public consciousness of the United States especially but, in varying forms, other societies too. As if being modern were not difficult enough, liberal democrats are now being asked to take positions on issues that would tax anyone's moral capacities.

Although the rise of new moral issues has contributed to the polarization of modern politics and increased demagoguery, one positive benefit can stem from the breakdown of the moral consensus. The very newness of such issues means that often no preestablished rules exist on which people can rely for answers. Morality, in that sense, is "in the making"[2]—part of a process by which people try to make sense out of the dilemmas, experiences, conversations, and stories in which they participate. When morality is in the making, individuals are far more likely to construct their own moral rules out of their interactions with others. The new moral issues speak to the social construction of morality, and the social construction of morality speaks to the new moral issues. Perhaps the most widely studied of the new moral issues—abortion—indicates why this is so.

As L. W. Sumner points out, at issue in most of the debates over abortion in which moral philosophers engage is a matter of principle: how one views the moral status of the fetus. To use a Kantian distinction, if the fetus is viewed as a person, then abortion is immoral, whereas if the fetus is considered a thing, a woman is justified in exercising control over her own body.[3] Opponents of abortion generally base their arguments on an obligation to a higher good, such as religious belief, and the resulting conviction that the fetus is a person from conception. A decision against abortion follows such a conviction, as in the following argument: "At some point between two and twelve weeks after conception, the fetus becomes a human being with all the rights to life (to use that phrase) belonging to such an entity. Thereafter—with the exception of one special case—it is wrong for the mother to abort the fetus, even if her life is threatened by its continued existence."[4]

Moral advice of this sort tells a woman that her obligations to a potential life are so great that she has no obligation at all to those in her present environment, including herself, her mate, or her children. (As John Noonan writes, "Feeling is notoriously an unsure guide to the humanity of others.")[5] This is a form of what I have called heroic morality in extremis. Not only are women expected to be ruled by nature—and thereby to reject modernity—but they are also expected to sacrifice themselves in the process. "There is no moral act that does not imply a sacrifice," Durkheim once wrote.[6] Indeed, some sacrifice, as I argued in Chapter 3, is clearly necessary for the strength of the moral order. Yet to ask people to sacrifice their own futures for the sake of a principle is more than modern people will bear.

On the point of principle, however, the liberal position on abortion echoes the conservative. Many supporters of unrestricted abortion, like their antagonists, also base their arguments on a principle—that of a woman's right to control her own body. In their view, the fetus is a thing rather than a life, and one of the principles of modern liberal democratic capitalism is that people have the right to dispose of the things that are theirs as they wish.[7] As Sumner (who takes a moderate liberal position) argues, because positions on these issues "must have a rational foundation," it follows that "personal feelings or sentiments cannot themselves count as reasons in favor of a moral view of abortion."[8] From this perspective, a principle of obligation to the self and its needs takes precedence over feelings toward potential future generations, again requiring something of a heroic attitude toward the stirrings of and bondings with the thing/person that exists in one's womb.

How principled are most abortion decisions? Judith Smetana, who has studied women's reasoning about abortion from Kohlbergian premises, divided her sample into those who made a "moral" decision that life begins with conception and those who made a "personal" decision involving autonomy and control over their own lives.[9] The problem is that such "domains", as she calls them, are rarely so bounded. For most women—indeed, for anyone—making a decision about when life begins is so demanding that abstract principles are not much help. Only by discussing these matters with others—by relying on practices rather than principles—can such an issue be resolved. The extensive sociological literature on abortion generally concludes that principles count for little in reaching this decision, while friends, feelings, and moral account-giving count very much. The ways by which people grow and develop as moral agents, through rules emphasizing situation, context, trust, reliance on others, and common sense, are in fact the ways by which most women make a decision regarding abortion.

Abortion decisions, first of all, rely on talk, and evidently a good deal of it. According to Arthur Shostak and Gary McLouth, approximately 85 percent of the women who obtain abortions tell the natural father of the fetus that they are pregnant and discuss what they are planning to do.[10] Despite the possibility of hostile reactions from parents or siblings, especially in the first years when abortion was legal, Mary Zimmerman found that 60 percent of her sample in a conservative Midwestern city discussed their situation with a parent, brother, or sister.[11] Many women turn to workers in family-planning clinics for advice on what to do.[12] Although careful to keep the relationship professional and clinical, doctors also counsel women who are making abortion decisions; and doctors themselves, caught between competing pressures, make their own decisions on whether to perform abortions not out of principle but based on what they hear.[13] Even political movements can be a source of information as, through social interaction, both pro-life and pro-choice positions are reinforced and strengthened.[14]

The conversations that inevitably take place during those formal episodes when people are forced to make decisions for which they have few guidelines are the very stuff of moral decision-making. Faced with conflicts for which principles are of little help, women construct the moral rules that regulate abortion socially in interaction with others. Thus do moral rules become the product of people's own activity as moral agents. Cultural sanctions are not fixed commands; with regard to abortion, what society views as morally unpermissible has changed, in large part because women took an active role in trying to change it. Nor are the decisions women make the result of fixed preferences that are somehow simply revealed; they are instead part of a learning process through which people make sense of the moral choices that face them. Civil society—ties of affection, friendship, and community—becomes, as I argued in the previous chapter, a kind of moral laboratory for resolving dilemmas for which existing moral codes seem inadequate.

If an issue such as abortion indicates why people need strong ties in civil society, it also indicates why, during moments of moral intensity, they look also to the market and the state to provide relief. The encountering of a new stage in the life cycle or a moment of sudden moral passage, in which moral dilemmas only dimly recognized before must quickly be grappled with, is not something people wish to experience often. Consequently, individuals often try to simplify the moral decision-making process by turning to government or the market. In the case of abortion, both the state and the market can ease access, thereby reducing the moral "costs" and making a decision to abort more routine. In the United States, despite ongoing contestation by conservative opponents, abortion has been medicalized and commodified, with largely beneficial results. Taking advantage of new opportunities becomes easier, the price drops, and the number of people who can avail themselves of the procedure increases. In Sweden, abortion is free on demand until the eighteenth week of pregnancy, and much of the stigma associated with the process has been removed.[15] Because abortion is viewed as a public good, it undergoes the dynamics of bureaucratization—available to all, at prices well below the market price, it is also safer and more trustworthy because regulated by public authority.

As a practice becomes routinized when treated as a private or a public good, the intensity of the moral decision it elicits will decline. Yet abortion, because it does involve an issue, not only of life but also of the life of future generations, is inevitably morally complicated. Wherever it has been treated either as a medical commodity or as a fundamental right guaranteed by the state, moments of moral passage have not been eliminated. In Scandinavia, the moral debate over abortion did not end with legislation establishing a legal right to it; despite free access to abortion in Sweden, for example, numerous women still experienced emotional disturbances and strong psychological reactions.[16] In the United States, mixed feelings about the commodification of abortion are well illustrated by Carole Joffe's study of family-planning workers, many of whom went into abortion counseling out of a principled commitment to a woman's right to control her own body. Many of these women found that all the ethical and social pressures on them presented almost inescapable dilemmas. "The only effective 'policy' for dealing with these tensions," Joffe concludes, "is to avoid, as much as possible, *any* rigid policy."[17] To live at the whim of decisions made without the experience of moments of moral epiphany may be an improvement over living in an age of intense moral scrutiny, but only partly.

Abortion decisions, then, represent in a sense a case study of how modernity, morality, and civil society relate. Abortion exemplifies the process by which people reach decisions when faced with an unprecedented number of choices to make and little sense of how to make them. Although a menu of options seems to be the modern definition of freedom—having choice where there once existed only sanction—choice is constrained by the natural bonds that exist between a woman and the potential life she carries within her. With the social and the natural in such conflict, most women do not seek some universally just principle to guide their decisions but turn instead to others in their immediate environment to find a way to balance what they understand to be their obligations—to themselves, to their intimate others, and to future generations. Thus, if civil society has been weakened by the tendency of modern liberal democrats to rely on markets and states, so has the capacity to act as a self-producing moral agent.

Markets, States, and New Moral Issues

Markets and states, which between them cannot resolve some of the older moral dilemmas of liberal democracy, are even less helpful in confronting the newer ones. Yet people, not always willing to experience the intensity of moral decision-making associated with civil society, will often look to them anyway for help in dealing with new moral issues. New moral issues, however, involve one major difference. When an issue concerns political economy, supporters of the state are usually on the left, while those who lean toward the market are on the right. In new moral issues, though, the positions are reversed: with respect to abortion, say, a free market is the preferred position of the left, while government regulation becomes that of the right. Since modern liberal democrats have only two major ways of thinking about their social obligations, when each no longer seems to work they simply flip them around.

One example of the inappropriateness of markets and states to the kinds of moral issues facing modern liberal democrats can be seen in the AIDS epidemic. Like abortion, AIDS poses difficult moral dilemmas, not only for those affected or potentially affected, but for the rest of society as well; in recalling the epidemics and plagues that characterized the premodern era, AIDS reminds us of how fragile, and recent, the civilizing process is.[18] Two Scandinavian countries, Sweden and Denmark, illustrate two different ways of responding to the moral challenges of AIDS: the former relies, to an unusual degree, on the state, whereas the latter, at least in its initial response, respected individual choice much as in the market.

As part of its efforts to protect public health and safety, the Swedish state, long before the advent of the AIDS epidemic, already possessed the authority to declare certain diseases part of a "sexual epidemic."[19] Once declared, governmental authority can be swiftly used to control it. Doctors are required by law to report to the authorities all patients diagnosed as having venereal disease. Those so diagnosed are given a certain period of time to report to the police, and if they do not the police will come and take them into custody. The purpose of meeting with public authorities is to make available to them a list of all the people with whom one has had sexual relations, so that the authorities can inform those partners of the situation. From the start of the process until the end of a quarantine, when the patient is declared free of disease, government is continuously involved.

The question facing Swedish authorities in the early 1980s was whether AIDS should be classified as a sexual epidemic. The problem was that AIDS is not like, for example, syphilis. Because AIDS has no cure, no limited period of quarantine after which matters will return to "normal" can be established. Moreover, one of the fears in using compulsion to deal with AIDS is that it might drive the behavior to be regulated underground, which is why many governments have recommended against compulsory AIDS testing. In the end, however, these concerns had little impact in Sweden. AIDS was classified as a sexual epidemic, and the full force of the state was brought to bear. The government announced that drug addicts and prostitutes affected with AIDS, for example, would be transferred to prison, and immediately come under the supervision of not only doctors but also psychologists.[20] Furthermore, the Ministry of Health, in November 1987, decided to convert a former mental hospital into a facility in which people whose behavior indicated that they were likely to spread AIDS to others would be confined.[21] The same tendency to want to head off potential antisocial behavior as therapists used in matters involving family violence or alcoholism was thus transferred to AIDS.

Not surprisingly, Swedes who want to know if they have been infected with the AIDS virus will travel to other, less restrictive, countries to find out. One place they often go is next door to Copenhagen, where confidentiality in AIDS testing is guaranteed. Indeed, the Danish response to AIDS could not be more dissimilar to the Swedish.[22] (The first Westerner known to have died of AIDS was a Danish doctor who had worked in Africa.) Just as Denmark is more liberal in economic matters than Sweden, it is also more laissez-faire in moral matters. When the Progress party, the most right-wing party in parliament, proposed applying Denmark's epidemic laws to AIDS, three of the other major political parties responded by proposing that the epidemic laws be abolished entirely. Yet the more marketlike respect for freedom and confidentiality in Denmark does not solve the problems of AIDS either. Danes were long reluctant to close bathhouses, for example, even when it became known that rapid transmission of the disease was because of them.[23] As in San Francisco, this approach to AIDS, emphasizing tolerance for the individual life-styles of gay men, courted disaster by refusing to take collective responsibility for a problem that transcended the individual's freedom to have sex in any way at any time.

Neither approach—the one based on the market's respect for individual choice, the other on the coercive powers inherent in the state—seems appropriate to resolve the moral dilemmas raised by AIDS.[24] Danish authorities, in viewing AIDS as a matter of individual choice, failed to recognize the need to move beyond immediate preferences, to use the conscience of society early enough and forcefully enough to create a moment of moral scrutiny. (Admittedly, once the crisis became more serious the government changed its policies, bringing gay voluntary organizations into the process and developing a public advertising campaign that stressed both the seriousness of AIDS to society and the idea that individuals themselves must be relied on to hear and act on the message.) Swedish authorities, in contrast, relied so much on government that individuals and their needs counted for little (although by leaving the country to be tested for AIDS, individual Swedes are reacting, in a fairly commonsense way, to a punitive approach that fails to respect individuals as able to understand their own moral dilemmas).

The notion that people with AIDS are suffering for their sins and we ought not give positive reinforcement for the behavior that got them into trouble seems as inappropriate as the idea that it is not our business to tell people how they ought to conduct their sex lives when sex is capable of killing others. To respond to a new moral issue such as AIDS, the institutions and practices of society have to allow room for moral growth by encouraging individuals to reach out to others during moments of passage. Modernity will continue to frustrate people if it raises ever more difficult issues and then relies on moral codes that distrust the ability of individuals to resolve those issues.

Abortion and AIDS by no means exhaust the range of moral issues facing modern liberal democrats. If the parents of an all but officially dead infant want to express their sense of altruism by donating its organs, should they be allowed to, despite rules that define their desire as murder? In a conflictful decision involving surrogate motherhood, is it the interests of the child, the natural mother, or the mother by contract that ought to prevail? Should new technologies be developed that will enable older people to live ten years longer when so doing may take away funds that could be used to cure childhood diseases?[25] There are few easy answers to any of these questions, for in most cases they involve a clash not between good and evil but between one good and another. We may, if we have to deal with such issues, want to turn them over either to the rational calculation of self-interest or to the rule-making capacity of bureaucratic agencies, but we will probably find out that with respect to issues so unprecedented in their moral demands, if people cannot decide for themselves what to do, no other methods will help them much either.

As so many of these moral dilemmas indicate, a certain hesitation ought to be involved in suggesting to people the moral courses they should take. A sociological approach to moral obligation involves a shift in our thinking about moral obligation. Rather than asking which of a number of possible courses of action is more moral (having an abortion or not having one, being sexually promiscuous or not), it seeks to clarify the conditions under which individuals can bring their own capacities as moral agents to bear on the decisions they must make. There is an obvious risk in doing so. Even if people experience a moment of moral passage in which they confront the views of others, they may decide to do what liberal humanitarian opinion would not have them do. (AIDS victims, for example, might continue to have unsafe sex; women who have had many abortions may have more.) Short of creating conditions under which no one could act as a moral agent—the one condition that clearly violates the standard of morality as a social practice (and a condition that is more than just a theoretical possibility when discussing AIDS)—this risk might be worth taking. If, for example, a person has been exposed to the issues of busing and school integration and, having heard and considered the views of others in intense moments of moral passage, such as a series of demonstrations and confrontations, still believes in neighborhood schools, it becomes difficult to judge that person's views or behavior as immoral, no matter how much it may violate one's own sense that racial integration is a moral imperative.[26] One hopes that self-producing moral agents do what one considers morally just, and people who are exposed to other positions through moments of moral passage often will, but it cannot be insisted on beyond a point.

A sociological approach to moral obligation is not, to use a philosophical term, consequentialist; it does not judge the morality of an action by the morality of its consequences. Nor is it proceduralist, seeking to find the proper rules within which moral judgments can be made. Moral obligation is instead found in process, in the degree to which the everyday conditions of ordinary life allow individuals to bring their social capacities to bear on the issues that confront them. Market-oriented societies tend to focus on procedures; in their concern for property rights or the rule of law, they emphasize formalism and specificity in moral obligation. Welfare states, especially those in Scandinavia, tend to be consequentialist: if government can produce morally attractive results, that is justification enough to rely on government. (That the Scandinavian societies have achieved such good results, yet in the process have sacrificed personal moral responsibility, explains my ambivalence toward them.) Even if the best of both worlds were combined—if proper procedures led to consequences generally agreed to be just—a moral dimension would still be missing so long as individuals did not mature and develop as agents through their interaction with others.

It is difficult for social scientists (who are nearly always moral philosophers in disguise) to stop telling people what rules they ought to follow and instead to concentrate on helping people make their own rules. Yet what we lose by doing so—a finely designed and morally just set of rules that most people will wind up altering anyway—may well be compensated for by a recognition of the important contribution a sociological approach to moral obligation can make to the paradoxes of modernity. The more modern we become, the more likely we are to rely on markets and states for our moral codes. And the more we rely on markets and states, the more the spaces within which relations in civil society flourish break down. Yet the weaker civil society becomes, the harder it is to be modern, for it becomes more difficult to find practical ways of balancing obligations in the near and distant spheres of society. Allowing people to be wrong may be less risky overall than insisting on rules by which they may be right, if so doing permits them to keep vibrant a place in which they can cultivate their social capacities to act as moral agents.

Joining, Waiting, Leaving

About the only thing that can be said with any confidence about the moral issues that future generations will have to face is that they cannot be predicted on the basis of the moral issues that we currently face. Just as issues involving AIDS would have astonished people twenty years ago, we simply cannot know what kinds of decisions people living twenty years in the future will be expected to make.

Whatever the moral issues that will define the social fabric of the future, their resolution will be smoother if individuals have a place in society that allows them to take personal responsibility for the moral decisions they make. The contribution of sociologists to an understanding of moral obligation in modern society should be to facilitate the process by which individuals come to recognize and appreciate the importance of civil society. Because the intimate sphere of society is fragile, modern liberal democrats need to think more about how they can preserve it. They will be better able to do so if they think about three aspects of the groups to which they belong: Who should and who should not be members, since membership brings in its wake obligation? How ought groups to establish rules for distributing the benefits they offer? And what are one's obligations to a group that one wishes to leave in order to join another? A sociological approach to moral obligation requires that we think about what can be called entrance rules, waiting rules, and exit rules.

Some people feel an obligation to all humanity, and sometimes even to all animals as well, but for most people moral obligation is more meaningful when obligations are limited in scope. Communities, Michael Walzer has written, "must have boundaries."[27] One of the most difficult issues in the business of defining moral obligation is deciding on *entrance rules,* criteria for determining who should belong to the group to which one is presumably obligated.

Entrance rules are now hotly contested in all modern liberal democracies. In Scandinavia, international movements—of both people and capital—have begun to have a strong effect on the welfare state.[28] As relatively small countries with relatively small economies, the Scandinavian states cannot be tempted by protectionist economic policies but must compete internationally; yet in this open arena, the level of expenditure that the welfare state can tolerate is necessarily affected by international currency movements, balances of trade, and other economic events outside the control of policy makers. Even more significant is the international movement of people, which in the Scandinavian context has considerably changed the ethnic and racial profile of these countries (see table 10). Because Scandinavian societies offer so many benefits, the question of who should be allowed into the country to take advantage of them becomes an emotionally charged issue;[29] meanwhile, the existence within the society of people from many different cultures makes it less likely that the welfare state can operate on the basis of informal understandings and more likely that its rules will be formally codified.

A major political issue facing Scandinavian society today concerns who has a right to belong. A feeling that society is being overwhelmed by foreigners has led to an increase in efforts at exclusion: Sweden, for example, decided that people from Lebanon are no longer to be considered political refugees seeking asylum, while the Social Democratic mayor of a working-class suburb of Copenhagen complained loudly that his city was turning into a Turkish one. It is relatively easy to condemn such actions and complaints as racist, yet the notion that everyone ought to be allowed in, while workable on a case by case basis, is hardly a satisfactory entrance rule. Not everyone who deserves admission to Sweden, Norway, or Denmark can buy the illegal transportation (generally through East Germany) to arrive at a Scandinavian airport and plead their case. Because citizenship is inherently exclusionary—one can be a citizen only if someone else is not—some method of closing borders will always be found.

The case of refugees to Scandinavia poses clearly the moral problem in-

TABLE 10. *Citizens of Selected Foreign Countries, Scandinavia, 1978–85*

	Citizens of Turkey		Citizens of Iran		Citizens of Vietnam	
	1978	*1985*	*1978*	*1985*	*1978*	*1985*
Denmark	11,989	20,408	246	4,727	421	3,675
Norway	1,736	3,359	131	249	432	5,179
Sweden	14,731	21,538	1,903	8,342	45	2,544

Source. *Yearbook of Nordic Statistics 1978* (Stockholm: Nordic Council, 1979), 42–43; *Yearbook of Nordic Statistics 1986* (Stockholm: Nordic Council, 1987), 40–41.

volved in most entrance rules. If such rules are drawn too tightly, obligations to people already in the group are more likely to be satisfied, but at the risk of ignoring any obligation to people outside. If, however, they are drawn too loosely, a commitment to people outside the group can cause a lessening sense of obligation to those inside. This is a real dilemma in Scandinavia, because fiscal limits on the welfare state mean that public resources spent on new members of society reduce the funds available for other kinds of programs. A position that everyone should be allowed into the country is as shortsighted as a position that no one ought to be allowed in.

These dilemmas over entrance rules apply not only to the borders of the nation-state, but also to the borders that define any group within the nation-state. In corporatist-type political systems such as the Scandinavian, group membership tends to be characterized by formal obligations and tightly drawn entrance rules, all of which reinforce a sense of belonging and of loyalty to others. But once again, when obligations within a group are tightly drawn, obligations to those outside the group suffer. On the one hand, life becomes more difficult for those who are not members of any group at all: when day care for small children is as well organized as it is in Scandinavia, the streets are extremely lonely for children not in day care; when unemployment compensation is administered by unions, life can be rough for women and young people who are unemployed and have never been in the labor market. On the other hand, each group demands what is best for itself—even at the expense of its own members. In Scandinavia, tightly organized politics falls victim to what Gunnar Heckscher has called "collective bribery": each group wields enough power to force consideration of its immediate needs.[30] Thus, for example, perfectly sensible reforms in the area of child care—such as relying more on older people to watch young children or encouraging part-time work for one parent when children are small[31]—are opposed, in this case by unions, because the rights of child-care workers take priority over any general sense of obligation to society as a whole, even though child-care workers themselves have children who will be affected by the inflexibility of the rules that their group membership demands. Similarly, both labor and capital share an interest in limiting the hours that stores can legally open, and both use their group power to prevent changes in the law, which results in inconvenience for everyone, including very members of the groups that block the changes.

American society represents a sharp contrast to Scandinavia in terms of entrance rules. While formal entry into the United States is often difficult to obtain, informal passage in and out of the country, especially by immigrant workers seeking low-paid jobs in the South and Southwest, is so easy that people constantly complain that there seems to be no border at all. Likewise, the existence of fifty different states, each with its own entrance rules, encourages liberal entry, for states compete with one another to welcome capital within their borders, making it more difficult for any one state to tighten its borders. Changes in political and social consciousness, such as the breakdown of clubs composed entirely of white male Protestants or the impact of first the civil rights and then the women's movement, have similarly contributed to a loosening of entrance rules within groups of all kinds. American interest-group liberalism, in contrast to Scandinavian corporatism, does not insist that every public policy be decided through negotiation with well-organized groups. (An exception involves New York City, where tightly organized groups such as public school custodians or taxi medallion owners can, much as in Scandinavia, protect their interests irrespective of the consequences for the rest of the city.) Even the entrance rules into families, traditionally the tightest groups of all, have been liberalized as people have been met with more choices, not only over birth control but also over adoption, surrogate motherhood, and other developments that make family membership less a matter of biology and more one of policy.[32]

This ease of entry, both into America and into the groups that compose its public life, constitutes one of the attractions of American society. It is surely a sign of progress when the ease of entry associated with the market replaces strictly defined entrance rules associated with caste and class. Yet when entrance rules are loosened, problems of moral obligation do not go away so much as change their character. It is not that those who are already members will ignore the needs of people outside the group, but rather that group membership itself will carry little sense of obligation toward those who already belong. I hope a personal example is not out of place. The group that pays me a salary, the City University of New York (CUNY), took the courageous step of opening its admissions to all, a step that I supported. Yet it seems clear to me now that in easing entry rules we seriously underestimated the effect our actions would have on institutional loyalty. By essentially announcing that joining CUNY did not entail any special qualities of character, we cheapened group membership for all those who did enter. A decline not only in academic standards but also in the meaning of the experience of education followed, not because poor and minority students took advantage of open admissions (actually the policy, especially at my own institution, led to a rise in the number of lower-middle-class whites who otherwise would have attended religious schools) but because no criteria of entry existed to define who we were and so commit us to be obligated in some sense toward one another.

If no group (or society) can let everyone in but also cannot keep everyone out, obligations to the self and to others can be kept in balance only when groups have entry rules strict enough to give their members a feeling that it means something to be a member, yet at the same time flexible enough to admit strangers and to prevent obligations from becoming so parochial as to be stifling. Somehow a balance will always be found, for modern liberal democracies have neither fully closed guilds nor completely open entry rules. Failure to address the issue out of the mistaken belief either that everyone deserves entry or that no one does means that money becomes the criterion of entry, either because a privileged group becomes expensive to join or because, if joining costs little, the benefits the group offers deteriorate and other groups costing more will be formed as a result.

Since some criteria will always be used to define entry, then, conceiving of entry as a moral passage may help liberal democrats steer a course between groups that are completely closed and groups that cannot define their boundaries. The benefits one obtains by becoming a member of the group ought to impose some costs so that membership is not a frivolous or cheap affair, but those costs can just as well involve membership rituals, time, and obligations to existing members as they can money. Groups ought to be allowed to differ in purpose and membership without being accused of elitism, but those differences can involve commitment and friendship as much as social class, gender, or income. It is certainly not easy to develop entrance rules that are simultaneously tight and loose, but if societies do not, then obligations to groups will come at the expense of obligations to strangers, or vice versa.

Waiting rules attempt to establish criteria for the distribution of scarce goods within any collectivity whose entrance rules have already been defined. Since scarce goods by definition cannot be distributed to everyone who wants them at exactly the moment they choose to want them, there will always be some rules that establish who goes to the front of the line and who waits at the rear. Effective waiting rules rely on a sense of obligation to strangers. If I wait for a benefit to which I am otherwise entitled now, I am allowing someone else to claim it and in that sense recognize that the moral claims of others have priority over mine. Such waiting rules presuppose substantial social trust. If everyone else is unwilling to wait, it makes little sense for me to do so. My freedom to allow others to get in line ahead of me so that I might in turn be allowed to advance in the line when I need to is dependent on extremely fragile social ties that are easily destroyed.

For much of their history, societies that relied on the market did not have to worry much about waiting rules. Those with the right kinds of funds did not need to wait at all, while those who lacked the proper funds had to wait so long that it made sense for them to give up waiting entirely. A market solution to the problem of waiting was as elegant as it was unfair: lines were shortened by eliminating the right of people to wait in them. But whatever its past advantages and disadvantages, reliance on the market to organize waiting rules under modern conditions of economic growth brings about new kinds of problems. Since place in line is literally a positional good, to use Fred Hirsch's term, the market, in lowering the costs of what is available, encourages people to believe they can cut in the line, thereby breaking down the order for which the line was formed in the first place.[33] It is perhaps metaphorical, but one of the consequences of Mrs. Thatcher's efforts to revitalize the market in Britain in the 1980s is much public discussion about the unwillingness of Britons to wait in line with the tolerance, patience, and deference they once showed.

Reliance on the state to organize waiting rules, by contrast, tends to be much fairer, because government acts as a referee to insure that people do not cut in line in front of others. Yet because everyone is guaranteed a place, the lines will obviously be longer. In Scandinavia, for example, even benefits that in theory are universal are in practice characterized by waiting periods that can be unusually long. Health care is generally the most discussed area in this regard. As table II indicates, Danes may wait as long as four years for an operation, and the difference between those who wait a long time and those who wait a short time can vary considerably (while the distribution of services is fairer when organized by the state than by the market, it is still not perfectly fair: middle-class people have better access to day care, and at least some of the variation in hospital waiting lists can be explained by class). It is for such reasons that two Norwegian writers have talked about Scandinavia as a *køsamfunn,* a society of lines.[34]

Although waiting rules are often fairer when organized by the state rather than the market, both markets and states can cause bottlenecks in other ways. Few politicians wish to risk arguing for priorities that will better organize waiting, because it is always safer politically to insist that the goal of universality can be met, even if everyone knows that it cannot. This situation is quite similar to Hirsch's "social limits to growth," only with government, not the market, as the focus. Without a consensus over waiting rules, everyone will claim the rights they have to benefits at the same time, which can have the paradoxical effect of reducing real access to such benefits by increasing the costs of providing them.

One area where a better understanding of waiting rules applies is in Scandinavian efforts to universalize day-care benefits. Because in most families both parents work, the need for day care is inexhaustible. Yet it is also expensive—about $10,000 a year for every Swedish child, for example.[35] Since universalization under these conditions is impossible, many areas have waiting lists for public day care so long that children will be in school before their turn to use preschool facilities comes up (two-thirds of Danish counties have waiting lists, especially for very young children).[36] People thus turn instead to various "gray markets," often with government encouragement. While this conflict between a universal principle and fiscal reality exists in theory, in actual practice it is softened by the fact that many families prefer to alter their claims while they have small children: women would rather work part time, have more maternity leave when their children are young, or stay home and watch their children themselves. The problem is that labor markets tend not to be flexible with respect to waiting rules: if a woman takes five years of her life to raise a small child, she will sacrifice advancement in her career. Here is a case where the state and the market, acting together, not only discourage people from doing what common sense tells them they ought to do, but also prove unable to supply satisfactory guidelines of moral obligation themselves.

Responding to problems of this sort, the American writer Neil Gilbert

TABLE II. *Waiting Lists, Selected Surgical Procedures, Denmark, 1983–85*

	Total Number Performed			Number on Waiting List, 30 June 1986	Long Wait (in months)	Short Wait (in months)	Average Wait (in months)
	1983	1984	1985				
Hernia	11,025	10,679	10,030	3,337	8.4	1.6	4.0
Varicose veins	6,238	5,743	4,885	2,942	42.0	3.7	7.2
Sterilization (men)	6,407	5,744	6,408	1,961	8.7	0.6	3.7
Sterilization (women)	6,831	5,843	5,326	3,705	24.9	1.5	8.3
Cataract	5,467	6,617	7,760	6,124	19.3	4.5	9.5
Knee transplant	902	1,027	1,039	1,635	44.2	10.8	18.9
Hip transplant	4,071	3,738	3,658	3,690	23.8	6.0	12.1

Source. Ventetider til sygehusbehandling (Copenhagen: Ministry of the Interior, 1986), 29.

has suggested awarding credits for childrearing that could be exchanged for a higher entry position in the labor force or for educational advancement later on in life.[37] Somewhat similarly, conservative parties in Scandinavia have proposed that women who choose to stay home with their children (and thereby offer to the public sector the gift of some fiscal relief) be paid for doing so. Such reforms would help to relieve the tension between universal claims and fiscal realities and at the same time would show respect for people's own commonsense understandings of what their obligations to others ought to be—a combination of advantages that should make them popular. Yet they remain off the public agenda. Women's groups oppose them on the grounds that they will interfere with the drive toward equality in the workplace; likewise, the general lack of a sense of reciprocity across time works against them, as individuals find it difficult to allow the claims of others to take precedence over their own claims, in return for similar favors later. People want strict rules and commonsense exceptions simultaneously, a difficult balance to find.

In both the United States and Scandinavia, reliance on markets and states has created new problems with respect to waiting rules. In the United States in the early 1980s, the social security system lost some of its popular support when fears that increasing longevity would combine with lower birth rates to deplete the system of money in the future. Although such fears turned out to be incorrect, they reflected the heritage of the otherwise brilliant popular legitimation for social security, first advanced by Franklin Roosevelt, that the system ought to appear to conform to the marketplace principle that people are getting equal benefits in return for what they are putting in.[38] In Scandinavia, the conflict between benefits that in theory are universally available but in practice require waiting has begun to put a strain on the consensus and sense of fairness that have always made the Scandinavian welfare state such a model. The task of establishing effective waiting rules is anything but easy, but at a minimum society should recognize that those who are willing to wait, whose common sense tells them not to exercise a claim even when the market and the state make a benefit available to them, ought not to be discouraged.

A third social practice that requires greater understanding if people are to use their capacity as social beings to create moral rules concerns *exit rules*. Ease of exit is always tied to ease of entrance: it is much easier to leave a group when you know that another is prepared to take you in. Yet although one group's entrance is always another's exit, it is often difficult to treat exit and entrance as moral equivalents. As Walzer puts it,

[The] right to control immigration does not include or entail the right to control emigration. The political community can shape its own population in the one way, not in the other. . . . The restraint of entry serves to defend the liberty and welfare, the politics and culture of a group of people committed to one another and to their common life. But the restraint of exit replaces commitment with coercion.[39]

Of course, Walzer is correct in the absolute sense of complete restraints on exit. Societies that use the powers of government to prevent people from leaving, such as the Soviet Union, deny the moral capacity of their members to participate in shaping the social practices that will govern them and thus force an obligation to the state, as symbolized by the police, rather than to society, as symbolized by obligations to others.[40]

Yet an unrestricted right to exit under any conditions is also morally problematic, if not to the same degree. If one has been the member of a group or political community and has received benefits from that group for some period of time, an automatic, unconditional right to exit is a right to escape from the obligations such benefits carry. Numerous examples exist of how the ease of exit so valued by the market corrodes moral obligation, nearly all of them involving firms that received benefits to locate in a particular place (including tax concessions, easements, public services, and the willingness of individuals to give time and effort) only to close up and move—not when profits disappeared, but when profits were not as great as they could be in some other place.[41] Societies need exit rules to prevent exactly this kind of thing from happening. It is not unreasonable to believe that Scandinavians who have received benefits from generous welfare states owe something to society if they decide to move to America to make more money, just as corporations should be allowed to leave communities only after some meaningful repayment of the gift the community offered them in the first place.

There is one final area where a sociological approach to moral obligation ought to search for rules that are neither as restrictive as those of the state nor as permissive as those of the market. Here the importance of exit rules applies not to those who plan to leave but to those who decide to stay behind. If exit rules are too loosely drawn, it becomes difficult for remaining members to invest much in their obligations to others, for those others can always escape. Moreover, obligations in society as a whole are not likely to be taken seriously when migration becomes so dominant a response to tight situations that it is continuously rewarded over staying. Leaving should, therefore, be made somewhat more difficult than automatic. This does not mean the use of state police force, merely that those who want to leave be asked to donate something in return. Whether we are talking of marriages, clubs, neighborhoods, or societies, separation anxieties ought, in fact, to be anxious. Leaving should not be prohibited, but exit rules should be established to remind both those taking their leave and those left behind that, because they once had obligations in the old group, they will likely have obligations to others in the new social arrangements that are formed when old ones change.

Under the influence of the market, we tend not to take seriously our group obligations but rather enter them and leave them as our self-interest demands. Under the influence of the state, groups become vital to the definition of who we are, identifying our rights and determining our obligations. Although quite different, both ways of thinking about the obligations that membership brings have one thing in common: neither asks that individuals themselves play an active role in determining the character of the groups to which they belong. Groups should not be viewed as if membership in them were, like birth, a biological act, but they also should not make up so much a part of our collective identity that we become prisoners to the political logic by which they operate. If modern liberal democrats are going to accept a greater role in shaping the rules that govern them, they will need to pay as much attention to the ways groups constitute and reconstitute themselves as political and economic approaches to moral obligation pay to the benefits that membership in groups can bring.

Ecologies: Natural and Social

The paradox of modernity, I argued in the Introduction, is that individuals whose sense of moral commitment in the small-scale world of civil society is being weakened need to develop rules to govern their obligations to strangers and even hypothetical others. By now it ought to be clear that demands of this sort are so difficult to meet that people quite possibly will not be able to, with consequences for the future (and for distant others in the present) that are painful to contemplate. It ought furthermore to be clear that if people *can* meet these demands, it will not be because they are furnished with a set of universally applicable moral rules that require only that they do their duty or claim their rights. Markets and states are good for many things, but when used for finding the right way to balance intimacy and distance they tend to overweight one or the other.

I have in this book suggested that a better way to find a balance between intimate and distant obligations is to view the construction of moral rules as a social practice, one that requires groups in civil society for the learning and development of moral rules, yet also requires that what is learned in the intimate realm be extended to people whom we will never personally know. It is not enough simply to praise civil society and condemn the market and the state. That path would surely lead to a situation in which obligations in small-scale worlds would be satisfied at the expense of obligations in the larger world—a situation just as frustrating to the paradox of modernity as one in which obligations to strangers took precedence over obligations to family members and friends.

This unsatisfactory result is even more likely to be the case because the intimate world in modern liberal democracies in fact *is,* as I have suggested throughout this book, threatened both by markets and by states. In Scandinavia, consequently, the language of community control and family integrity is used to protest every plan to close a school or a hospital during periods of fiscal restraint. One's instincts are to support such protests, but in so doing one fails to recognize that such efforts may deprive future generations of schools and hospitals, as well as prevent the construction of new institutions in areas that do not yet have them. (In a similar manner, the rise of what in the United States have been called "NIMBY" movements—for "not in my back yard"—tend to be accompanied by the attitude that so long as a nuclear power plant or highway extension is not built here, where exactly it is built need not concern us.) Individuals who use the language of civil society to protect in-group privileges against the claims of strangers thus forfeit the right to have strangers consider *their* needs. Civil society, viewed as an end in itself, leads directly to Hobbesian struggles over turf.

There is, however, evidence, some of which I have presented in this book, that the protection of the intimate sphere of society can act to give individuals a personal stake in the fate of others. When people have strong ties in the intimate sector, they are more likely to give to charity (in societies that emphasize the market) or to pay their taxes (in societies that emphasize the state). People who have experienced caring for others, no matter how difficult, tend to understand the importance of providing for the young and the old. (While caring is something that generally takes place in families, it need not; the extraordinary degree of caring shown by many homosexuals toward individuals dying of AIDS calls on emotional resources that few family members will ever need to muster.) When local communities are protected against the full intrusion of the market, greater voluntary activity and respect for others will result; when they are protected against the full intrusion of the state, not every response to every social problem need be an institutional response. When the satisfaction of self-interest becomes difficult to resist, reliance on common services—even when self-interest might dictate an exit—improves everyone else's capacity to rely on common services. When reliance on government to provide services becomes difficult to resist, individuals who can and want to provide for themselves can ease the fiscal burden involved in having government provide services for those who cannot. When people know that they share with others a common culture, restraints on self-interest (in market-oriented societies) or on claims to rights (in state-oriented societies) are more likely to exist. When, in short, civil society exists as a sphere alongside the market and the state, it contributes to the more effective working of both of them; when the market and the state exist without civil society, neither can work as promised. If the question is whether we use abstract rules that regulate our relationships with strangers to organize our relationships with intimates or we rely on the recognition of our dependency on intimates to help us codify our relationships with strangers, the latter seems to make more sense. Most people find it easier to move from the particular to the general than the reverse.

Still, when all is said and done there is not and can never be any guarantee that stronger relations in civil society will create the practices that enable people to take personal responsibility for the fate of abstract others. All the social scientist can do in such a circumstance is to remind modern liberal democrats that they do not live in tribal clans. If people are not aware of a world outside the intimate sphere, social science must make them aware of it. Sociology in particular ought to reinforce the idea that moral obligation can become a social practice only when—as the thinkers of the Scottish Enlightenment proposed and the classical tradition in sociology carried forward—society is understood as a gift. Moreover, it is a gift that we give to ourselves, since no one put it in place for us. It is difficult for modern people to remember these things, because we take for granted society's independence from nature in a way that eighteenth-century theorists never could. A social bond, now in place, is simply assumed to be. Society has become part of the scenery of modern life, the backdrop in front of which economics and politics play their roles.

If modern liberal democrats are going to learn to live with the difficulties of moral obligation, they will need to put behind them the temptations of Rousseau. We are not born free and corrupted by our institutions. If anything, as I argued in Chapter 8, we are born as selfish egoists, and only our institutions and practices save us from ourselves. A long tradition in social theory holds that individuals are anything but angels. Put them together with no rules to help them define their moral obligations—in prisons or market situations lacking any moral restraint—and they will act as pure market theorists or neo-Hobbesians assume. That they do not act that way all the time is because they have accepted the gift of society—which is why it is so risky to flirt with the idea of taking the gift back. Having rules to regulate our social interaction is what makes everything else possible.

It is only because modern liberal democrats take society for granted that they can even consider relying on the market or the state to structure rules of moral obligation. What makes the approach of the Chicago school of economics so tantalizing is its suggestion that we can do without society and all its difficulties. The issue is not that Chicago school theories are wrong in their description of how ubiquitous self-interest can become; it is the disturbing possibility that they may be right. When we make self-interest the guide to all our moral decisions, we are in a sense proclaiming that we no longer wish to enjoy the gift of society but wish instead to be ruled by something called human "nature," as if society were not put in place to prevent us from acting like selfish genes. To the degree that Chicago school economics describes what is taking place in society, it describes a society that is in decline because its members are not willing to adhere to the rules that make it work. The problem with the Chicago school recommendations is that if we choose to go back to "nature," it will take a social decision to do so. Nature, as Karl Polanyi emphasized, looks different when it is socially created.[42]

Much the same is true of neo-Hobbesian approaches to politics. The conditions of modern life are nowhere near the state they were at the time of the English civil war, when Hobbes was prompted to call for sovereign authority. But numerous reminders of the fragility of the social bond exist, even in the most modern of liberal democracies. The "normal accidents" of complex technology, the precariousness of the compromises between labor and capital, racial and ethnic hostilities, increasing homelessness and marginality, the savagery of urban life, and the transmission of AIDS (which shows that we are capable of killing each other through love just as Hobbes's Englishmen killed each other through war) are just a few reminders of how thin the line is between the natural and the social.[43]

The promise of the Hobbesian approach to social order is that government will protect us from our own animalistic instincts. To some degree, of course, this is true: instill enough fear in people, and they may well obey. Yet no society can rely on the police forever. In fact, it is not government that separates us from a state of nature, but society, the invisible links of trust and reliance on others that enable us not to carry guns whenever we face unknown others. When society makes civilized life possible we tend, as with the market, to assume its existence. We are thereby tempted to take the shortcut of keeping order through use of the state instead, forgetting that the state is a product of society, that substituting the former for the latter is to return us to the state of nature from which we have emerged. It is at this point that pure statists and pure market theorists recognize the need for each other: since both take society for granted, each reinforces the distrust that proves the other's view of human nature correct.[44]

Society and nature are radically different ecologies. It is a serious mistake to believe that respect for nature can help us develop rules for respecting society.[45] The common response of people concerned with protecting the natural environment is laissez-faire: intervention—to alter genes or redirect rivers, for example—is best not done, for who can tell what the consequences will be if we tamper? When the same notion is applied to society, however, the social order is understood to be so self-regulating that any effort to give it a conscious direction will be self-defeating. Yet while there is evolution in nature, there is no evolution in society—except in those movements that are the product of will and deliberation. By applying the rules of laissez-faire to society, we strip ourselves of the capacity to engage in social growth: we are forced to sit and watch as our social ecology crumbles. Then, when it seems almost too late to stop the process, we call on the authority of government to save us from our worst instincts; yet because government intervention is premised on the notion that our nature drives us to escape our obligations, we thereby acknowledge our inability to trust one another instead.

It seems strange to justify modernity on the basis of a premodern conception of moral agency in which individuals can control everything in society except their own natures, but that is essentially what we do when we rely on the rules of markets and states to codify our obligations for us. Under the rules of contemporary economics and politics, society, modernity's greatest invention, is brought into being to regulate our interactions with one another but then is stripped of its power to do so through deemphasis of the social skills we have at our disposal. In the constant shifting between economic and political rules, society has little role to play at all; the dialectic of freedom and constraint is fought out between individuals whose nature impels them to want more on the one hand and a Hobbesian source of authority that once in a while has to call a halt to the process on the other.

The gift society has given us lies in the benefits we receive—including high rates of economic growth, large and centralized economies, a government capable of delivering services, and rapid social and economic mobility—by coordinating our actions with those of others. Yet all gifts, even when altruistically offered, are given in the expectation that the receiver will reciprocate. In return for the gift of society, modern liberal democrats are asked only one thing: to recognize that in return for these benefits they relinquish "pure" freedom, the ability to do anything they want in any way at any time. It is in this sense that the constraints on freedom imposed by modernity are social, not natural; it is not our inability to transcend gravity or overcome the anarchy of a state of nature that restricts our freedom to do what we like, but our inability to transcend our dependence on others.

When we recognize society as a gift, we realize that we are free because our preferences can change through interaction with others, not because they are constant. We are free because we can give meaning to the way our situations are defined. We are free because we recognize that the condition of being modern sets internal limits on free-ridership, even if there were no external obstacles to impede us. We are free because we elevate loyalty over exit and voice, because we have strong intimate relations that enable us to resist mass society's pressure to conform. We are free because we fulfill our obligations to society because we want to, not because government does it for us. We are free, not to express our nature, but to create it. We are free because we accept the regulation and discipline needed to make social cooperation work but then challenge that regulatory process to take account of real people in real situations of time and space. We are free because we can grow and develop. We are free only when others are also free, and they are free only when we are.

The message that sociology offers modern liberal democrats is neither complacent nor apocalyptic. It is commonsensical: here is society; you have given it to yourself as a gift; if you do not take care of it, you should not be surprised when you can no longer find it. That message by itself cannot tell people how to satisfy their obligations to intimate and distant others simultaneously, but it at least makes it clear that if people themselves do not continue to try to meet those obligations, no one else will do it for them.

Notes

Notes to Introduction

1. For an overview, see Gabriel A. Almond, Marvin Chodorow, and Roy Harvey Pearce, eds., *Progress and Its Discontents* (Berkeley and Los Angeles: University of California Press, 1982).

2. See Michael Ignatieff, *The Needs of Strangers: An Essay on Privacy, Solidarity, and the Politics of Being Human* (New York: Penguin Books, 1985).

3. See Seyla Benhabib, "The Generalized and Concrete Other," in *Women and Moral Theory*, ed. Eva Kittay and Diane Meyers (Totowa, N.J.: Rowman and Littlefield, 1988), 154–77.

4. William Sullivan, *Reconstructing Public Philosophy* (Berkeley and Los Angeles: University of California Press, 1982), 95.

5. Robert E. Goodin, *Protecting the Vulnerable: A Reanalysis of Our Social Responsibilities* (Chicago: University of Chicago Press, 1985).

6. Lionel Trilling, *The Liberal Imagination* (New York: Viking Press, 1950), 222.

7. John Gardner, *On Moral Fiction* (New York: Basic Books, 1978).

8. E. M. Forster, *Two Cheers for Democracy* (New York: Harcourt, Brace, 1951), 57.

9. E. M. Forster, *Howard's End* (London: Penguin Books, 1971), 179.

10. Various explorations of the relationship between morality and the social sciences have recently begun to appear. See, e.g., Norma Haan, Robert Bellah, Paul Rabinow, and William M. Sullivan, *Social Science as Moral Inquiry* (New York: Columbia University Press, 1983); Amartya Sen, *On Ethics and Economics* (Oxford: Basil Blackwell, 1987); and the literature discussed at greater length in Chapter 8 below.

11. One work in modern social science which argues that too great a centralization of authority will undermine sources of regeneration is Joseph Schumpeter, *Capitalism, Socialism, and Democracy* (New York: Harper, 1950). For the views of an economist who argues the other point—that the sum total of anarchic individual

decisions can cause a breakdown of the capitalist order—see Fred Hirsch, *Social Limits to Growth* (Cambridge, Mass.: Harvard University Press, 1976).

12. Milton Friedman, *Capitalism and Freedom* (Chicago: University of Chicago Press, 1962), 13.

13. Geoffrey Brennan and James M. Buchanan, *The Reason of Rules: Constitutional Political Economy* (Cambridge: Cambridge University Press, 1985), 3.

14. Gary Becker, *The Economic Approach to Human Behavior* (Chicago: University of Chicago Press, 1976), 5.

15. Dennis H. Wrong, "The Oversocialized Conception of Man in Modern Sociology," *American Sociological Review* 26 (April 1961): 183–93.

16. Benjamin Barber, *Strong Democracy: Participatory Politics for a New Age* (Berkeley and Los Angeles: University of California Press, 1984), 173–78.

17. Charles Schultze, *The Public Use of Private Interest* (Washington, D.C.: Brookings Institution, 1977), 18.

18. Lawrence M. Baskir and William A. Strauss, *Chance and Circumstance: The Draft, the War, and the Vietnam Generation* (New York: Alfred Knopf, 1978).

19. Charles C. Moskos, "Citizen Soldier Versus Economic Man," in *The Social Fabric,* ed. James F. Short, Jr. (Beverly Hills, Calif.: Sage, 1986), 245.

20. Milton Friedman, "Why Not a Volunteer Army?" and Walter Oi, "The Costs and Implications of an All Volunteer Force," in *The Draft,* ed. Sol Tax (Chicago: University of Chicago Press, 1967), 200–207, 221–51.

21. This influence of the "only available job" is why the army became disproportionately black when it relied on the market to recruit. See Charles C. Moskos, "Social Considerations of the All-Volunteer Force," in *Military Service in the United States,* ed. Brent Scowcroft (Englewood Cliffs, N.J.: Prentice-Hall, 1982), 129–50; and Martin Binkin et al., *Blacks and the Military* (Washington, D.C.: Brookings Institution, 1982).

22. Morris Janowitz and Charles C. Moskos, "Five Years of the All-Volunteer Force: 1973–1978," *Armed Forces and Society* 5 (February 1979): 171–218; and Charles C. Moskos and John H. Faris, "Beyond the Marketplace: National Service and the AVF," in *Towards a Consensus on Military Policy,* ed. Andrew J. Goodpaster, Lloyd H. Elliott, and J. Allan Hovey (New York: Pergamon Press, 1981), 131–51.

23. Amy Gutmann, *Democratic Education* (Princeton, N.J.: Princeton University Press, 1987), 61.

24. Albert O. Hirschman, *Shifting Involvements: Private Interest and Public Action* (Princeton, N.J.: Princeton University Press, 1982).

25. Peter L. Berger, *The Capitalist Revolution: Fifty Propositions About Prosperity, Equality, and Liberty* (New York: Basic Books, 1986), 20.

26. Adam Ferguson, *An Essay on the History of Civil Society* (Philadelphia: Wm. Fry, 1819), 32.

27. Ibid., 33.

28. Quoted in David Frisby and Derek Sayer, *Society* (London: Tavistock, 1986), 23.

29. Quoted in Ignatieff, *Needs of Strangers,* 92.

30. Ignatieff (ibid., 83–87) recounts the story of Hume's secular death as told by Boswell and Adam Smith.

31. Alasdair MacIntyre, *A Short History of Ethics* (New York: Collier Books, 1966), 179.

32. David Hume, "An Inquiry Concerning Human Understanding," in *Essays: Moral, Political, and Literary,* ed. T. H. Greene and T. H. Grose (London: Longmans Green, 1875), 2:72–73.

33. T. M. Knox, *Hegel's Philosophy of Right* (New York: Oxford University Press, 1967), 123.

34. Among conservatives, for example, the concept of "mediating structures" bears some resemblance to civil society. See Peter Berger and Richard John Neuhaus, *To Empower People: The Role of Mediating Structures in Public Policy* (Washington, D.C.: American Enterprise Institute, 1977); for a left perspective, see John Keane, *Democracy and Civil Society* (London: Verso, 1988). Also relevant to this discussion are Torben Hviid Nielsen, "The State, the Market, and the Individual," *Acta Sociologica* 29, no. 4 (1986): 283–302, and Nielsen, *Samfund og magt* (Copenhagen: Akademisk Forlag, 1988), 81–101.

35. Claude Lefort, *The Political Forms of Modern Society* (Cambridge, Mass.: MIT Press, 1986), 285.

36. For a collection of writings emphasizing this point, see John Keane, ed., *Civil Society and the State* (London: Verso, 1988).

37. Georg Konrad, *Antipolitics* (London: Quartet Books, 1984), 92.

38. Adam Michnik, *Letters from Prison and Other Essays* (Berkeley and Los Angeles: University of California Press, 1985), 124.

39. For a review of a large body of literature showing the importance of social support networks organized by neither the market nor the state, see Marc Pilisuk and Susan Hillier Parks, *The Healing Web: Social Networks and Human Survival* (Hanover, N.H.: University Press of New England, 1986).

40. Jürgen Habermas, *Theory of Communicative Action,* vol. 1: *Reason and the Rationality of Society,* trans. Thomas McCarthy (Boston: Beacon Press, 1984).

Notes to Chapter 1

1. Adam Smith, *The Wealth of Nations* (New York: Modern Library, 1937), 17.

2. Bernard Barber, "Absolutization of the Market: Some Notes on How We Got From There to Here," in *Markets and Morals,* ed. Gerald Dworkin, Gordon Bermant, and Peter G. Brown (New York: John Wiley, 1977), 19–20.

3. An examination of the economy of Smith's Scotland reveals modest growth, but primarily in the agricultural sector. See T. C. Smout, "Where Had the Scottish Economy Got to by the Third Quarter of the Eighteenth Century?" in *Wealth and Virtue,* ed. Istvan Hont and Michael Ignatieff (Cambridge: Cambridge University Press, 1983), 45–72.

4. Nathan Rosenberg and L. E. Birdsell, Jr., *How The West Grew Rich: The Economic Transformation of the Industrial World* (New York: Basic Books, 1986), 183.

5. Irving Kristol, "Rationalism in Economics," in *The Crisis in Economic Theory,* ed. Daniel Bell and Irving Kristol (New York: Basic Books, 1981), 206.

6. It is now generally recognized that Adam Smith's moral philosophy was far more complex than a simple defense of self-interest. See, e.g., J. Ralph Lindgren, *The Social Philosophy of Adam Smith* (The Hague: Martinus Nijhoff, 1973); and Hans Medick, *Naturzustand und Naturgeschichte der bürgerlichen Gesellschaft* (Göttingen: Vandenhoeck and Ruprecht, 1973), 171–295. For a slightly different interpretation, see Nicholas Phillipson, "Adam Smith as Civil Moralist," in Hont and Ignatieff, *Wealth and Virtue,* 179–202.

7. Smith, *The Wealth of Nations,* 14, 13.

8. Adam Smith, *The Theory of Moral Sentiments,* ed. D. D. Raphael and A. L. Macfie (Oxford: Clarendon Press, 1976), 9, 21, 61.

9. Allan Silver, "Friendship in Social Theory: Personal Relations in Classical Liberalism" (unpublished paper, January 1987), 12, 29. The quotes from Smith are cited by Silver from *The Theory of Moral Sentiments.*

10. Among the important documents are Herbert A. Simon, "Theories of Decision-making in Economics and Behavioral Science," *American Economic Review* 49 (June 1959): 253–83; Kenneth Arrow, "Risk Perception in Psychology and Economics," *Economic Inquiry* 20 (January 1982): 1–9; Harvey Leibenstein, *Beyond Economic Man: A New Foundation for Economics* (Cambridge, Mass.: Harvard University Press, 1976); William J. Baumol, *Welfare Economics and the Theory of the State,* 2d rev. ed. (Cambridge, Mass.: Harvard University Press, 1965); and Francis M. Bator, "The Anatomy of Market Failure," *Quarterly Journal of Economics* 72 (August 1958): 351–79. The best critiques of neoclassical economic assumptions, in my opinion, are Martin Hollis and Edward J. Nell, *Rational Economic Man: A Philosophical Critique of Neo-classical Economics* (Cambridge: Cambridge University Press, 1975); and Amartya Sen, "Rational Fools," in *Choice, Welfare, and Measurement,* ed. Sen (Oxford: Basil Blackwell, 1982), 84–106.

11. On the question of perfect information, see Armen A. Alchian and Harold Demsetz, "Production, Information Costs, and Economic Information," *American Economic Review* 62 (December 1972): 777–95; and Sanford J. Grossman and Joseph E. Stiglitz, "On the Impossibility of Informationally Efficient Markets," *American Economic Review* 70 (June 1980): 393–408. On hierarchical and institutional decision-making, see, e.g., Oliver Williamson, *The Economic Institutions of Capitalism* (New York: Free Press, 1985).

12. This similarity of interest may help explain why at least some Marxist economists praise the research methodology of Chicago School economists. See John Roemer, ed., *Analytical Marxism* (Cambridge: Cambridge University Press, 1986).

13. On marriage, see Gary Becker, *The Economic Approach to Human Behavior* (Chicago: University of Chicago Press, 1976), 205–50; on immigration, Julian L. Simon, "Auction the Right to Be an Immigrant," *New York Times,* 28 January 1986,

A25; on credit, Stephen M. Crafton, "An Empirical Test of the Effect of Usury Laws," *Journal of Law and Economics* 23 (April 1980): 135–45; on selling body parts, Lori B. Andrews, "My Body, My Property," *Hastings Center Report* 16 (October 1986): 28–38; on service and long lines, Francis T. Lui, "An Equilibrium Queuing Model of Bribery," *Journal of Political Economy* 93 (August 1985): 760–81; on surrogate motherhood, Anthony D'Amato, "Surrogate Motherhood Should be Privatized" (letter), *New York Times,* 3 March 1987, A26; and on suicide, Daniel S. Hammermesh and Neal M. Soss, "An Economic Theory of Suicide," *Journal of Political Economy* 82 (January–February 1974): 83–98, quote p. 85.

14. On the Marxist approach to morality, see Steven Lukes, *Marxism and Morality* (Oxford: Clarendon Press, 1985).

15. Murray Rothbard, *Man, Economy, and State* (Princeton, N.J.: Van Nostrand, 1962), 1:443, cited in Robert Nozick, *Anarchy, State, and Utopia* (New York: Basic Books, 1974), 86; and Nozick, ibid., 85.

16. John Kay, "Discussion," *Economic Policy* 6 (April 1988): 187–89, quote p. 188; and David F. Larcker and Thomas Lys, "An Empirical Analysis of the Incentives to Engage in Costly Information Acquisition," *Journal of Financial Economics* 18, no. 1 (1987): 111–26.

17. My approach in this chapter both overlaps and differs from that of Amitai Etzioni in *The Moral Dimension: Toward a New Economics* (New York: Free Press, 1988), which appeared just as this book was going to press. Although our critiques of neoclassical economic assumptions are similar, Etzioni views rationality as artificial and nonrationality as natural, whereas I tend to see the matter the other way around (see Chapter 8). In addition, he posits a dichotomy between self-interested or pleasurable motivations and moral ones, while I tend to view advocates of rational egoism as engaged in a discussion about morality, if of a particular kind. Finally, Etzioni's approach to moral obligation is more deontological than mine, as will become clear in the chapters that follow.

18. See Marvin B. Sussman, Judith N. Cates, and David T. Smith, *The Family and Inheritance* (New York: Russell Sage Foundation, 1970); and John A. Brittain, *Inheritance and the Inequality of Material Wealth* (Washington, D.C.: Brookings Institution, 1978). On discrimination against daughters, see Carole Shammas, Marylynn Salmon, and Michael Dahlin, *Inheritance in America from Colonial Times to the Present* (New Brunswick, N.J.: Rutgers University Press, 1987), 204.

19. B. D. Bernheim, A. Shleifer, and L. H. Summers, "The Strategic Bequest Motive," *Journal of Political Economy* 93 (December 1985): 1071.

20. Timothy H. Hannan, "Bank Robberies and Bank Security Precautions," *Journal of Legal Studies* 11 (January 1982): 83–92.

21. Richard Titmuss, *The Gift Relationship: From Human Blood to Social Policy* (London: Allen and Unwin, 1970); a recent effort to reinterpret blood donation from an economic perspective is Robert Sugden, *Who Cares? An Economic and Ethical Analysis of Private Charity and the Welfare State* (London: Institute for Economic Affairs, 1983). For a far more balanced, indeed charitable, view, see Kenneth J.

Arrow, "Gifts and Exchanges," in *Altruism, Morality, and Economic Theory,* ed. Edmund S. Phelps (New York: Russell Sage Foundation, 1975), 13–28.

22. On dueling, W. F. Schwartz, K. Baxter, and D. Ryan, "The Duel: Can These Gentlemen Be Acting Efficiently?" *Journal of Legal Studies* 13 (June 1984): 321–55; on symbols and clan names, J. L. Carr and J. T. Landu, "The Economics of Symbols, Clan Names, and Religion," *Journal of Legal Studies* 12 (January 1983): 135–56; on blackmail, Richard A. Epstein, "Blackmail, Inc.," *University of Chicago Law Review* 50 (Spring 1983): 553–66; on plea bargaining, Frank H. Easterbrook, "Criminal Procedure and the Market System," *Journal of Legal Studies* 12 (June 1983): 289–332; on quackery, A.W.B. Simpson, "Quackery and Contract Law: The Case of the Carbolic Smoke Ball," *Journal of Legal Studies* 14 (June 1985): 345–89; on photocopying, William R. Johnson, "The Economics of Copying," *Journal of Political Economy* 93 (February 1985): 158–74; on academic life, George J. Stigler, *The Intellectual and the Market Place* (Glencoe, Ill.: Free Press, 1963); on Eichmann, Albert Breton and Ronald Wintrobe, "The Bureaucracy of Murder Revisited," *Journal of Political Economy* 94 (October 1986): 905–26.

23. Bruce Bueno de Mesquita, "The Costs of War: A Rational Expectations Approach," *American Political Science Review* 77 (June 1983): 347–57.

24. Becker, *Economic Approach,* 14. Becker claims that he is not trying to "downgrade" the other social sciences and is not even arguing for the superiority of economics. But he then proceeds to cite as evidence of the contribution made by other social sciences only those committed to the assumption of stable preferences, most especially, in his view, sociobiology. Recently Becker accepted an appointment in the sociology department at the University of Chicago to complement his appointment in economics.

25. Jack Hirshleifer, "The Expanding Domain of Economics," *American Economic Review* 75 (December 1985): 53–68.

26. Reuven Brenner, "Economics—An Imperialist Science?" *Journal of Legal Studies* 9 (January 1980): 179–88. A certain modesty in predictive claims might be entertained by the economics profession. One study compared the predictions made by economists concerning GNP, inflation, and the balance of trade against so-called naive methods, such as estimating the future based on a linear extrapolation from the immediate past. The naive methods performed better. See D. J. Smyth and J.C.K. Ash, "Forecasting Gross National Product, the Rate of Inflation, and the Balance of Trade: The OECD Performance," *The Economic Journal* 85 (June 1975): 361–64. See also the discussion in Alasdair MacIntyre, *After Virtue: A Study in Moral Theory* (South Bend, Ind.: University of Notre Dame Press, 1981), 89.

27. Donald N. McCloskey, *The Rhetoric of Economics* (Madison: University of Wisconsin Press, 1985), 76, 82.

28. See Milton Friedman, "The Methodology of Positive Economics," in *Essays in Positive Economics* (Chicago: University of Chicago Press, 1953), 3–46.

29. Gordon Tullock, "Economic Imperialism," in *The Theory of Public Choice,* ed. James M. Buchanan and Robert D. Tollison (Ann Arbor: University of Michigan Press, 1972), 324.

30. Michael S. McPherson, "Want Formation, Morality, and Some 'Interpretative' Aspects of Economic Inquiry," in *Social Science as Moral Inquiry,* ed. Norma Haan et al. (New York: Columbia University Press, 1983), 96–124.

31. George J. Stigler and Gary S. Becker, "De Gustibus Non Disputandum," *American Economic Review* 67 (March 1977): 76–90.

32. For a critique of Chicago school theory along similar lines, and moreover one that shows the linkages between behavioralism in psychology, sociobiology, and this version of economic theory, see Barry Schwartz, *The Battle for Human Nature: Science, Morality, and Modern Life* (New York: W.W. Norton, 1986).

33. For a discussion of the major ethical and moral issues raised by economic theories of the market, see Allen Buchanan, *Ethics, Efficiency, and the Market* (Oxford: Clarendon Press, 1985).

34. Becker, *Economic Approach,* 14.

35. Richard A. Posner, *The Economics of Justice* (Cambridge, Mass.: Harvard University Press, 1981), 2.

36. Elizabeth M. Landes and Richard A. Posner, "The Economics of the Baby Shortage," *Journal of Legal Studies* 7 (June 1978): 344–45.

37. Becker, *Economic Approach,* 8, 5, 14.

38. See, for example, Bernard Williams, "A Critique of Utilitarianism," in *Utilitarianism—For and Against,* ed. J.J.C. Smart and Bernard Williams (Cambridge: Cambridge University Press, 1973), 77–150.

39. Posner, *Economics of Justice,* 66.

40. Michael Walzer, *Spheres of Justice: A Defense of Pluralism and Equality* (New York: Basic Books, 1983).

41. Posner, *Economics of Justice,* 62.

42. Walzer, *Spheres of Justice,* 281–321.

43. Ibid., 119–20.

44. An interesting effort to argue that marketplace theories of rational choice are coercive may be found in Robin West, "Authority, Autonomy, and Choice: The Role of Consent in the Moral and Political Visions of Franz Kafka and Richard Posner," *Harvard Law Review* 99 (December 1985): 384–428. I also found helpful Larry M. Preston, "Freedom, Markets, and Voluntary Exchange," *American Political Science Review* 78 (December 1984): 959–70.

45. Charles Lindblom, "The Market as Prison," *Journal of Politics* 44 (May 1982): 324–36.

46. The novelist is Richard Powers, *Prisoner's Dilemma* (New York: William Morrow, 1988).

47. Robert Axelrod, *The Evolution of Cooperation* (New York: Basic Books, 1984).

48. Tournaments are of special interest to the Chicago school; see, for example,

Jerry R. Green and Nancy L. Stokey, "A Comparison of Tournaments and Contracts," *Journal of Political Economy* 91 (June 1983): 349–64.

49. Axelrod, *Evolution of Cooperation,* 193. Tullock evidently did not enter the second round.

50. For introductions to the economics of time, see Gordon C. Winston, *The Timing of Economic Activities* (Cambridge: Cambridge University Press, 1982); and Clifford H. Sharp, *The Economics of Time* (Oxford: Martin Robertson, 1981).

51. See Robert Frank, *Choosing the Right Pond: Human Behavior and the Quest for Status* (New York: Oxford University Press, 1985), 42–55, for an explication of this point.

52. Murray Malbin, *Night as Frontier: Colonizing the World After Dark* (New York: Free Press, 1987), 105.

53. Eviatar Zerubavel, *The Seven-Day Circle: The History and Meaning of the Week* (New York: Free Press, 1985), 88, 109.

54. See Gary Becker, "A Theory of the Allocation of Time," *Economic Journal* 75 (September 1965): 493–517.

55. Axelrod, *Evolution of Cooperation,* 126–32.

56. Leon Mann, "Queue Culture: The Waiting Line as a Social System," *American Journal of Sociology* 75 (November 1969): 341.

57. Niklas Luhmann, *Trust and Power* (New York: John Wiley, 1979), 20.

58. Mann, "Queue Culture," 342. For another sociological study in the same vein, one that (in my opinion) concedes too much importance to economic theories, see Barry Schwartz, *Queuing and Waiting: Studies in the Social Organization of Access and Delay* (Chicago: University of Chicago Press, 1975).

59. Charles W. Smith, *Auctions: The Social Construction of Value* (New York: Free Press, 1989).

60. A standard work in the economics of space is R. W. Vickerman, *Spatial Economic Behavior* (London: Macmillan, 1970).

61. Jon P. Nelson, "Residential Choice, Hedonic Prices, and the Demand for Urban Air Quality," *Journal of Urban Economics* 5 (July 1978): 357–69; and Douglas E. Hough and Charles G. Kratz, "Can 'Good' Architecture Meet the Market Test?" *Journal of Urban Economics* 14 (July 1983): 40–54.

62. Larry A. Sjaastad, "The Costs and Returns of Human Migration," *Journal of Political Economy* 70 (October 1962 supplement): 80.

63. Charles M. Tiebout, "A Pure Theory of Local Expenditures," *Journal of Political Economy* 64 (October 1956): 416–24.

64. Donald Lowe, *History of Bourgeois Perception* (Chicago: University of Chicago Press, 1983), 55–60.

65. Kwang-kuo Hwang, "Face and Favor: The Chinese Power Game," *American Journal of Sociology* 92 (January 1987): 944–74, esp. 963.

66. Posner, *Economics of Justice,* 146–227.

67. Harold Garfinkel, *Studies in Ethnomethodology* (Englewood Cliffs, N.J.: Prentice-Hall, 1967).

68. Jon Elster, *Ulysses and the Sirens: Studies in Rationality and Irrationality* (Cambridge: Cambridge University Press, 1979).

69. Charles Taylor, *Hegel* (Cambridge: Cambridge University Press, 1975), 561, 563.

70. Steffan B. Linder, *The Harried Leisure Class* (New York: Columbia University Press, 1979), and Tibor Scitovsky, *The Joyless Economy: An Inquiry into Human Satisfaction and Consumer Dissatisfaction* (New York: Oxford University Press, 1976), explore this theme.

71. E. M. Forster, *Howard's End* (London: Penguin Books, 1971), 316.

Notes to Chapter 2

1. I owe to Adam Przeworski and Michael Wallerstein the notion that the bourgeoisie never completed its first revolution. See "Democratic Capitalism at the Crossroads," *democracy* 2 (July 1982): 52–68.

2. An interesting study of the anticapitalist inclinations of many British capitalists may be found in Martin J. Weiner, *English Culture and the Decline of the Industrial Spirit, 1850–1980* (Cambridge: Cambridge University Press, 1981).

3. Joan W. Scott and Louise A. Tilly, "Women's Work and the Family in Nineteenth Century Europe," *Comparative Studies in Society and History* 17 (January 1975): 36–64.

4. Ibid., 50, 59.

5. Louise A. Tilly and Joan W. Scott, *Women, Work, and Family* (New York: Holt, Rinehart and Winston, 1978), 214.

6. See Diana Pearce, "The Feminization of Poverty: Women, Work, and Welfare," *Urban and Social Change Review* 11 (Winter–Summer 1978): 28–36; and Barbara Ehrenreich and Frances Fox Piven, "The Feminization of Poverty: When the Family Wage System Breaks Down," *Dissent* 31 (Spring 1984): 162–70.

7. Paul Blumberg, *Inequality in an Age of Decline* (New York: Oxford University Press, 1980), 90, 92.

8. Kathleen Gerson, *Hard Choices: How Women Decide About Work, Career, and Motherhood* (Berkeley and Los Angeles: University of California Press, 1985), 70–74, 77–80.

9. For a study of how women decide among different contraceptive (and noncontraceptive) options, see Kristin Luker, *Taking Chances: Abortion and the Decision Not to Contracept* (Berkeley and Los Angeles: University of California Press, 1975). In the 1980s, however, worries about the pill, corporate efforts to remove IUDs from the market, and changing attitudes toward abortion have made completely free choice in birth control a thing of the past for many women.

10. Rosanna Hertz, *More Equal Than Others: Women and Men in Dual-Career Marriages* (Berkeley and Los Angeles: University of California Press, 1986), 118. On delayed childbearing in demographic terms, see Roland R. Rindfuss, S. Philip Morgan, and Gary Swicegood, *First Births in America: Changes in the Timing of Parenthood* (Berkeley and Los Angeles: University of California Press, 1988), 65–74.

11. Gerson, *Hard Choices,* 167–68.

12. Linda J. Waite and Ross M. Stolzenberg, "Intended Childbearing and Labor Force Participation of Young Women," *American Sociological Review* 41 (April 1976): 235–52; and James C. Cramer, "Fertility and Female Employment: Problems of Causal Direction," *American Sociological Review* 45 (April 1980): 167–90.

13. David M. Schneider and Raymond T. Smith, *Class Differences and Sex Roles in American Kinship and Family Structure* (Englewood Cliffs, N.J.: Prentice-Hall, 1973), 42.

14. Shirley S. Angrist, Judith R. Lave, and Richard Mickelsen, "How Working Mothers Manage: Socioeconomic Differences in Work, Childcare, and Household Tasks," *Social Science Quarterly* 56 (March 1976): 631–37.

15. Andrew J. Cherlin and Frank R. Furstenberg, Jr., *The New American Grandparent: A Place in the Family, a Life Apart* (New York: Basic Books, 1986), 127–31.

16. Schneider and Smith, *Class Differences,* 42.

17. Gerson, *Hard Choices,* 185.

18. Hertz, *More Equal Than Others,* 151.

19. Andrew J. Cherlin, *Marriage, Divorce, Remarriage* (Cambridge, Mass.: Harvard University Press, 1981), 34.

20. Glen H. Elder, Jr., *Children of the Great Depression: Social Change in the Life Experience* (Chicago: University of Chicago Press, 1974).

21. Glen H. Elder, Jr., and Richard C. Rockwell, "Economic Depression and Postwar Opportunity in Men's Lives," in *Research on Community Mental Health,* ed. R. A. Simmons (Greenwich, Conn.: JAI Press, 1979), 1:249–303.

22. Glen H. Elder, Jr., "Social History and the Life Experience," in *Present and Past in Middle Life,* ed. Dorothy H. Eichorn et al. (New York: Academic Press, 1981), 3–31.

23. Jeffrey K. Liker and Glen H. Elder, Jr., "Economic Hardship and Marital Relations in the 1930s," *American Sociological Review* 48 (June 1983): 343–59.

24. Carol B. Stack, *All Our Kin: Strategies for Survival in a Black Community* (New York: Harper and Row, 1974).

25. Philip Blumstein and Pepper Schwartz, *American Couples: Money, Work, Sex* (New York: William Morrow, 1983), 189.

26. Lenore J. Weitzman, *The Divorce Revolution: The Unexpected Social and Economic Consequences for Women and Children in America* (New York: Free Press, 1985), x, 370.

27. Ibid., 374.

28. Cherlin, *Marriage, Divorce,* 74.

29. Judith S. Wallerstein and Joan Berlin Kelly, *Surviving the Breakup: How Children and Parents Cope with Divorce* (New York: Basic Books, 1980), 206–34.

30. Cherlin, *Marriage, Divorce,* 79.

31. Frank F. Furstenberg et al., "The Life Course of Children of Divorce," *American Sociological Review* 48 (October 1983): 667.

32. Arthur Kornhaber, "Grandparenthood and the 'New Social Contract,'" in *Grandparenthood,* ed. Vern L. Bengston and Joan F. Robertson (Beverly Hills, Calif.: Sage, 1985), 159.

33. Lillian Troll and Vern Bengston, "Generations and the Family," in *Contemporary Theories of the Family,* ed. Wesley R. Burr et al. (New York: Free Press, 1979), 1:127–61; Amy Horowitz, "Sons and Daughters as Caregivers to Older Parents," *The Gerontologist* 25 (December 1985): 612–17; and Bertram J. Cohler and Henry V. Grunebaum, *Mothers, Grandmothers, Daughters* (New York: John Wiley, 1981).

34. Cherlin and Furstenberg, *New American Grandparent,* 51.

35. Ibid., 57, 41, 96, 167, 176, 206.

36. All these factors may help explain why the gap in happiness between married and unmarried couples has been decreasing. See Norval D. Glenn and Charles N. Weaver, "The Changing Relationship of Marital Status to Reported Happiness," *Journal of Marriage and the Family* 50 (May 1988): 817–24.

37. Included here is, most prominently, Gary Becker; see *A Treatise on the Family* (Cambridge, Mass.: Harvard University Press, 1981).

38. William J. Goode, perhaps the leading theorist of the family in American sociology, "welcomes" what he calls the Chicago school "invasion" of sociology, yet also warns sociologists to "turn away from the deficiencies in that approach and instead build into our basic schema of action itself the variables and factors that economics leaves out." For his welcome, see "Comment: The Economics of Nonmonetary Variables," in *The Economics of the Family,* ed. Theodore W. Schultz (Chicago: University of Chicago Press, 1974), 346; for his warning, see "Individual Choice and the Social Order," in *The Social Fabric: Dimensions and Issues,* ed. James F. Short (Beverly Hills, Calif.: Sage, 1986), 58.

39. Joseph Veroff, Elizabeth Douvan, and Richard A. Kulka, *The Inner American: A Self-portrait from 1957 to 1976* (New York: Basic Books, 1981), 140–41.

40. Kai Erikson, *Everything in Its Path: Destruction of Community in the Buffalo Creek Flood* (New York: Simon and Schuster, 1976), 13.

41. Actually, given the inclination of most sociologists to want to counter conventional wisdom, there is a strain in the field that emphasizes how much small-town life was affected by the *Gesellschaft* features of modern life. See Arthur Vidich and Joseph Bensman, *Small Town in Mass Society: Class, Power, and Religion in a Rural Community* (Princeton, N.J.: Princeton University Press, 1968).

42. William Kornblum, *Blue Collar Community* (Chicago: University of Chicago Press, 1974); Gerald D. Suttles, *The Social Order of the Slum: Ethnicity and Territory in the Inner City* (Chicago: University of Chicago Press, 1968); and Her-

bert Gans, *The Urban Villagers: Group and Class in the Life of Italian-Americans* (New York: Free Press, 1962).

43. On the claim that the advance of modernity need not lead to the decline of community, see Thomas Bender, *Community and Social Change in America* (Baltimore: Johns Hopkins Press, 1982); Claude Fischer, *To Dwell Among Friends: Personal Networks in Town and City* (Chicago: University of Chicago Press, 1982); and the literature cited by both. Other recent treatments include Barry Wellman, "The Community Question: The Intimate Networks of East Yorkers," *American Journal of Sociology* 84 (March 1979): 1201–31, which deals with Toronto; and Barrett A. Lee et al., "Testing the Decline of Community Thesis," *American Journal of Sociology* 89 (March 1984): 1161–88.

44. Bender, *Community and Social Change*, 7, 113–14.

45. Peter M. Wolf, *Land in America: Its Value, Use, and Control* (New York: Pantheon Books, 1981), 19.

46. Henry J. Aaron, *Shelter and Subsidies: Who Benefits from Federal Housing Projects?* (Washington, D.C.: Brookings Institution, 1972).

47. Gwendolyn Wright, *Building the Dream: A Social History of Housing in America* (New York: Pantheon Books, 1981), 244.

48. Quoted in Matthew Edel, Elliott D. Sclar, and Daniel Luria, *Shaky Palaces: Homeownership and Social Mobility in Boston's Suburbanization* (New York: Columbia University Press, 1984), 345.

49. David Harvey, "The Political Economy of Urbanization in Advanced Capitalism," in *The Social Economy of Cities,* ed. Gary Gappbert and Harold M. Rose (Beverly Hills, Calif.: Sage, 1975), 153.

50. Fischer, *To Dwell Among Friends,* 216.

51. Mark S. Granovetter, "The Strength of Weak Ties," *American Journal of Sociology* 78 (May 1973): 1378.

52. Fischer, *To Dwell Among Friends,* 88.

53. *Freddie Mac Reports* (May 1984): 6.

54. Ibid. (June 1987): 4.

55. Data collected from *Freddie Mac Reports,* all issues 1984–86; Marshall Dennis, *Residential Mortgage Lending* (Reston, Va.: Reston Publishing Company, 1985); and "Adjustable Rate Financing in Mortgage and Consumer Credit Markets," *Federal Reserve Bulletin* 71 (November 1985): 823–35. It has been reported that 70 percent of new home loans in early 1988 were adjustable; see Francine Schwadel and Robert Johnson, "More Consumers Find Variable-Rate Loans a Burden as Rates Rise," *Wall Street Journal,* 3 June 1988, 1.

56. *Freddie Mac Reports* (November 1985): 2.

57. Ibid. (June 1987): 6.

58. Ibid. (December 1984): 6.

59. Harvey Molotch and John R. Logan, "Urban Dependencies: New Forms of Use and Exchange in U.S. Cities," *Urban Affairs Quarterly* 21 (December 1985):

143–69. See also Logan and Molotch, *Urban Futures: The Political Economy of Place* (Berkeley and Los Angeles: University of California Press, 1987).

60. For comments by San Franciscans worried about Manhattanization, see David M. Hummon, "Urban Views: Popular Perspectives on City Life," *Urban Life* 15 (April 1986): 23.

61. An ethnographic account of the implications of the economic downturn for Elizabeth is contained in Katherine S. Newman, "Turning Your Back on Tradition: Symbolic Analysis and Moral Critique in a Plant Shutdown," *Urban Anthropology* 14 (Spring–Summer–Fall 1985): 109–50, esp. p. 141. Similar comments concerning the area around Elizabeth can be found in David Halle, *America's Working Man: Work, Home, and Politics Among Blue-Collar Property Owners* (Chicago: University of Chicago Press, 1984).

62. William R. Freudenberg, "Boomtown's Youth: The Differential Impacts of Rapid Community Growth on Adolescents and Adults," *American Sociological Review* 49 (October 1984): 697–705.

63. Richard S. Krannich, Thomas Greider, and Ronald L. Little, "Rapid Growth and Fear of Crime," *Rural Sociology* 50 (Summer 1985): 193–209.

64. Alan C. Acock and Forrest A. Deseran, "Off-Farm Employment by Women and Marital Instability," *Rural Sociology* 51 (Fall 1986): 314–27.

65. J. Lynn England and Stan L. Albrecht, "Boomtowns and Social Disruption," *Rural Sociology* 49 (Summer 1984): 230–46.

66. P. D. Rosenblatt and L. O. Keller, "Economic Vulnerability and Economic Stress in Farm Couples," *Family Relations* 32 (October 1983): 567–73.

67. See Kenneth P. Wilkinson, "Rurality and Patterns of Social Disruption," *Rural Sociology* 49 (Spring 1984): 23–36; and Steven Stack, "The Effects of Marital Dissolution on Suicide," *Journal of Marriage and the Family* 42 (February 1980): 83–91.

68. U.S. Department of Agriculture, *Economic Indicators of the Farm Sector: State Financial Summary, 1985* (Washington, D.C.: Government Printing Office, 1987), 112; and American Banker's Association data, cited in U.S. Department of Agriculture, *Agricultural Finance: Situation and Outlook Report* (March 1986): 20 and (March 1987): 26.

69. Kenneth P. Wilkinson, "In Search of Community in the Changing Countryside," *Rural Sociology* 51 (Spring 1986): 1–17. See also Wilkinson, "Changing Rural Communities," in *Handbook of Community Mental Health,* ed. Peter A. Keller and J. Dennis Murray (New York: Human Sciences Press, 1982), 20–28.

70. Gary P. Green, "Credit and Agriculture: Some Consequences of the Centralization of the Banking System," *Rural Sociology* 49 (Winter 1984): 568–79.

71. Andrew H. Malcolm, *Final Harvest: An American Tragedy* (New York: Times Books, 1986), 28.

72. For elaborations on these points, see James S. Duncan, ed., *Housing and Identity: Cross-cultural Perspectives* (New York: Holmes and Meier, 1982).

73. Constance Perin, *Everything in Its Place: Social Order and Land Use in America* (Princeton, N.J.: Princeton University Press, 1977), 3.

74. Herbert J. Gans, *The Levittowners: Ways of Life and Politics in a New Suburban Community* (New York: Vintage Books, 1967), 179.

75. Mark Baldassare, *Trouble in Paradise: The Suburban Transformation in America* (New York: Columbia University Press, 1986), 101–68.

76. See Dirk Johnson, "Suburban Fire and Rescue Services Have Worrisome Volunteer Shortage," *New York Times,* 19 May 1986, pt. 2, p. 1.

77. Kenneth B. Perkins, "Volunteer Firefighters in the United States" (Unpublished report to the National Volunteer Fire Council, Department of Sociology and Anthropology, Longwood College, Farmville, Virginia, 13 August 1987).

78. Ira Katznelson and Margaret Weir, *Schooling for All: Class, Race, and the Decline of the Democratic Ideal* (New York: Basic Books, 1985), 24.

79. The leading historian of this effort is Michael Katz, from *The Irony of Early School Reform: Educational Innovation in Mid-Nineteenth-Century Massachusetts* (Cambridge, Mass.: Harvard University Press, 1968) to *Reconstructing American Education* (Cambridge, Mass.: Harvard University Press, 1987).

80. The major critique of the revisions may be found in Diana Ravitch, *The Revisionists Revised: A Critique of the Radical Attack on the Schools* (New York: Basic Books, 1978). I also found helpful in correcting an overemphasis on economic explanations of educational institutions Richard Rubinson, "Class Formation, Politics, and Institutions: Schooling in the United States," *American Journal of Sociology* 92 (November 1986): 519–48.

81. David Tyack and Elizabeth Hansot, *Managers of Virtue: Public School Leadership in America, 1820–1980* (New York: Basic Books, 1982), 28–62.

82. John W. Meyer et al., "Public Education as Nation Building in America," *American Journal of Sociology* 85 (November 1979): 601.

83. James S. Coleman, Thomas Hoffer, and Sally Kilgore, *High School Achievement: Public, Private, and Catholic High Schools Compared* (New York: Basic Books, 1982). For updated data, see Coleman and Hoffer, *Public and Private High Schools: The Impact of Communities* (New York: Basic Books, 1987).

84. The critical literature on the Coleman study is in fact voluminous, and not all or even a substantial part of it can be cited here. For a representative sample of the debate, see Karl L. Alexander and Aaron M. Pallas, "Private Schools and Public Policy," *Sociology of Education* 56 (October 1983): 170–82; and Sally Kilgore, "Schooling Effects: Reply to Alexander and Pallas," *Sociology of Education* 57 (January 1984): 59–61.

85. Among the most exclusive private schools—the boarding schools that train the predominantly Protestant elite—parents purchase private education, often at high cost; paradoxically, though, the schools teach not individualistic values associated with the market, but instead rituals, bonding, loyalty, and other primarily "nonrational" values. See Peter W. Cookson, Jr., and Caroline Hodges Persell, *Pre-*

paring for Power: America's Elite Boarding School (New York: Basic Books, 1985), 22–26, 106.

86. Barbara Falsey and Barbara Heyns, "The College Channel," *Sociology of Education* 57 (April 1984): 111–22.

87. Laura Hersh Salganik and Nancy Karweit, "Voluntarism and Governance in Education," *Sociology of Education* 55 (April–July 1982): 152–61.

88. Bruce S. Cooper, "The Changing Universe of U.S. Private Schools" (Stanford University, Institute for Research on Educational Finance and Governance, November 1985, mimeo), 30, 34.

89. See Alan Peshkin, *God's Choice: The Total World of a Fundamentalist Christian School* (Chicago: University of Chicago Press, 1986).

90. Thomas James and Henry M. Levin, eds., *Public Dollars for Private Schools: The Case of Tuition Tax Credits* (Philadelphia: Temple University Press, 1983). See also Henry M. Levin, "Education as a Public and Private Good," *Journal of Policy Analysis and Management* 6 (Summer 1987): 628–41; and Michael Krashinsky, "Why Educational Vouchers May Be Bad Economics," *Teachers College Record* 88 (Winter 1986): 139–51.

91. Katznelson and Weir, *Schooling for All,* 216.

92. Arthur G. Powell, Eleanor Farrar, and David K. Cohen, *The Shopping Mall High School* (Boston: Houghton Mifflin, 1985), 77.

93. Noah Lewin-Epstein, *Youth Employment During High School* (Washington: National Center for Education Statistics, 1981), cited in Ellen Greenberger and Laurence Steinberg, *When Teenagers Work: The Psychological and Social Costs of Adolescent Employment* (New York: Basic Books, 1986), 16.

94. Before children became "priceless" in America, they were often expected to turn over any wages they made in a sealed envelope to their parents; see Viviana Zelizer, *Pricing the Priceless Child: The Changing Social Value of Children* (New York: Basic Books, 1985), 101.

95. Greenberger and Steinberg, *When Teenagers Work,* 10–46.

96. Powell, Farrar, and Cohen, *Shopping Mall High School,* 77.

97. Greenberger and Steinberg, *When Teenagers Work,* 51.

98. Powell, Farrar, and Cohen, *Shopping Mall High School,* 39, 41.

99. Ibid., 56, 93.

100. Robert Hampel, *The Last Little Citadel: American High Schools Since 1940* (Boston: Houghton Mifflin, 1986), 2.

101. In general, see Robert W. Poole, Jr., and Philip E. Fixler, Jr., "Privatization of Public-Sector Services in Practice," *Journal of Policy Analysis and Management* 6 (Summer 1987): 612–25; and Stephen H. Hanke, ed., *Prospects for Privatization* (New York: Academy of Political Science, 1987). On prisons, see Joan Mullen, "Corrections and the Private Sector," *Research in Brief* (National Institute of Justice) (March 1985): 4. Biotherapeutics, Inc., which opened in 1985, is the only private for-profit cancer research business in the United States; see Robin Marantz Henig,

"In Business to Treat Cancer," *New York Times Magazine*, 23 November 1986, 68–70, 78–86.

102. Stuart M. Butler, *Privatizing Public Spending: A Strategy to Eliminate the Deficit* (New York: Universe Books, 1985), 136–40.

103. Poole and Fixler, "Privatization," 620–21. Sweden has already begun to implement such a technology; see *International Herald Tribune*, 17 March 1988, 2.

104. See, e.g., Isabel Wilkerson, "Schools of Social Work Swamped by Applicants," *New York Times*, 9 November 1987, A18.

105. For evidence on this point, see Norval D. Glenn, "Social Trends in the United States: Evidence from Sample Surveys," *Public Opinion Quarterly* (Winter 1987), S109–S126.

106. Veroff, Douvan, and Kulka, *Inner American*, 118.

Notes to Chapter 3

1. Thomas Schelling, *Micromotives and Macrobehavior* (New York: W. W. Norton, 1978).

2. Marian Wright Edelman, *Families in Peril: An Agenda for Social Change* (Cambridge, Mass.: Harvard University Press, 1987), 27. A study published by the Center on Budget and Public Priorities concluded that the number of poor families with children grew 35 percent between 1979 and 1987; see the *New York Times*, 8 September 1987, B7.

3. These figures come from Alvin L. Schorr, *Common Decency: Domestic Policies After Reagan* (New Haven, Conn.: Yale University Press, 1986), 79.

4. W. Norton Grubb and Marvin Lazerson, *Broken Promises: How Americans Fail Their Children* (New York: Basic Books, 1982), 52.

5. See George Masnick and Mary Jo Bane, *The Nation's Families: 1960–1990* (Boston: Auburn House, 1980), 47–50; and Sar A. Levitan, Richard S. Belous, and Frank Gallo, *What's Happening to the American Family? Tensions, Hopes, Realities*, rev. ed. (Baltimore: Johns Hopkins University Press, 1988), 107–24. A clear presentation of 1980 census figures is contained in James A. Sweet and Larry L. Bumpers, *American Families and Households* (New York: Russell Sage Foundation, 1987).

6. U.S. House of Representatives, Select Committee on Children, Youth, and Families, *Children, Youth, and Families, 1983;* cited in Eric R. Kingson, Barbara A. Hirshorn, and John M. Cormann, *Ties That Bind: The Interdependence of Generations* (Washington, D.C.: Seven Locks Press, 1986), 119. See also Harrell R. Rodgers, Jr., *Poor Women, Poor Families: The Economic Plight of America's Female-headed Households* (Armonk, N.Y.: M.E. Sharpe, 1986).

7. Martha S. Hill, "Trends in the Economic Situation of U.S. Families and Children: 1970–1980," in *American Families and the Economy*, ed. Richard R. Nelson and Felicity Skidmore (Washington, D.C.: National Academy Press, 1983), 48.

8. Phyllis Moen, Edward L. Kain, and Glen H. Elder, Jr., "Economic Conditions and Family Life," in Nelson and Skidmore, *American Families,* 236.

9. Ibid., 244.

10. The material cited in this paragraph comes from Janet S. Hansen, "Student Loans: Are They Overburdening a Generation?" (Washington, D.C.: Joint Economic Committee, U.S. Congress, December 1986); quotes pp. 21, 37.

11. Judith Gussler and L. Eugene Arnold, "Feeding Patterns and the Changing Family," in *Parents, Children, and Change,* ed. L. Eugene Arnold (Lexington, Mass.: D.C. Heath, 1985), 117.

12. National Commission on Youth, *The Transition of Youth to Adulthood* (Boulder, Colo.: Westview Press, 1980), 186; cited in Jerold M. Starr, "American Youth in the 1980s," *Youth and Society* 17 (June 1986): 342.

13. Starr, "American Youth," 340. A further study sponsored by the Center for Disease Control reported that between 1970 and 1980 the suicide rate among men aged between fifteen and twenty-four increased from 13.5 per 100,000 population to 20.2; the increase in female suicide was negligible. See "Youth Suicide is Rising," *New York Times,* 22 February 1987, pt. 1, p. 28.

14. Emile Durkheim, *Suicide* (New York: Free Press, 1966), 215.

15. Starr, "American Youth."

16. T. R. Forstenzer, "Tomorrow in North America: Youth Between the American Dream and Reality," in *Youth in the 1980s* (New York: UNESCO Press, 1981), 65–86. On political knowledge in general, see W. Russell Neuman, *The Paradox of Mass Politics: Knowledge and Opinion in the American Electorate* (Cambridge, Mass.: Harvard University Press, 1986), 14–25.

17. Raymond A. Eve and Francis B. Harrold, "Creationism, Cult Archaeology, and Other Pseudoscientific Beliefs," *Youth and Society* 17 (June 1986): 396–421.

18. One study, however, did not find that 1982 students were more pessimistic toward the future; see Guy J. Manaster, Donald L. Greer, and Douglas A. Kleiber, "Youth's Outlook on the Future III," *Youth and Society* 17 (September 1985): 97–112.

19. Angela A. Aidala and Cathy Stein Greenblatt, "Changes in Moral Judgement Among Student Populations, 1929–83," *Youth and Society* 17 (March 1986): 221–35.

20. American Council on Education, *The American Freshman: National Norms for Fall 1987* (Los Angeles: Higher Education Research Institute, UCLA, 1988). College officials, however, have begun to talk of a rebirth of voluntarism and idealistic spirit on campus at the end of the 1980s; see the *New York Times,* 3 December 1986, 24.

21. Pamela Doty, "Family Care of the Elderly: The Role of Public Policy," *Milbank Quarterly* 64, no. 1 (1986): 34–75.

22. Andrew Cherlin and Frank F. Furstenberg, *The New American Grandparent: A Place in the Family, a Life Apart* (New York: Basic Books, 1986), 110. The

relationship between proximity and care giving is discussed in Judith A. Hays, "Aging and Family Resources: Availability and Proximity of Kin," *The Gerontologist* 24 (April 1984): 149–53.

23. Sarah H. Matthews and Jetse Sprey, "The Impact of Divorce on Grandparenthood," *The Gerontologist* 24 (February 1984): 41–47. See also Cherlin and Furstenberg, *New American Grandparent*, 136–64.

24. William Rakowski and Noreen M. Clark, "Future Outlook, Caregiving, and Care-receiving in the Family Context," *The Gerontologist* 25 (December 1985): 618–23.

25. For evidence that reciprocity matters to relations between generations, see Amy Horwitz and Lois W. Shindelman, "Reciprocity and Affection: Past Influences on Current Caregiving," *Journal of Gerontological Social Work* 5 (Spring 1983): 5–20; and Peggy Hawley and John D. Chamley, "Older Person's Perceptions of the Quality of Their Human Support Systems," *Aging and Society* 6 (September 1986): 295–312.

26. Doty, "Family Care of the Elderly," 39.

27. Henry J. Pratt, *The Gray Lobby* (Chicago: University of Chicago Press, 1976).

28. Some of the pitfalls of the interest-group strategy are discussed in Fernando Torres-Gil and Jon Pynoos, "Long-Term Care Policy and Interest Group Struggles," *The Gerontologist* 26 (October 1986): 488–95.

29. Phillip Longman, *Born to Pay: The New Politics of Aging in America* (Boston: Houghton Mifflin, 1987), 27–32.

30. Daniel Yankelovich, *New Rules: Searching for Self-fulfillment in a World Turned Upside Down* (New York: Random House, 1981), 104; cited in Daniel Callahan, *Setting Limits: Medical Goals in an Aging Society* (New York: Simon and Schuster, 1987), 86.

31. Callahan, *Setting Limits*, 30.

32. Annette Baier, "The Rights of Past and Future Generations," in *Responsibilities to Future Generations: Environmental Ethics*, ed. Ernest Partridge (Buffalo, N.Y.: Prometheus Books, 1981), 177.

33. "Pressure on time, like pressure on geographic or social space, adds to the consumption activities that have to be undertaken as means to other forms of consumption" (Fred Hirsch, *The Social Limits to Growth* [Cambridge, Mass.: Harvard University Press, 1978], 75).

34. Recognition of the importance of the third sector has been stimulated by a series of studies out of Yale University concerning "nonprofit" activities. See, e.g., Paul J. DiMaggio, ed., *Non-Profit Enterprise in the Arts: Studies in Mission and Constraint* (New York: Oxford University Press, 1986); and Walter W. Powell, ed., *The Non-Profit Sector: A Research Handbook* (New Haven, Conn.: Yale University Press, 1987).

35. Commission on Private Philanthropy and Public Needs, *Giving in America: Toward a Stronger Voluntary Sector* (Washington, D.C.: Filer Commission, 1975), 11; hereafter cited as Filer Commission, *Giving*.

36. There are to my knowledge only a few serious efforts to discuss the political theory of the third sector and to contrast it to the free market liberalism of economics: Franklin I. Gamwell, *Beyond Preference: Liberal Theories of Independent Associations* (Chicago: University of Chicago Press, 1984); and Susan A. Ostrander, Stuart Longton, and Jon Van Til, eds., *Shifting the Debate: Public/Private Sector Relations in the Modern Welfare State* (New Brunswick, N.J.: Transaction Books, 1987).

37. Virginia Ann Hodgkinson and Murray A. Weitzman, *Dimensions of the Independent Sector* (Washington, D.C.: Independent Sector, 1986).

38. Waldemar Nielsen, *The Endangered Sector* (New York: Columbia University Press, 1979), 10; Ralph L. Nelson, "Private Giving in the American Economy," Filer Commission Research Papers (Washington, D.C.: U.S. Treasury Department, 1977), 115–55; and Charles T. Clotfelter, *Federal Tax Policy and Charitable Giving* (Chicago: University of Chicago Press, 1985), 17–18.

39. On the antipathy toward government as a source of altruistic inclinations in the Reagan years, see Renee A. Berger, "Private-Sector Initiatives in the Reagan Era: New Actors Rework an Old Theme," in *The Reagan Presidency and the Governing of America,* ed. Lester M. Salamon and Michael S. Lund (Washington, D.C.: Urban Institute, 1985), 181–211.

40. Wendy Kaminer, *Women Volunteering: The Pleasure, Pain, and Politics of Unpaid Work from 1830 to the Present* (Garden City, N.Y.: Doubleday, 1984), 15–16; and Barry Kosmin, "The Political Economy of Gender in Jewish Federations" (Paper presented at the conference "Women and Philanthropy," CUNY Graduate Center, June 1987).

41. Alan Pifer, *Philanthropy in an Age of Transition: The Essays of Alan Pifer* (New York: The Foundation Center, 1984), 231.

42. Filer Commission, *Giving,* 56–57.

43. Donald I. Warren and Rachelle B. Warren, "U.S. National Patterns of Problem Coping Networks," *Journal of Voluntary Action Research* 14 (April–September 1985): 31–53.

44. Hodgkinson and Weitzman, *Dimensions of the Independent Sector,* 74.

45. See the interview with Virginia Hodgkinson reported in *Fund Raising Management* 17 (August 1986): 68.

46. Patricia Klobus Edwards and Ann DeWitt Watts, "Volunteerism in Human Service Organizations: Trends and Prospects," *Journal of Applied Social Sciences* 7 (Spring–Summer 1983): 225–45. See also Arlene Kaplan Daniels, *Invisible Careers: Women Civic Leaders From the Volunteer World* (Chicago: University of Chicago Press, 1988).

47. Vicki R. Schram and Marilyn M. Dunsing, "Influences on Married Women's Volunteer Work Participation," *Journal of Consumer Research* 7 (March 1981): 372–79.

48. Patricia Klobus Edwards, John N. Edwards, and Ann DeWitt Watts, "Women, Work, and Social Participation," *Journal of Voluntary Action Research* 13

(January–March 1984): 17; and Barbara Hargrove, Jean Miller Schmidt, and Sheila Greeve Davaney, "Religion and the Changing Role of Women," *Annals of the American Academy of Political and Social Science* 480 (July 1985): 117–31.

49. Edwards, Edwards, and Watts, "Women, Work, and Social Participation."

50. The substantial role played by women in the voluntary aspects of American associational life is brought out in Anne Firor Scott, "Women's Voluntary Associations: From Philanthropy to Reform" (Paper presented at the conference "Women and Philanthropy," CUNY Graduate Center, June 1987).

51. Ronald S. Burt, "Corporate Philanthropy as a Cooptive Relationship," *Social Forces* 62 (December 1983): 419–49. A study of business philanthropy more based on economic models, especially transaction costs economics, than my own approach is Joseph Galaskiewicz, *The Social Organization of an Urban Grants Economy* (New York: Academic Press, 1985).

52. See Lester M. Salamon and Alan J. Abramson, *The Federal Budget and the Non-Profit Sector* (Washington, D.C.: Urban Institute, 1982). See also Lester Salamon, "Non-Profit Organizations: The Lost Opportunity," in *The Reagan Record: An Assessment of America's Changing Domestic Priorities,* ed. John C. Palmer and Isabel V. Sawhill (Washington, D.C.: Urban Institute, 1984), 261–68.

53. The Conference Board, *Annual Survey of Corporate Contributions* (New York: The Conference Board, 1980–85).

54. The figures and quotes in this paragraph all come from Kathleen Teltsch, "Corporate Pressures Slowing Gifts to Charity," *New York Times,* 8 July 1987, 1.

55. Hervé Varenne, *Americans Together: Structured Diversity in a Midwestern Town* (New York: Teachers College Press, 1977), 32. Had Varenne researched the matter further, he would have discovered that the American Farm Bureau Federation is the prototype of private agencies serving public functions. The lack of public interest that he found in its affairs, therefore, may be due to its quasi-official relationship to the state. See Grant McConnell, *The Decline of Agrarian Democracy* (Berkeley and Los Angeles: University of California Press, 1959).

56. Michel Crozier, *The Trouble with America: Why the System Is Breaking Down* (Berkeley and Los Angeles: University of California Press, 1984), 85.

57. Richard M. Merelman, *Making Something of Ourselves: On Culture and Politics in the United States* (Berkeley and Los Angeles: University of California Press, 1984).

58. Isabel Wilkerson, "Code of Highway: Finders Keepers," *New York Times,* 24 November 1987, A16.

59. "From Watergate, Training in Ethics," *New York Times,* 21 March 1988, A16.

60. Mary Douglas and Baron Isherwood, *The World of Goods: Towards an Anthropology of Consumption* (London: Penguin Books, 1980).

61. On apprenticeship, see William J. Rorabaugh, *The Craft Apprenticeship: From Franklin to the Machine Age in America* (New York: Oxford University Press, 1986); on ethnic family ties, see Pyong Gap Min, *Ethnic Business Enterprise: Korean Small Business in Atlanta* (New York: Center for Migration Studies, 1988), 91–95.

62. T. J. Jackson Lears, "From Salvation to Self-Realization," in T. J. Jackson

Lears and Richard Wrightman Fox, *The Culture of Consumption: Critical Essays in American History, 1880–1980* (New York: Pantheon Books, 1983), 3–38, esp. p. 20.

63. Roland Marchand, *Advertising the American Dream: Making Way for Modernity, 1920–1940* (Berkeley and Los Angeles: University of California Press, 1985), 89–94.

64. Stephen Fox, *The Mirror Makers: A History of Advertising and Its Creators* (New York: William Morrow, 1984), 316–17.

65. Tom Engelhardt, "Children's Television: The Shortcake Strategy," in *Watching Television: A Pantheon Guide to Popular Culture,* ed. Todd Gitlin (New York: Pantheon Books, 1986), 68–110.

66. Merelman, *Making Something of Ourselves,* 124.

67. Quoted in Fox, *Mirror Makers,* 326.

68. Marchand, *Advertising the American Dream,* 206–34.

69. Michael Schudson, *Advertising: The Uneasy Persuasion* (New York: Basic Books, 1984), 221.

70. See, e.g., Ralph Miliband, *The State in Capitalist Society: An Analysis of Western Systems of Power* (New York: Basic Books, 1969), 215–18.

71. Clifford Geertz, *The Interpretation of Cultures: Selected Essays* (New York: Basic Books, 1973); see also James Clifford and George Marcus, *Writing Culture: The Poetics and Politics of Ethnography* (Berkeley and Los Angeles: University of California Press, 1986).

72. Merelman, *Making Something of Ourselves,* 134.

73. Varda Langholz Leymore, *Hidden Myth: Structure and Symbol in Advertising* (New York: Basic Books, 1975); cited in Merelman, *Making Something of Ourselves,* 140–41.

74. Stanley Hauerwas, *A Community of Character: Toward a Constructive Christian Social Ethic* (Notre Dame, Ind.: University of Notre Dame Press, 1981), 84.

75. David L. Gutmann, *Reclaimed Powers: Towards a New Psychology of Men and Women in Later Life* (New York: Basic Books, 1987), esp. 246–49.

76. For a discussion of some of these issues, see Norman Daniels, *Am I My Parents' Keeper? An Essay on Justice Between the Young and the Old* (New York: Oxford University Press, 1988).

77. John Rawls, *A Theory of Justice* (Cambridge, Mass.: Harvard University Press, 1971), 140, 288.

78. Karl Mannheim, "The Problem of Generations," in *Essays on the Sociology of Knowledge* (London: Routledge and Kegan Paul, 1952), 287.

79. Joseph Addison, in *The Spectator,* no. 381 (20 August 1714); cited in Robert E. Goodin, *Protecting the Vulnerable: A Reanalysis of Our Social Responsibilities* (Chicago: University of Chicago Press, 1985), 177.

80. Thomas Schwartz, "Obligations to Posterity," in *Obligations to Future Generations,* ed. R. I. Sikora and Brian Barry (Philadelphia: Temple University Press, 1978), 3–13.

81. See, e.g., Gary S. Becker, "Altruism, Egoism, and Genetic Fitness," *Journal*

of Economic Literature 14 (September 1976): 817–26; and Howard Margolis, *Selfishness, Altruism, and Rationality* (Cambridge: Cambridge University Press, 1982). The essays in Edmund S. Phelps, *Altruism, Morality, and Economic Theory* (New York: Russell Sage Foundation, 1975), especially Phelps's introduction, view some degree of altruism, independent of economic motivations, as necessary for the social order. An effort to use economic methods to increase altruism is David Collard, *Altruism and Economy: A Study in Non-selfish Economics* (Oxford: Martin Robertson, 1978).

82. Marcel Mauss, *The Gift* (New York: W.W. Norton, 1967); Richard Titmuss, *The Gift Relationship: From Human Blood to Social Policy* (New York: Pantheon Books, 1971); Marshall Sahlins, *Stone Age Economics* (Chicago: Aldine, 1972); and Lewis Hyde, *The Gift: Imagination and the Erotic Life of Poetry* (New York: Vintage Books, 1983).

83. See Roberta G. Simmons, Susan D. Klein, and Richard L. Simmons, *Gift of Life: The Social and Psychological Impact of Organ Transplantation* (New York: John Wiley, 1977).

84. E.g., Allan Bloom, *The Closing of the American Mind: How Higher Education Has Failed Democracy and Impoverished the Souls of Today's Students* (New York: Simon and Schuster, 1987).

Notes to Chapter 4

1. Theodore J. Lowi, *The End of Liberalism: The Second Republic of the United States,* 2d ed. (New York: W.W. Norton, 1979), 267.

2. Kenneth H. F. Dyson, *The State Tradition in Western Europe* (New York: Oxford University Press, 1980), 139.

3. "This very well-being of the State is secured not solely through power, but also through ethics and justice; and in the last resort the disruption of these can endanger the maintenance of power itself" (Friedrich Meineicke, *Machiavellianism* [New Haven, Conn.: Yale University Press, 1957], 3).

4. Albert Hirschman, *The Passions and the Interests: Political Arguments for Capitalism Before Its Triumph* (Princeton, N.J.: Princeton University Press, 1977), 50.

5. David Hume, "Of the Original Contract," in *Essays: Moral, Political, and Literary,* ed. T. H. Greene and T. H. Grose (London: Longmans, Green, 1907), 1:443–60; see esp. p. 456.

6. John Dunn, *Western Political Theory in the Face of the Future* (Cambridge: Cambridge University Press, 1979), 54.

7. A. John Simmons, *Moral Principles and Political Obligations* (Princeton, N.J.: Princeton University Press, 1979), 192.

8. Carole Pateman, *The Problem of Political Obligation: A Critical Analysis of Liberal Theory* (Cambridge: Polity Press, 1985), 180.

9. See Stephen Holmes, *Benjamin Constant and the Making of Modern Liber-*

alism (New Haven, Conn.: Yale University Press, 1984); and Nancy L. Rosenblum, *Another Liberalism: Romanticism and the Reconstruction of Liberal Thought* (Cambridge, Mass.: Harvard University Press, 1987).

10. Gregory S. Kavka, *Hobbesian Moral and Political Theory* (Princeton, N.J.: Princeton University Press, 1986), 179–244.

11. Thomas Hobbes, *Leviathan,* ed. C. B. MacPherson (New York: Penguin Books, 1961), 209.

12. Ibid., 119–47.

13. John Dunn, *The Political Thought of John Locke: An Historical Account of the Argument of "The Two Treatises of Government"* (Cambridge: Cambridge University Press, 1969), 100.

14. Sheldon Wolin, *Politics and Vision* (Boston: Little, Brown, 1960), 335.

15. Hirschman, *Passions and Interests.*

16. See Chapter 1 above and Allan Silver, "Friendship and Trust as Moral Ideals" (paper presented at the 1985 meetings of the American Sociological Association).

17. Anthony Arblaster, *The Rise and Decline of Western Liberalism* (Oxford: Basil Blackwell, 1984), 17.

18. See Steven Seidman, *Liberalism and the Origins of European Social Theory* (Berkeley and Los Angeles: University of California Press, 1983).

19. Quoted in Charles Camic, "The Utilitarians Revisited," *American Journal of Sociology* 85 (November 1979): 533.

20. For background, see Michael Freeden, *The New Liberalism: An Ideology of Social Reform* (Oxford: Clarendon Press, 1978); and Peter F. Clarke, *Liberals and Social Democrats* (Cambridge: Cambridge University Press, 1978).

21. Stefan Collini, *Liberalism and Sociology: L. T. Hobhouse and Political Argument in England, 1880–1914* (Cambridge: Cambridge University Press, 1979).

22. Arthur Vidich and Stanford Lyman, *American Sociology: Worldly Rejections of Religion and Their Directions* (New Haven, Conn.: Yale University Press, 1985).

23. T. H. Marshall, "Citizenship and Social Class," in *Class, Citizenship, and Social Development: Essays by T. H. Marshall,* ed. S. M. Lipset (Garden City, N.Y.: Anchor Books, 1965), 71–134.

24. Emile Durkheim, *The Division of Labor in Society* (New York: Free Press, 1964), 28.

25. Cited in David Nichols, *Three Varieties of Pluralism* (New York: St. Martins Press, 1974), 8.

26. William Kornhauser, *The Politics of Mass Society* (Glencoe, Ill.: Free Press, 1959).

27. Wolin, *Politics and Vision,* 343.

28. David B. Truman, *The Governmental Process: Political Interests and Public Opinion* (New York: Alfred Knopf, 1951), 16, 18, 25, 53, 54, 56, 61, 166, 316, 340, 512, 524.

29. Donald R. Matthews, *U.S. Senators and Their World* (Chapel Hill: University of North Carolina Press, 1960), 92–117.

30. William S. White, *Citadel* (Boston: Houghton Mifflin, 1968), 81–94.

31. Arthur Maass, *Muddy Waters: The Army Engineers and the Nation's Rivers* (Cambridge, Mass.: Harvard University Press, 1951), set the standard for this kind of research. On clientelism in anthropology, see S. N. Eisenstadt and L. Roniger, *Patrons, Clients, and Friends: Interpersonal Relations and the Structure of Trust in Society* (Cambridge: Cambridge University Press, 1984).

32. Edward C. Banfield and James Q. Wilson, *City Politics* (Cambridge, Mass.: Harvard University Press, 1963), 116.

33. Hadley Arkes, *The Philosopher in the City: The Moral Dimensions of Politics* (Princeton, N.J.: Princeton University Press, 1981), 304.

34. Sidney Verba and Norman H. Nie, *Participation in America: Political Democracy and Social Equality* (New York: Harper and Row, 1972), 116.

35. Angus Campbell et al., *The American Voter* (New York: John Wiley, 1960), 128.

36. The literature on trust is very large, since it seems to be amenable to survey research. For recent statements, see Paul R. Abramson and Ada W. Finifter, "On the Meaning of Political Trust: New Evidence from Items Introduced in 1978," *American Journal of Political Science* 25 (May 1981): 297–307; Geraint Parry, "Trust, Distrust, and Consensus," *British Journal of Political Science* 6 (April 1976): 129–42; and the discussion in Richard M. Merelman, *Making Something of Ourselves: On Culture and Politics in the United States* (Berkeley and Los Angeles: University of California Press, 1984), 12.

37. Gabriel Almond and Sidney Verba, *The Civic Culture: Political Attitudes and Democracy in Five Nations* (Princeton, N.J.: Princeton University Press, 1963), and all the books spawned by this work, too numerous to list here.

38. The inability of large and bureaucratic groups to act like individuals has not generally been discussed in the political science literature, but one scholar who recognizes that the classic pluralist notion of membership groups no longer applies to the interest-group struggles of large-scale institutions is Robert H. Salisbury; see his "Interest Representation: The Dominance of Institutions," *American Political Science Review* 78 (March 1984): 64–76.

39. Fred J. Greenstein, "The Changing Pattern of Urban Politics," *Annals of the American Academy of Political and Social Science* 353 (May 1964): 1–13; and Robert H. Salisbury, "Urban Politics: The New Convergence of Power," *Journal of Politics* 26 (November 1964): 775–97.

40. A convenient summary of the evidence in favor of the decline of political parties is William J. Crotty and Gary C. Jacobson, *American Parties in Decline* (Boston: Little, Brown, 1980). For an alternative view, see Xandra Kayden and Eddie Mahe, Jr., *The Party Goes On: The Persistence of the Two-Party System in the United States* (New York: Basic Books, 1985).

41. Edward R. Tufte, *Political Control of the Economy* (Princeton, N.J.: Princeton University Press, 1978).

42. See Larry J. Sabato, *The Rise of Political Consultants: New Ways of Winning Elections* (New York: Basic Books, 1981).

43. Benjamin Ginsberg, *The Captive Public: How Mass Opinion Promotes State Power* (New York: Basic Books, 1986), 86–148.

44. This lack of reciprocity is one of the major themes of Michael J. Malbin, *Unelected Representatives: Congressional Staff and the Future of Representative Government* (New York: Basic Books, 1980).

45. Stephen S. Smith, "New Patterns of Decisionmaking in Congress," in *The New Direction in American Politics,* ed. John E. Chubb and Paul E. Peterson (Washington, D.C.: Brookings Institution, 1985), 223–30.

46. Burdett A. Loomis, "The 'Me Decade' and the Changing Context of House Leadership," in *Understanding Congressional Leadership,* ed. Frank H. Mackaman (Washington, D.C.: Congressional Quarterly Press, 1981), 157–79. See also Thomas E. Mann and Norman J. Ornstein, eds., *The New Congress* (Washington, D.C.: American Enterprise Institute, 1981).

47. Samuel Kernell, "Campaigning, Governing, and the Contemporary Presidency," in Chubb and Peterson, *New Direction in American Politics,* 140.

48. For an overview of these changes, see James Q. Wilson, ed., *The Politics of Regulation* (New York: Basic Books, 1980); and Martha Derthick and Paul J. Quirk, *The Politics of Deregulation* (Washington, D.C.: Brookings Institution, 1985).

49. Mancur Olson, Jr., *The Logic of Collective Action,* rev. ed. (New York: Schocken Books, 1971), 12, 13.

50. For an overview of the literature, see Peter H. Aranson, *American Government: Strategy and Choice* (Boston: Little, Brown, 1981). That behind this research does lie a normative theory is one of the points made by Peter H. Aranson and Peter C. Ordeshook, "Public Interest, Private Interest, and the Democratic Polity," in *The Democratic State,* ed. Roger Benjamin and Stephen L. Elkin (Lawrence: University Press of Kansas, 1985), 87–177.

51. John Plamanatz, *The English Utilitarians,* 2d rev. ed. (Oxford: Basil Blackwell, 1958), 173–75: cited in Brian Barry, *Sociologists, Economists, and Democracy* (Chicago: University of Chicago Press, 1978), 176.

52. See, e.g., Oliver E. Williamson, *Markets and Hierarchies, Analysis and Anti-Trust Implications: A Study in the Economics of Internal Organization* (New York: Free Press, 1975); James M. Buchanan and Gordon Tullock, *The Calculus of Consent: Logical Foundations of Constitutional Democracy* (Ann Arbor: University of Michigan Press, 1971); and William H. Riker, *Liberalism Against Populism: A Confrontation Between the Theory of Democracy and the Theory of Social Choice* (San Francisco: W.H. Freeman, 1982).

53. Buchanan and Tullock, *Calculus of Consent,* 291.

54. James M. Buchanan and Richard E. Wagner, *Democracy in Deficit: The Political Legacy of Lord Keynes* (New York: Academic Press, 1977), 175.

288 Notes to Pages 122–28

55. H. Geoffrey Brennan and James M. Buchanan, *Monopoly in Money and Infla-tion* (London: Institute of Economic Affairs, 1981), 65.

56. H. Geoffrey Brennan and James M. Buchanan, *The Reason of Rules: Consti-tutional Political Economy* (Cambridge: Cambridge University Press, 1985), 150.

57. Ronald H. Coase, "The Nature of the Firm," *Economia* 4 (November 1937): 386–405.

58. Oliver E. Williamson, *Economic Organization: Firms, Markets, and Policy Control* (New York: New York University Press, 1986), 147, 163, 174. See also the discussion in Samuel Bowles and Herbert Gintis, *Democracy and Capitalism: Prop-erty, Community, and the Contractions of Modern Social Thought* (New York: Basic Books, 1986), 196–97.

59. John Rawls, *A Theory of Justice* (Cambridge, Mass.: Harvard University Press, 1971), 360.

60. Ibid., 468.

61. Ibid., 471.

62. Ibid., 474.

63. Lawrence Kohlberg, *The Philosophy of Moral Development* (New York: Harper and Row, 1981).

64. Rawls, *Theory of Justice*, 490.

65. Ibid., 474.

66. Ibid., 475, 490.

67. Ibid., 533.

68. Carol Gilligan, *In a Different Voice: Psychological Theory and Women's Devel-opment* (Cambridge, Mass.: Harvard University Press, 1982), 19.

69. For a criticism of Rawls and Kohlberg that emphasizes the paucity of story-telling capacity in their liberal theory, see Stanley Hauerwas, *A Community of Char-acter: Toward a Constructive Christian Social Ethic* (Notre Dame, Ind.: University of Notre Dame Press, 1981).

70. Rawls, *Theory of Justice*, 454.

71. Michael J. Sandel, *Liberalism and the Limits of Justice* (Cambridge: Cam-bridge University Press, 1982), 183, 175.

72. Rawls, *Theory of Justice*, 115, 337.

73. Pateman, *Problem of Political Obligation*, 113, points out some of the simi-larities between Rawls and Hegel on these issues.

74. Lawrence Mead, *Beyond Entitlement: The Social Obligations of Citizenship* (New York: Free Press, 1986), 6, 8.

75. Ibid., 228.

76. See James T. Kloppenberg, *Uncertain Victory: Social Democracy and Progres-sivism in European and American Thought, 1870–1920* (New York: Oxford University Press, 1986).

77. See, e.g., the essay entitled "Social Welfare and the Art of Giving," in *The*

Philosophy of Welfare: Selected Writings of Richard M. Titmuss, ed. Brian Abel-Smith and Kay Titmuss (London: Allen and Unwin, 1987), 113–27.

78. Marshall, "Citizenship and Social Class," 101.

79. Gösta Rehn, "The Wages of Success," in *Norden—The Passion for Equality,* ed. Stephen R. Graubard (Oslo: Norwegian University Press, 1986), 173.

80. Ronald Dworkin, "Liberalism," in *Public and Private Morality,* ed. Stuart Hampshire (Cambridge: Cambridge University Press, 1978), 142. See also Dworkin's essay "Neutrality, Equality and Liberalism," reprinted in *Liberalism Reconsidered,* ed. Douglas MacLean and Claudia Mills (Totowa, N.J.: Rowman and Allenheld, 1983), 1–11.

81. Bruce A. Ackerman, *Social Justice in the Liberal State* (New Haven, Conn.: Yale University Press, 1980), 368; cited in Sandel, *Liberalism and the Limits of Justice,* 176.

82. Russell L. Hanson, *The Democratic Imagination in America: Conversations with Our Past* (Princeton, N.J.: Princeton University Press, 1985), 258.

83. Sheldon S. Wolin, "The New Public Philosophy," *democracy* 1 (October 1981): 36.

84. John D. Stephens, *The Transition from Capitalism to Socialism* (Urbana: University of Illinois Press, 1986).

85. Stein Ringen, *The Possibility of Politics: A Study in the Political Economy of the Welfare State* (Oxford: Clarendon Press, 1987), 207.

86. Richard J. Estes, *The Social Progress of Nations* (New York: Praeger, 1984).

Notes to Chapter 5

1. Ole P. Kristensen, *Væksten i den offentlige sektor* (Copenhagen: Danish Union of Lawyers and Economists, 1987), 15. Translations of titles from the Scandinavian languages will be found in the bibliography.

2. Stein Kuhnle, "Offentlige utgifter og velferdsutgifter," in *Velferdsstaten: Vekst og omstilling,* ed. Stein Kuhnle and Liv Solheim (Oslo: Tano, 1985), 56.

3. Lars Nørby Johansen and Jon Eivind Kolberg, "Welfare State Regression in Scandinavia?" in *The Welfare State and Its Aftermath,* ed. S. N. Eisenstadt and Ora Ahimeir (London: Croom Held, 1985), 153.

4. The most comprehensive account of the growth, accomplishments, and dilemmas of the Scandinavian welfare states available in English is Peter Flora, ed., *Growth to Limits,* vol. 1: *Sweden, Norway, Finland, Denmark* (Berlin: Walter de Gruyter, 1988).

5. Quoted in Seppo Hentilä, "The Origins of the *Folkhem* Ideology in Swedish Social Democracy," *Scandinavian Journal of History* 3, no. 1 (1978): 327.

6. For data on the degree to which welfare programs become part of the "claims" that families can make to support their claims in the market, see Lee Rain-

water, Martin Rein, and Joseph Schwartz, *Income Packaging in the Welfare State: A Comparative Study of Family Income* (Oxford: Clarendon Press, 1986), 12–24.

7. Kari Wærness and Stein Ringen, "Women in the Welfare State," in *The Scandinavian Model: Welfare States and Welfare Research,* ed. Robert Erikson et al. (Armonk, N.Y.: Sharpe, 1986), 162.

8. On the various Swedish child-allowance programs, see Åke Elmér, *Svensk socialpolitik* (Lund: LiberLäromedel, 1981), 97; on the Danish, see Lars Nørby Johansen, *The Danish Welfare State, 1945–1980* (Odense: Institute for Social Science, 1982), 29–35.

9. Kuhnle, "Offentlige utgifter," 61.

10. Olav Sunnanå, *Det ikkje-offentlege skoleverket* (Oslo: Institute for Educational Research, 1984).

11. Niels Egelund, *Privatskole kontra folkeskole* (Hørsholm, Den.: Educational Psychology Publishers, 1988), 9.

12. The 1980 studies are, for Sweden, Elisabet Näsman, Kerstin Nordström, and Ruth Hammarström, *Föräldrars arbete och barns villkor* (Stockholm: LiberTryck, 1983), 50; and, for Denmark, Bjarne Hjorth Andersen and Per Schultz Jørgensen, *Dagpasning for de 6–10 årige* (Copenhagen: Danish Social Research Institute, 1987), 30. The 1984 figures for both countries may be found in Björn Flising and Inge Johansson, *Fritidshem i Norden* (Stockholm: Nordic Council, 1987), 96.

13. Such programs in Denmark are analyzed in Per Schultz Jørgensen, Birthe Gamst, and Bjarne Hjorth Andersen, *Efter skoletid* (Copenhagen: Danish Social Research Institute, 1986). The extent of after-school activities in Sweden is discussed in *Skolbarnsomsorgen* (Stockholm: Government Official Reports, 1985). Kurt Klaudi Klausen, *Per Ardua ad Astra* (Odense: Odense University Press, 1988), 41, discusses public funding of sports clubs.

14. Lars Grue, *Barns levekår: En faktasamling* (Oslo: Institute for Applied Social Research, 1987), 18. In Denmark, the question of whether newspaper boys ought to be organized in labor unions was widely debated in the fall of 1987.

15. See, e.g., Gustav Jonsson, *Att bryta det sociala arvet* (Stockholm: Tiden-Folksam, 1973); or Erik Jørgen Hansen, *Hvem bryder den sociale arv?* 2 vols. (Copenhagen: Danish Social Research Institute, 1982).

16. Turid Vogt Grinde, *Barnevern i Norden* (Stockholm: Nordic Council, 1985), 107; and *Barns behov och föräldrars rätt* (Stockholm: Government Official Reports, 1986), 79.

17. *Barns behov och föräldrars rätt,* 71.

18. This citation is from a Swedish translation of the *Spiegel* article in *Göteborg-Posten,* 13 November 1983, 34.

19. Grinde, *Barnevern i Norden,* 124–25.

20. Merete Watt Boolsen, Jill Mehlbye, and Lisbeth Sparre, *Børns opvækst uden for hjemmet* (Copenhagen: Local Government Research Institute on Public Fi-

nance and Administration, 1986). In December 1984, 14,640 Danish children or young people were living outside their homes (p. 9).

21. How this works in Norway is described in Karen Hassel, "Psykologen som sakkyndig i barneverns-og barnefordelingssaker," *Nordisk psykologi* 36, no. 4 (1984): 237–47.

22. Gunilla Larsson, Gunilla Ekenstein, and Ewa Rasch, "Are the Social Workers Prepared to Assist a Changing Population of Dysfunctional Parents in Sweden?" *Child Abuse and Neglect* 8 (1984): 9–14; and Gunilla Larsson and Gunilla Ekenstein, "Institutional Care of Infants in Sweden," *Child Abuse and Neglect* 7 (1983): 11–16; both cited in Grinde, *Barnevern i Norden*, 118. My emphasis.

23. Jürgen Habermas, "Law as Medium and Law as Institution," in *Dilemmas of Law in the Welfare State*, ed. Gunther Teubner (Berlin: Walter de Gruyter, 1986), 203–20, quote p. 210.

24. Lise Togeby, "Notat om børnepasningsdækning i de nordiske lande" (Århus University, Institute for Political Science, October 1987, photocopy), 18.

25. Mogens Nygaard Christoffersen, Ole Bertelsen, and Poul Vestergaard, *Hvem passer vore børn?* (Copenhagen: Danish Social Research Institute, 1987), 40.

26. Ole Langsted and Dion Sommer, *Småbørns livsvilkår i Danmark* (Copenhagen: Hans Reitzels, 1988), 100–101.

27. Näsman, Nordström, and Hammarström, *Föräldrars arbete*, 49, 51. See also Mårten Lagergren et al., *Tid för omsorg* (Stockholm: LiberFörlag/Institute for Future Studies, 1982), 137–45. A 1982–83 study showed somewhat greater reliance on public day care; see Berit Kemvall-Ljung, *Statistiska uppgifter om småbarns livsvillkor i Sverige* (Stockholm: Childhood, Society, and Development in the Nordic Countries Project, 1986), 27.

28. Stein Ringen, *The Possibility of Politics: A Study in the Political Economy of the Welfare State* (Oxford: Clarendon Press, 1987), 130. The best study of the changing Swedish family in English is David Popenoe, *Disturbing the Net: Family Change and Decline in Modern Societies* (Hawthorne, N.Y.: Aldine de Gruyter, 1988).

29. Mogens Nygaard Christoffersen, *Familien under forandring* (Copenhagen: Danish Social Research Institute, 1987), 19, 21, 30.

30. Grinde, *Barnevern i Norden*, 95.

31. On Norway, see Jan Erik Kristiansen, "Familien i endring: Et demografisk perspektiv," in *Familien i endring*, ed. Jan Erik Kristiansen and Tone Schou Wetlesen (Oslo: Institute for Sociology, 1986), 25; on Denmark, Christoffersen, *Familien under forandring* 23–24; and on Sweden, Neil Gilbert, "Sweden's Disturbing Family Trends," *Wall Street Journal*, 22 June 1987, 6.

32. Inger Koch-Neilsen, *Skilsmisser* (Copenhagen: Danish Social Research Institute, 1983), 116–18.

33. Inger Koch-Nielsen and Henning Transgaard, *Familiemønstre efter skilsmisse* (Copenhagen: Danish Social Research Institute, 1987), 21; Lennart Köhler et al.,

292   Notes to Pages 141–43

Health Implications of Family Breakdown (Stockholm: Nordic School of Public Health, 1987), 19–20; Svend Heinild and Frode Muldkjær, *Skilsmissens børn* (Copenhagen: Rhodos, 1982); and Inger Myhr Lunde and Liv Else Schjelderup, *Etter skilsmisse* (Stavanger: Norwegian University Press, 1985). A long-term study of Danish divorce concluded that while the price was high, children were able to cope, in some cases better than adults, who tended to use their children as pawns in struggles with their ex-spouses. See Morten Nissen, *Skilsmissens pris* (Copenhagen: Danish Social Research Institute, 1988).

34. Michael T. Hannan, Nancy Brandon Tuma, and Lyle Groeneveld, "Income and Marital Events: Evidence from an Income Maintenance Experiment," *American Journal of Sociology* 82 (May 1977): 1186–1211.

35. Lars Guldbrandsen and Catherine Ulstrup Tønnessen, *Barnetilsyn og yrkesdeltakelse blant småbarnsmødre* (Oslo: Institute for Social Research, 1987), 10.

36. Natalie Rogoff Ramsøy and Lise Kjølsrød, *Velferdsstatens yrker* (Oslo: Institute for Applied Social Research, 1985), 10.

37. Bent Rold Andersen, "Rationality and Irrationality of the Nordic Welfare State," in *Norden: The Passion for Equality,* ed. Stephen R. Graubard (Oslo: Norwegian University Press, 1986), 137.

38. See Helga Maria Hernes, "Women and the Welfare State: The Transition from Private to Public Dependence," in *Patriarchy in a Welfare Society,* ed. Harriet Holter (Oslo: Norwegian University Press, 1984), 26–45.

39. Anette Borchorst and Birte Siim, *Kvinder i velfærdsstaten* (Ålborg: Ålborg University Press, 1984); see also Birte Siim, "The Scandinavian Welfare States: Towards Sexual Equality or a New Kind of Male Domination?" *Acta Sociologica* 30, no. 3/4 (1987): 255–70.

40. Anna Hedborg and Rudolf Meidner, *Folkhemsmodellen* (Stockholm: Raben and Sjögren, 1984).

41. Quoted in Hentilä, "Origins of the *Folkhem* Ideology," 327.

42. Johan Borgen, *Barndommens rike;* quoted in Vigdis Christie, "Nœrmiljøet," in *Det moderne Norge,* vol. 2: *Samliv og nærmiljø,* ed. Kari Wærness and Vigdis Christie (Oslo: Gyldendal, 1982), 274.

43. Gösta Esping-Andersen, *Politics Against Markets: The Social Democratic Road to Power* (Princeton, N.J.: Princeton University Press, 1985), 49–50.

44. Natalie Rogoff Ramsøy, "From Necessity to Choice: Social Change in Norway," in Erikson et al., *The Scandinavian Model,* 100.

45. Harry Haue, Jørgen Olsen, and Jørn Aarup-Kristiansen, *Det ny Danmark, 1890–1985* (Copenhagen: Munksgaard, 1985), 219; and Hans Christian Johansen, *Dansk historisk statistik, 1814–1980* (Copenhagen: Gyldendal, 1985), 119.

46. Esping-Andersen, *Politics Against Markets,* 187.

47. Mats Franzén and Eva Sandstedt, *Grannskap och stadsplanering* (Uppsala: Institute for Sociology, 1981), 228–29.

48. Thomas J. Anton, *Administered Politics: Elite Political Culture in Sweden* (The Hague: Martinus Nijhoff, 1980), 2.

49. Ramsøy, "From Necessity to Choice," 100.

50. See Esping-Andersen, *Politics Against Markets,* 179–90, on the differences between Danish and Swedish housing policies.

51. Bent Rold Andersen, "Rationality and Irrationality," 133.

52. Ringen, *The Possibility of Politics,* 121–40; and Rehn, "The Wages of Success," in Graubard, *Norden,* 164–65.

53. All these data are from Christina Axelsson, "Family and Social Integration," in *Welfare in Transition,* ed. Robert Erikson and Rune Åberg (Oxford: Clarendon Press, 1987), 217–32.

54. *Levnadsförhållanden* (Stockholm: Central Statistical Department, 1987), 181–95.

55. Cecilla Henning, Mats Lieberg, and Karin Palm Lindén, *Boende, omsorg och sociala nätverk* (Stockholm: Institute for Construction Research, 1987), 174–75.

56. Mogens Kjær Jensen et al., *Sociale netværk og socialpolitik* (Copenhagen: Danish Social Research Institute, 1987), 104–13, 162–65.

57. Per Nyberg, *Sociala nätverk och problemlösning* (Lund: Center for Social Medicine, 1987).

58. Thomas Hjortsjö, *Självmord i Stockholm* (Göteborg: School of Public Health, 1983), 112.

59. *Statistisk årbog för Sverige 1988* (Stockholm: Central Statistical Department, 1988), 327.

60. For data and analysis, see Nils Retterstøl, *Selvmord* (Oslo: Norwegian University Press, 1985), 26–29.

61. See Jacques Blum, *De grimme ællinger* (Copenhagen: Aschehoug, 1985), 116. The degree to which figures like the suicide rate ought to be taken seriously has become the subject of some debate in Denmark. Jacques Blum and Michael Porsager, in their recent book *Det andet Danmark* (Copenhagen: Politiken, 1987), argue that by nearly all accounts—from suicide to drug addiction to crime—Denmark is far worse off now than ever before, but the reliability of their data can be, and has been, challenged. For a critical review, see Berl Kutchinsky, "Sensationslyst skæmmer rapport om vor elendighed," *Weekendavisen,* 6–12 November 1987, 10.

62. For Sweden, see *Rapport 87: Alkohol-och-narkotika utvecklingen i Sverige* (Stockholm: Center for Alcohol and Narcotics Information, 1987), 190; for Norway, see Sverre Brun-Gulbrandsen, "Våre forfedres alkoholbruk," in *Alkohol i Norge,* ed. Oddvar Arner, Ragnar Hauge, and Ole-Jørgen Skog (Oslo: Norwegian University Press, 1985), 39. Figures on Denmark are contained in *Dansk alkoholstatistik,* 5th ed. (Copenhagen: Danish Temperance Organization, 1986), 7.

63. On tobacco use in Sweden, see *Tobaksvanor i Sverige* (Stockholm: Social Commission, 1986), 29; on narcotics, *Rapport 87,* 224–40.

64. Hanns von Hofer, *Nordisk kriminalstatistik 1950–1980* (Copenhagen: Nordic Statistical Secretariat, 1982), 50, 72.

65. Hjorstjö, *Självmord*, 36–37, 96; and Bjørn Bjørnsen et al., *Alkohol og vold* (Oslo: Norwegian University Press, 1985).

66. Siri Næss, *Selvmord, ensomhet, og samfunnsutvikling* (Oslo: Institute for Applied Social Research, 1987). Næss attributes the higher suicide rates in Denmark and Norway compared to Sweden as being due to the later urbanization of the former.

67. Blum, *De grimme ællinger*, 116–24.

68. An epidemiological study of suicides in Sweden, however, indicated that a surprisingly large number of socially alienated people were in recent contact with the state in the form of psychiatric care; see Socialstyrelsen Redovisar, *Självmord inom den psykiatriska vården* (Stockholm: Social Commission, 1985).

69. Erik Jørgen Hansen, *Danskernes levevilkår* (Copenhagen: Hans Reitzels, 1986), 70.

70. Gösta Esping-Andersen and Walter Korpi, "From Poor Relief to Institutional Welfare States," in Erikson et al., *The Scandinavian Model*, 40, 42. My sense is that Esping-Andersen and Korpi mean by "civil society" the economic sector, not, as I have been using the term in this book, the social and moral sector.

71. Helga Maria Hernes, *Welfare State and Woman Power* (Oslo: Norwegian University Press, 1987), 159.

72. Esping-Andersen and Korpi, "From Poor Relief to Institutional Welfare States," 69.

73. The consolidation of the older welfare state is discussed in Sven E. Olsson, "Toward a Transformation of the Swedish Welfare State," in *Modern Welfare States: A Comparative View of Trends and Prospects*, ed. Robert R. Friedman, Neil Gilbert, and Moshe Sherer (Brighton, Eng.: Wheatsheaf Books, 1987), 78.

74. Andreas Hompland, ed., *Scenarier 2000* (Oslo: Norwegian University Press, 1987), 40.

75. The lack of a legitimacy crisis in the Scandinavian welfare state is well documented. For Denmark, see Jørgen Goul Andersen, "Vælgernes holdninger til den offentlige udgiftspolitik," in *Fra vækst til omstilling*, ed. Karl-Henrik Bentzon (Copenhagen: News from Political Science, 1988), 145–90. For Sweden, see Sören Holmberg, *Väljare i förändring* (Stockholm: Publica, 1984), 170; and Sören Holmberg and Mikael Gilljam, *Väljare och val i Sverige* (Stockholm: Bonniers, 1987), 265. For Norway, see Jon Eivind Kolberg and Per Arnt Pettersen, "Om velferdsstatens politiske basis," *Tidsskrift for samfunnsforskning* 22, no. 2/3 (1981): 193–222.

76. For an argument that the welfare state does raise economic problems—all of them attributable to politics—see Gunnar Eliasson, "Is the Swedish Welfare State in Trouble?" Industrial Institute for Economic and Social Research, Working Paper no. 151 (Stockholm, 1985).

77. Bent Rold Andersen, "Rationality and Irrationality," 116. For a much more

conservative expression of a similar point of view, see David Gress, "Daily Life in the Danish Welfare State," *The Public Interest* 69 (Fall 1982): 33–44.

78. Staffan B. Linder, *Den härtlösa välfärdsstaten* (Stockholm: Timbro, 1983).

79. See the discussions in Anne Showstack Sassoon, ed., *Women and the State* (London: Hutchinson, 1987).

80. Niels Ole Finnemann, *I broderskabets aand* (Copenhagen: Gyldendal, 1985), 81.

81. See, e.g., Kari Wærness, "Caring as Women's Work in the Welfare State," in Holter, *Patriarchy in a Welfare Society,* 67–87.

82. Kari Wærness, "A Feminist Perspective on the New Ideology of 'Community Care' for the Elderly," *Acta Sociologica* 30, no. 2 (1987): 149.

83. The day-care center in Denmark that is watching my two children as I write this chapter has been severely hurt by personnel cutbacks, but the people who work there try their best and my children are (most days) happy for the experience. Any criticisms I make of day-care centers in this and the following chapter should be balanced against the fact that, if they did not exist, these chapters would have been less thorough.

84. Christoffersen, Bertelsen, and Vestergaard, *Hvem passer vore børn?* 110–22, 137–45.

85. On Norway, see Agnes Andenæs and Hanne Haavind, *Små barns livsvilkår i Norge* (Oslo: Norwegian University Press, 1987), 66; and Christie, "Nærmiljøet," 233. On Sweden, see Marianne Sundström, *A Study in the Growth of Part-Time Work in Sweden* (Stockholm: Center for Working Life, 1987). In recent years the percentage of part-time work among Swedish women has begun to decline.

86. Ramsøy, "From Necessity to Choice," 102.

87. Esping-Andersen and Korpi, "From Poor Relief to Institutional Welfare States," 40.

88. For a review of the issues in Great Britain, Australia, and the United States, see Robert E. Goodin and Julian LeGrand, eds., *Not Only the Poor: The Middle Class and the Welfare State* (London: Allen and Unwin, 1987).

89. Ringen, *The Possibility of Politics,* 76.

90. On Denmark, see Christoffersen, Bertelsen, and Vestergaard, *Hvem passer vore børn?* 57; on Sweden, see Kemvall-Ljung, *Statistika uppgifter,* 33. For a general overview in English, see Arnlaug Leira, *Day Care for Children in Denmark, Norway, and Sweden* (Oslo: Institute for Social Research, 1987), 82, 118.

91. Oddbjørn Knutsen, "Sosiale klasser og politiske verdier i Norge," *Tidsskrift for samfunnsforskning* 27, no. 4 (1986): 263–87.

92. Jørgen Goul Andersen, "Konservatismen, vælgerne og velfærdsstaten," (Århus University, Institute for Political Science, 1987), 5.

93. Stefan Svallfors, "Kampen om välfärdstaten," *Zenit* 4, no. 4 (1986): 5–24.

94. Esping-Andersen, *Politics Against Markets,* 31–36.

95. Steven Kelman, *Regulating America, Regulating Sweden: A Comparative*

Study of Occupational Safety and Health Policy (Cambridge, Mass.: MIT Press, 1981).

96. Erik Allardt, *Att ha, att älska, att vara* (Lund: Argos, 1975), 27–35, quote p. 30.

Notes to Chapter 6

1. An interesting effort to capture the generational character of social democracy lies in the portrait of two fictional Swedes drawn by Hans L. Zetterberg, "The Rational Humanitarians," in *Norden: The Passion for Equality,* ed. Stephen R. Graubard (Oslo: Norwegian University Press, 1986), 80–86.

2. This statement is more true of Denmark than of Sweden, where age is not as important a factor in determining support for social democracy (Sören Holmberg and Mikael Gilljam, *Väljare och val i Sverige* [Stockholm: Bonniers, 1987], 176). In Denmark, only 15 percent of the voters between eighteen and twenty-four voted for the Social Democrats in the elections of 1987, while 35 percent voted for more leftist parties and 50 percent voted for the conservative parties (figures supplied by Lise Togeby).

3. *Levnadsförhållanden* (Stockholm: Central Statistical Bureau, 1987), 281–83.

4. Myrdal's "birth strike" is cited in Gösta Rehn, "The Wages of Success," in Graubard, *Norden,* 159. On the future, see Magne Raundalen and Ole Johan Finnøy, "Barn og unges syn på framtiden," *Barn* 4, no. 1 (1984): 8–26, which reported that of a sample of Norwegian children between twelve and eighteen years old, 75 percent were pessimistic about the world in which they would live as adults.

Youth unemployment is far more of a problem in Denmark than in the other Scandinavian countries; for background, see Lise Togeby, *Ung og arbejdsløs* (Århus: Politica, 1982). In Sweden, youth unemployment rose rapidly in the early 1980s but since then has dropped substantially; see Eksil Wadensjö, *The Youth Labor Market in Sweden* (Stockholm: Institute for Social Research, 1987), 99.

On drugs, see Oddvar Arner, Mona Duckert, and Ragnar Hauge, *Ungdom og narkotika* (Oslo: Norwegian University Press, 1980). On crime, see Kjersti Ericson, Geir Lundby, and Monika Rudberg, *Mors nest beste barn* (Oslo: Norwegian University Press, 1985) for Norway; and *Berlingske tidende,* 16 October 1987, 1, for Denmark.

For background on the "youth revolt," see, e.g., Erling Bjurstrøm, *Generasjonsopprøret* (Oslo: Norwegian University Press, 1982); and Carsten Jensen, ed., *BZ Europa* (Copenhagen: Tiderne Skifter, 1982).

5. Ivar Frønes, *Generasjoner, solidaritet, og fordeling* (Oslo: Institute for Applied Social Research, 1985), 29; and Inger Koch-Nielsen, "Fremtidens familiemønstre," in *Næste generation,* ed. Inger Koch-Nielsen, Birthe Kyng, Laurits Lauritsen, Bente Ørum, and Ebbe Kløvedal Reich (Copenhagen: Aschehoug, 1985), 42.

6. Ivar Frønes, "Generasjoner og livsløp," in *Det norske samfunn,* ed. Lars Alldén, Natalie Rogoff Ramsøy, and Mariken Vaa (Oslo: Gyldendal, 1986), 180.

7. Lars Dencik, "Opvækst i postmodernismen," in *Børn i nye familie mønstre,* ed. Per Schultz Jørgensen (Copenhagen: Hans Reitzels, 1987), 12–45.

8. Bengt-Erik Andersson, *Home Care or External Care? A Study of the Effects of*

Public Child Care on Children's Development When Eight Years Old (Stockholm: Swedish Institute of Educational Research, 1986).

9. On autonomy, see Erik Sigsgaard, "Om småbørns udvikling af personlig og kollektiv autonomi," in *Småbørn, familie, samfund,* ed. Charlotte Bøgh and Per Schultz Jørgensen (Copenhagen: Hans Reitzels, 1985), 177–86. On the broader social experience obtainable through day care, see, for Sweden, Karin Edenhammar, *Äldersblandade barngrupper* (Stockholm: LiberFörlag, 1982); and for Denmark, Jytte Juul Jensen and Ole Langsted, "Aldersintegrerende institutioner," in Bøgh and Schultz Jørgensen, *Småbørn, familie, samfund,* 187–97.

10. On personnel turnover, see Paul Pedersen and Reidnar J. Pettersen, "Virkninger av personalgjennomtrekk i barnehage," *Nordisk pedagogisk tidsskrift* 69, no. 2 (1985): 102–11. On lack of quality time with the family, see Oddbjørn Evanshaug and Dag Hallen, "Pedagogisk ansvars-fordeling: Mor-far-barnehagen," *Nordisk pedagogisk tidsskrift* 69, no. 2 (1985): 84–91; Mogens Nygaard Christoffersen, Ole Bertelsen, and Poul Vestergaard, *Hvem passer vore børn?* (Copenhagen: Danish Social Research Institute, 1987), 110–15; and Ole Langsted and Dion Sommer, *Småbørns livsvilkår i Danmark* (Copenhagen: Hans Reitzels, 1988), 93–95.

11. Ivar Frønes, *Jevnaldermiljø, sosialisering, og lokalsamfunn* (Oslo: Institute for Social Research, 1987); and Christoffersen, Bertelsen, and Vestergaard, *Hvem passer vore børn?* 129–35. Langsted and Sommer, *Småbørns livsvilkår,* 107, cite research which shows that more than half of Danish parents feel their children do not have enough playmates.

12. The findings on infants in a new environment are summarized in Andersson, *Home Care or External Care,* 2–3. For more on aggressiveness, see the discussion in Birthe Kyng, "Børns personlighedsudvikling: Et fremtidsperspektiv," in Koch-Neilsen, et al., *Næste generation,* 73–74.

13. Kyng, "Børns personlighedsudvikling," 73.

14. *Børnekommissionens betænkning* (Copenhagen: Commission on Children, 1981), 103.

15. Lis Bjørnø, Vagn Dalgård, and Bente Madsen, *Børnekommissionens betænkning: Den nye børnekarakter og skolepsykologi,* School Psychology Monograph Series, no. 21 (Copenhagen, 1982), 16. For a somewhat similar point of view, see Margot Jørgensen and Peter Schreiner, *Fighterrelationen* (Copenhagen: Hans Reitzels, 1985).

16. Kyng, "Børns personlighedsudvikling," 73.

17. Søren Surland, *Har børnene taget magten from os?* (Copenhagen: Aschehoug, 1988).

18. Helga Maria Hernes, *Welfare State and Woman Power* (Oslo: Norwegian University Press, 1987), 15–16.

19. Svein Olav Daatland and Gerdt Sundström, *Gammal i Norden* (Stockholm: Initiatives for Service and Housing Sectors for the Elderly Project, 1985), 25.

20. Gerdt Sundström, "Family and State: Recent Trends in the Care of the Aged in Sweden," *Aging and Society* 6 (June 1986): 172.

21. Tor Inge Romøren, "Midlertidig sykehjemsopphold blant eldre," *Tidsskrift for samfunnsforskning* 26, no. 1/2 (1985): 177–99.

22. Kari Wærness, "A Feminist Perspective on the New Ideology of 'Community Care' for the Elderly," *Acta Sociologica* 30, no. 2 (1987): 133–50. For a basically similar Swedish view, see Ritva Gough, *Hemhjälp til gamla* (Stockholm: Center for Working Life, 1987).

23. This is one of the main themes of Martin Bulmer, *The Social Basis of Community Care* (London: Allen and Unwin, 1987), dealing primarily with the British context.

24. As far as the improvement in the situation of the elderly is concerned, a study of Danes born 1906–1910 indicated that between 1976 and 1986, both their housing situation and their feeling of social connectedness improved (Erik Jørgen Hansen, *Generationer og livsforløb i Danmark* [Copenhagen: Hans Reitzels, 1988], 172).

25. Inger Hilde Nordhus, "Begrepet omsorgsbyrde," *Tidsskrift for samfunnsforskning* 27, no. 4 (1986): 304.

26. A study of two neighborhoods in Oslo, for example, indicated that (at least in one of them) women in full-time work generally were less available to help their parents; see Susan Lingsom, *I eget hjem med andres hjelp* (Oslo: Institute for Social Research, 1987), 93.

27. Sundström, "Family and State," 173.

28. For the American case, see Chapter 2, and Andrew Cherlin and Frank Furstenberg, *The New American Grandparent: A Place in the Family, a Life Apart* (New York: Basic Books, 1986). The notion of "intimacy at a distance" comes from Leopold Rosenmayr and Eva Køckeis, "Propositions for a Sociological Theory of Aging and the Family," *International Social Science Journal* 15, no. 3 (1963): 410–26.

29. Sundström, "Family and State," 176.

30. Bent Rold Andersen, "Creating Coherent Public Policy for the Elderly in a Welfare State," in *Two Essays on the Nordic Welfare State* (Copenhagen: Local Government Research Institute on Public Finance and Administration, 1983), 65.

31. For a discussion of the strains involved in caring for the elderly, see Nordhus, "Begrepet omsorgsbyrde."

32. Susan Lingsom, "Omsorg for ektefellen," *Tidsskrift for samfunnsforskning* 25, no. 3 (1984): 245–68.

33. See Svein Olav Daatland, "Eldreomsorg i en småby," *Tidsskrift for samfunnsforskning* 24, no. 2 (1983): 155–73.

34. Vernon L. Bengston and J. A. Kuypers, "Psycho-Social Issues in the Aging Family" (Paper presented at the Twelfth International Congress of Gerontology, Hamburg, 1981); cited in Svein Olav Daatland, "Care Systems," *Aging and Society* 3 (March 1983): 13.

35. For research that demonstrates the importance of informal care for the

elderly, see Warren A. Peterson and Jill Quadagno, eds., *Social Bonds in Later Life: Aging and Interdependence* (Beverly Hills, Calif.: Sage, 1985).

36. See, e.g., Charlotte Nusberg, Mary Jo Greson, and Sheila Peace, *Innovative Aging Programs Abroad: Implications for the United States* (Westport, Conn.: Greenwood Press, 1984), esp. 130–31.

37. Sundström, "Family and State," 176.

38. Tine Eiby, "Da børnene vandt over de gamle," *Weekendavisen*, 8–14 April 1988, 1. In previous years pensions in Scandinavia tended to be better funded than day-care centers; this change can therefore be viewed as a historic correction.

39. Susan Lingsom, "Fragmeneter i samspill," in *Gammel i eget hjem*, ed. Svein Olav Daatland (Copenhagen: Nordic Council, 1987), 200.

40. Gunhild Hammarström, *Solidaritetsmönster mellan generationer* (Uppsala: The Elderly in Society Before, Now, and in the Future Project, 1986), 86–90, 205–29.

41. Merete Platz, *Længst muligt i eget hjem* . . . (Copenhagen: Danish Social Research Institute, 1987), 92–97.

42. Lise Widding Isaksen, "Om krenking av den personlige bluferdighet," *Tidsskrift for samfunnsforskning* 28, no. 1 (1987): 33–46.

43. Erik Jørgen Hansen, *Generationer og livsforløb*, 172, shows that between 1976 and 1986 the number of elderly Danes who missed having strong friendships decreased slightly, but for those non-working-class elderly without children the feeling of missing friends nearly doubled.

44. Wærness, "A Feminist Perspective," 146. For American data, see Gunhild O. Hagestad, "Problems and Promises in the Social Psychology of Intergenerational Relations," in *Aging*, ed. Robert Fogel et al. (New York: Academic Press, 1981), 11–46.

45. Bent Rold Andersen, "Creating Coherent Public Policy," 65.

46. Richard Titmuss, *The Gift Relationship: From Human Blood to Social Policy* (New York: Pantheon Books, 1971).

47. Merete Watt Boolsen, *Frivillige i socialt arbejde* (Copenhagen: Danish Social Research Institute, 1988), 19.

48. Mirdza Brivkalne, "Fritid," in *Perspektiv på välfärden 1987* (Stockholm: Central Statistical Bureau, 1987), 257.

49. Michael Tåhlin, *Fritid i välfärden* (Stockholm: Riksförbundet Sveriges Fritids-och Hemgårder, 1985), 55–78.

50. Peter Winai, *Gränsorganisationer* (Stockholm: Finance Department, 1987), and Winai, *Organisationer på gränsen mellan privat och offentlig sektor* (Stockholm: Finance Department, 1985).

51. See the following studies by Håkon Lorentzen, all published in 1987 by the Institute for Applied Social Research, Oslo: *Frivillig sosialt arbeid i organisasjoner for syke, handicappede, og funksjonshemmede; Frivillige sosiale ytelser i menighetenes regi;* and *Frivillig sosialt arbeid og ytelser i noen humanitære organisasjoner.*

52. The report of the examination of voluntary organizations is Ulla Habermann and Ingrid Parsby, *Myter og realiteter i det frivillige sociale arbejde* (Copenhagen: Danish Social Ministry, 1987); see also Kirsten Just Jeppesen and Dorte Høeg, *Private hjælpeorganisationer på det sociale område* (Copenhagen: Danish Social Research Institute, 1987). On the "third network" and its role, see Ulla Habermann, *Det tredje netværk* (Copenhagen: Akademisk Forlag, 1987); and Kurt Klaudi Klausen, "Organisationer mellem stat og marked" (Photocopy).

53. Such a pregnancy was the subject of one of the most famous twentieth-century Danish novels, Martin Andersen Nexø's *Ditte Menneskebarn* (Copenhagen: Gyldendal, 1963; first published in 1917–21).

54. As in the United States, women in Scandinavia have played a leading role in the voluntary sector. See Hernes, *Welfare State and Woman Power*, 56–61.

55. Vera Skalts and Magna Nørgaard, *Mødrehjælpens epoke* (Copenhagen: Rhodos, n.d.), 22–30, 49, 57–79.

56. Victor Pürschel; cited in ibid., 29.

57. Dansk Mødrehjælpen af 1983, *Årsberetning 1986.*

58. Anne Køppe, *Evaluering af Mødrehjælpen af 1983* (Copenhagen: Institute for Social Medicine, 1987).

59. Ralph Kramer, *Voluntary Agencies in the Welfare State* (Berkeley and Los Angeles: University of California Press, 1981), emphasizes how private organizations receive state support, especially in Holland, in contrast to the American pattern. Scandinavian societies represent yet another alternative, where private organizations, as in Holland, receive government funds but, unlike in Holland, are not extensively relied upon.

60. Danmarks Frivillige Bloddonorer, *Festskrift 1932–1982*, 6–7.

61. Axel Hadenius, *A Crisis of the Welfare State?* (Stockholm: Almqvist and Wiksell, 1986), 23. For a comparison of Denmark, Sweden, and three other countries, see Douglas A. Hibbs, Jr., and Henrik Jess Madsen, "Public Reactions to the Growth of Taxation and Government Expenditure," *World Politics* 33 (April 1981): 413–35.

62. Recent figures are contained in Organization for Economic Cooperation and Development, *Revenue Statistics of Member Countries* (Paris: OECD, 1986), 83. In the late 1980s, Denmark may pass Sweden and become first in the world in taxation, in part because of tax reform in Sweden and in part because a conservative government in Denmark has chosen not to cut back welfare state activities aggressively.

63. Gunnar Heckscher, *The Welfare State and Beyond: Success and Problems in Scandinavia* (Minneapolis: University of Minnesota Press, 1984), 106. For a different point of view, see Stein Ringen, *The Possibility of Politics: A Study in the Political Economy of the Welfare State* (Oxford: Clarendon Press, 1987), 68.

64. Einar Øverbye, *Skatteprogresjon og skattereduserende strategier* (Oslo: Institute for Applied Social Research, 1984), 123, 137.

65. Einar Øverbye, *Den skjulte inntekten* (Oslo: Institute for Applied Social Research, 1985), 84.

66. Ibid., 90. Øverbye (p. 89) does point out that his data are not good enough to establish a life-cycle or generational effect in tax obligations. Young Swedes were also found to be more likely to indicate dissatisfaction with tax rates; see Hadenius, *Crisis of the Welfare State?* 38.

67. Joachim Vogel, *Aspirationer, möjligheter, och skattemoral* (Stockholm: Government Official Reports, 1970), 145; the 1980–81 data are in Hadenius, *Crisis of the Welfare State?* 35.

68. Øverbye, *Den skjulte inntekten*, 85.

69. Although Americans are thought of as individualistic and Scandinavians as collectivistic, it is my experience that pure rational-choice models of action tend to apply, particularly with regard to the behavior of organizations, better in Scandinavia than in the United States. On cultural rather than economic issues—such as smoking in public or driving without respect for others—Danes engage in "self-interested" behavior to a far greater degree than Americans.

70. Vogel, *Aspirationer*, 73, 147.

71. Pekka Kosonen, "From Collectivity to Individualism in the Welfare State?" *Acta Sociologica* 30, no. 3/4 (1987): 281–93.

72. Gunnar Viby Mogensen, *Sort arbejde i Danmark* (Viborg, Den.: Arnold Busck, 1985), 32.

73. Edgar L. Feige, "Sweden's Underground Economy," Industrial Institute for Economic and Social Research, Working Paper no. 161 (Stockholm, 1986), 16.

74. Arne Jon Isachsen, Jan Tore Klovland, and Steinar Strøm, "The Hidden Economy in Norway," in *The Underground Economy in the United States and Abroad*, ed. Vito Tanzi (Lexington, Mass.: Lexington Books, 1982), 209–32; and Arne Isachsen and Steiner Strøm, "The Size and Growth of the Hidden Economy in Norway," *Review of Income and Wealth* 31 (March 1985): 21–38.

75. For an application of this approach to Scandinavia, see Friedrich Schneider and Jens Lundager, "The Development of the Shadow Economies for Denmark, Norway, and Sweden" (Institute for Economics, Århus University, 1986), which shows increases over time for all three countries, the largest shadow economy being in Sweden.

76. See B. S. Frey and Hannelore Weck, "Estimating the Shadow Economy," *Oxford Economic Papers* 35 (March 1983): 23–44.

77. Mogensen, *Sort arbejde*, 71.

78. See Jens Bonke, *Formelt og informelt byggeri* (Copenhagen: Government Institute for Construction Research, 1986).

79. Mogensen, *Sort arbejde*, 65–76.

80. Ibid., 76–87.

81. Hans Magnus Enzensberger, *Svensk höst* (Stockholm: Dagens Nyheter,

1982), 17. Enzensberger also visited Norway, the results of which trip were published as *Norsk utakt* (Oslo: Norwegian University Press, 1984).

82. The most conspicuous conservative critic is Roland Huntford; see his *The New Totalitarians* (London: Allen Lane, 1972). Danes, who are of a more liberal bent than Swedes, also marvel at the Swedish state; one, using Enzensberger's own formulation, has written that the Swedish state has "a kind of moral immunity that no other society has" (Mogens Behrendt, *Tilfældet Sverige* [Copenhagen: Erichsen, 1983], 21). For a Norwegian effort to understand Sweden, see Lars Hellberg, *Det nye Sverige* (Oslo: Cappalens, 1981).

83. A point made by Gösta Rehn in *Towards a Society of Free Choice*, Stockholm: Institute for Social Research, 1978.

84. The most poetic account of Grundtvig's life and accomplishments is Ebbe Kløvedal Reich, *Frederik* (Copenhagen: Gyldendal, 1981). For a collection of Grundtvig's writings in English, see *A Grundtvig Anthology*, ed. Niels Lynhe Jensen (Cambridge: James Clarke, 1984).

85. Arne Ruth, "The Second New Nation: The Mythology of Modern Sweden," in Graubard, *Norden*, 279.

86. Olof Holm, *Kooperation i ofärd och välfärd* (Stockholm: Department of Education, University of Stockholm, 1984).

87. Hilding Johansson, *Folkrörelserna i Sverige* (Stockholm: Sober, 1980); and Sven Lundqvist, *Folkrörelserna i det svenska samhället 1850–1920* (Stockholm: Sober, 1977).

88. Quoted in Heckscher, *The Welfare State and Beyond*, 45.

89. The best history of the early Norwegian welfare state is Anna-Lise Seip, *Socialhjelpstaten blir til* (Oslo: Gyldendal, 1984).

90. Bo Rothstein, "Managing the Welfare State: Lessons from Gustav Möller," in *Velfærdsstaten i krise*, ed. Ann-Dorte Christiansen, Erik Christiansen, Karin Hansen, Morten Lassen, and Børge Rasmussen (Ålborg: Center for Welfare State Studies, 1986), 2:225–58.

91. Ruth, "Second New Nation," 273.

92. The relevance of the Grundtvigian moral vision is a constant theme of discussion in Danish cultural life. See Ejvind Larsen, *Det levende ord* (Copenhagen: Rosinante, 1983); and Henrik S. Nissen, ed., *Efter Grundtvig* (Copenhagen: Gyldendal, 1983).

93. Holm, *Kooperation*, 128–72, 183–98.

94. Bo Rothstein, *Den socialdemokratiska staten*, Dissertation Series, no. 21 (Lund, 1986), 161–96.

95. Ruth, "Second New Nation," 278–79.

96. Bent Rold Andersen, "Rationality and Irrationality of the Nordic Welfare State," in Graubard, *Norden*, 132.

97. Heckscher, *The Welfare State and Beyond*, 160.

98. Michael Walzer, "Socialism and the Gift Relationship," *Dissent* 29 (Fall 1982): 432.

99. Michael Walzer, *Spheres of Justice: A Defense of Pluralism and Equality* (New York: Basic Books, 1983), 94.

100. Ulrich K. Preuss, "The Concept of Rights and the Welfare State," in *Dilemmas of Law in the Welfare State,* ed. Gunther Teubner (Berlin: Walter de Gruyter, 1986), 156, 160.

101. Gösta Esping-Andersen and Walter Korpi, "From Poor Relief to Institutional Welfare States," in *The Scandinavian Model: Welfare States and Welfare Research,* ed. Robert Erikson et al. (Armonk, N.Y.: M.E. Sharpe, 1986), 53.

Notes to Chapter 7

1. One who does insist on including the realm of the social within discussions of political economy is Philippe Schmitter, "Neo-Corporatism and the State," in *The Political Economy of Corporatism,* ed. Wyn Grant (New York: St. Martins Press, 1985), 32–62, esp. p. 52.

2. Charles Lindblom, *Politics and Markets: The World's Political Economic Systems* (New York: Basic Books, 1977); and Gösta Esping-Andersen, *Politics Against Markets: The Social Democratic Road to Power* (Princeton, N.J.: Princeton University Press, 1985).

3. See Albert O. Hirschman, *Exit, Voice, and Loyalty: Responses to Decline in Firms, Organizations, and States* (Cambridge, Mass.: Harvard University Press, 1970); and Hirschman, "Exit and Voice: Some Further Distinctions," in *Essays in Trespassing: Economics to Politics and Beyond* (Cambridge: Cambridge University Press, 1981), 236–45.

4. Albert O. Hirschman, *Shifting Involvements: Private Interest and Public Action* (Princeton, N.J.: Princeton University Press, 1982).

5. Anthony Giddens, *The Constitution of Society: Outline of the Theory of Structuration* (Berkeley and Los Angeles: University of California Press, 1984), 281–84.

6. See Gary Becker, *The Economic Approach to Human Behavior* (Chicago: University of Chicago Press, 1976), 5.

7. See Jon Elster, *Making Sense of Marx* (Cambridge: Cambridge University Press, 1985).

8. Emile Durkheim, *The Division of Labor in Society* (New York: Free Press, 1964), 28.

9. Emile Durkheim, *Moral Education* (New York: Free Press, 1973), 43, 54.

10. Emile Durkheim, *Suicide* (New York: Free Press, 1966), 248.

11. Ferdinand Tönnies, *Community and Association,* trans. Charles P. Loomis (London: Routledge and Kegan Paul, 1974), 261.

12. The best of these antimodern moralists is, in this writer's opinion, Alasdair

Notes to Pages 192–99

MacIntyre; see his *After Virtue: A Study in Moral Theory* (South Bend, Ind.: University of Notre Dame Press, 1981).

13. Brigitte Berger and Peter L. Berger, *The War over the Family: Capturing the Middle Ground* (Garden City, N.Y.: Doubleday, 1983), 141, 154.

14. For an exploration of this theme, see Stephen P. Turner and Mark L. Wardell, eds., *Sociological Theory in Transition* (Boston: Allen and Unwin, 1986).

15. Peter M. Blau, *Exchange and Power in Social Life* (New York: John Wiley, 1964).

16. Two books that deal with that approach more generally, including the work of George Homans (whom I have not discussed) are Anthony Heath, *Rational Choice and Social Exchange* (Cambridge: Cambridge University Press, 1976); and Peter Ekeh, *Social Exchange Theory: The Two Traditions* (London: Heinemann, 1974).

17. Blau, *Exchange and Power*, 62.

18. Ibid., 92; see also 93–97.

19. Ibid., 259.

20. Ibid., 92, 260.

21. Ibid., 92; see Alvin W. Gouldner, "The Norm of Reciprocity," *American Sociological Review* 25 (April, 1960): 161–78.

22. Blau, *Exchange and Power*, 62.

23. See ibid., 97.

24. Ibid., 70–71.

25. Morris Janowitz, *The Reconstruction of Patriotism: Education for Civic Consciousness* (Chicago: University of Chicago Press, 1983), xi, 2.

26. See Morris Janowitz, "Sociological Theory and Social Control," *American Journal of Sociology* 81 (July 1975): 82–108. In this article Janowitz argues that the concept of social control developed in direct opposition to theories of economic man, as an effort "to identify the limitations of marginal–utility analysis" (p. 84).

27. Morris Janowitz, *The Last Half Century: Societal Change and Politics in America* (Chicago: University of Chicago Press, 1978), 235. Despite his distaste for Chicago school models of rational choice, Janowitz concludes, contrary to my own arguments in Chapter 1 of this book, that "the emergence of economic analysis of crime by Gary Becker . . . supplies not a substitute but rather a continuity with traditional sociological observations" (pp. 372–73).

28. The last two of these points are elaborated more fully in *The Reconstruction of Patriotism* than in *The Last Half Century*.

29. Morris Janowitz, *Social Control of the Welfare State* (New York: Elsevier, 1976), 107–8.

30. "There is one association that among all others enjoys a genuine preeminence and that represents the end, par excellence, of moral conduct. This is political society, i.e., the nation—but the nation conceived of as a partial embodiment of the idea of humanity" (Durkheim, *Moral Education*, 80).

31. Janowitz, *The Last Half Century,* 370, 368, 14.

32. Janowitz, *Reconstruction of Patriotism,* 14, 194.

33. Ibid., xi. Janowitz's identification of himself as a social democrat is in *Social Control of the Welfare State,* xvi.

34. Janowitz, *Reconstruction of Patriotism,* 99, 105, 106, 111, 138.

35. The notion that Parsons was a moralist is, of course, at the heart of Alvin Gouldner's critique of his work; see his *The Coming Crisis of Western Sociology* (New York: Basic Books, 1970), esp. 140–41, 144–48, 178–95, and 254–57.

36. Talcott Parsons, *The Social System* (New York: Free Press, 1964), 540.

37. Ibid., 14.

38. Ibid., 429.

39. Ibid., 464.

40. Allan Silver, "'Trust' in Social and Political Theory," in *The Challenge of Social Control,* ed. Gerald D. Suttles and Mayer N. Zald (Norwood, N.J.: Ablex, 1985), 52.

41. Niklas Luhmann has written the best account of trust as a socially binding force: see his *Trust and Power* (New York: John Wiley, 1979). Other recent works on the sociology of trust include Bernard Barber, *The Logic and Limits of Trust* (New Brunswick, N.J.: Rutgers University Press, 1983); and J. David Lewis and Andrew Weigert, "Trust as a Social Reality," *Social Forces* 63 (June 1985): 967–85.

42. Parsons, *The Social System,* 41.

43. William Buxton, *Talcott Parsons and the Capitalist Nation-State* (Toronto: University of Toronto Press, 1985), 146–64.

44. Talcott Parsons, "'Voting' and the Equilibrium of the American Political System," in *Politics and Social Structure* (New York: Free Press, 1969), 205.

45. Talcott Parsons, "The Political Aspect of Social Structure and Process," in *Politics and Social Structure,* 318.

46. See Michael Hechter, *Principles of Group Solidarity* (Berkeley and Los Angeles: University of California Press, 1987); and Michael Taylor, *The Possibility of Cooperation,* rev. ed. (Cambridge: Cambridge University Press, 1987).

47. On contemporary structural-functionalism, see Jeffrey Alexander, ed., *Neo-Functionalism* (Beverly Hills, Calif.: Sage, 1985). Representative works on the theory of the state include Theda Skocpol, *States and Social Revolutions: A Comparative Analysis of France, Russia, and China* (Cambridge: Cambridge University Press, 1979); Charles Tilly, ed., *The Development of the State in Western Europe* (Princeton, N.J.: Princeton University Press, 1975); and Michael Mann, *The Sources of Social Power: A History of Power from the Beginning to A.D. 1760* (Cambridge: Cambridge University Press, 1986). My own contribution to the theory of the state is *The Limits of Legitimacy: Political Contractions of Contemporary Capitalism* (New York: Free Press, 1977).

48. One exception to this generalization is what could be called the "Bellah" school. See, e.g., Richard Madsen, *Morality and Power in a Chinese Village* (Berke-

ley and Los Angeles: University of California Press, 1984); Stephen J. Tipton, *Getting Saved from the Sixties: Moral Meaning in Conversion and Cultural Change* (Berkeley and Los Angeles: University of California Press, 1982); and Robert Wuthnow, *Meaning and Moral Order: Explorations in Cultural Analysis* (Berkeley and Los Angeles: University of California Press, 1987).

49. Robert K. Merton, *Sociological Ambivalence and Other Essays* (New York: Free Press, 1976).

50. Donald McCloskey, *The Rhetoric of Economics* (Madison: University of Wisconsin Press, 1985).

51. Arlie Russell Hochschild, *The Managed Heart: Commercialization of Human Feeling* (Berkeley and Los Angeles: University of California Press, 1983); and Robert Bellah et al., *Habits of the Heart: Individualism and Commitment in American Life* (Berkeley and Los Angeles: University of California Press, 1985).

52. For the first position, see Robert Nisbet, *Emile Durkheim* (Englewood Cliffs, N.J.: Prentice-Hall, 1965); for the second, Stephen Seidman, *Liberalism and the Origins of European Social Theory* (Berkeley and Los Angeles: University of California Press, 1983); and for the third, Steve Fenton, *Durkheim and Modern Social Theory* (Cambridge: Cambridge University Press, 1985).

53. For Lukács's views, see his *The Destruction of Reason,* trans. Peter Palmer (Atlantic Highlands, N.J.: Humanities Press, 1981).

Notes to Chapter 8

1. The essays contained in Jon Elster, ed., *The Multiple Self* (Cambridge: Cambridge University Press, 1986), explore this general assumption, but with greater emphasis on self-deception than on the social aspects of the self. See also Thomas Schelling, "Ethics, Law, and the Exercise of Self-Command," in *Choice and Consequence: Perspectives of an Errant Economist* (Cambridge, Mass.: Harvard University Press, 1984), 83–112.

2. Virginia Held, *Rights and Goods: Justifying Social Action* (New York: Free Press, 1984), 25.

3. Amitai Etzioni, *The Moral Dimension: Toward a New Economics* (New York: Free Press, 1988), 36–41.

4. Harold Garfinkel, *Studies in Ethnomethodology* (Englewood Cliffs, N.J.: Prentice-Hall, 1967).

5. Alfred Schutz, "Phenomenology and the Social Sciences"; cited in Jeffrey Alexander, *Twenty Lectures: Sociological Theory Since World War II* (New York: Columbia University Press, 1987), 250. In his most famous work, Schutz wrote: "I thus presuppose that at any given time we are both referring to the same objects, which transcend the subjective experience of either of us" (*The Phenomenology of the Social World* [Evanston, Ill.: Northwestern University Press, 1967], 105).

6. John Heritage, *Garfinkel and Ethnomethodology* (Cambridge: Polity Press, 1984), 100.

7. Eugene Rochberg-Halton, *Meaning and Modernity: Social Theory in Pragmatic Attitude* (Chicago: University of Chicago Press, 1986), 114.

8. Ibid., 164.

9. Victor Turner, *The Ritual Process: Structure and Anti-Structure* (Chicago: Aldine, 1969), 127, 129.

10. Ibid., 203.

11. On political freedom, see Randall Collins, *Weberian Sociological Theory* (Cambridge: Cambridge University Press, 1986), 261–62.

12. Turner, *The Ritual Process,* 116.

13. Rom Harré and Paul Secord, *The Explanation of Social Behavior* (Totowa, N.J.: Littlefield, Adams, 1972), 13.

14. Of the many critiques of sociobiology that have been published, I have found of most help Philip Kitcher, *Vaulting Ambition: Sociobiology and the Quest for Human Nature* (Cambridge, Mass.: MIT Press, 1985), esp. 396–434.

15. Drew Westen, *Self and Society: Narcissism, Collectivism, and the Development of Morals* (Cambridge: Cambridge University Press, 1985), 176.

16. A recent contribution to the debate on human nature is Thomas Sowell, *A Conflict of Visions: Ideological Origins of Political Struggles* (New York: William Morrow, 1987).

17. The need to recognize social creatures as living in social institutions, especially in contrast to some theories of rational-choice individualism, is one of Mary Douglas's themes in *How Institutions Think* (Syracuse, N.Y.: Syracuse University Press, 1986).

18. Harré and Secord, *Explanation of Social Behavior,* 89.

19. Erving Goffman, *Asylums: Essays on the Social Situation of Mental Patients and Other Inmates* (London: Penguin Books, 1968), 119.

20. Kathryn Pyne Addelson, "Moral Passages," in *Women and Moral Theory,* ed. Eva Kittay and Diane Meyers (Totowa, N.J.: Rowman and Littlefield, 1988), 87–110.

21. Besides illustrating the sociological concern with "deviance," Becker is also one who emphasizes "doing things together"; see Howard S. Becker, *Doing Things Together: Selected Papers* (Evanston, Ill.: Northwestern University Press, 1986).

22. One recent effort to relate the study of deviance to the reproduction of the moral order in Durkheimian fashion is Nachman Ben-Yehuda's *Deviance and Moral Boundaries: Witchcraft, the Occult, Science Fiction, Deviant Sciences, and Scientists* (Chicago: University of Chicago Press, 1985).

23. George Herbert Mead, *Mind, Self, and Society: From the Standpoint of a Social Behavioralist* (Chicago: University of Chicago Press, 1962), 162. Goffman goes even further: the self, he writes, "is not a property of the person to whom it is attributed, but dwells rather in the pattern of social control that is exercised in connection with the person by himself and those around him" (*Asylums,* 154).

24. Niklas Luhmann, *Trust and Power* (New York: John Wiley, 1979), 63.

25. The "exit" option, of course, is the invention of Albert Hirschman; see *Exit, Voice, and Loyalty: Responses to Decline in Firms, Organizations, and States* (Cambridge, Mass.: Harvard University Press, 1970). The phrase "concentration of the mind" appears on p. 21.

26. Samuel Bowles and Herbert Gintis, *Democracy and Capitalism: Property, Community, and the Contractions of Modern Social Thought* (New York: Basic Books, 1986), 127.

27. On the immortality of the self, see Raymond L. Schmidt and W. M. Leonard, "Immortalizing the Self Through Sport," *American Journal of Sociology* 91 (March 1986): 1088–1111.

28. Amy Gutmann, "What's The Use of Going to School?" in *Utilitarianism and Beyond,* ed. Amartya Sen and Bernard Williams (Cambridge: Cambridge University Press, 1982), 261–77.

29. On this point, see Harry Frankfurt, "Freedom of the Will and the Concept of a Person," in *The Importance of What We Care About: Philosophical Essays* (Cambridge: Cambridge University Press, 1988), 11–25.

30. Robert E. Lane, "Market Thinking and Political Thinking," in *Dilemmas of Liberal Democracies: Studies in Fred Hirsch's "Social Limits to Growth,"* ed. Adrian Ellis and Krishan Kumar (London: Tavistock, 1983), 140–41.

31. I develop these points at greater length in "Inauthentic Democracy," *Studies in Political Economy* 21 (Autumn 1986): 57–81.

32. Robert Bellah et al., *Habits of the Heart: Individualism and Commitment in American Life* (Berkeley and Los Angeles: University of California Press, 1985).

33. Bowles and Gintis, *Democracy and Capitalism,* 124–27.

34. Michel Foucault, *Discipline and Punish: The Birth of the Prison,* trans. Alan Sheridan (New York: Vintage Books, 1979).

35. Alasdair MacIntyre, *After Virtue: A Study in Moral Theory* (South Bend, Ind.: University of Notre Dame Press, 1981), 175.

36. Mitchell Aboulafia, *The Mediating Self: Mead, Sartre, and Self-Determination* (New Haven, Conn.: Yale University Press, 1986), 73–101.

37. Emile Durkheim, *Moral Education* (New York: Free Press, 1973), 11, 34, 42.

38. Emile Durkheim, *The Elementary Forms of Religious Life* (New York: Free Press, 1965), 492, 495.

39. Emile Durkheim, "Pragmatism and Sociology," in Kurt H. Wolff, ed., *Essays on Sociology and Philosophy* (New York: Harper and Row, 1964), 433; cited in Derek L. Phillips, *Toward a Just Social Order* (Princeton, N.J.: Princeton University Press, 1986), 22.

40. Phillips, *Toward a Just Social Order,* 51.

41. Freud, of course, was certainly a moral thinker; see Philip Rieff, *Freud: The Mind of a Moralist,* 3d ed. (Chicago: University of Chicago Press, 1979). On more recent work, see Jean Piaget, *The Moral Judgement of the Child* (New York: Free

Press, 1965); Lawrence Kohlberg, *The Philosophy of Moral Development* (New York: Harper and Row, 1983); Elliot Turiel, *The Development of Social Knowledge: Morality and Convention* (Cambridge: Cambridge University Press, 1983); and Leonard W. Doob, *Slightly Beyond Skepticism: Social Science and the Search for Morality* (New Haven, Conn.: Yale University Press, 1987). Criticisms of the Kolhbergian approach can be found in Carol Gilligan, *In a Different Voice: Psychological Theory and Women's Development* (Cambridge, Mass.: Harvard University Press, 1982); and Norma Haan, Elaine Aerts, and Bruce A. B. Cooper, *On Moral Grounds: The Search for Practical Morality* (New York: New York University Press, 1985).

42. See Ervin Staub et al., *Development and Maintenance of Prosocial Behavior* (New York: Plenum, 1984); J. P. Rushton, *Altruism, Socialization, and Society* (Englewood Cliffs, N.J.: Prentice-Hall, 1980); Melvin J. Lerner and Sally C. Lerner, *The Justice Motive in Social Behavior: Adapting to Times of Scarcity and Change* (New York: Plenum, 1981); and Morton Deutsch, *Distributive Justice: A Social-psychological Perspective* (New Haven, Conn.: Yale University Press, 1985).

43. The economists include Kenneth J. Arrow, *Social Choice and Individual Values* (New York: John Wiley, 1963); William J. Baumol, *Welfare Economics and the Theory of the State,* 2d ed. (Cambridge, Mass.: Harvard University Press, 1965); and Amartya K. Sen, *Collective Choice and Social Welfare* (San Francisco: Holden Day, 1970). On utilitarianism, see R. M. Hare, *Moral Thinking: Its Levels, Methods, and Point* (Oxford: Clarendon Press, 1981); on rational-choice theory, David P. Gauthier, *Morals by Agreement* (Oxford: Clarendon Press, 1986), and John C. Harsanyi, "Morality and the Theory of Rational Behavior," in Sen and Williams, *Utilitarianism and Beyond,* 39–62; and on state-of-nature assumptions, Robert Nozick, *Anarchy, State, and Utopia* (New York: Basic Books, 1974).

44. It is an obvious oversimplification to posit a dichotomy between philosophical and sociological approaches to morality. Although Jürgen Habermas, for example, accepts the notion of universally valid truth claims (see below), many philosophers have quite a bit in common with sociologists. See, e.g., Maria Ossowska, *Social Determinants of Moral Ideas* (Philadelphia: University of Pennsylvania Press, 1970); Nel Noddings, *Caring: A Feminist Approach to Ethics and Moral Education* (Berkeley and Los Angeles: University of California Press, 1984); and Nicholas Rescher, *Unselfishness: The Role of Vicarious Affects in Moral Philosophy and Social Theory* (Pittsburgh: University of Pittsburgh Press, 1975).

45. James S. Fishkin, *Beyond Subjective Morality: Ethical Reasoning and Political Philosophy* (New Haven, Conn.: Yale University Press, 1984).

46. Allan Gewirth, *Reason and Morality* (Chicago: University of Chicago Press, 1978), 24.

47. See Kohlberg's "The Future of Liberalism as the Dominant Ideology of the West," in *Moral Development and Politics,* ed. Richard W. Wilson and Gordon J. Schochet (New York: Praeger, 1980), 64.

48. Gauthier, *Morals by Agreement,* 269. For an opposing point of view, defend-

ing "intuition over arguments," see Thomas Nagel, *Mortal Questions* (Cambridge: Cambridge University Press, 1979), x.

49. This point is stressed by Charles Taylor in *Philosophical Papers*, vol. 2: *Philosophy and the Human Sciences* (Cambridge: Cambridge University Press, 1985), 211–47.

50. On having children, see Onora O'Neill and William Ruddick, *Having Children: Philosophical and Legal Reflections on Parenthood* (New York: Oxford University Press, 1979); on abortion, see L. W. Sumner, *Abortion and Moral Theory* (Princeton, N.J.: Princeton University Press, 1981); and on death, see Nagel, *Mortal Questions*, 1–10. Peter Singer, ed., *Applied Ethics* (New York: Oxford University Press, 1986), contains a succinct essay on Singer's defense of animal rights, plus other articles on controversial topics such as overpopulation. On nuclear weapons, the environment, and world hunger, see Anthony Kenny, *The Logic of Deterrence* (Chicago: University of Chicago Press, 1985); Paul W. Taylor, *Respect for Nature: A Theory of Environmental Ethics* (Princeton, N.J.: Princeton University Press, 1986); William W. Aiken and Hugh LaFollette, eds., *World Hunger and Moral Obligation* (Englewood Cliffs, N.J.: Prentice-Hall, 1977); and Onora O'Neill, *Faces of Hunger: An Essay on Poverty, Justice, and Development* (London: Allen and Unwin, 1986).

51. Phillips, *Toward a Just Social Order*, 175.

52. Discussion of the ambiguity of language is particularly evident in the work of social psychologists influenced by Wittgenstein, such as Rom Harré and Paul Secord, *The Explanation of Social Behavior*. On the nature of real experience, see Richard Rorty, *Philosophy and the Mirror of Nature* (Princeton, N.J.: Princeton University Press, 1979); on how humans make moral judgments, see Charles E. Larmore, *Patterns of Moral Complexity* (Cambridge: Cambridge University Press, 1987); and, on the human manufacture of symbolic worlds, see Kathryn Pyne Addelson, "Why Philosophers Must Become Sociologists" (Photocopy).

53. Joseph Raz, *The Morality of Freedom* (Oxford: Clarendon Press, 1986), 309.

54. Geoffrey Brennan and James Buchanan, *The Reason of Rules: Constitutional Political Economy* (Cambridge: Cambridge University Press, 1985), 105.

55. F. A. Hayek, *Rules and Order*, vol. 1: *Law, Liberty, and Legislation* (Chicago: University of Chicago Press, 1973), 36, 44 (quotes); on the last point, see, e.g., p. 18.

56. Lon L. Fuller, *The Morality of Law*, rev. ed. (New Haven, Conn.: Yale University Press, 1964), 178, 5, 9, 17.

57. Tom R. Burns and Helena Flam, *The Shaping of Social Organization: Social Rule System Theory with Application* (Beverly Hills, Calif.: Sage, 1987), 12.

58. Brennan and Buchanan, *The Reason of Rules*, 109.

59. See Wayne E. Baker, "The Social Structure of a National Securities Market," *American Journal of Sociology* 89 (January 1984): 775–811; and Wayne E. Baker, "Floor Trading and Crowd Dynamics," in *The Social Dynamics of Financial Markets*, ed. Patricia A. Adler and Peter Adler (Greenwich, Conn.: JAI Press, 1984), 107–28.

60. Clifford Geertz, *Local Knowledge: Further Essays in Interpretive Anthropology* (New York: Basic Books, 1983), 73–120.

61. For an argument of how judges interpret legal rules sociologically, see Gordon L. Clark, *Judges and the Cities: Interpreting Local Autonomy* (Chicago: University of Chicago Press, 1985).

62. Duncan Kennedy, "Form and Substance in Private Law Adjudication," *Harvard Law Review* 89 (June 1976): 1685–1778. Whether rules are primarily associated with egoistic theories of self-interest, and standards with theories of altruism and cooperation, is not as important in this context as the fact that all rules presume standards and all standards presume rules.

63. Brennan and Buchanan, *The Reason of Rules*, 7.

64. Lon L. Fuller, "Two Principles of Human Association," in *The Principles of Social Order: Selected Essays of Lon L. Fuller,* ed. Kenneth I. Winston (Durham, N.C.: Duke University Press, 1981), 67–85, quote p. 71.

65. For a general discussion, see John P. Burke, *Bureaucratic Responsibility* (Baltimore: Johns Hopkins University Press, 1986).

66. Fuller, *The Morality of Law*, 153.

67. Lawrence Kohlberg, "From Is to Ought," in *Cognitive Development and Epistemology,* ed. Theodore Mischel (New York: Academic Press, 1971), 215.

68. See William N. Nelson, *On Justifying Democracy* (London: Routledge and Kegan Paul, 1980).

69. For an effort to develop a moral theory around the idea that we must recognize ambiguity, not only in the language we use to express moral ideals, but even in the ideals themselves, see Burton Zweibach, *The Common Life: Ambiguity, Agreement, and the Structure of Morals* (Philadelphia: Temple University Press, 1988).

70. On the "traditional model" of administrative law, see Richard B. Stewart, "The Reformation of American Administrative Law," *Harvard Law Review* 88 (June 1975): 1667–1813, esp. p. 1676.

71. Ronald Dworkin, *Law's Empire* (Cambridge, Mass.: Harvard University Press, 1986), 85.

72. Jürgen Habermas, *Theory of Communicative Action,* vol. 1: *Reason and the Rationality of Society,* trans. Thomas McCarthy (Boston: Beacon Press, 1984). For a critique of Habermas along similar lines to mine, see Iris Marion Young, "Impartiality and the Civic Public" in *Feminism as Critique: On the Politics of Gender,* ed. Seyla Benhabib and Drucilla Cornell (Minneapolis: University of Minnesota Press, 1987), 57–76.

73. Kristin Luker, *Abortion and the Politics of Motherhood* (Berkeley and Los Angeles: University of California Press, 1984); and Jonathan Rieder, *Canarsie: The Jews and Italians of Brooklyn Against Liberalism* (Cambridge, Mass.: Harvard University Press, 1985).

Notes to Chapter 9

1. Claus Offe, "Competitive Party Democracy and the Welfare State," *Policy Sciences* 15 (June 1983): 225–46.

2. I borrow this term from Helen Weinreich-Haste and Don Locke, eds., *Morality in the Making: Thought, Action, and the Social Context* (New York: John Wiley, 1983).

3. L. W. Sumner, *Abortion and Moral Theory* (Princeton, N.J.: Princeton University Press, 1981), 15.

4. Baruch Brody, *Abortion and the Sanctity of Human Life* (Cambridge, Mass.: MIT Press, 1975), 116. For the curious, the one exception Brody admits is as follows: "It is permissible to take B's life to save A's life if B is going to die anyway in a relatively short time, taking B's life is the only way of saving A's life, and either (1) taking A's life (or doing anything else) will not save B's life or (2) taking A's life (or doing anything else) will save B's life, but one has, by some fair random method, determined to save A's life rather than B's life" (p. 23).

5. John T. Noonan, "An Almost Absolute Value in History," in *The Morality of Abortion: Legal and Historical Perspectives,* ed. John T. Noonan (Cambridge, Mass.: Harvard University Press, 1970), 53.

6. Emile Durkheim, "The Dualism of Human Nature and Its Social Conditions," in *Emile Durkheim on Morality and Society,* ed. Robert Bellah (Chicago: University of Chicago Press, 1973), 152.

7. The relationship between the principle of a woman's right to control her own body and the political theory of "possessive individualism" is explored in Jean Bethke Elshtain, "Reflections on Abortion, Values, and the Family," in *Abortion: Understanding Differences,* ed. Sidney Callahan and Daniel Callahan (New York: Plenum, 1984), 53–54.

8. Sumner, *Abortion and Moral Theory,* 34, 38.

9. Judith G. Smetana, *Concepts of Self and Morality: Women's Reasoning About Abortion* (New York: Praeger, 1982).

10. Arthur B. Shostak and Gary McLouth, *Men and Abortion: Lessons, Losses, and Love* (New York: Praeger, 1984), 17.

11. Mary K. Zimmerman, *Passage Through Abortion: The Personal and Social Reality of Women's Experience* (New York: Praeger, 1977), 126.

12. See Carole Joffe, *The Regulation of Sexuality: Experiences of Family Planning Workers* (Philadelphia: Temple University Press, 1986), for a discussion of the experiences of such workers.

13. Jonathan B. Imber, *Abortion and the Private Practice of Medicine* (New Haven, Conn.: Yale University Press, 1986), 119.

14. Kristin Luker, *Abortion and the Politics of Motherhood* (Berkeley and Los Angeles: University of California Press, 1984).

15. For a comprehensive history of the 1974 Swedish decision to liberalize its abortion laws, see Stefan Swärd, *Varför Sverige fick fri abort* (Stockholm: Political Science Department, Stockholm University, 1984).

16. For a study of the experiences of more than a hundred Swedish women who had abortions, see Anne-Christine Trost, *Abort och psykiska besvär* (Västerås, Swe.: International Library, 1982).

17. Joffe, *The Regulation of Sexuality,* 161.

18. Johan Goudsblom, "Public Health and the Civilizing Process," *Milbank Quarterly* 64, no. 2 (1986): 161–88.

19. For information on the Swedish approach to AIDS, I have relied on Benny Henriksson, *AIDS: Föreställingar om en verklighet* (Stockholm: Glacio, 1987), 55–61. "AIDS i Norden," *Nordisk Kontakt* 32, no. 8 (1987): 6–13, gives an overview of the treatment of AIDS in all the Nordic countries.

20. *International Herald Tribune,* 20 November 1987, 5.

21. Ibid., 26 November 1987, 6.

22. The Danish approach to AIDS is described in Vagn Greve and Annika Snare, *AIDS: Nogle retspolitiske spørgsmål* (Copenhagen: Institute of Criminology, 1987).

23. Randy Shilts, *And the Band Played On: Politics, People, and the AIDS Epidemic* (New York: St. Martins Press, 1987), 565–66.

24. For a similar conclusion, see Ronald Bayer, *Private Acts, Social Consequences: AIDS and the Politics of Public Health* (New York: Free Press, 1989).

25. The kinds of moral dilemmas posed by advances in medical technology are discussed in Ruth Macklin, *Mortal Choices: Bioethics in Today's World* (New York: Pantheon Books, 1987).

26. For a different conclusion, emphasizing that the morality of integrated schools ought to be chosen over the morality of a community's wishes, see Jennifer Hochschild, *The New American Dilemma: Liberal Democracy and School Desegregation* (New Haven, Conn.: Yale University Press, 1984). That participants in Boston's school wars, on all sides, did experience moments of moral passage is shown by J. Anthony Lukas, *Common Ground: A Turbulent Decade in the Lives of Three American Families* (New York: Alfred Knopf, 1985).

27. Michael Walzer, *Spheres of Justice: A Defense of Pluralism and Equality* (New York: Basic Books, 1983), 50.

28. See Göran Therborn, "Den svenska välfärdsstatens särart och framtid," in *Lycksalighetens halvö* (Stockholm: Institute for Future Studies, 1987), 13–44.

29. A Danish study of attitudes toward immigrants and refugees found great polarization of opinion: those who were hostile tended to become more hostile, while those who were accepting tended to become more accepting. See Eszter Körmendi, *Os og de andre* (Copenhagen: Danish Social Research Institute, 1986).

30. Gunnar Heckscher, *The Welfare State and Beyond: Success and Problems in Scandinavia* (Minneapolis: University of Minnesota Press, 1984), 140.

31. Bent Rold Andersen describes his frustrations as social minister in trying to achieve some of these reforms in "Creating Coherent Public Policy for the Elderly in a Welfare State," in *Two Essays on the Nordic Welfare State* (Copenhagen: Local Government Research Institute on Public Finance and Administration, 1983), 73–75.

32. For this last point I am indebted to discussions with Barbara Katz Rothman.

33. Fred Hirsch, *The Social Limits to Growth* (Cambridge, Mass.: Harvard University Press, 1978), 52, 54.

34. Bernt Hagtvet and Erik Rudeng, "Scandinavia: Achievements, Dilemmas, Challenges," in *Norden: The Passion for Equality,* ed. Stephen R. Graubard (Oslo: Norwegian University Press, 1986), 301.

35. Neil Gilbert, "Sweden's Disturbing Family Trends," *Wall Street Journal,* 22 June 1987, 6.

36. Ole Bertelsen and Peter Linde, *Efterspørgsel efter offentlig dagpasning* (Copenhagen: Danish Social Research Institute, 1985), 33–34.

37. Neil Gilbert, *Capitalism and the Welfare State: Dilemmas of Social Benevolence* (New Haven, Conn.: Yale University Press, 1983), 110–14.

38. For a refutation of the aged-dependency ratio, see Merton C. Bernstein and Joan Brodshaug Bernstein, *Social Security: The System That Works* (New York: Basic Books, 1988), 70–89.

39. Walzer, *Spheres of Justice,* 39.

40. For a thorough examination of these issues, see Alan Dowty, *Closed Borders* (New Haven, Conn.: Yale University Press, 1987).

41. For examples and analysis, see Barry Bluestone and Bennett Harrison, *The Deindustrialization of America: Plant Closings, Community Abandonment, and the Dismantling of Basic Industry* (New York: Basic Books, 1982).

42. Karl Polanyi, *The Great Transformation: The Political and Economic Origin of Our Times* (Boston: Beacon Press, 1957), 141.

43. The term *normal accidents* comes from Charles Perrow, *Normal Accidents: Living with High-Risk Technologies* (New York: Basic Books, 1984).

44. On how free-market economics can be linked to strong government, especially in the British context, see Andrew Gamble, *The Free Economy and the Strong State* (Durham, N.C.: Duke University Press, 1988).

45. For a different point of view, see William R. Catton, Jr., Gerhard Lenski, and Frederick H. Buttel, "To What Degree Is a Social System Dependent on Its Resource Base?" in *The Social Fabric,* ed. James F. Short (Beverly Hills, Calif.: Sage, 1986), 166.

Bibliography

Aaron, Henry J. 1972. *Shelter and Subsidies: Who Benefits from Federal Housing Policies?* Washington, D.C.: Brookings Institution.

Aboulafia, Mitchell. 1986. *The Mediating Self: Mead, Sartre, and Self-Determination.* New Haven, Conn.: Yale University Press.

Abramson, Paul R., and Ada W. Finifter. 1981. "On the Meaning of Political Trust: New Evidence from Items Introduced in 1978." *American Journal of Political Science* 25 (May): 297–307.

Ackerman, Bruce A. 1980. *Social Justice in the Liberal State.* New Haven, Conn.: Yale University Press.

Acock, Alan C., and Forrest A. Deseran. 1986. "Off-Farm Employment by Women and Marital Instability." *Rural Sociology* 51 (Fall): 314–27.

Addelson, Kathryn Pyne. N.d. "Why Philosophers Must Become Sociologists." Photocopy.

———. 1988. "Moral Passages." In *Women and Moral Theory,* edited by Eva Kittay and Diane Meyers, 87–110. Totowa, N.J.: Rowman and Littlefield.

"Adjustable Rate Financing in Mortgage and Consumer Credit Markets." 1985. *Federal Reserve Bulletin* 71:823–35.

Aidala, Angela A., and Cathy Stein Greenblatt. 1986. "Changes in Moral Judgments Among Youth Populations, 1929–83." *Youth and Society* 17 (March): 221–35.

"AIDS i Norden" (AIDS in the Nordic countries). 1987. *Nordisk kontakt* 32 (8): 6–13.

Aiken, William W., and Hugh LaFollette, eds. 1977. *World Hunger and Moral Obligation.* Englewood Cliffs, N.J.: Prentice-Hall.

Alchian, Arman A., and Harold Demsetz. 1972. "Production, Information Costs, and Economic Information." *American Economic Review* 62 (December): 777–95.

Alexander, Jeffrey. 1987. *Twenty Lectures: Sociological Theory Since World War II.* New York: Columbia University Press.

————, ed. 1985. *Neo-Functionalism*. Beverly Hills, Calif.: Sage.

Alexander, Karl L., and Aaron M. Pallas. 1983. "Private Schools and Public Policy." *Sociology of Education* 56 (October): 170–82.

Allardt, Erik. 1975. *Att ha, att älska, att vara* (To have, to love, to be). Lund: Argos.

Almond, Gabriel A., and Sidney Verba. 1963. *The Civic Culture: Political Attitudes and Democracy in Five Nations*. Princeton, N.J.: Princeton University Press.

Almond, Gabriel A., Marvin Chodorow, and Roy Harvey Pearce, eds. 1982. *Progress and Its Discontents*. Berkeley and Los Angeles: University of California Press.

American Association of Fund Raising Councils. 1986. *Giving USA: Estimates of Philanthropic Giving in 1985 and the Trends They Show*. New York: AAFRC.

American Council on Education. 1988. *The American Freshman: National Norms for Fall 1987*. Los Angeles: Higher Education Research Institute.

Andenæs, Agnes, and Hanne Haavind. 1987. *Små barns livsvilkår i Norge* (The living conditions of small children in Norway). Oslo: Norwegian University Press.

Andersen, Bent Rold. 1983. "Creating Coherent Public Policy for the Elderly in a Welfare State." In *Two Essays on the Nordic Welfare State*, 53–76. Copenhagen: Local Government Research Institute on Public Finance and Administration.

————. 1986. "Rationality and Irrationality of the Nordic Welfare State." In *Norden: The Passion for Equality*, edited by Stephen R. Graubard, 112–42. Oslo: Norwegian University Press.

Andersen, Bjarne Hjorth, and Per Schultz Jørgensen. 1987. *Dagpasning for de 6–10 årige* (Day care for six- to ten-year-olds). Copenhagen: Danish Social Research Institute.

Andersen, Jørgen Goul. 1987. "Konservatismen, vælgerne og velfærdsstaten" (Conservatism, voters, and the welfare state). Århus: Institute for Political Science.

————. 1988. "Vælgernes holdninger til den offentlige udgiftspolitik" (The electorate's opinion on public spending). In *Fra vækst til omstilling* (From growth to change), edited by Karl-Henrik Bentzon, 145–90. Copenhagen: News from Political Science.

Andersson, Bengt-Erik. 1986. *Home Care or External Care? A Study of the Effects of Public Child Care on Children's Development When Eight Years Old*. Stockholm: Swedish Institute of Educational Research.

Andrews, Lori B. 1986. "My Body, My Property." *Hastings Center Report* 16 (October): 28–38.

Angrist, Shirley S., Judith R. Lave, and Richard Mickelsen. 1976. "How Working Mothers Manage: Socioeconomic Differences in Work, Childcare, and Household Tasks." *Social Science Quarterly* 56 (March): 631–37.

Anton, Thomas J. 1980. *Administered Politics: Elite Political Culture in Sweden*. The Hague: Martinus Nijhoff.

Aranson, Peter H. 1981. *American Government: Strategy and Choice*. Boston: Little, Brown.

Aranson, Peter H., and Peter C. Ordeshook. 1985. "Public Interest, Private Interest, and the Democratic Polity." In *The Democratic State,* edited by Roger Benjamin and Stephen L. Elkin, 87–177. Lawrence: University Press of Kansas.

Arblaster, Anthony. 1984. *The Rise and Decline of Western Liberalism.* Oxford: Basil Blackwell.

Arkes, Hadley. 1981. *The Philosopher in the City: The Moral Dimensions of Politics.* Princeton, N.J.: Princeton University Press.

Arner, Oddvar, Ragnar Hauge, and Ole-Jørgen Skog. 1985. *Alkohol i Norge* (Alcohol in Norway). Oslo: Norwegian University Press.

Arner, Oddvar, Mona Duckert, and Ragnar Hauge. 1980. *Ungdom og narkotika* (Youth and narcotics). Oslo: Norwegian University Press.

Arnold, L. Eugene, ed. 1985. *Parents, Children, and Change.* Lexington, Mass.: D. C. Heath.

Arrow, Kenneth J. 1963. *Social Choice and Individual Values.* New York: John Wiley.

————. 1975. "Gifts and Exchanges." In *Altruism, Morality, and Economic Theory,* edited by Edmund S. Phelps, 13–28. New York: Russell Sage Foundation.

————. 1982. "Risk Perception in Psychology and Economics." *Economic Inquiry* 20 (January): 1–9.

Axelrod, Robert. 1984. *The Evolution of Cooperation.* New York: Basic Books.

Axelsson, Christina. "Family and Social Integration." In *Welfare in Transition,* edited by Robert Erikson and Rune Åberg, 217–32. Oxford: Clarendon Press.

Baier, Annette. 1981. "The Rights of Past and Future Generations." In *Responsibilities to Future Generations: Environmental Ethics,* edited by Ernest Partridge, 171–83. Buffalo, N.Y.: Prometheus Books.

Baker, Wayne E. 1984. "Floor Trading and Crowd Dynamics." In *The Social Dynamics of Financial Markets,* edited by Patricia A. Adler and Peter Adler, 107–28. Greenwich, Conn.: JAI Press.

————. 1984. "The Social Structure of a National Securities Market." *American Journal of Sociology* 89 (January): 775–811.

Baldassare, Mark. 1986. *Trouble in Paradise: The Suburban Transformation in America.* New York: Columbia University Press.

Banfield, Edward C., and James Q. Wilson. 1963. *City Politics.* Cambridge, Mass.: Harvard University Press.

Barber, Benjamin. 1984. *Strong Democracy: Participatory Politics for a New Age.* Berkeley and Los Angeles: University of California Press.

Barber, Bernard. 1977. "Absolutization of the Market: Some Notes on How We Got from There to Here." In *Markets and Morals,* edited by Gerald Dworkin, Gordon Bermant, and Peter G. Brown, 15–32. New York: John Wiley.

————. 1983. *The Logic and Limits of Trust.* New Brunswick, N.J.: Rutgers University Press.

Barns behov och föräldrars rätt (Children's needs and parents' rights). 1986. Stockholm: Government Official Reports.

Barry, Brian. 1978. *Sociologists, Economists, and Democracy.* Chicago: University of Chicago Press.

Baskir, Lawrence M., and William A. Strauss. 1978. *Chance and Circumstance: The Draft, the War, and the Vietnam Generation.* New York: Alfred Knopf.

Bator, Francis M. 1958. "The Anatomy of Market Failure." *Quarterly Journal of Economics* 72 (August): 351–79.

Baumol, William J. 1965. *Welfare Economics and the Theory of the State.* 2d rev. ed. Cambridge, Mass.: Harvard University Press.

Bayer, Ronald. 1989. *Private Acts, Social Consequences: AIDS and the Politics of Public Health.* New York: Free Press.

Becker, Gary S. 1965. "A Theory of the Allocation of Time." *Economic Journal* 75 (September): 493–517.

———. 1976. "Altruism, Egoism, and Genetic Fitness." *Journal of Economic Literature* 14 (September): 817–26.

———. 1976. *The Economic Approach to Human Behavior.* Chicago: University of Chicago Press.

———. 1981. *A Treatise on the Family.* Cambridge, Mass.: Harvard University Press.

Becker, Howard S. 1986. *Doing Things Together: Selected Papers.* Evanston, Ill.: Northwestern University Press.

Behrendt, Mogens. 1983. *Tilfældet Sverige* (The Swedish case). Copenhagen: Erichsen.

Bellah, Robert, Richard Madsen, William M. Sullivan, Ann Swidler, and Steven M. Tipton. 1985. *Habits of the Heart: Individualism and Commitment in American Life.* Berkeley and Los Angeles: University of California Press.

Bender, Thomas. 1982. *Community and Social Change in America.* Baltimore: Johns Hopkins University Press.

Bengston, Vernon L., and J. A. Kuypers. 1983. "Psycho-Social Issues in the Aging Family." Paper presented at the 12th International Congress of Gerontology, Hamburg, 1981.

Benhabib, Seyla. 1988. "The Generalized and Concrete Other." In *Women and Moral Theory,* edited by Eva Kittay and Diane Meyers, 154–77. Totowa, N.J.: Rowman and Littlefield.

Ben-Yehuda, Nacham. 1985. *Deviance and Moral Boundaries: Witchcraft, the Occult, Science Fiction, Deviant Sciences, and Scientists.* Chicago: University of Chicago Press.

Berger, Brigitte, and Peter L. Berger. 1983. *The War over the Family: Capturing the Middle Ground.* Garden City, N.Y.: Doubleday.

Berger, Peter L. 1986. *The Capitalist Revolution: Fifty Propositions About Prosperity, Equality, and Liberty.* New York: Basic Books.

Berger, Peter L., and Richard John Neuhaus. 1977. *To Empower People: The Role of Mediating Structures in Public Policy.* Washington, D.C.: American Enterprise Institute.

Berger, Renee A. 1985. "Private-Sector Initiatives in the Reagan Era: New Actors Rework an Old Theme." In *The Reagan Presidency and the Governing of Amer-*

ica, edited by Lester M. Salamon and Michael S. Lund, 181–211. Washington, D.C.: Urban Institute.

Bernheim, B. D., A. Shleifer, and L. H. Summers. 1985. "The Strategic Bequest Motive." *Journal of Political Economy* 93 (December): 1045–76.

Bernstein, Merton C., and Joan Brodshaug Bernstein. 1988. *Social Security: The System That Works.* New York: Basic Books.

Bertelsen, Ole, and Peter Linde. 1985. *Efterspørgsel efter offentlig dagpasning* (Demand for public day care). Copenhagen: Danish Social Research Institute.

Binkin, Martin, Mark J. Eitelberg, Alvin J. Schneider, and Marvin M. Smith. 1982. *Blacks and the Military.* Washington, D.C.: Brookings Institution.

Bjørnø, Lis, Vagn Dalgård, and Bente Madsen. 1982. *Børnekommissionens betænkning: Den nye børnekarakter og skolepsykologi* (The report of the Commission on Children: The new children's character and school psychology). School Psychology Monograph Series, no. 21. Copenhagen.

Bjørnsen, Bjørn, et al. 1985. *Alkohol og vold* (Alcohol and violence). Oslo: Norwegian University Press.

Bjurstrøm, Erling. 1982. *Generasjonsopprøret* (The revolt of the generations). Oslo: Norwegian University Press.

Blau, Peter M. 1964. *Exchange and Power in Social Life.* New York: John Wiley.

Bloom, Allan. 1987. *The Closing of the American Mind: How Higher Education Has Failed Democracy and Impoverished the Souls of Today's Students.* New York: Simon and Schuster.

Bluestone, Barry, and Bennett Harrison. 1982. *The Deindustrialization of America: Plant Closings, Community Abandonment, and the Dismantling of Basic Industry.* New York: Basic Books.

Blum, Jacques. 1985. *De grimme ællinger* (The ugly ducklings). Copenhagen: Aschehoug.

Blum, Jacques, and Michael Porsager. 1987. *Det andet Danmark* (The other Denmark). Copenhagen: Politiken.

Blumberg, Paul. 1980. *Inequality in an Age of Decline.* New York: Oxford University Press.

Blumstein, Philip, and Pepper Schwartz. 1983. *American Couples: Money, Work, Sex.* New York: William Morrow.

Bonke, Jens. 1986. *Formelt og informelt byggeri* (Formal and informal construction). Copenhagen: Government Institute for Construction Research.

Boolsen, Merete Watt. 1988. *Frivillige i socialt arbejde* (Volunteers in social work). Copenhagen: Danish Social Research Institute.

Boolsen, Merete Watt, Jill Mehlbye, and Lisbeth Sparre. 1986. *Børns opvækst uden for hjemmet* (Childrearing outside the home). Copenhagen: Local Government Research Institute on Public Finance and Administration.

Borchorst, Anette, and Birte Siim. 1984. *Kvinder i velfærdstaten* (Women in the welfare state). Ålborg: Ålborg University Press.

Bowles, Samuel, and Herbert Gintis. 1986. *Democracy and Capitalism: Property, Community and the Contractions of Modern Social Thought*. New York: Basic Books.

Brennan, Geoffrey H., and James M. Buchanan. 1981. *Monopoly in Money and Inflation*. London: Institute of Economic Affairs.

———. 1985. *The Reason of Rules: Constitutional Political Economy*. Cambridge: Cambridge University Press.

Brenner, Reuven. 1980. "Economics: An Imperialist Science?" *Journal of Legal Studies* 9 (June): 179–88.

Breton, Albert, and Ronald Wintrobe. 1986. "The Bureaucracy of Murder Revisited." *Journal of Political Economy* 94 (October): 905–26.

Brittain, John A. 1978. *Inheritance and the Inequality of Material Wealth*. Washington, D.C.: Brookings Institution.

Brivkalne, Mirdza. 1987. "Fritid" (Leisure). In *Perspektiv på välfärden 1987* (Perspective on welfare 1987), 249–69. Stockholm: Central Statistical Bureau.

Brody, Baruch. 1975. *Abortion and the Sanctity of Human Life*. Cambridge, Mass.: MIT Press.

Brun-Gulbrandsen, Sverre. 1985. "Våre forfedres alkoholbruk" (Our ancestors' use of alcohol). In *Alkohol i Norge* (Alcohol in Norway), edited by Oddvar Arner, Ragnar Hauge, and Ole-Jørgen Skog, 25–45. Oslo: Norwegian University Press.

Buchanan, Allen. 1985. *Ethics, Efficiency, and the Market*. Oxford: Clarendon Press.

Buchanan, James M., and Gordon Tullock. 1971. *The Calculus of Consent: Logical Foundations of Constitutional Democracy*. Ann Arbor: University of Michigan Press.

Buchanan, James M., and Richard E. Wagner. 1977. *Democracy in Deficit: The Political Legacy of Lord Keynes*. New York: Academic Press.

Bulmer, Martin. 1987. *The Social Basis of Community Care*. London: Allen and Unwin.

Burke, John P. 1986. *Bureaucratic Responsibility*. Baltimore: Johns Hopkins University Press.

Burns, Tom R., and Helena Flam. 1987. *The Shaping of Social Organization: Social Rule System Theory with Applications*. Beverly Hills, Calif.: Sage.

Burt, Ronald S. 1983. "Corporate Philanthropy as a Cooptive Relationship." *Social Forces* 62 (December): 419–49.

Butler, Stuart M. 1985. *Privatizing Public Spending: A Strategy to Eliminate the Deficit*. New York: Universe Books.

Buxton, William. 1985. *Talcott Parsons and the Capitalist Nation-State*. Toronto: University of Toronto Press.

Bøgh, Charlotte, and Per Schultz Jørgensen, eds. 1985. *Småbørn, familie, samfund* (Small children, family, society). Copenhagen: Hans Reitzels.

Børnekommissionens betænkning (Report of the Commission on Children). 1981. Copenhagen: Commission on Children.

Callahan, Daniel. 1987. *Setting Limits: Medical Goals in an Aging Society.* New York: Simon and Schuster.

Camic, Charles. 1979. "The Utilitarians Revisited." *American Journal of Sociology* 85 (November): 516–50.

Campbell, Angus, Philip E. Converse, Warren E. Miller, and Donald E. Stokes. 1960. *The American Voter.* New York: John Wiley.

Carr, J. L., and J. T. Landu. 1983. "The Economics of Symbols, Clan Names, and Religion." *Journal of Legal Studies* 12 (January): 135–56.

Catton, William R., Jr. 1986. "To What Extent Is a Social System Dependent on Its Resource Base?" In *The Social Fabric,* edited by James F. Short, 165–86. Beverly Hills, Calif.: Sage.

Cherlin, Andrew J. 1981. *Marriage, Divorce, Remarriage.* Cambridge, Mass.: Harvard University Press.

Cherlin, Andrew J., and Frank R. Furstenberg, Jr. 1986. *The New American Grandparent: A Place in the Family, a Life Apart.* New York: Basic Books.

Christiansen, Ann-Dorte, Erik Christiansen, Karin Hansen, Morten Lassen, and Børge Rasmussen. 1986. *Velfærdsstaten i krise,* vol. 2. (The welfare state in crisis). Ålborg: Center for Welfare State Studies.

Christie, Vigdis. 1982. "Nærmiljøet" (The local community). In *Det moderne Norge* (Modern Norway). Vol. 2: *Samliv og nærmiljø* (Social life and the local community), edited by Kari Wærness and Vigdis Christie, 187–317. Oslo: Gyldendal.

Christoffersen, Mogens Nygaard. 1987. *Familien under forandring* (The family in transition). Copenhagen: Danish Social Research Institute.

Christoffersen, Mogens Nygaard, Ole Bertelsen, and Poul Vestergaard. 1987. *Hvem passer vore børn?* (Who's watching our children?). Copenhagen: Danish Social Research Institute.

Chubb, John E., and Paul E. Peterson, eds. 1985. *The New Direction in American Politics.* Washington, D.C.: Brookings Institution.

Clark, Gordon L. 1985. *Judges and the Cities: Interpreting Local Autonomy.* Chicago: University of Chicago Press.

Clarke, Peter F. 1978. *Liberals and Social Democrats.* Cambridge: Cambridge University Press.

Clifford, James, and George Marcus. 1986. *Writing Culture: The Poetics and Politics of Ethnography.* Berkeley and Los Angeles: University of California Press.

Clotfelter, Charles T. 1985. *Federal Tax Policy and Charitable Giving.* Chicago: University of Chicago Press.

Coase, Ronald H. 1937. "The Nature of the Firm." *Economia* 4 (November): 386–405.

Cohler, Bertram J., and Henry V. Grunebaum. 1981. *Mothers, Grandmothers, Daughters.* New York: John Wiley.

Coleman, James S., and Thomas Hoffer. 1987. *Public and Private High Schools: The Impact of Communities.* New York: Basic Books.

Coleman, James S., Thomas Hoffer, and Sally Kilgore. 1982. *High School Achievement: Public, Private, and Catholic High Schools Compared.* New York: Basic Books.

Collard, David. 1978. *Altruism and Economy: A Study in Non-selfish Economics.* Oxford: Martin Robertson.

Collini, Stefan. 1979. *Liberalism and Sociology: L. T. Hobhouse and Political Argument in England, 1880–1914.* Cambridge: Cambridge University Press.

Collins, Randall. 1986. *Weberian Sociological Theory.* Cambridge: Cambridge University Press.

Commission on Private Philanthropy and Public Need. 1975. *Giving in America: Toward a Stronger Voluntary Sector.* Washington, D.C.: Filer Commission.

Conference Board. 1980–85. *Annual Survey of Corporate Contributions.* New York: Conference Board.

Cookson, Peter W., Jr., and Caroline Hodges Persell. 1985. *Preparing for Power: America's Elite Boarding Schools.* New York: Basic Books.

Cooper, Bruce S. 1985. "The Changing Universe of U.S. Private Schools." Institute for Research on Educational Finance and Governance, Stanford University. Mimeo.

Crafton, Stephen M. 1980. "An Empirical Test of the Effect of Usury Laws." *Journal of Law and Economics* 23 (April): 135–45.

Cramer, James C. 1980. "Fertility and Female Employment: Problems of Causal Direction." *American Sociological Review* 45 (April): 167–90.

Crotty, William J., and Gary C. Jacobson. 1980. *American Parties in Decline.* Boston: Little, Brown.

Crozier, Michel. 1984. *The Trouble with America: Why the System Is Breaking Down.* Berkeley and Los Angeles: University of California Press.

Daatland, Svein Olav. 1983. "Eldreomsorg i en småby" (Care of the elderly in a small town). *Tidsskrift for samfunnsforskning* 24 (2): 155–73.

———. 1983. "Care Systems." *Aging and Society* 3 (March): 1–21.

———, ed. 1987. *Gammel i eget hjem* (The elderly in their own homes). Copenhagen: Nordic Council.

Daatland, Svein Olav, and Gerdt Sundström. 1985. *Gammal i Norden* (The elderly in the Nordic countries). Stockholm: Initiatives for Service and Housing Sectors for the Elderly Project.

Daniels, Arlene Kaplan. 1988. *Invisible Careers: Women Civic Leaders from the Volunteer World.* Chicago: University of Chicago Press.

Daniels, Norman. 1988. *Am I My Parents' Keeper? An Essay on Justice Between the Young and the Old.* New York: Oxford University Press.

Danmarks Frivillige Bloddonorer (Denmark's voluntary blood donors). 1982. *Festskrift 1932–1982.*

———. 1986. *Årsberetning 1986* (Annual Report 1986).

Danmarks statistisk årbog (Yearbook of Danish statistics). Various years.

Dansk alkohol-statistisk (Danish alcohol statistics). 1986. 5th ed. Copenhagen: Danish Temperance Organization.

Dansk Folkekirkens Nødhjælp (Emergency Relief Fund of the Danish State Church). 1980–86. *Årsberetninger* (Annual reports).

Dansk Mødrehjælpen af 1983 (Danish Mothers' Help of 1983). 1986. *Årsberetning* (Annual report).

Dansk Red Barnet (Danish Save the Children). 1980–86. *Årsberetninger* (Annual reports).

Dansk Røde Kors (Danish Red Cross). 1980–86. *Årsberetninger* (Annual reports).

Dencik, Lars. 1987. "Opvækst i postmodernismen" (Growing up postmodern). In *Børn i nye familie mønstre* (Children in new family patterns), edited by Per Schultz Jørgensen, 12–45. Copenhagen: Hans Reitzels.

Dennis, Marshall. 1985. *Residential Mortgage Lending*. Reston, Va.: Reston Publishing.

Derthick, Martha, and Paul J. Quirk. 1985. *The Politics of Deregulation*. Washington, D.C.: Brookings Institution.

Deutsch, Morton. 1985. *Distributive Justice: A Social-psychological Perspective*. New Haven, Conn.: Yale University Press.

DiMaggio, Paul J., ed. 1986. *Non-Profit Enterprise in the Arts: Studies in Mission and Constraint*. New York: Oxford University Press.

Doob, Leonard W. 1987. *Slightly Beyond Skepticism: Social Science and the Search for Morality*. New Haven, Conn.: Yale University Press.

Doty, Pamela. 1986. "Family Care of the Elderly: The Role of Public Policy." *Milbank Quarterly* 64 (1): 34–75.

Douglas, Mary. 1986. *How Institutions Think*. Syracuse, N.Y.: Syracuse University Press.

Douglas, Mary, and Baron Isherwood. 1980. *The World of Goods: Towards an Anthropology of Consumption*. London: Penguin Books.

Dowty, Alan. 1987. *Closed Borders*. New Haven, Conn.: Yale University Press.

Duncan, James S., ed. 1982. *Housing and Identity: Cross-cultural Perspectives*. New York: Holmes and Meier.

Dunn, John. 1969. *The Political Thought of John Locke: An Historical Account of the Argument of "The Two Treatises of Government."* Cambridge: Cambridge University Press.

———. 1979. *Western Political Theory in the Face of the Future*. Cambridge: Cambridge University Press.

Durkheim, Emile. 1964. *The Division of Labor in Society*. New York: Free Press.

———. 1964. "Pragmatism and Sociology." In *Essays on Sociology and Philosophy*, edited by Kurt H. Wolff, 386–436. New York: Harper and Row.

———. 1965. *The Elementary Forms of Religious Life*. New York: Free Press.

———. 1966. *Suicide*. New York: Free Press.

———. 1973. "The Dualism of Human Nature and Its Social Conditions." In *Emile*

Durkheim on Morality and Society, edited by Robert Bellah, 149–63. Chicago: University of Chicago Press.

———. 1973. *Moral Education.* New York: Free Press.

Dworkin, Ronald. 1978. "Liberalism." In *Public and Private Morality,* edited by Stuart Hampshire, 113–43. Cambridge: Cambridge University Press.

———. 1983. "Neutrality, Equality and Liberty." In *Liberalism Reconsidered,* edited by Douglas MacLean and Claudia Mills, 1–11. Totowa, N.J.: Rowman and Allenheld.

———. 1986. *Law's Empire.* Cambridge, Mass.: Harvard University Press.

Dyson, Kenneth H. F. 1980. *The State Tradition in Western Europe.* New York: Oxford University Press.

Easterbrook, Frank H. 1983. "Criminal Procedure and the Market System." *Journal of Legal Studies* 12 (June): 289–332.

Edel, Matthew, Elliott D. Sclar, and Daniel Luria. 1984. *Shaky Palaces: Homeownership and Social Mobility in Boston's Suburbanization.* New York: Columbia University Press.

Edelman, Marian Wright. 1987. *Families in Peril: An Agenda for Social Change.* Cambridge, Mass.: Harvard University Press.

Edenhammer, Karin. 1982. *Åldersblandade barngrupper* (Children groups of mixed age). Stockholm: LiberFörlag.

Edwards, Patricia Klobus, and Ann DeWitt Watts. 1983. "Volunteerism in Human Service Organizations: Trends and Prospects." *Journal of Applied Social Sciences* 7 (Spring–Summer): 225–45.

Edwards, Patricia Klobus, John N. Edwards, and Ann DeWitt Watts. 1984. "Women, Work, and Social Participation." *Journal of Voluntary Action Research* 13 (January–March): 7–22.

Egelund, Niels. 1988. *Privatskole kontra folkeskole* (Private schools versus public schools). Hørsholm, Den.: Educational Psychology Publishers.

Ehrenreich, Barbara, and Frances Fox Piven. 1984. "The Feminization of Poverty: When the Family Wage Breaks Down." *Dissent* 31 (Spring): 162–70.

Eisenstadt, S. N., and L. Roniger. 1984. *Patrons, Clients, and Friends: Interpersonal Relations and the Structure of Trust in Society.* Cambridge: Cambridge University Press.

Ekeh, Peter. 1974. *Social Exchange Theory: The Two Traditions.* London: Heinemann.

Elder, Glen H., Jr. 1974. *Children of the Great Depression: Social Change in the Life Experience.* Chicago: University of Chicago Press.

———. 1981. "Social History and the Life Experience." In *Present and Past in Middle Life,* edited by Dorothy H. Eichorn, John A. Clausen, Norma Haan, Marjorie P. Honzik, and Paul H. Mussen, 3–31. New York: Academic Press.

Elder, Glen H., Jr., and Russell C. Rockwell. 1979. "Economic Depression and Postwar Opportunity in Men's Lives." In *Research on Community Mental Health,* edited by R. A. Simmons, 249–304. Greenwich, Conn.: JAI Press.

Eliasson, Gunnar. 1985. "Is the Swedish Welfare State in Trouble?" Industrial Institute for Economic and Social Research, Working Paper no. 151. Stockholm.

Elmér, Åke. 1981. *Svensk socialpolitik* (Swedish social policy). Lund: Liber-Läromedel.

Elshtain, Jean Bethke. 1984. "Reflections on Abortion, Values, and the Family." In *Abortion: Understanding Differences,* edited by Sidney Callahan and Daniel Callahan, 47–72. New York: Plenum.

Elster, Jon. 1979. *Ulysses and the Sirens: Studies in Rationality and Irrationality.* Cambridge: Cambridge University Press.

———. 1985. *Making Sense of Marx.* Cambridge: Cambridge University Press.

———, ed. 1986. *The Multiple Self.* Cambridge: Cambridge University Press.

Engelhardt, Tom. 1986. "Children's Television: The Shortcake Strategy." In *Watching Television: A Pantheon Guide to Popular Culture,* edited by Todd Gitlin, 68–110. New York: Pantheon Books.

England, J. Lynn, and Stan L. Albrecht. 1984. "Boomtowns and Social Disruption." *Rural Sociology* 49 (Summer): 230–46.

Enzensberger, Hans Magnus. 1982. *Svensk höst* (Swedish autumn). Stockholm: Dagens Nyheter.

———. 1984. *Norsk utakt* (Norway out of tune). Oslo: Norwegian University Press.

Epstein, Richard A. 1983. "Blackmail, Inc." *University of Chicago Law Review* 50 (Spring): 553–66.

Ericson, Kjersti, Geir Lundby, and Monika Rudberg. 1985. *Mors nest beste barn* (Mother's second-best child). Oslo: Norwegian University Press.

Erikson, Kai. 1976. *Everything in Its Path: Destruction of Community in the Buffalo Creek Flood.* New York: Simon and Schuster.

Esping-Andersen, Gösta. 1985. *Politics Against Markets: The Social Democratic Road to Power.* Princeton, N.J.: Princeton University Press.

Esping-Andersen, Gösta, and Walter Korpi. 1986. "From Poor Relief to Institutional Welfare States." In *The Scandinavian Model: Welfare States and Welfare Research,* edited by Robert Erikson, Erik Jørgen Hansen, Stein Ringen, and Hannu Uusitalo, 39–74. Armonk, N.Y.: M.E. Sharpe.

Estes, Richard J. 1984. *The Social Progress of Nations.* New York: Praeger.

Etzioni, Amitai. 1988. *The Moral Dimension: Toward a New Economics.* New York: Free Press.

Evanshaug, Oddbjørn, and Dag Hallen. 1985. "Pedagogisk ansvars-fordeling: Mor-far-barnehagen" (Division of educational responsibility: Mother–father–daycare center). *Nordisk Pedagogisk Tidsskrift* 69 (2): 84–91.

Eve, Raymond A., and Francis B. Harrold. 1986. "Creationism, Cult Archeology, and Other Pseudoscientific Beliefs." *Youth and Society* 17 (June): 396–421.

Falsey, Barbara, and Barbara Heyns. 1984. "The College Channel." *Sociology of Education* 57 (April): 111–22.

Federal Reserve Bank of New York. 1986. *Quarterly Review.*

Feige, Edgar L. 1986. "Sweden's Underground Economy." Industrial Institute for Economic and Social Research, Working Paper no. 161. Stockholm.

Fenton, Steve. 1985. *Durkheim and Modern Social Theory.* Cambridge: Cambridge University Press.

Ferguson, Adam. 1819. *An Essay on the History of Civil Society.* Philadelphia: William Fry.

Finnemann, Niels Ole. 1985. *I broderskabets aand* (In the spirit of brotherhood). Copenhagen: Gyldendal.

Fischer, Claude. 1982. *To Dwell Among Friends: Personal Networks in Town and City.* Chicago: University of Chicago Press.

Fishkin, James S. 1984. *Beyond Subjective Morality: Ethical Reasoning and Political Philosophy.* New Haven, Conn.: Yale University Press.

Flising, Björn, and Inge Johansson. 1987. *Fritidshem i Norden* (After-school centers in the Nordic countries). Stockholm: Nordic Council.

Flora, Peter, ed. 1988. *Growth to Limits.* Vol. 1: *Sweden, Norway, Finland, Denmark.* New York: Walter de Gruyter.

Forstenzer, T. R. 1980. "Tomorrow in North America: Youth Between the American Dream and Reality." In *Youth in the 1980s,* 65–86. New York: UNESCO Press.

Forster, E. M. 1951. *Two Cheers for Democracy.* New York: Harcourt, Brace.

———. 1971. *Howard's End.* London: Penguin Books.

Foucault, Michel. 1979. *Discipline and Punish: The Birth of the Prison.* Translated by Alan Sheridan. New York: Vintage Books.

Fox, Stephen. 1984. *The Mirror Makers: A History of Advertising and Its Creators.* New York: William Morrow.

Frank, Robert. 1985. *Choosing the Right Pond: Human Behavior and the Quest for Status.* New York: Oxford University Press.

Frankfurt, Harry. 1988. *The Importance of What We Care About: Philosophical Essays.* Cambridge: Cambridge University Press.

Franzén, Mats, and Eva Sandstedt. 1981. *Grannskap och stadsplanering* (Neighborhood and town planning). Uppsala: Institute for Sociology.

Freddie Mac Reports. 1984–88.

Freeden, Michael. 1978. *The New Liberalism: An Ideology of Social Reform.* Oxford: Oxford University Press.

Freudenberg, William R. 1984. "Boomtown's Youth: The Differential Impacts of Rapid Community Growth on Adolescents and Adults." *American Journal of Sociology* 49 (October): 697–705.

Frey, B. S., and Hannelore Weck. 1983. "Estimating the Shadow Economy." *Oxford Economic Papers* 35 (March): 23–44.

Friedman, Milton. 1953. "The Methodology of Positive Economics." In *Essays in Positive Economics,* 3–46. Chicago: University of Chicago Press.

———. 1962. *Capitalism and Freedom.* Chicago: University of Chicago Press.

————. 1967. "Why Not a Volunteer Army?" In *The Draft,* edited by Sol Tax, 200–207. Chicago: University of Chicago Press.

Friedman, Robert R., Neil Gilbert, and Moshe Sherer, eds. 1987. *Modern Welfare States: A Comparative View of Trends and Prospects.* Brighton, Eng.: Wheatsheaf Books.

Frisby, David, and Derek Sayer. 1986. *Society.* London: Tavistock.

Frønes, Ivar. 1985. *Generasjoner, solidaritet, og fordeling* (Generations, solidarity, and distribution). Oslo: Institute for Applied Social Research.

————. 1986. "Generasjoner og livsløp" (Generations and the life course). In *Det norske samfunn* (Norwegian society), edited by Lars Alldén, Natalie Rogoff Ramsøy, and Mariken Vaa, 169–96. Oslo: Gyldendal.

————. 1987. *Jevnaldermiljø, sosialisering, og lokalsamfunn* (Peer group environment, socialization, and local community). Oslo: Institute for Social Research.

Fuller, Lon L. 1964. *The Morality of Law.* Rev. ed. New Haven, Conn.: Yale University Press.

————. 1981. "Two Principles of Human Association." In *Two Principles of Social Order: Selected Essays of Lon L. Fuller,* edited by Kenneth I. Winston, 67–85. Durham, N.C.: Duke University Press.

Furstenberg, Frank F., Christine W. Nord, James L. Peterson, and Nicholas Zill. 1983. "The Life Course of Children of Divorce." *American Sociological Review* 48 (October): 656–68.

Galaskiewicz, Joseph. 1985. *The Social Organization of an Urban Grants Economy.* New York: Academic Press.

Gamwell, Franklin I. 1984. *Beyond Preference: Liberal Theories of Independent Associations.* Chicago: University of Chicago Press.

Gamble, Andrew. 1988. *The Free Economy and the Strong State.* Durham, N.C.: Duke University Press.

Gans, Herbert J. 1962. *The Urban Villagers: Group and Class in the Life of Italian-Americans.* New York: Free Press.

————. 1967. *The Levittowners: Ways of Life and Politics in a New Suburban Community.* New York: Vintage Books.

Gardner, John. 1978. *On Moral Fiction.* New York: Basic Books.

Garfinkel, Harold. 1967. *Studies in Ethnomethodology.* Englewood Cliffs, N.J.: Prentice-Hall.

Gauthier, David P. 1986. *Morals by Agreement.* Oxford: Clarendon Press.

Geertz, Clifford. 1973. *The Interpretation of Cultures: Selected Essays.* New York: Basic Books.

————. 1983. *Local Knowledge: Further Essays in Interpretive Anthropology.* New York: Basic Books.

Gerson, Kathleen. 1985. *Hard Choices: How Women Decide About Work, Career, and Motherhood.* Berkeley and Los Angeles: University of California Press.

Gewirth, Allan. 1978. *Reason and Morality.* Chicago: University of Chicago Press.

Giddens, Anthony. 1984. *The Constitution of Society: Outline of the Theory of Structuration.* Berkeley and Los Angeles: University of California Press.

Gilbert, Neil. 1983. *Capitalism and the Welfare State: Dilemmas of Social Benevolence.* New Haven, Conn.: Yale University Press.

Gilligan, Carol. 1982. *In a Different Voice: Psychological Theory and Women's Development.* Cambridge, Mass.: Harvard University Press.

Ginsberg, Benjamin. 1986. *The Captive Public: How Mass Opinion Promotes State Power.* New York: Basic Books.

Glenn, Norval D. 1987. "Social Trends in the United States: Evidence from Sample Surveys." *Public Opinion Quarterly* 51 (Winter): S109–S126.

Glenn, Norval D., and Charles W. Weaver. 1988. "The Changing Relationship of Marital Status to Reported Happiness." *Journal of Marriage and the Family* 50 (May): 317–24.

Goffman, Erving. 1968. *Asylums: Essays on the Social Situation of Mental Patients and Other Inmates.* London: Penguin Books.

Goode, William J. 1974. "Comment." In *Economics of the Family,* edited by Theodore W. Schultze, 345–51. Chicago: University of Chicago Press.

———. 1986. "Individual Choice and the Social Order." In *The Social Fabric: Dimensions and Issues,* edited by James F. Short, 39–62. Beverly Hills, Calif.: Sage.

Goodin, Robert E. 1985. *Protecting the Vulnerable: A Reanalysis of Our Social Responsibilities.* Chicago: University of Chicago Press.

Goodin, Robert E., and Julian LeGrand. 1987. *Not Only the Poor: The Middle Class and the Welfare State.* London: Allen and Unwin.

Goudsblom, Johan. 1986. "Public Health and the Civilizing Process." *Milibank Quarterly* 64 (2): 161–88.

Gough, Ritva. 1987. *Hemhjälp til gamla* (Home care for the elderly). Stockholm: Center for Working Life.

Gouldner, Alvin W. 1960. "The Norm of Reciprocity." *American Sociological Review* 25 (April): 161–78.

———. 1970. *The Coming Crisis of Western Sociology.* New York: Basic Books.

Granovetter, Mark S. 1973. "The Strength of Weak Ties." *American Journal of Sociology* 78 (May): 1360–80.

Graubard, Stephen R., ed. 1986. *Norden: The Passion for Equality.* Oslo: Norwegian University Press.

Green, Gary P. 1984. "Credit and Agriculture: Some Consequences of the Centralization of the Banking System." *Rural Sociology* 49 (Winter): 568–79.

Green, Jerry R., and Nancy L. Stokey. 1983. "A Comparison of Tournaments and Contracts." *Journal of Political Economy* 91 (June): 349–64.

Greenberger, Ellen, and Laurence Steinberg. 1986. *When Teenagers Work: The Psychological and Social Costs of Adolescent Employment.* New York: Basic Books.

Greenstein, Fred J. 1964. "The Changing Pattern of Urban Politics." *Annals of the American Academy of Political and Social Science* 353 (May): 1–13.

Gress, David. 1982. "Daily Life in the Danish Welfare State." *The Public Interest* 69 (Fall): 33–44.

Greve, Vagn, and Annika Snare. 1987. *AIDS: Nogle retspolitiske spørgsmål* (AIDS: Some civil liberties issues). Copenhagen: Institute of Criminology.

Grinde, Turid Vogt. 1985. *Barnevern i Norden* (Child welfare authorities in the Nordic countries). Stockholm: Nordic Council.

Grossman, Sanford J., and Joseph E. Stiglitz. 1980. "On the Impossibility of Informationally Efficient Markets." *American Economic Review* 70 (June): 393–408.

Grubb, W. Norton, and Marvin Lazerson. 1982. *Broken Promises: How Americans Fail Their Children*. New York: Basic Books.

Grue, Lars. 1987. *Barns levekår: En faktasamling* (The life conditions of children: A fact sheet). Oslo: Institute for Applied Social Research.

Grundtvig, N.F.S. 1984. *A Grundtvig Anthology*, edited by Niels Lynhe Jensen. Cambridge: James Clarke.

Guldbrandsen, Lars, and Catherine Ulstrup Tønnessen. 1987. *Barnetilsyn og yrkesdeltakelse blant småbarnsmødre* (Child supervision and work frequency of mothers with small children). Oslo: Institute for Social Research.

Gussler, Judith, and L. Eugene Arnold. 1985. "Feeding Patterns and the Changing Family." In *Parents, Children, and Change*, edited by L. Eugene Arnold, 115–32. Lexington, Mass.: D.C. Heath.

Gutmann, Amy. 1982. "What's the Use of Going to School?" In *Utilitarianism and Beyond*, edited by Amartya Sen and Bernard Williams, 261–77. Cambridge: Cambridge University Press.

———. 1987. *Democratic Education*. Princeton, N.J.: Princeton University Press.

Gutmann, David L. 1987. *Reclaimed Powers: Towards a New Psychology of Men and Women in Later Life*. New York: Basic Books.

Haan, Norma, Elaine Aerts, and Bruce A. B. Cooper, eds. 1985. *On Moral Grounds: The Search for Practical Morality*. New York: New York University Press.

Haan, Norma, Robert Bellah, Paul Rabinow, and William M. Sullivan, eds. 1983. *Social Science as Moral Inquiry*. New York: Columbia University Press.

Habermann, Ulla. 1987. *Den tredje netværk* (The third network). Copenhagen: Akademisk Forlag.

Habermann, Ulla, and Ingrid Parsby. 1983. *Myter og realiteter i det frivillige sociale arbejde* (Myths and realities in voluntary social work). Copenhagen: Danish Social Ministry.

Habermas, Jürgen. 1984. *The Theory of Communicative Action*. Vol. 1: *Reason and the Rationality of Society*. Translated by Thomas McCarthy. Boston: Beacon Press.

———. 1986. "Law as Medium and Law as Institution." In *Dilemmas of Law in the Welfare State*, edited by Gunther Teubner, 203–20. Berlin: de Gruyter.

Hadenius, Axel. 1986. *A Crisis of the Welfare State?* Stockholm: Almqvist and Wiksell.

Hagestad, Gunhild O. 1981. "Problems and Promises in the Social Psychology of

Intergenerational Relations." In *Aging*, edited by Robert Fogel, Elaine Hatfield, Sara B. Kiesler, and Ethel Shanas, 11–46. New York: Academic Press.

Hagtvet, Bernt, and Erik Rudeng. 1986. "Scandinavia: Achievements, Dilemmas, Challenges." In *Norden: The Passion for Equality*, edited by Stephen R. Graubard, 288–308. Oslo: Norwegian University Press.

Halle, David. 1984. *America's Working Man: Work, Home, and Politics Among Blue-Collar Property Owners*. Chicago: University of Chicago Press.

Hammarström, Gunhild. 1986. *Solidaritetsmönster mellan generationer* (Solidarity patterns between generations). Uppsala: The Elderly in Society Before, Now, and in the Future Project, 1986.

Hammermesh, Daniel S., and Neal. M. Soss. 1974. "An Economic Theory of Suicide." *Journal of Political Economy* 82 (January–February): 83–98.

Hampel, Robert. 1986. *The Last Little Citadel: American High Schools Since 1940*. Boston: Houghton Mifflin.

Hanke, Stephen H., ed. 1987. *Prospects for Privatization*. New York: Academy of Political Science.

Hannan, Michael T., Nancy Brandon Tuma, and Lyle Groeneveld. 1977. "Income and Marital Events: Evidence from an Income Maintenance Experiment." *American Journal of Sociology* 82 (May): 1186–1211.

Hannan, Timothy H. 1982. "Bank Robberies and Bank Security Precautions." *Journal of Legal Studies* 11 (January): 83–92.

Hansen, Erik Jørgen. 1982. *Hvem bryder den sociale arv?* (Who breaks the social inheritance?). 2 vols. Copenhagen: Danish Social Research Institute.

———. 1986. *Danskernes levevilkår* (The living conditions of Danes). Copenhagen: Hans Reitzels.

———. 1988. *Generationer og livsforløb i Danmark* (Generations and the lifecourse in Denmark). Copenhagen: Hans Reitzels.

Hansen, Janet S. 1986. "Student Loans: Are They Overburdening a Generation?" Washington, D.C.: U.S. Congress, Joint Economic Committee. Photocopy.

Hanson, Russell L. 1985. *The Democratic Imagination in America: Conversations with Our Past*. Princeton, N.J.: Princeton University Press.

Hare, R. M. 1981. *Moral Thinking: Its Levels, Methods, and Point*. Oxford: Clarendon Press.

Hargrove, Barbara, Jean Miller Schmidt, and Sheila Greeve Davaney. 1985. "Religion and the Changing Role of Women." *Annals of the American Academy of Political and Social Science* 480 (July): 117–31.

Harré, Rom, and Paul Secord. 1972. *The Explanation of Social Behavior*. Totowa, N.J.: Littlefield, Adams.

Harsanyi, John C. 1982. "Morality and the Theory of Rational Behavior." In *Utilitarianism and Beyond*, edited by Amartya Sen and Bernard Williams, 39–62. Cambridge: Cambridge University Press.

Harvey, David. 1975. "The Political Economy of Urbanization in Advanced Capitalism." In *The Social Economy of Cities,* edited by Gary Gappbert and Harold M. Rose, 119–63. Beverly Hills, Calif.: Sage.

Hassel, Karen. 1984. "Psykologen som sakkyndig i barneverns- og barnefordelingssaker" (The psychologist as an expert witness in custody and divorce cases). *Nordisk Psykologi* 36 (4): 237–47.

Haue, Harry, Jørgen Olsen, and Jørn Aarup-Kristiansen. 1985. *Det ny Danmark, 1890–1985* (The new Denmark, 1890–1985). Copenhagen: Munksgaard.

Hauerwas, Stanley. 1981. *A Community of Character: Toward a Constructive Christian Social Ethic.* Notre Dame, Ind.: University of Notre Dame Press.

Hawley, Peggy, and John D. Chamley. 1986. "Older Persons' Perceptions of the Quality of Their Human Support Systems." *Aging and Society* 6 (September): 295–312.

Hayek, F. A. 1973. *Rules and Order.* Vol. 1: *Law, Liberty, and Legislation.* Chicago: Chicago University Press.

Hays, Judith A. 1984. "Aging and Family Resources: Availability and Proximity of Kin." *The Gerontologist* 24 (April): 149–53.

Heath, Anthony. 1976. *Rational Choice and Social Exchange.* Cambridge: Cambridge University Press.

Hechter, Michael. 1987. *Principles of Group Solidarity.* Berkeley and Los Angeles: University of California Press.

Heckscher, Gunnar. 1984. *The Welfare State and Beyond: Success and Problems in Scandinavia.* Minneapolis: University of Minnesota Press.

Hedborg, Anna, and Rudolf Meidner. 1984. *Folkhemsmodellen* (The "people's home" model). Stockholm: Raben and Sjögren.

Heinild, Svend, and Frode Muldkjær. 1982. *Skilsmissens børn* (Children of divorce). Copenhagen: Rhodos.

Held, Virginia. 1984. *Rights and Goods: Justifying Social Action.* New York: Free Press.

Hellberg, Lars. 1981. *Det nye Sverige* (The new Sweden). Oslo: Cappalens.

Henning, Cecilia, Mats Lieberg, and Karin Palm Lindén. 1987. *Boende, omsorg och sociala nätverk* (Housing, care, and social networks). Stockholm: Institute for Construction Research.

Henrik, S. Nissen, ed. 1983. *Efter Grundtvig* (After Grundtvig). Copenhagen: Gyldendal.

Henriksson, Benny. 1987. *AIDS: Föreställingar om en verklighet* (AIDS: Some conceptions about a reality). Stockholm: Glacio.

Hentilä, Seppo. 1978. "The Origins of the *Folkhem* Ideology in Swedish Social Democracy." *Scandinavian Journal of History* 3 (1): 323–45.

Heritage, John. 1984. *Garfinkel and Ethnomethodology.* Cambridge: Polity Press.

Hernes, Helga Maria. 1984. "Women and the Welfare State: The Transition from Private to Public Dependence." In *Patriarchy in a Welfare Society,* edited by Harriet Holter, 26–45. Oslo: Norwegian University Press.

———. 1987. *Welfare State and Woman Power.* Oslo: Norwegian University Press.

Hertz, Rosanna. 1986. *More Equal than Others: Women and Men in Dual-Career Marriages.* Berkeley and Los Angeles: University of California Press.

Hibbs, Douglas A., Jr., and Henrik Jess Madsen. 1981. "Public Reactions to the Growth of Taxation and Government Expenditure." *World Politics* 33 (April): 413–35.

Hill, Martha S. 1983. "Trends in the Economic Situation of U.S. Families and Children." In *American Families and the Economy,* edited by Richard R. Nelson and Felicity Skidmore, 9–53. Washington, D.C.: National Academy Press.

Hirsch, Fred. 1976. *The Social Limits to Growth.* Cambridge, Mass.: Harvard University Press.

Hirschman, Albert O. 1970. *Exit, Voice, and Loyalty: Responses to Decline in Firms, Organizations, and States.* Cambridge, Mass.: Harvard University Press.

———. 1977. *The Passions and the Interests: Political Arguments for Capitalism Before Its Triumph.* Princeton, N.J.: Princeton University Press.

———. 1981. *Essays in Trespassing: Economics to Politics and Beyond.* Cambridge: Cambridge University Press.

———. 1982. *Shifting Involvements: Private Interest and Public Action.* Princeton, N.J.: Princeton University Press.

Hirshleifer, Jack. 1985. "The Expanding Domain of Economics." *American Economic Review* 75 (December): 53–68.

Hjortsjö, Thomas. 1983. *Självmord i Stockholm* (Suicide in Stockholm). Göteborg: School of Public Health.

Hobbes, Thomas. 1961. *Leviathan.* Edited by C. B. MacPherson. New York: Penguin Books.

Hochschild, Arlie Russell. 1983. *The Managed Heart: Commercialization of Human Feeling.* Berkeley and Los Angeles: University of California Press.

Hochschild, Jennifer. 1984. *The New American Dilemma: Liberal Democracy and School Desegregation.* New Haven, Conn.: Yale University Press.

Hodgkinson, Virginia Ann, and Murray A. Weitzman. 1986. *Dimensions of the Independent Sector.* Washington, D.C.: Independent Sector.

Hofer, Hanns von. 1982. *Nordisk kriminalstatistik 1950–1980* (Scandinavian criminal statistics 1950–1980). Copenhagen: Nordic Statistical Secretariat.

Hollis, Martin, and Edward J. Nell. 1975. *Rational Economic Man: A Philosophical Critique of Neo-classical Economics.* Cambridge: Cambridge University Press.

Holm, Olof. 1984. *Kooperation i ofärd och välfärd* (Cooperation in hard times and good times). Stockholm: Department of Education, University of Stockholm.

Holmberg, Sören. 1984. *Väljare i förändring* (Changing voters). Stockholm: Publica.

Holmberg, Sören, and Mikael Gilljam. 1987. *Väljare och val i Sverige* (Voters and elections in Sweden). Stockholm: Bonniers.

Holmes, Stephen. 1984. *Benjamin Constant and the Making of Modern Liberalism.* New Haven, Conn.: Yale University Press.

Hompland, Andreas, ed. 1987. *Scenarier 2000* (Scenarios for the year 2000). Oslo: Norwegian University Press.

Hont, Istvan, and Michael Ignatieff, eds. 1983. *Wealth and Virtue: The Shaping of Political Economy in the Scottish Enlightenment.* Cambridge: Cambridge University Press.

Horowitz, Amy. 1985. "Sons and Daughters as Caregivers to Older Parents." *The Gerontologist* 25 (December): 612–17.

Horowitz, Amy, and Lois W. Shindelman. 1983. "Reciprocity and Affection: Past Influences on Current Caregiving." *Journal of Gerontological Social Work* 5 (Spring): 5–20.

Hough, Douglas E., and Charles G. Kratz. 1983. "Can 'Good' Architecture Meet the Market Test?" *Journal of Urban Economics* 14 (July): 40–54.

Hume, David. 1875. "An Inquiry Concerning Human Understanding." In *Essays: Moral, Political, and Literary,* edited by T. H. Greene and T. H. Grose, 2:2–135. London: Longmans, Green.

———. 1907. "Of the Original Contract." In *Essays: Moral, Political, and Literary,* edited by T. H. Greene and T. H. Grose, 1:443–60. London: Longmans, Green.

Hummon, David M. 1986. "Urban Views: Popular Perspectives on City Life." *Urban Life* 15 (April): 3–36.

Huntford, Roland. 1972. *The New Totalitarians.* London: Allen Lane.

Hwang, Kwang-kuo. 1987. "Face and Favor: The Chinese Power Game." *American Journal of Sociology* 92 (January): 944–74.

Hyde, Lewis. 1983. *The Gift: Imagination and the Erotic Life of Poetry.* New York: Vintage Books.

Ignatieff, Michael. 1985. *The Needs of Strangers: An Essay on Privacy, Solidarity, and the Politics of Being Human.* New York: Penguin Books.

Imber, Jonathan B. 1986. *Abortion and the Private Practice of Medicine.* New Haven, Conn.: Yale University Press.

Isachsen, Arne Jon, and Steiner Strøm. 1985. "The Size and Growth of the Hidden Economy in Norway." *Review of Income and Wealth* 31 (March): 21–38.

Isachsen, Arne Jon, Jan Tore Klovland, and Steinar Strøm. 1982. "The Hidden Economy in Norway." In *The Underground Economy in the United States and Abroad,* edited by Vito Tanzi, 209–32. Lexington, Mass.: Lexington Books.

Isaksen, Lise Widding. 1987. "Om krenking av den personlige bluferdighet" (Violations of personal modesty). *Tidsskrift for samfunnsforskning* 28 (1): 33–46.

James, Thomas, and Henry M. Levin, eds. 1983. *Public Dollars for Private Schools: The Case of Tuition Tax Credits.* Philadelphia: Temple University Press.

Janowitz, Morris. 1975. "Sociological Theory and Social Control." *American Journal of Sociology* 81 (July): 82–108.

————. 1976. *Social Control of the Welfare State*. New York: Elsevier.

————. 1978. *The Last Half Century: Societal Change and Politics in America*. Chicago: University of Chicago Press.

————. 1983. *The Reconstruction of Patriotism: Education for Civic Consciousness*. Chicago: University of Chicago Press.

Janowitz, Morris, and Charles C. Moskos. 1979. "Five Years of the All-Volunteer Force: 1973–1978." *Armed Forces and Society* 5 (February): 171–218.

Jensen, Carsten, ed. 1982. *BZ Europa* (Squatters Europe). Copenhagen: Tiderne Skifter.

Jensen, Jytte Juul, and Ole Langsted. 1985. "Aldersintegrerende institutioner" (Age-integrated institutions). In *Småbørn, familie, samfund* (Small children, family, society), edited by Charlotte Bøgh and Per Schultz Jørgensen, 187–97. Copenhagen: Hans Reitzels.

Jensen, Mogens Kjær, Dines Andersen, Torben Fridberg, and Keld Anker Nielsen. 1987. *Sociale netværk og socialpolitik* (Social networks and social policy). Copenhagen: Danish Social Research Institute.

Jeppesen, Kirsten Just, and Dorte Høeg. 1987. *Private hjælpeorganisationer på det sociale område* (Private helping organizations in the social sphere). Copenhagen: Danish Social Research Institute.

Joffe, Carole. 1986. *The Regulation of Sexuality: Experiences of Family Planning Workers*. Philadelphia: Temple University Press.

Johansen, Hans Christian. 1985. *Dansk historisk statistik, 1814–1980* (Danish historical statistics, 1814–1980). Copenhagen: Gyldendal.

Johansen, Lars Nørby. 1982. *The Danish Welfare State, 1945–1980*. Odense: Institute for Social Science.

Johansen, Lars Nørby, and Jon Eivind Kolberg. 1985. "Welfare State Regression in Scandinavia?" In *The Welfare State and Its Aftermath*, edited by S. N. Eisenstadt and Ora Ahimeir, 143–76. London: Croom Held.

Johansson, Hilding. 1980. *Folkrörelserna i Sverige* (Popular movements in Sweden). Stockholm: Sober.

Johnson, William R. 1985. "The Economics of Copying." *Journal of Political Economy* 93 (February): 158–74.

Jonsson, Gustav. 1973. *Att bryta det sociala arvet* (To break the social inheritance). Stockholm: Tiden\Folksam.

Jørgensen, Margot, and Peter Schreiner. 1985. *Fighterrelationen* (Fighter relations). Copenhagen: Hans Reitzels.

Jørgensen, Per Schultz, Birthe Gamst, and Bjarne Hjorth Andersen. 1986. *Efter Skoletid* (After schooltime). Copenhagen: Danish Social Research Institute.

Kaminer, Wendy. 1984. *Women Volunteering: The Pleasure, Pain, and Politics of Unpaid Work from 1830 to the Present*. Garden City, N.Y.: Doubleday.

Kattay, Eva, and Diane Keyes, eds. 1988. *Women and Moral Theory*. Totowa, N.J.: Rowman and Littlefield.

Katz, Michael. 1968. *The Irony of Early School Reform: Educational Innovation in Mid-Nineteenth-Century Massachusetts*. Cambridge, Mass.: Harvard University Press.

———. 1987. *Reconstructing American Education*. Cambridge, Mass.: Harvard University Press.

Katznelson, Ira, and Margaret Weir. 1985. *Schooling for All: Class, Race, and the Decline of the Democratic Ideal*. New York: Basic Books.

Kavka, Gregory S. 1986. *Hobbesian Moral and Political Theory*. Princeton, N.J.: Princeton University Press.

Kay, John. 1988. "Discussion." *Economic Policy* 6 (April): 187–89.

Kayden, Xandra, and Eddie Mahe, Jr. 1985. *The Party Goes On: The Persistence of the Two-Party System in the United States*. New York: Basic Books.

Keane, John. 1988. *Democracy and Civil Society*. London: Verso.

———, ed. 1988. *Civil Society and the State*. London: Verso.

Kelman, Steven. 1981. *Regulating America, Regulating Sweden: A Comparative Study of Occupational Safety and Health Policy*. Cambridge, Mass.: MIT Press.

Kemvall-Ljung, Berit. 1986. *Statistiska uppgifter om småbarns livsvillkor i Sverige* (Statistical information on the living conditions of small children in Sweden). Stockholm: Childhood, Society, and Development in the Nordic Countries Project.

Kennedy, Duncan. 1976. "Form and Substance in Private Law Adjudication." *Harvard Law Review* 89 (June): 1685–1778.

Kenny, Anthony. 1985. *The Logic of Deterrence*. Chicago: University of Chicago Press.

Kernell, Samuel. 1985. "Campaigning, Governing, and the Contemporary Presidency." In *The New Direction in American Politics*, edited by John E. Chubb and Paul E. Peterson, 117–41. Washington, D.C.: Brookings Institution.

Kilgore, Sally. 1984. "Schooling Effects: Reply to Alexander and Pallas." *Sociology of Education* 57 (January): 59–61.

Kingson, Eric R., Barbara A. Hirshorn, and John M. Cormann. 1986. *Ties That Bind: The Interdependence of Generations*. Washington, D.C.: Seven Locks Press.

Kitcher, Philip. 1985. *Vaulting Ambition: Sociobiology and the Quest for Human Nature*. Cambridge, Mass.: MIT Press.

Klausen, Kurt Klaudi. 1989. "Frivillige organisationer mellem stat og marked." In *Stat og marked: Fra Leviathan og usynlig hånd til forhandlingsøkonomi* (State and Market: From Leviathan and the Invisible Hand to the Managed Economy), eds. Kurt Klaudi Klausen and Torben Hviid Nielsen. Copenhagen: Danish Union of Lawyers and Economists, 227–82.

———. 1988. *Per ardua ad astra*. Odense: Odense University Press.

Kloppenberg, James T. 1986. *Uncertain Victory: Social Democracy and Progressivism in European and American Thought, 1870–1920*. New York: Oxford University Press.

Knox, T. M. 1967. *Hegel's Philosophy of Right*. New York: Oxford University Press.

Knutsen, Oddbjørn. 1986. "Sosiale klasser og politiske verdier i Norge" (Social classes and political values in Norway). *Tidsskrift for samfunnsforskning* 27 (4): 263–87.

Koch-Neilsen, Inger. 1983. *Skilsmisser* (Divorces). Copenhagen: Danish Social Research Institute.

———. 1985. "Fremtidens familiemønstre" (Future family patterns). In *Næste generation* (Next generation), edited by Inger Koch-Nielsen et al., 13–49. Copenhagen: Aschehoug.

Koch-Nielsen, Inger, and Henning Transgaard. 1987. *Familiemønstre efter skilsmisse* (Family patterns after divorce). Copenhagen: Danish Social Research Institute.

Koch-Nielsen, Inger, Birthe Kyng, Laurits Lauritsen, Bente Ørum, and Ebbe Kløvedal Reich. 1985. *Næste generation* (Next generation). Copenhagen: Aschehoug.

Kohlberg, Lawrence. 1971. "From is to ought." In *Cognitive Development and Epistemology,* edited by Theodore Mischel, 151–236. New York: Academic Press.

———. 1980. "The Future of Liberalism as the Dominant Ideology of the West." In *Moral Development and Politics,* edited by Richard W. Wilson and Gordon J. Schochet, 55–68. New York: Praeger.

———. 1981. *The Philosophy of Moral Development.* New York: Harper and Row.

Kolberg, Jon Eivind, and Per Arnt Pettersen. 1981. "Om velferdsstatens politiske basis" (On the political basis of the welfare state). *Tidsskrift for samfunnsforskning* 22 (2/3): 193–222.

Konrad, Georg. 1984. *Antipolitics.* London: Quartet Books.

Kornblum, William. 1974. *Blue Collar Community.* Chicago: University of Chicago Press.

Kornhaber, Arthur. 1985. "Grandparenthood and the 'New Social Contract.'" In *Grandparenthood,* edited by Vern L. Bengston and Joan F. Robertson, 159–71. Beverly Hills, Calif.: Sage.

Kornhauser, William. 1959. *The Politics of Mass Society.* Glencoe, Ill.: Free Press.

Kosmin, Barry. 1987. "The Political Economy of Gender in Jewish Federations." Paper presented to the Conference on Women and Philanthropy, CUNY Graduate Center.

Kosonen, Pekka. 1987. "From Collectivity to Individualism in the Welfare State?" *Acta Sociologica* 30 (3/4): 281–93.

Kramer, Ralph M. 1981. *Voluntary Agencies in the Welfare State.* Berkeley and Los Angeles: University of California Press.

Krannich, Richard S., Thomas Greider, and Ronald L. Little. 1985. "Rapid Growth and Fear of Crime." *Rural Sociology* 50 (Summer): 193–209.

Krashinsky, Michael. 1986. "Why Educational Vouchers May Be Bad Economics." *Teachers College Record* 88 (Winter): 139–51.

Kristensen, Ole P. 1987. *Væksten i den offentlige sektor* (The expansion of the public sector). Copenhagen: Danish Union of Lawyers and Economists.

Kristiansen, Jan Erik. 1986. "Familien i endring: Et demografisk perspektiv" (Changes in the family: A demographic perspective). In *Familien i endring*

(Changes in the family), edited by Jan Erik Kristiansen and Tone Schou Wetlesen, 17–45. Oslo: Institute for Sociology.

Kristol, Irving. 1981. "Rationalism in Economics." In *The Crisis in Economic Theory*, edited by Daniel Bell and Irving Kristol, 201–18. New York: Basic Books.

Kuhnle, Stein. 1985. "Offentlige utgifter og velferdsutgifter" (Public Expenditures and Welfare Expenditures). In *Velferdsstaten: Vekst og omstilling* (The welfare state: Growth and change), edited by Stein Kuhnle and Liv Solheim, 54–65. Oslo: Tano.

Kyng, Birthe. 1985. "Børns personlighedsudvikling: Et fremtidsperspektiv" (The personality development of children: A future perspective). In *Næste generation* (Next generation), edited by Inger Koch-Neilsen et al., 51–113. Copenhagen: Aschehoug.

Köhler, Lennart, Bengt Lindström, Keith Barnard, and Hovda Itani. 1987. *Health Implications of Family Breakdown*. Stockholm: Nordic School of Public Health.

Køppe, Anne. 1987. *Evaluering af Mødrehjælpen af 1983* (Evaluation of Mothers' Help of 1983). Copenhagen: Institute for Social Medicine.

Körmendi, Eszter. 1986. *Os og de andre* (Us and the others). Copenhagen: Danish Social Research Institute.

Lagergren, Mårten, Leda Lundh, Mingo Okran, and Christer Sanne. 1982. *Tid för omsorg* (Time for care). Stockholm: LiberFörlag/Institute for Future Studies.

Landes, Elizabeth M., and Richard A. Posner. 1978. "The Economics of the Baby Shortage." *Journal of Legal Studies* 7 (June): 323–48.

Lane, Robert E. 1983. "Market Thinking and Political Thinking." In *Dilemmas of Liberal Democracies: Studies in Fred Hirsch's "Social Limits to Growth,"* edited by Adrian Ellis and Krishan Kumar, 122–47. London: Tavistock.

Langsted, Ole, and Dion Sommer. 1988. *Småbørns livsvilkår i Danmark* (The living condition of small children in Denmark). Copenhagen: Hans Reitzels.

Larcker, David F., and Thomas Lys. 1987. "An Empirical Analysis of the Incentives to Engage in Costly Information Acquisition." *Journal of Financial Economics* 18 (1): 111–26.

Larmore, Charles E. 1987. *Patterns of Moral Complexity*. Cambridge: Cambridge University Press.

Larsen, Ejvind. 1983. *Det levende ord* (The living word). Copenhagen: Rosinante.

Lears, T. J. Jackson. 1983. "From Salvation to Self-Realization." In *The Culture of Consumption: Critical Essays in American History, 1880–1980,* edited by T. J. Jackson Lears and Richard Wrightman Fox, 1–38. New York: Pantheon Books.

Lee, Barrett A., R. S. Oropesa, Barbara J. Metch, and Avery M. Guest. 1984. "Testing the Decline of Community Thesis." *American Journal of Sociology* 89 (March): 1161–88.

Lefort, Claude. 1986. *The Political Forms of Modern Society*. Cambridge, Mass.: MIT Press.

Leibenstein, Harvey. 1976. *Beyond Economic Man: A New Foundation for Economics*. Cambridge, Mass.: Harvard University Press.

Leira, Arnlaug. 1987. *Day Care for Children in Denmark, Norway, and Sweden*. Oslo: Institute for Social Research.

Lerner, Melvin J., and Sally C. Lerner. 1981. *The Justice Motive in Social Behavior: Adapting to Times of Scarcity and Change*. New York: Plenum.

Levin, Henry M. 1987. "Education as Public and Private Good." *Journal of Policy Analysis and Management* 6 (Summer): 628–41.

Levitan, Sar A., Richard S. Belous, and Frank Gallo. 1988. *What's Happening to the American Family? Tensions, Hopes, Realities*. Rev. ed. Baltimore: Johns Hopkins University Press.

Levnadsförhållanden (Living conditions). 1987. Stockholm: Central Statistical Bureau.

Lewin-Epstein, Noah. 1981. *Youth Employment During High School*. Washington, D.C.: National Center for Education Statistics.

Lewis, J. David, and Andrew Weigert. 1985. "Trust as a Social Reality." *Social Forces* 63 (June): 967–85.

Liker, Jeffrey K., and Glen H. Elder, Jr. 1983. "Economic Hardship and Marital Relations in the 1930s." *American Sociological Review* 48 (June): 343–59.

Lindblom, Charles. 1977. *Politics and Markets: The World's Political Economic Systems*. New York: Basic Books.

———. 1982. "The Market as Prison." *Journal of Politics* 44 (May): 324–36.

Linder, Staffan B. 1979. *The Harried Leisure Class*. New York: Columbia University Press.

———. 1983. *Den härtlösa välfärdsstaten* (The heartless welfare state). Stockholm: Timbro.

Lindgren, J. Ralph. 1973. *The Social Philosophy of Adam Smith*. The Hague: Martinus Nijhoff.

Lingsom, Susan. 1984. "Omsorg for ektefellen" (Caring for an ailing spouse). *Tidsskrift for samfunnsforskning* 25 (3): 245–68.

———. 1987. "Fragmenter i samspill: Den offentlige og private hjelpen i eldres hverdag" (Working together: Public and private help in the everyday life of the elderly). In *Gammel i eget hjem* (The elderly in their own homes), edited by Svein Olav Daatland, 196–220. Copenhagen: Nordic Council.

———. 1987. *I eget hjem med andres hjelp* (In one's own home with help from others). Oslo: Institute for Social Research.

Logan, John R., and Harvey L. Molotch. 1987. *Urban Fortunes: The Political Economy of Place*. Berkeley and Los Angeles: University of California Press.

Longman, Phillip. 1987. *Born to Pay: The New Politics of Aging in America*. Boston: Houghton Mifflin.

Loomis, Burdett A. 1981. "The 'Me Decade' and the Changing Context of House

Leadership." In *Understanding Congressional Leadership,* edited by Frank H. Mackaman, 157–79. Washington, D.C.: Congressional Quarterly Press.

Lorentzen, Håkon. 1987. *Frivillige sosiale ytelser i menighetenes regi* (Voluntary social contribution in the parish). Oslo: Institute for Applied Social Research.

———. 1987. *Frivillig sosialt arbeid i organisasjoner for syke, handicappede, og funksjonshemmede* (Voluntary social work in organizations for the sick, handicapped, and functionally disabled). Oslo: Institute for Applied Social Research.

———. 1987. *Frivillig sosialt arbeid og ytelser i noen humanitære organisasjoner* (Voluntary social work and contributions in some humanitarian organizations). Olso: Institute for Applied Social Research.

Lowe, Donald. 1983. *History of Bourgeois Perception.* Chicago: University of Chicago Press.

Lowi, Theodore J. 1979. *The End of Liberalism: The Second Republic of the United States.* 2d ed. New York: W. W. Norton.

Luhmann, Niklas. 1979. *Trust and Power.* New York: John Wiley.

Lui, Francis T. 1985. "An Equilibrium Queuing Model of Bribery." *Journal of Political Economy* 93 (August): 760–81.

Lukács, Georg. 1981. *The Destruction of Reason.* Translated by Peter Palmer. Atlantic Highlands, N.J.: Humanities Press.

Lukas, J. Anthony. 1985. *Common Ground: A Turbulent Decade in the Lives of Three American Families.* New York: Alfred Knopf.

Luker, Kristin. 1975. *Taking Chances: Abortion and the Decision Not to Contracept.* Berkeley and Los Angeles: University of California Press.

———. 1984. *Abortion and the Politics of Motherhood.* Berkeley and Los Angeles: University of California Press.

Lukes, Steven. 1985. *Marxism and Morality.* Oxford: Clarendon Press.

Lunde, Inger Myhr, and Liv Else Schjelderup. 1985. *Etter skilsmisse* (After divorce). Stavanger: Norwegian University Press.

Lundqvist, Sven. 1977. *Folkrörelserna i det svenska samhället 1850–1920* (Popular Movements in Swedish Society 1850–1920). Stockholm: Sober.

Maass, Arthur. 1951. *Muddy Waters: The Army Engineers and the Nation's Rivers.* Cambridge, Mass.: Harvard University Press.

McCloskey, Donald N. 1985. *The Rhetoric of Economics.* Madison: University of Wisconsin Press.

McConnell, Grant. 1959. *The Decline of Agrarian Democracy.* Berkeley and Los Angeles: University of California Press.

MacIntyre, Alasdair. 1966. *A Short History of Ethics.* New York: Collier Books.

———. 1981. *After Virtue: A Study in Moral Theory.* South Bend, Ind.: University of Notre Dame Press.

Macklin, Ruth. 1987. *Mortal Choices: Bioethics in Today's World.* New York: Pantheon Books.

McPherson, Michael S. 1983. "Want Formation, Morality, and Some 'Interpretative' Aspects of Economic Inquiry." In *Social Science as Moral Inquiry,* edited by Norma Haan, Robert N. Bellah, Paul Rabinow, and William M. Sullivan, 96–124. New York: Columbia University Press.

Madsen, Richard. 1984. *Morality and Power in a Chinese Village.* Berkeley and Los Angeles: University of California Press.

Malbin, Michael J. 1980. *Unelected Representatives: Congressional Staff and the Future of Representative Government.* New York: Basic Books.

Malbin, Murray. 1987. *Night as Frontier: Colonizing the World After Dark.* New York: Free Press.

Malcolm, Andrew H. 1986. *Final Harvest: An American Tragedy.* New York: Times Books.

Manaster, Guy J., Donald L. Greer, and Douglas A. Kleiber. 1985. "Youth's Outlook on the Future III." *Youth and Society* 17 (September): 97–112.

Mann, Leon. 1969. "Queue Culture: The Waiting Line as a Social System." *American Journal of Sociology* 75 (November): 340–54.

Mann, Michael. 1986. *The Sources of Social Power: A History of Power from the Beginning to A.D. 1760.* Cambridge: Cambridge University Press.

Mann, Thomas E., and Norman J. Ornstein, eds. 1981. *The New Congress.* Washington, D.C.: American Enterprise Institute.

Mannheim, Karl. 1952. "The Problem of Generations." In *Essays on the Sociology of Knowledge,* 276–320. London: Routledge and Kegan Paul.

Marchand, Roland. 1985. *Advertising the American Dream: Making Way for Modernity, 1920–1940.* Berkeley and Los Angeles: University of California Press.

Margolis, Howard. 1982. *Selfishness, Altruism, and Rationality.* Cambridge: Cambridge University Press.

Marshall, T. H. 1964. "Citizenship and Social Class." In *Class, Citizenship, and Social Development,* edited by S. M. Lipset, 71–134. Garden City, N.Y.: Anchor Books.

Masnick, George, and Mary Jo Bane. 1980. *The Nation's Families: 1960–1990.* Boston: Auburn House.

Matthews, Donald R. 1960. *U.S. Senators and Their World.* Chapel Hill: University of North Carolina Press.

Matthews, Sarah H., and Jetse Sprey. 1984. "The Impact of Divorce on Grandparenthood." *The Gerontologist* 24 (February): 41–47.

Mauss, Marcel. 1967. *The Gift.* New York: W. W. Norton.

Mead, George Herbert. 1962. *Mind, Self, and Society: From the Standpoint of a Social Behavioralist.* Chicago: University of Chicago Press.

Mead, Lawrence. 1986. *Beyond Entitlement: The Social Obligations of Citizenship.* New York: Free Press.

Medick, Hans. 1973. *Naturzustand und Naturgeschichte der bürgerlichen Gesellschaft.* Göttingen: Vandenhoeck and Ruprecht.

Meineicke, Friedrich. 1957. *Machiavellianism*. New Haven, Conn.: Yale University Press.

Merelman, Richard M. 1984. *Making Something of Ourselves: On Culture and Politics in the United States*. Berkeley and Los Angeles: University of California Press.

Merton, Robert K. 1976. *Sociological Ambivalence and Other Essays*. New York: Free Press.

Mesquita, Bruce Bueno de. 1983. "The Costs of War: A Rational Expectations Approach." *American Political Science Review* 77 (June): 347–57.

Meyer, John W., David Tyack, Joane Nagel, and Audri Gordon. 1979. "Public Education as Nation Building in America." *American Journal of Sociology* 85 (November): 591–613.

Michnik, Adam. 1985. *Letters from Prison and Other Essays*. Berkeley and Los Angeles: University of California Press.

Miliband, Ralph. 1969. *The State in Capitalist Society: An Analysis of Western Systems of Power*. New York: Basic Books.

Min, Pyong Gap. 1988. *Ethnic Business Enterprise: Korean Small Business in Atlanta*. New York: Center for Migration Studies.

Moen, Phyllis, Edward L. Kain, and Glen H. Elder, Jr. 1983. "Economic Conditions and Family Life." In *American Families and the Economy,* edited by R. R. Nelson and F. Skidmore, 213–59. Washington, D.C.: National Academy Press.

Mogensen, Gunnar Viby. 1985. *Sort arbejde i Danmark* (Illegal work in Denmark). Viborg, Den.: Arnold Busck.

Molotch, Harvey, and John R. Logan. 1985. "Urban Dependencies: New Forms of Use and Exchange in U.S. Cities." *Urban Affairs Quarterly* 21 (December): 143–69.

Moskos, Charles C. 1982. "Social Considerations of the All-Volunteer Force." In *Military Service in the United States,* edited by Brent Scowcraft, 129–50. Englewood Cliffs, N.J.: Prentice-Hall.

———. 1986. "Citizen Soldier Versus Economic Man." In *The Social Fabric,* edited by James F. Short, Jr., 243–53. Beverly Hills, Calif.: Sage.

Moskos, Charles C., and J. H. Faris. 1981. "Beyond the Marketplace: National Service and the AVF." In *Towards a Consensus on Military Policy,* edited by Andrew J. Goodpaster, Lloyd H. Elliott, and J. Allan Hovey, 131–51. New York: Pergamon Press.

Mullen, Joan. 1985. "Corrections and the Private Sector." *Research in Brief* (National Institute of Justice) (March).

Nagel, Thomas. 1979. *Mortal Questions*. Cambridge: Cambridge University Press.

National Commission on Youth. 1980. *The Transition of Youth to Adulthood*. Boulder, Colo.: Westview Press.

Nelson, Jon P. 1978. "Residential Choice, Hedonic Prices, and the Demand for Urban Air Quality." *Journal of Urban Economics* 5 (July): 357–69.

Nelson, Ralph L. 1977. "Private Giving in the American Economy." Filer Commission Research Papers, 115–55. Washington, D.C.: Treasury Department.

Nelson, Richard R., and Felicity Skidmore, eds. 1983. *American Families and the Economy: The High Costs of Living.* Washington, D.C.: National Academic Press.

Nelson, William N. 1980. *On Justifying Democracy.* London: Routledge and Kegan Paul.

Neuman, W. Russell. 1986. *The Paradox of Mass Politics: Knowledge and Opinion in the American Electorate.* Cambridge, Mass.: Harvard University Press.

Newman, Katherine S. 1985. "Turning Your Back on Tradition: Symbolic Analysis and Moral Critique in a Plant Shutdown." *Urban Anthropology* 14 (Spring–Summer–Fall): 109–50.

Nexø, Martin Andersen. 1963. *Ditte menneskebarn* (Ditte, child of man). Copenhagen: Gyldendal.

Nichols, David. 1974. *Three Varieties of Pluralism.* New York: St. Martins Press.

Nielsen, Torben Hviid. 1986. "The State, the Market, and the Individual." *Acta Sociologica* 29 (4): 283–302.

———. 1988. *Samfund og magt* (Society and power). Copenhagen: Akademisk Forlag.

Nielsen, Waldemar. 1979. *The Endangered Sector.* New York: Columbia University Press.

Nisbet, Robert. 1965. *Emile Durkheim.* Englewood Cliffs, N.J.: Prentice-Hall.

Nissen, Henrik S., ed. 1983. *Efter Grundtvig* (After Grundtvig). Copenhagen: Gyldendal.

Nissen, Morten. 1988. *Skilsmissens pris* (The costs of divorce). Copenhagen: Danish Social Research Institute.

Noddings, Nel. 1984. *Caring: A Feminist Approach to Ethics and Moral Education.* Berkeley and Los Angeles: University of California Press.

Noonan, John T. 1970. "An Almost Absolute Value in History." In *The Morality of Abortion: Legal and Historical Perspectives,* edited by John T. Noonan, 1–59. Cambridge, Mass.: Harvard University Press.

Nordhus, Inger Hilde. 1986. "Begrepet omsorgsbyrde" (The burden of caregiving). *Tidsskrift for samfunnsforskning* 27 (4): 288–311.

Nordic Council. 1979. *Yearbook of Nordic Statistics 1978.* Stockholm: Nordic Council.

———. 1987. *Yearbook of Nordic Statistics 1986.* Stockholm: Nordic Council.

Nordic Statistical Secretariat. 1986. *Social tryghed i de Nordiske lande* (Social security in the Nordic countries). Copenhagen: NSS.

Norsk Kirkens Nødhjelp (Norwegian State Church Emergency Relief). 1980–86. *Årsrapport* (Annual reports).

Norsk Redd Barna (Norwegian Save the Children). 1980–86. *Årsmelding og regnskap* (Annual reports and budgets).

Nozick, Robert. 1974. *Anarchy, State, and Utopia.* New York: Basic Books.

Nusberg, Charlotte, Mary Jo Greson, and Sheila Peace. 1984. *Innovative Aging Pro-*

grams Abroad: Implications for the United States. Westport, Conn.: Greenwood Press.

Nyberg, Per. 1987. *Sociala nätverk och problemlösning* (Social networks and problem solving). Lund: Center for Social Medicine.

Näsman, Elisabet, Kerstin Nordström, and Ruth Hammarström. 1983. *Föräldrars arbete och barns villkor* (Parental work and child welfare). Stockholm: LiberTryck.

Næss, Siri. 1987. *Selvmord, ensomhet, og samfunnsutvikling* (Suicide, loneliness, and social development). Oslo: Institute for Applied Social Research.

Offe, Claus. 1983. "Competitive Party Democracy and the Welfare State." *Policy Science* 15 (June): 225–46.

Oi, Walter. 1967. "The Costs and Implications of an All-Volunteer Force." In *The Draft,* edited by Sol Tax, 221–51. Chicago: University of Chicago Press.

Olson, Mancur, Jr. 1971. *The Logic of Collective Action.* Rev. ed. New York: Schocken Books.

Olsson, Sven E. 1987. "Toward a Transformation of the Swedish Welfare State." In *Modern Welfare States: A Comparative View of Trends and Prospects,* edited by Robert R. Friedman, Neil Gilbert, and Moshe Sherer, 44–82. Brighton, Eng.: Wheatsheaf Books.

O'Neill, Onora. 1986. *Faces of Hunger: An Essay on Poverty, Justice, and Development.* London: Allen and Unwin.

O'Neill, Onora, and William Rudick. 1979. *Having Children: Philosophical and Legal Reflections on Parenthood.* New York: Oxford University Press.

Organization for Economic Cooperation and Development. 1986. *Revenue Statistics of Member Countries.* Paris: OECD.

Ossowska, Maria. 1970. *Social Determinants of Moral Ideas.* Philadelphia: University of Pennsylvania Press.

Ostrander, Susan, Stuart Langton, and Jon Van Til. 1987. *Shifting the Debate: Public/Private Sector Relations in the Modern Welfare State.* New Brunswick, N.J.: Transaction Books.

Parry, Geraint. 1976. "Trust, Distrust, and Consensus." *British Journal of Political Science* 6 (April): 129–42.

Parsons, Talcott. 1964. *The Social System.* New York: Free Press.

———. 1969. *Politics and Social Structure.* New York: Free Press.

Pateman, Carole. 1985. *The Problem of Political Obligation: A Critical Analysis of Liberal Theory.* Cambridge: Polity Press.

Pearce, Diana. 1978. "The Feminization of Poverty: Women, Work, and Welfare." *Urban and Social Change Review* 11 (Winter–Summer): 28–36.

Pedersen, Paul, and Reidnar J. Pettersen. 1985. "Virkninger av personalgjennomtrekk i barnehage" (Effects of personnel turnovers in day-care centers). *Nordisk Pedagogisk Tidskrift* 69 (2): 102–11.

Perin, Constance. 1977. *Everything in Its Place: Social Order and Land Use in America*. Princeton, N.J.: Princeton University Press.

Perkins, Kenneth B. 1987. "Volunteer Firefighters in the United States: A Report to the National Volunteer Fire Council." Department of Sociology and Anthropology, Longwood College, Farmville, Va. Mimeo.

Perrow, Charles. 1984. *Normal Accidents: Living with High-Risk Technologies*. New York: Basic Books.

Peshkin, Alan. 1986. *God's Choice: The Total World of a Fundamentalist Christian School*. Chicago: University of Chicago Press.

Peterson, Warren A., and Jill Quadagno, eds. 1985. *Social Bonds in Later Life: Aging and Interdependence*. Beverly Hills, Calif.: Sage.

Phelps, Edmund S., ed. 1975. *Altruism, Morality, and Economic Theory*. New York: Russell Sage Foundation.

Phillips, Derek L. 1986. *Toward a Just Social Order*. Princeton, N.J.: Princeton University Press.

Phillipson, Nicholas. 1983. "Adam Smith as Civil Moralist." In *Wealth and Virtue*, edited by Istvan Hont and Michael Ignatieff, 179–202. Cambridge: Cambridge University Press.

Piaget, Jean. 1965. *The Moral Judgement of the Child*. New York: Free Press.

Pifer, Alan. 1984. *Philanthropy in an Age of Transition: The Essays of Alan Pifer*. New York: The Foundation Center.

Pilisuk, Marc, and Susan Hillier Parks. 1986. *The Healing Web: Social Networks and Human Survival*. Hanover, N.H.: University Press of New England.

Plamanatz, John. 1958. *The English Utilitarians*. 2d rev. ed. Oxford: Basil Blackwell.

Platz, Merete. 1987. *Længst muligt i eget hjem . . .* (As long as possible in one's own home . . .). Copenhagen: Danish Social Research Institute.

Polanyi, Karl. 1957. *The Great Transformation: The Political and Economic Origin of Our Times*. Boston: Beacon Press.

Poole, Robert W., Jr., and Philip E. Fixler, Jr. 1987. "Privatization of Public-Sector Services in Practice." *Journal of Policy Analysis and Management* 6 (Summer): 612–25.

Popenoe, David. 1988. *Disturbing the Nest: Family Change and Decline in Modern Societies*. Hawthorne, N.Y.: Aldine de Gruyter.

Posner, Richard A. 1981. *The Economics of Justice*. Cambridge, Mass.: Harvard University Press.

Powell, Arthur G., Eleanor Farrar, and David K. Cohen, 1985. *The Shopping Mall High School*. Boston: Houghton Mifflin.

Powell, Walter W., ed. 1987. *The Non-Profit Sector: A Research Handbook*. New Haven, Conn.: Yale University Press.

Powers, Richard. 1988. *Prisoner's Dilemma*. New York: William Morrow.

Pratt, Henry J. 1976. *The Gray Lobby*. Chicago: University of Chicago Press.

Preston, Larry M. 1984. "Freedom, Markets, and Voluntary Exchange." *American Political Science Review* 78 (December): 959–70.

Preuss, Ulrich K. 1986. "The Concept of Rights and the Welfare State." In *Dilemmas of Law in the Welfare State*, edited by Gunther Teubner, 151–72. Berlin: Walter de Gruyter.

Przeworski, Adam, and Michael Wallerstein. 1982. "Democratic Capitalism at the Crossroads." *Democracy* 2 (July): 52–68.

Rainwater, Lee, Martin Rein, and Joseph Schwartz. 1986. *Income Packaging in the Welfare State: A Comparative Study of Family Income*. Oxford: Clarendon Press.

Rakowski, William, and Noreen M. Clark. 1985. "Future Outlook, Caregiving, and Caregiving in the Family Context." *The Gerontologist* 25 (December): 618–23.

Ramsøy, Natalie Rogoff. 1986. "From Necessity to Choice: Social Change in Norway." In *The Scandinavian Model: Welfare States and Welfare Research*, edited by Robert Erikson, Erik Jørgen Hansen, Stein Ringen, and Hannu Uusitalo, 75–105. Armonk, N.Y.: M.E. Sharpe.

Ramsøy, Natalie Rogoff, and Lise Kjølsrød. 1985. *Velferdsstatens yrker* (Occupations in the welfare state). Oslo: Institute for Applied Social Research.

Rapport 87: Alkohol-och-narkotika utvecklingen i Sverige (Report 87: Alcohol and narcotic trends in Sweden). 1987. Stockholm: Center for Alcohol and Narcotics Information.

Raundalen, Magne, and Ole Johan Finnøy. 1984. "Barn og unges syn på framtiden" (Children's and young people's view of the future). *Barn* 4 (1): 8–26.

Ravitch, Diane. 1978. *The Revisionists Revised: A Critique of the Radical Attack on the Schools*. New York: Basic Books.

Rawls, John. 1971. *A Theory of Justice*. Cambridge, Mass.: Harvard University Press.

Raz, Joseph. 1986. *The Morality of Freedom*. Oxford: Clarendon Press.

Rehn, Gösta. 1978. *Towards a Society of Free Choice*. Stockholm: Institute for Social Research.

———. 1986. "The Wages of Success." In *Norden: The Passion for Equality*, edited by Stephen R. Graubard, 143–75. Oslo: Norwegian University Press.

Reich, Ebbe Kløvedal. 1981. *Frederik*. Copenhagen: Gyldendal.

Rescher, Nicholas. 1975. *Unselfishness: The Role of Vicarious Affects in Moral Philosophy and Social Theory*. Pittsburgh: University of Pittsburgh Press.

Retterstøl, Nils. 1985. *Selvmord* (Suicide). Oslo: Norwegian University Press.

Rieder, Jonathan. 1985. *Canarsie: The Jews and Italians of Brooklyn Against Liberalism*. Cambridge, Mass.: Harvard University Press.

Rieff, Philip. 1979. *Freud: The Mind of a Moralist*. 3d ed. Chicago: University of Chicago Press.

Riker, William H. 1982. *Liberalism Against Populism: A Confrontation Between the Theory of Democracy and the Theory of Social Choice*. San Francisco: W. H. Freeman.

Rindfuss, Ronald R., J. Philip Morgan, and Gary Swicegood. 1988. *First Births in America: Changes in the Timing of Parenthood*. Berkeley and Los Angeles: University of California Press.

Ringen, Stein. 1987. *The Possibility of Politics: A Study in the Political Economy of the Welfare State.* Oxford: Clarendon Press.

Rochberg-Halton, Eugene. 1986. *Meaning and Modernity: Social Theory in Pragmatic Attitude.* Chicago: University of Chicago Press.

Rodgers, Harrell R., Jr. 1986. *Poor Women, Poor Families: The Economic Plight of America's Female-headed Households.* Armonk, N.Y.: M.E. Sharpe.

Roemer, John, ed. 1986. *Analytical Marxism.* Cambridge: Cambridge University Press.

Romøren, Tor Inge. 1985. "Midlertidig sykehjemsopphold blant eldre" (The nursing home as a temporary residence for the elderly). *Tidsskrift for samfunnsforskning* 26 (1–2): 177–99.

Rorabaugh, William J. 1986. *The Craft Apprenticeship: From Franklin to the Machine Age in America.* New York: Oxford University Press.

Rorty, Richard. 1979. *Philosophy and the Mirror of Nature.* Princeton, N.J.: Princeton University Press.

Rosenberg, Nathan, and L. E. Birdsell, Jr. 1986. *How the West Grew Rich: The Economic Transformation of the Industrial World.* New York: Basic Books.

Rosenblatt, P. D., and L. O. Keller. 1983. "Economic Vulnerability and Economic Stress in Farm Couples." *Family Relations* 32 (October): 567–73.

Rosenblum, Nancy L. 1987. *Another Liberalism: Romanticism and the Reconstruction of Liberal Thought.* Cambridge, Mass.: Harvard University Press.

Rosenmayr, Leopold, and Eva Køckeis. 1963. "Propositions for a Sociological Theory of Aging and the Family." *International Social Science Journal* 15 (3): 410–26.

Rothbard, Murray. 1962. *Man, Economy, and State.* Princeton, N.J.: Van Nostrand.

Rothstein, Bo. 1986. "Managing the Welfare State: Lessons from Gustav Möller." In *Velferdsstaten i krise* (The crisis of the welfare state), edited by Ann-Dorte Christiansen et al., 2:225–58. Ålborg: Center for Welfare State Studies.

———. 1986. *Den socialdemokratiska staten* (The social-democratic state). Dissertation Series, no. 21. Lund.

Rubinson, Richard. 1986. "Class Formation, Politics, and Institutions: Schooling in the United States." *American Journal of Sociology* 92 (November): 519–48.

Rushton, J. P. 1980. *Altruism, Socialization, and Society.* Englewood Cliffs, N.J.: Prentice-Hall.

Ruth, Arne. 1986. "The Second New Nation: The Mythology of Modern Sweden." In *Norden: The Passion for Equality,* edited by Stephen R. Graubard, 240–82. Oslo: Norwegian University Press.

Sabato, Larry J. 1981. *The Rise of Political Consultants: New Ways of Winning Elections.* New York: Basic Books.

Sahlins, Marshall. 1972. *Stone Age Economics.* Chicago: Aldine.

Salamon, Lester. 1984. "Non-Profit Organizations: The Lost Opportunity." In *The Reagan Record: An Assessment of America's Changing Domestic Priorities,* edited by John C. Palmer and Isabel V. Sawhill, 261–68. Washington, D.C.: Urban Institute.

Salamon, Lester M., and Alan J. Abramson. 1982. *The Federal Budget and the Non-Profit Sector.* Washington, D.C.: Urban Institute.

Salganik, Laura Hersh, and Nancy Karweit. 1982. "Voluntarism and Governance in Education." *Sociology of Education* 54 (April–July): 152–61.

Salisbury, Robert H. 1964. "Urban Politics: The New Convergence of Power." *Journal of Politics* 26 (November): 775–97.

————. 1984. "Interest Representation: The Dominance of Institutions." *American Political Science Review* 78 (March): 64–76.

Sandel, Michael J. 1982. *Liberalism and the Limits of Justice.* Cambridge: Cambridge University Press.

Sassoon, Anne Showstack, ed. 1987. *Women and the State.* London: Hutchinson.

Schelling, Thomas. 1978. *Micromotives and Macrobehaviors.* New York: W. W. Norton.

————. 1984. *Choice and Consequence: Perspectives of an Errant Economist.* Cambridge, Mass.: Harvard University Press.

Schmidt, Raymond L., and W. M. Leonard. 1986. "Immortalizing the Self Through Sport." *American Journal of Sociology* 91 (March): 1088–1111.

Schmitter, Philippe. 1985. "Neo-Corporatism and the State." In *The Political Economy of Corporatism,* edited by Wyn Grant, 32–62. New York: St. Martins Press.

Schneider, David M., and Raymond T. Smith. 1973. *Class Differences and Sex Roles in American Kinship and Family Structure.* Englewood Cliffs, N.J.: Prentice-Hall.

Schneider, Friedrich, and Jens Lundager. 1986. *The Development of the Shadow Economies for Denmark, Norway, and Sweden.* Århus: Institute for Economics, Århus University.

Schorr, Alvin L. 1986. *Common Decency: Domestic Policies After Reagan.* New Haven, Conn.: Yale University Press.

Schram, Vicki, and Marilyn M. Dunsing. 1981. "Influences on Married Women's Volunteer Work Participation." *Journal of Consumer Research* 7 (March): 372–79.

Schudson, Michael. 1984. *Advertising: The Uneasy Persuasion.* New York: Basic Books.

Schultze, Charles. 1977. *The Public Use of Private Interest.* Washington, D.C.: Brookings Institution.

Schumpeter, Joseph. 1950. *Capitalism, Socialism, and Democracy.* New York: Harper and Row.

Schutz, Alfred. 1967. *The Phenomenology of the Social World.* Translated by G. Walsh and F. Lehnert. Evanston, Ill.: Northwestern University Press.

Schwartz, Barry. 1975. *Queuing and Waiting: Studies in the Social Organization of Access and Delay.* Chicago: University of Chicago Press.

Schwartz, Barry. 1986. *The Battle for Human Nature: Science, Morality, and Modern Life.* New York: W. W. Norton.

Schwartz, Thomas. 1978. "Obligations to Posterity." In *Obligations to Future Generations,* edited by R. I. Sikora and Brian Barry, 3–13. Philadelphia: Temple University Press.

Schwartz, W. F., K. Baxter, and D. Ryan. 1984. "The Duel: Can These Gentlemen Be Acting Efficiently?" *Journal of Legal Studies* 13 (June): 321–55.

Scitovsky, Tibor. 1976. *The Joyless Economy: An Inquiry into Human Satisfaction and Consumer Dissatisfaction.* New York: Oxford University Press.

Scott, Anne Firor. 1987. "Women's Voluntary Associations: From Philanthropy to Reform." Paper presented at the Conference on Women and Philanthropy, CUNY Graduate Center, New York.

Scott, Joan W., and Louise A. Tilly. 1975. "Women's Work and the Family in Nineteenth Century Europe. *Comparative Studies in Society and History* 17 (January): 36–64.

Seidman, Steven. 1983. *Liberalism and the Origins of European Social Theory.* Berkeley and Los Angeles: University of California Press.

Seip, Anna-Lise. 1984. *Socialhjelpstaten blir til* (The coming of the social help state). Oslo: Gyldendal.

Sen, Amartya. 1970. *Collective Choice and Social Welfare.* San Francisco: Holden Day.

———. 1982. "Rational Fools." In *Choice, Welfare, and Measurement,* edited by Amartya Sen, 84–106. Oxford: Basil Blackwell.

———. 1987. *On Ethics and Economics.* Oxford: Basil Blackwell.

Shammas, Carole, Marylynn Salmon, and Michael Dahlin. 1987. *Inheritance in America from Colonial Times to the Present.* New Brunswick, N.J.: Rutgers University Press.

Sharp, Clifford H. 1981. *The Economics of Time.* Oxford: Martin Robertson.

Shilts, Randy. 1987. *And the Band Played On: Politics, People, and the AIDS Epidemic.* New York: St. Martins Press.

Shostak, Arthur B., and Gary McLouth. 1984. *Men and Abortion: Lessons, Losses, and Love.* New York: Praeger.

Sigsgaard, Erik. 1985. "Om småbørns udvikling af personlig og kollektiv autonomi" (On the personal and collective autonomous development of small children). In *Småbørn, familie, samfund* (Small children, family, society), edited by Charlotte Bøgh and Per Schultz Jørgensen, 177–86. Copenhagen: Hans Reitzels.

Siim, Birte. 1987. "The Scandinavian Welfare States: Towards Sexual Equality or a New Kind of Male Domination?" *Acta Sociologica* 30 (3/4): 255–70.

Silver, Allan. 1985. "Friendship and Trust as Moral Ideals." Paper presented at the annual meeting of the American Sociological Association.

———. 1985. "'Trust' in Social and Political Theory." In *The Challenge of Social Control,* edited by Gerald D. Suttles and Mayer N. Zald, 52–67. Norwood, N.J.: Ablex.

———. 1987. "Friendship in Social Theory: Personal Relations in Classical Liberalism." Mimeo.

Simmons, A. John. 1979. *Moral Principles and Political Obligations*. Princeton, N.J.: Princeton University Press.

Simmons, Roberta G., Susan D. Klein, and Richard L. Simmons. 1977. *Gift of Life: The Social and Psychological Impact of Organ Transplantation*. New York: John Wiley.

Simon, Herbert A. 1959. "Theories of Decision-Making in Economics and Behavioral Science." *American Economic Review* 49 (June): 253–83.

Simpson, A.W.B. 1985. "Quackery and Contract Law: The Case of the Carbolic Smoke Ball." *Journal of Legal Studies* 14 (June): 345–89.

Singer, Peter, ed. 1986. *Applied Ethics*. New York: Oxford University Press.

Sjaastad, Larry A. 1962. "The Costs and Returns of Human Migration." *Journal of Political Economy* 70 (October supplement): 80–93.

Skalts, Vera, and Magna Nørgaard. N.d. *Mødrehjælpens epoke* (The epoch of Mothers' Help). Copenhagen: Rhodos.

Skocpol, Theda. 1979. *States and Social Revolutions: A Comparative Analysis of France, Russia, and China*. Cambridge: Cambridge University Press.

Skolbarnsomsorgen (The care of school children). 1985. Stockholm: Government Official Reports.

Smetana, Judith G. 1982. *Concepts of Self and Morality: Women's Reasoning About Abortion*. New York: Praeger.

Smith, Adam. 1937. *The Wealth of Nations*. New York: Modern Library.

———. 1976. *The Theory of Moral Sentiments*. Edited by D. D. Raphael and A. L. Macfie. Oxford: Clarendon Press.

Smith, Charles W. 1989. *Auctions: The Social Construction of Value*. New York: Free Press.

Smith, Stephen S. 1985. "New Patterns of Decision-Making in Congress." In *The New Direction in American Politics*, edited by John E. Chubb and Paul E. Peterson, 223–30. Washington, D.C.: Brookings Institution.

Smout, T. C. 1983. "Where Had the Scottish Economy Got to by the Third Quarter of the Eighteenth Century?" In *Wealth and Virtue*, edited by Istvan Hont and Michael Ignatieff, 45–72. Cambridge: Cambridge University Press.

Smyth, D. J., and J.C.K. Ash. 1975. "Forecasting Gross National Product, the Rate of Inflation, and the Balance of Trade: The OECD Performance." *Economic Journal* 85 (June): 361–64.

Socialstyrelsen Redovisar. 1985. *Självmord inom den psykiatriska vården* (Suicide in the psychiatric ward). Stockholm: Social Commission.

Sowell, Thomas. 1987. *A Conflict of Visions: Ideological Origins of Political Struggles*. New York: William Morrow.

Stack, Carol B. 1974. *All Our Kin: Strategies for Survival in a Black Community*. New York: Harper and Row.

Stack, Steven. 1980. "The Effects of Marital Dissolution on Suicide." *Journal of Marriage and the Family* 42 (February): 83–91.

Starr, Jerold M. 1986. "American Youth in the 1980s." *Youth and Society* 17 (June): 323–45.

Statistisk årbog för Sverige 1988 (Swedish statistical yearbook 1988). 1988. Stockholm: Central Statistical Department.

Staub, Ervin, Daniel Bar-Tal, Jerzy Karylowski, and Janusz Reykowski. 1984. *Development and Maintenance of Prosocial Behavior.* New York: Plenum.

Stephens, John D. 1986. *The Transition from Capitalism to Socialism.* Urbana: University of Illinois Press.

Stewart, Richard B. 1975. "The Reformation of American Administrative Law." *Harvard Law Review* 88 (June): 1667–1813.

Stigler, George J. 1963. *The Intellectual and the Market Place.* Glencoe, Ill.: Free Press.

Stigler, George J., and Gary S. Becker. 1977. "De Gustibus Non Disputandum." *American Economic Review* 67 (March): 76–90.

Sugden, Robert. 1983. *Who Cares? An Economic and Ethical Analysis of Private Charity and the Welfare State.* London: Institute of Economic Affairs.

Sullivan, William. 1982. *Reconstructing Public Philosophy.* Berkeley and Los Angeles: University of California Press.

Sumner, L. W. 1981. *Abortion and Moral Theory.* Princeton, N.J.: Princeton University Press.

Sundström, Gerdt. 1986. "Family and State: Recent Trends in the Care of the Aged in Sweden." *Aging and Society* 6 (June): 169–96.

Sundström, Marianne. 1987. *A Study in the Growth of Part-Time Work in Sweden.* Stockholm: Center for Working Life.

Sunnanå, Olav. 1984. *Det ikkje-offentlege skoleverket* (The nonpublic school system). Oslo: Institute for Educational Research.

Surland, Søren. 1988. *Har børnene taget magten fra os?* (Have children taken power from us?) Copenhagen: Aschehoug.

Sussman, Marvin B., Judith N. Cates, and David T. Smith. 1970. *The Family and Inheritance.* New York: Russell Sage Foundation.

Suttles, Gerald D. 1968. *The Social Order of the Slum: Ethnicity and Territory in the Inner City.* Chicago: University of Chicago Press.

Svallfors, Stefan. 1986. "Kampen om välfärdstaten" (The struggle over the welfare state). *Zenit* 4 (4): 5–24.

Svensk Lutherhjälpen (Lutheran Church of Sweden). 1980–86. *Årsbok* (Yearbook).

Svensk Rädda Barnen (Swedish Save the Children). 1980–86. *Barnen och vi* (Children and us).

Svensk Röda Korset (Swedish Red Cross). 1980–86. *Årsbok* (Yearbook).

Sweet, James A., and Larry L. Bumpers. 1987. *American Families and Households.* New York: Russell Sage Foundation.

Swärd, Stefan. 1984. *Varför Sverige fick fri abort* (Why Sweden got abortion on demand). Stockholm: Political Science Department, Stockholm University.

Taylor, Charles. 1975. *Hegel*. Cambridge: Cambridge University Press.

————. 1985. *Philosophical Papers*. Vol. 2: *Philosophy and the Human Sciences*. Cambridge: Cambridge University Press.

Taylor, Michael. 1987. *The Possibility of Cooperation*. Rev. ed. Cambridge: Cambridge University Press.

Taylor, Paul W. 1986. *Respect for Nature: A Theory of Environmental Ethics*. Princeton, N.J.: Princeton University Press.

Therborn, Göran. 1987. "Den svenska välfärdsstatens särart och framtid" (The distinctiveness and future of the Swedish welfare state). In *Lycksalighetens halvö* (The blessed peninsula), 13–44. Stockholm: Institute for Future Studies.

Tiebout, Charles M. 1956. "A Pure Theory of Local Expenditures." *Journal of Political Economy* 64 (October): 416–24.

Tilly, Charles, ed. 1975. *The Development of the State in Western Europe*. Princeton, N.J.: Princeton University Press.

Tilly, Louise A., and Joan W. Scott. 1978. *Women, Work, and Family*. New York: Holt, Rinehart and Winston.

Tipton, Stephen J. 1982. *Getting Saved from the Sixties: Moral Meaning in Conversion and Cultural Change*. Berkeley and Los Angeles: University of California Press.

Titmuss, Richard M. 1971. *The Gift Relationship: From Human Blood to Social Policy*. New York: Pantheon.

————. 1987. "Social Welfare and the Art of Giving." In *The Philosophy of Welfare: Selected Writings of Richard M. Titmuss*, edited by Brian Abel-Smith and Kay Titmuss, 113–27. London: Allen and Unwin.

Tobaksvanor i Sverige (Smoking habits in Sweden). 1986. Stockholm: Social Commission.

Togeby, Lise. 1982. *Ung og arbejdløs* (Young and unemployed). Århus: Politica.

————. 1987. "Notat om børnepasningsdækning i de nordiske lande" (Memorandum on day-care coverage in the Nordic countries). Institute for Political Science, Århus University.

Torres-Gil, Fernando, and Jon Pynoos. 1986. "Long-Term Care Policy and Interest Group Struggles." *The Gerontologist* 26 (October): 488–95.

Trilling, Lionel. 1950. *The Liberal Imagination*. New York: Viking Press.

Troll, Lillian, and Vern Bengston. 1979. "Generations and the Family." In *Contemporary Theories About the Family*, edited by Wesley R. Burr, Reuben Hill, F. Ivan Nye, and Ira L. Reiss, 1:127–61. New York: Free Press.

Trost, Anne-Christine. 1982. *Abort och psykiska besvär* (Abortion and psychological problems). Västerås, Swe.: International Library.

Truman, David B. 1951. *The Governmental Process: Political Interests and Public Opinion*. New York: Alfred Knopf.

Tufte, Edward. 1978. *Political Control of the Economy*. Princeton, N.J.: Princeton University Press.

Tullock, Gordon. 1972. "Economic Imperialism." In *The Theory of Public Choice,* edited by James M. Buchanan and Robert D. Tollison, 317–29. Ann Arbor: University of Michigan Press.

Turiel, Elliot. 1983. *The Development of Social Knowledge: Morality and Convention.* Cambridge: Cambridge University Press.

Turner, Stephen P., and Mark L. Wardell, eds. 1986. *Sociological Theory in Transition.* Boston: Allen and Unwin.

Turner, Victor. 1969. *The Ritual Process: Structure and Anti-Structure.* Chicago: Aldine.

Tyack, David, and Elizabeth Hansot. 1982. *Managers of Virtue: Public School Leadership in America, 1820–1980.* New York: Basic Books.

Tönnies, Ferdinand. 1974. *Community and Association.* Translated by Charles P. Loomis. London: Routledge and Kegan Paul.

Tåhlin, Michael. 1985. *Fritid i Välfärden* (Leisure in a Welfare Society). Stockholm: Riksförbundet Sveriges Fritids-och Hemgårder Forlag.

U.S. Census Bureau. 1976–86. *Statistical Abstracts of the United States.* Washington, D.C.: Government Printing Office.

————. 1987. *Current Population Reports. Consumer Income, Series P-60. Money Income and Poverty Status of Families and Persons in U.S.* Washington, D.C.: Government Printing Office.

U.S. Department of Agriculture. 1986, 1987. *Agricultural Finance: Situation and Outlook Report.* Washington, D.C.: Government Printing Office.

————. 1987. *Economic Indicators of the Farm Sector: State Financial Summary, 1985.* Washington, D.C.: Government Printing Office.

U.S. House of Representatives. Select Committee on Children, Youth, and Families. 1983. *Children, Youth, and Families, 1983.* Washington, D.C.: Government Printing Office.

Varenne, Hervé. 1977. *Americans Together: Structured Diversity in a Midwestern Town.* New York: Teachers College Press.

Ventetider til sygehusbehandling (Waiting times for hospital treatment). 1986. Copenhagen: Ministry of the Interior.

Verba, Sidney, and Norman H. Nie. 1972. *Participation in America: Political Democracy and Social Equality.* New York: Harper and Row.

Veroff, Joseph, Elizabeth Douvan, and Richard A. Kulka. 1981. *The Inner American: A Self-portrait from 1957 to 1976.* New York: Basic Books.

Vickerman, R. W. 1970. *Spatial Economic Behavior.* London: Macmillan.

Vidich, Arthur, and Joseph Bensman. 1968. *Small Town in Mass Society: Class, Power, and Religion in a Rural Community.* Princeton, N.J.: Princeton University Press.

Vidich, Arthur, and Stanford Lyman. 1985. *American Sociology: Worldly Rejections of Religion and Their Directions.* New Haven, Conn.: Yale University Press.

Vogel, Joachim. 1970. *Aspirationer, möjligheter, och skattemoral* (Aspirations, possibilities, and taxpayer morality). Stockholm: Government Official Reports.

Wadensjö, Eksil. 1987. *The Youth Labor Market in Sweden.* Stockholm: Institute for Social Research.

Waite, Linda J., and Ross M. Stolzenberg. 1976. "Intended Childbearing and Labor Force Participation of Young Women." *American Sociological Review* 41 (April): 235–52.

Wallerstein, Judith S., and Joan Berlin Kelly. 1980. *Surviving the Breakup: How Children and Parents Cope with Divorce.* New York: Basic Books.

Walzer, Michael. 1982. "Socialism and the Gift Relationship." *Dissent* 29 (Fall): 431–41.

———. 1983. *Spheres of Justice: A Defense of Pluralism and Equality.* New York: Basic Books.

Warren, Donald I., and Rachelle B. Warren. 1985. "U.S. National Patterns of Problem Coping Networks." *Journal of Voluntary Action Research* 14 (April–September): 31–53.

Weiner, Martin J. 1981. *English Culture and the Decline of the Industrial Spirit, 1850–1980.* Cambridge: Cambridge University Press.

Weinreich-Haste, Helen, and Don Locke, eds. 1983. *Morality in the Making: Thought, Action and the Social Context.* New York: John Wiley.

Weitzman, Lenore J. 1985. *The Divorce Revolution: The Unexpected Social and Economic Consequences for Women and Children in America.* New York: Free Press.

Wellman, Barry. 1979. "The Community Question: The Intimate Networks of East Yorkers." *American Journal of Sociology* 84 (March): 1201–31.

West, Robin. 1985. "Authority, Autonomy, and Choice: The Role of Consent in the Moral and Political Visions of Franz Kafka and Richard Posner." *Harvard Law Review* 99 (December): 384–428.

Westen, Drew. 1985. *Self and Society: Narcissism, Collectivism, and the Development of Morals.* Cambridge: Cambridge University Press.

White, William S. 1968. *Citadel.* Boston: Houghton Mifflin.

Wilkinson, Kenneth P. 1982. "Changing Rural Communities." In *Handbook of Community Mental Health,* edited by Peter A. Keller and J. Dennis Murray, 20–28. New York: Human Sciences Press.

———. 1984. "Rurality and Patterns of Social Disruption." *Rural Sociology* 49 (Spring): 23–36.

———. 1986. "In Search of Community in the Changing Countryside." *Rural Sociology* 51 (Spring): 1–17.

Williams, Bernard. 1973. "A Critique of Utilitarianism." In *Utilitarianism—For and Against,* edited by J.J.C. Smart and Bernard Williams, 77–150. Cambridge: Cambridge University Press.

Williamson, Oliver E. 1975. *Markets and Hierarchies, Analysis and Anti-Trust Implications: A Study in the Economics of Internal Organization.* New York: Free Press.

———. 1985. *The Economic Institutions of Capitalism: Firms, Markets, and Relational Contracting.* New York: Free Press.

———. 1986. *Economic Organization: Firms, Markets, and Policy Control.* New York: New York University Press.

Wilson, James Q., ed. 1980. *The Politics of Regulation.* New York: Basic Books.

Winai, Peter. 1985. *Organisationer på gränsen mellan privat och offentlig sektor* (Organizations on the border between the private and public sectors). Stockholm: Finance Department.

———. 1987. *Gränsorganisationer* (Border organizations). Stockholm: Finance Department.

Winston, Gordon C. 1982. *The Timing of Economic Activities.* Cambridge: Cambridge University Press.

Wolf, Peter M. 1981. *Land in America: Its Value, Use, and Control.* New York: Pantheon Books.

Wolfe, Alan. 1977. *The Limits of Legitimacy: Political Contractions of Contemporary Capitalism.* New York: Free Press.

———. 1986. "Inauthentic Democracy." *Studies in Political Economy* 21 (Autumn): 57–81.

Wolin, Sheldon S. 1960. *Politics and Vision.* Boston: Little, Brown.

———. 1981. "The New Public Philosophy." *democracy* 1 (October): 23–36.

Wright, Gwendolyn. 1981. *Building the Dream: A Social History of Housing in America.* New York: Pantheon Books.

Wrong, Dennis H. 1961. "The Oversocialized Conception of Man in Modern Sociology." *American Sociological Review* 26 (April): 183–93.

Wuthnow, Robert. 1987. *Meaning and Moral Order: Explorations in Cultural Analysis.* Berkeley and Los Angeles: University of California Press.

Wærness, Kari. 1984. "Caring as Women's Work in the Welfare State." In *Patriarchy in a Welfare Society,* edited by Harriet Holter, 67–87. Oslo: Norwegian University Press.

———. 1987. "A Feminist Perspective on the New Ideology of 'Community Care' for the Elderly." *Acta Sociologica* 30 (2): 133–50.

Wærness, Kari, and Stein Ringen. 1987. "Women in the Welfare State." In *The Scandinavian Model,* edited by Robert Erikson, Erik Jørgen Hansen, Stein Ringen, and Hannu Uusitalo, et al., 161–70. Armonk, N.Y.: M.E. Sharpe.

Yankelovich, Daniel. 1981. *New Rules: Searching for Self-fulfillment in a World Turned Upside Down.* New York: Random House.

Young, Iris Marion. 1987. "Impartiality and the Civic Public." In *Feminism as Critique: On the Politics of Gender,* edited by Seyla Benhabib and Drucilla Cornell, 57–76. Minneapolis: University of Minnesota Press.

Zelizer, Viviana. 1985. *Pricing the Priceless Child: The Changing Social Value of Children.* New York: Basic Books.

Zerubavel, Eviatar. 1985. *The Seven-Day Circle: The History and Meaning of the Week.* New York: Free Press.

Zetterberg, Hans L. 1986. "The Rational Humanitarians." In *Norden: The Passion for Equality*, edited by Stephen R. Graubard, 79–96. Oslo: Norwegian University Press.

Zimmerman, Mary K. 1977. *Passage Through Abortion: The Personal and Social Reality of Women's Experience*. New York: Praeger.

Zweibach, Burton. 1988. *The Common Life: Ambiguity, Agreement, and the Structure of Morals*. Philadelphia: Temple University Press.

Øverbye, Einar. 1984. *Skatteprogresjon og skattereduserende strategier* (Progressive taxation and tax reduction strategies). Oslo: Institute for Applied Social Research.

———. 1985. *Den skjulte inntekten* (Hidden income). Oslo: Institute for Applied Social Research.

Subject Index

Name Index